WORTH FIGHTING FOR

WORTH FIGHTING FOR

CANADA'S TRADITION OF WAR RESISTANCE FROM 1812 TO THE WAR ON TERROR

LARA CAMPBELL, MICHAEL DAWSON, AND
CATHERINE GIDNEY, EDITORS

Between the Lines
Toronto

Worth Fighting For:
Canada's Tradition of War Resistance from 1812 to the War on Terror

© 2015

First published in 2015 by: Between the Lines
401 Richmond St. W., Studio 277
Toronto, Ontario   M5V 3A8
1-800-718-7201
www.btlbooks.com

Every reasonable effort has been made to identify copyright holders. Between the Lines would be pleased to have any errors or omissions brought to its attention.

Library and Archives Canada Cataloguing in Publication

Main entry under title:

Worth fighting for : Canada's tradition of war resistance from 1812 to the war on terror – Lara Campbell, Michael Dawson, Catherine Gidney, editors.

Includes bibliographical references and index.
ISBN 978-1-77113-179-7 (pbk.).
ISBN 978-1-77113-180-3 (epub).
ISBN 978-1-77113-181-0 (pdf).

1. Peace movements – Canada – History.   2. Pacifism – Canada – History.
3. Government, Resistance to – Canada – History.   I. Dawson, Michael, 1971–, editor
II. Campbell, Lara, 1970–, editor   III. Gidney, Catherine (Catherine Anne), 1969–, editor

JZ5584.C3W63 2015   327.1'720971   C2014-906717-8
                                                         C2014-906718-6

Cover design by Jennifer Tiberio.
Cover image: "Ban-the-Bomb Demonstration on Parliament Hill." n.d. Library and Archives Canada, Ted Grant fonds, e010836559.
Page preparation and text design by Steve Izma.
Printed in Canada.

As winner of the 2012 Wilson Prize for Publishing in Canadian History, Between the Lines thanks the Wilson Institute for Canadian History for its recognition of our contribution to Canadian history and its generous support of this book.

Between the Lines gratefully acknowledges assistance for its publishing activities from the Canada Council for the Arts, the Ontario Arts Council, the Government of Ontario through the Ontario Book Publishers Tax Credit program and through the Ontario Book Initiative, and the Government of Canada through the Canada Book Fund.

Canada Council   Conseil des Arts
for the Arts   du Canada

Canadä

ONTARIO ARTS COUNCIL
CONSEIL DES ARTS DE L'ONTARIO
an Ontario government agency
un organisme du gouvernement de l'Ontario

Contents

Acknowledgements

We wish to thank the staff at Between the Lines, especially Amanda Crocker, whose vision was central to the publication of this collection. We would also like to thank our copy editor Cameron Duder, whose hard work and attention to detail improved the manuscript, as well as the many anonymous peer reviewers for their expertise and constructive feedback. Thank you also to Eric Wredenhagen for his support. Most of all we'd like to thank the contributing authors. It's been a pleasure working with you on this project.

Lara Campbell, Michael Dawson, and Catherine Gidney

Introduction

War Resistance in Canadian History

LARA CAMPBELL, MICHAEL DAWSON,
AND CATHERINE GIDNEY

IF YOU HAVE TAKEN A RECENT Canadian citizenship test, attempted to answer a Dominion Institute history quiz, charted a course through Ottawa's public museums, relaxed on your couch in front of any number of History Television or CBC prime time offerings, or walked through the aisles of any major bookstore, you will be well aware that the experience of war is a fundamental category of Canadian history. A now familiar and predominantly English-Canadian narrative chronicles the forging of the nation state and of Canadian national identity through the experience of war. This narrative generally emphasizes the First World War as a defining moment in the development of Canadian autonomy and national pride, celebrating the sacrifices (and successes) at iconic battles such as Vimy Ridge. From this perspective, the forging of the Canadian nation is understood as a process of increased independence from British foreign policy, shored up by wartime sacrifices mainly in the First and Second World Wars.[1]

The place of war in Canada's history is a key element of our political culture – one that is expanding with commemorations marking Canada's participation in the First World War. Critics of the current Conservative government's emphasis on military history argue that the determination to portray Canada as a nation steeped in military strength and tradition has directly influenced both policy and commemoration projects. From the scale and scope of the recent War of 1812 bicentennial commemorations, to the rewriting of the citizenship guide, to the renaming of the armed services, they argue, the federal government is actively trying to (re)shape Canadians' conceptions of their (military) history.[2]

Popular and academic debates persist about the underlying *reasons* for this endeavour. Is this a reclamation of Canada's imperial ties to the British Empire and a rejection of the country's Trudeau-era multicultural policy orientation? Is it an attempt to reconstruct a particular Anglo-Canadian national identity that exists apart from both Quebec and the United States? Does it stem from a desire to rewrite and rebrand Canadian

1

national identity in order to justify increased spending on military technology? Or is it best understood as an attempt to reinforce support for Canada's role in a U.S.-British alliance in an era profoundly shaped by the War on Terror? Whatever the rationale, the result has been a reinforcement of Canada's military heritage that too often celebrates heroic sacrifices at the expense of alternative visions that emphasize the horrors of war and its victims.[3]

It might be tempting to dismiss such concerns as being "merely" the product of academic debates or partisan laments about whose pet projects secure federal funding. But the decisions we make about the place of war in Canadian history have real consequences. Beyond determining funding and space priorities in public museums they shape notions of what is acceptable or normal in settings as varied as our schools (the prominence of military voices at Remembrance Day assemblies), strip-mall parking lots (where yellow ribbons urging us to "Support Our Troops" beckon from store windows), and on our television and tablet screens (where Toronto Blue Jays players sport camouflage caps and jerseys at their home ballpark to celebrate the U.S. Memorial Day holiday). The prominence of the nation-forged-by-war narrative also helps to silence alternative voices and visions – a silence so strong that it is often difficult to imagine the shape and form a November 11 peace service might take, or how one might promote civic discourse that encourages us to recognize and distinguish between the vastly different forms of Canada's military engagements over the past two hundred years. Finally, this narrative glosses over deep differences, especially in English- and French-Canadian collective memories, over the meaning and value of Canadian participation in war and the divisions created by its commemoration.

This collection was conceived in part as a response to the current acceleration of military commemoration. But its broader aim is to help recalibrate our understanding of Canadian history by documenting Canada's long tradition of war resistance. The chapters tackle vastly different topics including pacifist campaigns to secure war service exemptions, anti-imperial dissent, protests against the sale of children's war toys, anti-nuclear demonstrations, assistance for American draft-dodgers and military deserters during the Vietnam, Iraq, and Afghanistan wars, and the inclusion of antiwar perspectives in public schools. Taken together, however, these chapters highlight three key points: they underscore the consistent presence of an antiwar tradition in Canada from the late eighteenth century to the present day; they speak to the wide-ranging and complex nature of this resistance; and they encourage us to grant war resistance a central place in Canadian history.

A Consistent Tradition

Canada boasts a long tradition of war resistance. Canadians (and their antecedents in British North America) have resisted wars and conflicts since the late eighteenth century, including the Revolutionary War, the War of 1812, the South African War, the First and Second World Wars, the Cold War, and the recent wars in Iraq and Afghanistan. Many Canadians are likely familiar with pacifists motivated by religious or spiritual commitments. The influential work of historian Thomas Socknat foregrounds the role of these spiritually motivated Conscientious Objectors (COs) in Canadian antiwar history. In the eighteenth and nineteenth centuries, for example, the historic peace churches (Quaker, Mennonite, and Brethren in Christ) sought accommodation from state-mandated militia service. Socknat argues that COs influenced by religious ethics remained at the heart of the antiwar movement throughout the twentieth century, maintaining a strong commitment to pacifism and antiwar work in the face of government oppression, popular support for "just wars," and changing perspectives on support for war in political organizations and feminist groups.[4]

Until the Second World War and the introduction of noncombatant service, claiming conscientious objector status was reserved for members of the historic peace churches. Moreover, the cost of seeking such status, especially before the 1940s, could be grave: state sanctions included imprisonment or disenfranchisement. Public media and many "patriots" vilified men who refused to fight, particularly in the twentieth century. After all, pacifists and COs challenged not only the authority of the state but also dominant ideals of masculinity. Front line war service was reserved for men; propaganda drew connections between the protection of home and family and war service. War service, in turn, supported soldiers' demands for state entitlements as rewards for patriotic loyalty.[5] This connection between service, citizenship, and masculinity meant that resisting war was often viewed as fundamentally unmanly, cowardly, or even treasonous. However, if we take seriously the promises made to the historic peace churches in the eighteenth and nineteenth centuries, as Ross Fair and Jonathan Seiling outline in this collection, then long-standing state accommodation of antiwar sentiments is foundational to what would eventually become the Canadian nation.

While faith-based war resistance has remained central to antiwar activities for over two centuries, by the early twentieth century war resistance efforts included direct challenges to imperial motivations for war. During both the South African War (1899–1902) and the First World War, determined voices, including organized labour and socialist parties, challenged the idea that Canada had an automatic imperial and moral duty to participate in these conflicts at Britain's side and insisted that wartime government demands were exacerbating rather than ameliorating economic, linguistic, and social disparities among Canadians. Many First Nations communities during the First World War pointed to the hypocrisy of a federal government asking them to fight in an imperial war while they faced disenfranchisement and dispossession in Canada.[6] As Amy Shaw and Geoff Keelan note in their chapters, then, Canada boasts an important history of anti-imperial war resistance. French-Canadian nationalists, in particular, challenged Canadian participation and protested against conscription in both world wars. Politician Henri Bourassa, a staunch opponent of Canada's participation in both the South African War and the First World War, remains perhaps the best-known champion of this anti-imperialist critique. The contested question of conscription in both wars, and especially the Easter riots of 1918 in Quebec which resulted in the death of four civilians, has shaped the historical memory of war in Quebec francophone history.[7]

Perhaps buoyed by these voices, peace work became more popular in the interwar years as Canadians joined with others in grappling with the enormous loss of millions of civilian and soldiers' lives. The peace movement drew on a number of traditions, including liberal pacifists who hoped for disarmament and international co-operation as a means to achieve peace among nations and "social radicals" who merged social gospel religious precepts with radical left critiques of the war, militarism, imperialism, and capitalism.[8] Many leading social democratic and social gospel women (including Laura Hughes, Agnes Macphail, Beatrice Brigden, Laura Jamieson, and Lucy Woodsworth) were leaders in the Canadian wing of the transnational organization Women's International League for Peace and Freedom (WILPF) which was established in The Hague in 1915 and began its Canadian operations shortly thereafter. WILPF focused not simply on ending war, but on building peace and justice-based societies. The organization criticized militarism in Canada, for example, by opposing cadet training – an activity, Cynthia Comacchio notes in her chapter, riven with controversy in the interwar years.[9]

While most historians argue that Canadians faced the prospect of another world war with resignation, perhaps the lingering public feeling that, in face of the looming threat of fascism, the Second World War was "just" – or at least understandable – explains why resistance to that conflict has been historically downplayed or dismissed. In fact, many different groups actively resisted the war effort, opposed conscription, or spoke against the curtailment of civil liberties, including pacifists and COs, francophones, farmers, feminists, and progressives. J.S. Woodsworth's opposition to the Second World War, which emphasized the horror of human suffering, demonstrates the intersecting critiques of war from an anti-capitalist, anti-imperialist, social gospel, and social justice perspective. For social democrats and pacifists like Woodsworth, war was intimately connected to the workings of capitalism and state-sponsored violence.[10] As Conrad Stoesz and Linda Ambrose demonstrate in their contributions to this volume, pacifist religious minorities in Canada endured an awkward but also sometimes transformative experience amid the Second World War, struggling to balance individual, spiritual, and state definitions of CO status or to define the place of alternative service in war resistance.

In the decades that followed, a number of Canadian peace organizations emerged to critique Cold War policies, lobby against Canadian participation in the nuclear arms race, and promote nuclear disarmament. Many of these organizations worked within a transnational scope, connecting with similar movements across North America and Europe. Increasing concerns about the health effects of radiation fallout from nuclear testing combined with the spectre of total nuclear annihilation to call the survival of humanity itself into question. Like critiques of war offered earlier in the century, a critical stance toward Canadian foreign and military policy during the Cold War entailed great risk as governments used the fear of communism to paint peace activists as either naïve or dangerous; either way, they were seen as threats to North American security whose political stances justified state surveillance campaigns.[11]

As the chapters by Ian McKay and Marie Hammond-Callaghan attest, women's peace work re-emerged during the Cold War in a variety of forms including ban-the-bomb campaigns and activism against the testing of nuclear weapons. One of the most prominent Canadian peace organizations of the period, and one which had political and grassroots connections across generations and in both anglophone and francophone communities, was Voice of Women/La Voix des femmes (VOW). This organization, formed in 1960, drew on maternalist discourses emphasizing women's special concern for children and families to critique Cold War policy and called on women in the West and the USSR to fight nuclear arms proliferation.[12] Its members collected baby teeth, for example, to send to scientists for radiation testing, participated in a campaign to knit dark-coloured clothing for children in Vietnam to protect them from American bombers, and, as Braden Hutchinson explores in his chapter, campaigned to end the selling of war toys to children.

Cold War antinuclear groups like VOW and Combined Universities Campaign for Nuclear Disarmament (CUCND), later succeeded by Student Union for Peace Action (SUPA), gradually made connections between antiwar and social justice issues. They developed transnational connections with other peace organizations and attempted to forge coalitions between Anglo-Canadian and francophone Quebecois activists; as Bruce Douville illustrates in his contribution to this volume, protests against the housing of nuclear missiles at La Macaza military base in Quebec joined together socialists, progressive Christians, separatists, and students. The protests drew on the language of nonviolent resistance to the threat of nuclear war as well as the right of Quebec, as a nation, to resist federal government and American military imposition. Montreal became a centre for such peace activism and boasted leading peace publications such as *Sanity: Peace Oriented News and Comment* and *Our Generation Against Nuclear War*.[13]

New social justice issues, in turn, reshaped the nature of the peace movement. Though women's peace groups of the early 1960s developed complex political critiques concerning the limits of liberal internationalism, their claims to activism often rested on women's traditional responsibilities for home and family.[14] Such work certainly challenged mid-century conceptions of women as either apolitical or quiescent. However, over the course of the 1960s and early 1970s, the women's liberation movement encouraged women protesting against war to incorporate into their campaigns explicit critiques of patriarchy and hegemonic masculinity and their role in supporting militarism and imperialism in the affairs of "Third World" countries.[15]

In recent decades, war resistance in Canada has followed a number of different paths. Antiwar and peace activists have, since the Vietnam War in particular, been highly vocal critics of Canada's military, economic, and political ties to the United States. The Vietnam War inspired a broad range of antiwar activism throughout the country by high school students and teachers, the student movement, university faculty, religious and peace organizations, women's groups, and New Left social movements. Though Canada did not commit armed forces to the conflict, activists decried Canada's "complicity" in the war and challenged the Canadian government to speak more clearly against American political hegemony in both North American and international affairs.[16] A number of the chapters that follow attest to the broad range of anti-Vietnam activism among antiwar, anti-draft, and New Left activists.

Peace activists have continued to critique Canada's ongoing involvement in Cold War and post-Cold War conflicts. In the 1980s, peace activists demanded that Prime Minister Pierre Trudeau "Refuse the Cruise" and prevent American cruise missile testing in northern Canada. Demonstrations occurred across the country, activists set up a Peace Camp on Parliament Hill for two years, and communities nation-wide, led in part by Project Ploughshares, declared themselves "Nuclear Weapon-Free Zones."[17] Debates raged over participation in the Gulf War (1991), the Iraq War (which began in 2003), and the War in Afghanistan (2001–11). Some of the largest antiwar demonstrations occurred in 2003, especially in Montreal, as Prime Minister Jean Chrétien weighed Canadian involvement in the Iraq War. In light of Canada's decision not to commit troops to that conflict, Canadian antiwar work turned to supporting American war resisters who faced military punishment for refusing to serve in Iraq.[18]

Finally, critics of Canadian participation in both the invasion of Afghanistan and the supposed "rebuilding" of that country cannot be separated from larger and ongoing debates surrounding the politics of the post-9/11 "War on Terror." Criticism of the motives and impact of this vaguely defined "war" is multifaceted. Many have pointed to the effects of the war on Afghan citizens, including high civilian casualties and Canadian military complicity in human rights abuses and the torture of prisoners. Others argue that participation in the war has allowed Canada to deepen a domestic security state that impinges on civil liberties and shores up Canada's role in American-led global "alliances" against terrorism. Still others have argued that far from leading to either the "democratization" of Afghanistan's political culture or the "liberation" of women from the oppression of the Taliban, the war has led to increased political and economic destabilization in the region.[19]

Canada's war resistance tradition thus encompasses opposition to conflicts fought on North American soil and in distant locations around the globe. It is a tradition that has addressed regional conflicts, imperial aggression, "hot" global wars, and the nuclear threat posed by the Cold War. From the War of 1812 to today's War on Terror a long line of Canadians have staunchly asserted their opposition to military conflict.

A Complex History

Forms of war resistance in Canada have varied greatly across time and also within particular communities. As several of the chapters in this collection demonstrate, churches did not have a monolithic perspective on religious objection to war. In times of conscription, pacifists faced the question of whether COs should embrace complete resistance to all military service or accept that alternative (noncombatant) service would honour one's obligation to both one's faith and the state.[20] Moreover, even within these religious communities some individuals willingly volunteered for military service – a fact that underscores the awkward and contested nature of both military service and war resistance.

Pacifists and COs generally opposed violence and war in principle, but others restricted their antiwar efforts to certain types of state-sanctioned violence or even to the waging of particular wars. A broad definition of war resistance, then, must include those who offered political critiques of the power of the Canadian state to conscript war recruits. This played out in the First and Second World Wars, when the unpopularity of the war effort was made clear in Quebec, resulting, for example, in conscription riots. Workers and farmers also resisted the power of the state to conscript. In some cases, as David Tough explains in his chapter, this resistance rested on larger political questions about the fairness of the sacrifices that citizens were asked to make in the name of the war: would business and industry be asked to make equal or greater economic sacrifices for the nation state?[21] War, from these perspectives, was understood and critiqued as an exercise in either British or capitalist imperialism.

This rhetoric of fairness is important to consider, for while it might not be specifically rooted in a pacifist perspective, it did raise the question of the extent to which citizens were obligated to sacrifice their income, their safety, and perhaps even their lives in times of war. And such protest also helped to shape government responses to critiques of its military policies. For example, the government responded differently to problems of reintegration following the end of the Second World War, partly in response to the social and political conflict after 1918, which resulted in the impoverishment and frustration of First World War veterans. As Ian Mosby has recently argued, the perception of "fairness" was crucial during the Second World War: when Canadians perceived restrictions such as food rationing as equally shared, support for them grew; conversely, when they understood them to be unfair and unjust, resistance was evident.[22]

Moreover, many who opposed the war in Vietnam were not necessarily pacifists, but they strongly believed that that conflict was unnecessary, unjust, and a product of American imperialism and Cold War power politics. Canadian and American antiwar activists shared this perspective but, as the chapters by Jessica Squires and Luke Stewart demonstrate, Canadians often expanded their antiwar work to include support for draft resisters, draft dodgers, and military deserters. Antiwar activists also critiqued what many felt was Canadian complicity in the war, particularly in terms of defence sharing agreements and weapons and chemical development – an issue Tarah Brookfield explores in her contribution to this volume. This critique of American foreign policy and pressure to facilitate the immigration of draft resisters peaked in the late 1960s and early 1970s as tens of thousands of young Americans immigrated to Canada to avoid the draft, but the issue re-emerged in the first decade of the twenty-first century as deserters from the American military attempted to gain sanctuary in Canada in response to the ongoing war in Iraq.

Thus, an important part of Canadian antiwar work has been a sustained and ongoing critique of American military intervention, not just in Vietnam but also in Central America and South America in the 1970s and 1980s. This sort of antiwar activism was (and remains) politically complex, including those who might self-identify as pacifists but also those motivated to protest such wars because they were (and are) expressions of American imperial power. War resistance, then, might also include resisting the power of the American military state as well as American influence on Canadian culture and political policy.[23]

Finally, resistance campaigns have been remarkably heterogeneous. Certainly, some took the form of well-organized and sustained protests or political marches. Others were comprised of both lobbying campaigns and individual actions – to assist American war resisters seeking asylum, for example. Some religious groups emphasized one's individual moral conscience before God and the duty to separate from the secular world, while others emphasized the responsibility to bring Christian perspectives on peace and justice to humanitarian work and policy reform. In other circumstances, the rhetorical battle between prowar and antiwar activists occurred within and about educational institutions expected to shape the nation's youth – a phenomenon explored in a number of chapters including those by Rose Fine-Meyer and Michael Dawson and Catherine Gidney.

Who, then, "counts" as a war resister? The traditional definition of pacifism as an "unconditional rejection of all forms of warfare" is a precise, if narrow, interpretation, as is a man who is conscripted into the armed forces but refuses to obey this directive.[24] Many more historians would also include those who actively promoted the rights of COs, those who refused to pay a portion of their taxes to the military, and those who critiqued the social, economic, and political impact of war. But as this collection highlights it also includes pacifist and educational movements against war, organized campaigns against specific wars, and organizations and individuals that criticized the cultural and economic militarization of Canadian society. This broad and multifaceted understanding of war resistance allows for a more inclusive and accurate category that includes the values, actions, and ideologies of younger and older men who would not qualify for war service (or be conscripted) as well as all women, who were neither allowed to serve in combat roles (until 1989) nor subject to conscription. Not everyone who opposed war in these circumstances was opposed to nonviolent resistance in *all* situations, but all were, and are, part of Canada's historical tradition of war resistance.

A Central Concern

How might acknowledging this long and complex tradition of war resistance reshape the way we think about Canadian history? Most historians would likely agree that both popular and academic histories of Canada's military accomplishments abound. And many historians have taken up the subject of war to tell us about the changing social and political landscape of Canadian society. Social and women's historians have repeatedly demonstrated that war must be understood beyond the battlefront. They have shown us how the social, political, and economic changes wrought by government support for massive war efforts in turn intersect with existing social movements (such as temperance or suffrage) to create new legislation and social policy. Historians have also moved beyond seeing how battles themselves are constitutive of national identity to emphasize the ways in which mobilizing for war changes the relationship between citizens and the state. Hence, the acceptance of increased government regulation, the emergence of permanent income tax, the development of minimum wage policies, and the establishment of government subsidized health and welfare for veterans.[25]

But the chapters in this collection suggest that when we look at stories of war in Canadian history, we must look beyond participation in battles, foreign policy decisions, or even changes on the home front, to the underlying history of resistance. While traditional historical narratives of Canadian nation-state development acknowledge anti-conscription protests in Quebec and among farmers in the First and Second World Wars, they have not yet adequately integrated peace movements, state accommodation for COs, political critiques of foreign policy and militarization, or feminists organizing against war into the dominant historical frameworks. The complex and nuanced resistance to war thus remains fragmented and separate from the stories that we, as Canadians, tell ourselves about our relationship to both war and peace.

The chapters in this collection tell us, convincingly, that over-emphasizing military history while ignoring resistance to war is a simplification of our past, and that the debates over the way we should think about the relationships among citizens, dissenters, resisters, activists, the military, and the state are far from settled. Moreover, while there are a significant number of publications on war resistance, ranging in focus from pacifism to ban-the-bomb movements, this is the first Canadian collection to bring such studies together as a cohesive resource for scholars, teachers, and the general public.[26] Together, these wide-ranging studies demonstrate that resistance to war in a variety of forms has a long trajectory and should therefore be deeply embedded in historical narratives about Canadian history and identity. Rather than seeing war resistance as tangential to Canada's wartime experience, this collection places it at the centre in order to illustrate its long and complex history.

Military conflict and mobilization in Canada have never gone unchallenged or unquestioned. Thus, while it is tempting to see wars as revolutionary or transformative episodes in Canadian history we must acknowledge that war resistance has always played a central role in the process of our national development. It has been central to the building of the nation-state, to the demand for independent foreign policy, to the notion of individual rights of conscience, and to the right of political dissent and critique. Canada's war resisters were a complex, active, and multifaceted group, and theirs is a legacy *worth fighting for*.

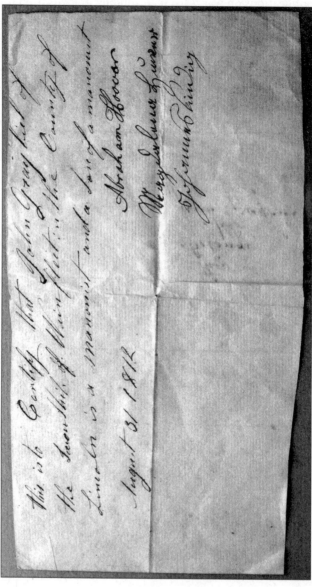

"Mennonite Exemption Certificate – John Graybiel, 1812." Port Colborne Historical and Marine Museum [2008.6.1].

1

"Scruples of Conscience" and the Historic Peace Churches in the War of 1812

JONATHAN SEILING

T HE WAR OF 1812 IS A RATHER COMPLEX TALE to tell.[1] While many Canadians still consider it the war in which the invading United States armies failed to annex Canada, the experience of residents in Upper Canada was more complicated. For settlers in Upper Canada, the conflict was not a Canadian-American war but a rekindling or an extension of the American Revolutionary War, one in which they might have sided with the revolutionaries. The United States' continued quest for greater sovereignty combined with the imperial ambitions of both the Americans and the British in the early 1800s to fuel a conflict that was contested primarily at sea. The invasion of Upper and Lower Canada was simply one strategic factor within a greater international military and commercial agenda. The land battles, however, were a devastating experience, especially for Upper Canadian settlers in Niagara, who proportionately saw a far greater level of combat and destruction than residents of any other region in North America. The recognition of the complex social and political contexts of the War of 1812 has significant implications for what we mean by "war resistance" in this particular war. And while it was an international rather than a civil war, resistance during the war might indicate either one's partisanship or one's religious principles about war and nonviolence.

What often captures the interest of Canadians is the fact that some "proto-Canadians" living in both Upper and Lower Canada participated in defending the land that later became the Dominion of Canada. Although fantasies about the settler militia's role as being anything but a minor auxiliary to the British army and Native allies have now been largely dispelled in more recent accounts of the war, a populist and patriotic "militia myth" evolved soon after the war ended.[2] According to this myth, the settlers played a fundamental role in defeating the invading Americans. Yet historians have demonstrated that many settlers actually welcomed the invading Americans, whether on the basis of affinity to a republican political ideology, dislike of the autocratic governance of the British regime in Upper Canada, or simply because many settlers were economic migrants from the United States and had only a nominal allegiance to the Crown. Most settlers came in the interests of free land and lower taxes and some on either side of the "border" resisted the war to protect commercial or trading interests.[3] Therefore, what the British perceived as widespread resistance to assisting them militarily cannot be reduced to a principle of pacifist war resistance. And yet while historians have debunked the myth of aversion to American invasion on the basis of Canadian patriotism, it continues to shape Canadian commemoration celebrations of the War of 1812.[4]

It was certainly no secret to either the colonial administration of Upper Canada or the U.S. government that Upper Canadians were a potentially uncooperative bunch when it came to defending British interests in North America. In addition to the British army and naval forces involved, various First Nations had agreed to defend British interests in the war in exchange for military protection and assurance of their sovereignty. Yet some Canadian settlers eventually heeded the call by Americans who had taken control of Fort Erie in 1813 not to resist their armed forces and joined with the Americans in turncoat militia bands such as the "Canadian Volunteers."[5] At the same time, American noncombatant raiders or marauders arrived in occupied areas of Upper Canada for the sake of plundering the inhabitants.

Because any of these warring groups could either "impress" or conscript settlers or their property for combatant and noncombatant service, resisting war participation was complex, difficult, and, indeed, a greater feat than many of us today could muster. Resistance could have meant opposing the Upper Canadian militia or "billeting" laws, the British military and Native allies, occupying American soldiers, turncoat Canadian contingents who joined the American forces, and American raiders who sought to steal property in anticipation of winning the war. Some exceptionally unfortunate communities were recipients of, and to some degree also resisted, all of these parties in the War of 1812. The historic peace churches – today called Quakers, Mennonites, and Brethren in Christ – made great efforts to be "nonresistant" by refusing to support violence in any form. The government muster rolls, local court records, and petitions for war losses are helpful sources for exploring the experiences of the peace churches when used alongside genealogical records. Minutes of the meeting houses are helpful for Quaker history, but little material survives from the early meetings of the Mennonites or Brethren in Christ. Historians can also rely on family history, which provides some of the more salient details handed down through oral tradition.[6]

By examining how religious beliefs about nonviolence informed both military resistance (militia service and fines) and domestic resistance (billeting and property conscription), this chapter demonstrates that faith-based war resistance and state exemptions for conscientious objection have a long tradition in Canadian history. Detailed glimpses are offered of the social experience of these early war resisters – people whose stories rarely fit into contemporary celebrations of this infamous war but whose actions profoundly shaped the legal foundations of modern recognition of conscientious objection.

Background

The historic peace church pacifists have been respected in the militia acts in Upper Canada since their inception, and, partly for this reason, these war resisters deserve special attention, even though the broader question of popular resistance to the war is important to keep in mind.[7] This history of Canada's pioneering war resisters offers examples of resistance such as lobbying for greater legislative provisions to ensure respect for religious convictions, acts of resistance related to the noncombatant duties of men and the domestic duties of women, and the refusal to pay militia exemption fees or to allow property to be used for the war effort.

Beginning with the 1793 *Militia Act*, the government of Upper Canada made provisions for Quakers (Society of Friends), Tunkers (now called the Brethren in Christ), and Menonists (Mennonites). Due to their "scruples of conscience," the *Act* exempted them from fighting in the military but enforced a number of penalties in lieu of military service. Upon demonstrating proof of eligibility they were required to pay an additional tax in order to gain the privilege of being conscientious objectors to combatant militia duty. However, they were still required to support the military effort through various noncombatant means, such as allowing for conscription of goods and property.

The ethical requirements of each of the historic peace churches were clearly spelled out in their statements of faith and practice. Mennonites in North America officially claimed the Dordrecht Confession (1632) as their statement of faith, and they submitted an English translation of this document printed in Niagara, Upper Canada, by Joseph Willcocks in 1811.[8] The Mennonite confession states:

> We must not inflict pain, harm, or sorrow upon any one, but seek the highest welfare and salvation of all men, and even, if necessity require it, flee for the Lord's sake from one city or country into another, and suffer the spoiling of our goods; that we must not harm any one, and, when we are smitten, rather turn the other cheek also, than take revenge or retaliate . . . we must pray for our enemies, feed and refresh them whenever they are hungry or thirsty, and thus convince them by well-doing, and overcome all ignorance.[9]

Like the other historic peace churches, Mennonites had no reluctance in stating their full loyalty to the British Crown.[10] In Europe, Mennonites were resigned to the practice of paying an additional tax in return for exemption from conscription; in Upper Canada, then, neither the requirement of noncombatant service nor the payment of additional taxes was disagreeable in principle. Similarly, the Brethren in Christ (a relatively new denomination founded in Pennsylvania in the 1770s) concurred with the compromise to pay taxes and perform noncombatant service.[11]

Notably, the Quakers differed from the Mennonites and Brethren in Christ on the question of payment of taxes in support of the military. By 1790, the Quaker *Discipline* included an injunction against paying a fine or tax "levied on account of their refusal to serve in the militia." Compliance with the militia exemption tax laws would lead eventually to exclusion from the Quaker society meetings.[12] As British citizens, however, Quakers were careful to appear loyal to the governing authority. In 1806, the Yonge Street meeting sent a petition to Lieutenant-Governor Francis Gore stating their nuanced position of loyalty to the Crown while also clarifying their refusal to fight:

> Although we cannot for conscience sake join with many of our fellow mortals in complimentary customs of man, neither in taking up the sword to shed human blood . . . we feel concerned for the welfare and the prosperity of the province, hoping your administration may be such as to be a terror to the evil-minded and a pleasure to them that do well, then will your province flourish and prosper under your direction, which is the earnest desire and prayer of your sincere friends.[13]

Differences between the pacifist sects rooted in national origin, history, language, culture, and theology likely account in part for their diverse responses to the war. The Mennonites and Brethren in Christ primarily spoke German and had a more separatist or even sectarian relationship to society compared to the more politically engaged Quakers. One text that speaks of a "quietistic" approach to nonresistance appeared on a folk art (*Fraktur*) drawing found among the Mennonite settlers in Niagara, entitled "Verschwiegenheit ist meine Ruhe" (Quietness is my Peace). Originally written in Germany, the verses speak of various examples of injustice and suffering, ending each stanza with the refrain "I hear much, yet remain silent."[14] Despite a penchant for disengaging from the political world, members of the historic peace churches demonstrated their willingness to protest, lobby, and advocate for peace. The difference between those church members who were willing to pay the militia tax and those who refused is a noteworthy aspect of the experience of war resisters during the War of 1812.[15]

Moreover, the historic peace churches' resistance to the War of 1812 can be seen in their generally loyalist orientation in the American Revolution, where they did not support American independence in principle or practice, and certainly not through violent revolution. In 1780 the Quaker writer James Moore wrote "A Lamentation for Pennsylvania," which expressed the sentiment shared by many members of the historic peace churches who felt compelled to leave their homes because of protracted civil conflict:

> Pennsylvania! ... Doth not thy land mourn to see so many of her young men slain by the sword, thy fine buildings plundered, and many burned with fire, and thy widows and fatherless children mourning? Are not thy horses forcibly taken from the stalls, and thy cattle and sheep from the fields, thy barns plundered, and the produce of thy lands taken to support the anti-christian practice of war, and the destruction of men's lives?[16]

While the decision to flee Pennsylvania was rarely made exclusively on any single ground – to be sure, economic opportunity was a prime factor for most settlers – the prospect of peace under King George was a key factor that encouraged their migration from the revolutionary United States. As a result, the historic peace churches of Pennsylvania were generally considered enemies of the newly formed country.

Exemption and Resistance

The religious beliefs of the pacifist groups shaped their response to the War of 1812. The militia in Upper Canada was divided into two corps, the incorporated (active combat) militia and the sedentary militia, the latter rarely serving in battle, being more akin to an alternative service corps.[17] Young men were the most sought after candidates for active combat service in the incorporated militia where they were trained as soldiers and used as a buffer army to hold off the American invaders until the British regular soldiers arrived. Many saw active battle while positioned at the extreme ends ("flanks") of the battalions and were thus given honours after the war, including land grants.

In the years just prior to the war, it had become clear that for Mennonites and Brethren in Christ, the exemption laws in the *Militia Act* (1808) did not extend to minors. While Quakers were members of their religious society from birth, Mennonites and Brethren in Christ became members by choice and usually did not join the church until the age of twenty-one. This meant that males between ages sixteen and twenty-one were not exempt until baptized. As a result of advocacy by ministers, elders, and members, in 1810 Upper Canadian law provided an exemption for these minors, provided their fathers were eligible.[18] This lobbying process is remarkable both because these German-speaking pioneers were well organized and willing to confront political authorities and because the authorities would grant further exemptions. While Ross Fair's chapter in this collection describes this legislative provision as a "mixed blessing," it may also demonstrate a good degree of sincerity on the part of the government, its respect for the presence and contribution of these industrious peace church settlers, and the Assembly's commitment to religious liberty.[19]

Another part of the laws concerning preparations for the war required duties which placed heavy demands on women as well as men. In an 1809 *Act for Quartering and Billeting, on Certain Occasions, his Majesty's Troops, and the Militia of this Province*,[20] settlers were required to provide lodging and a means to cook for militia or soldiers. In many cases they were also required to provide food, for which they hoped to receive compensation after the war. Further domestic requirements stated that owners of boats were to render them for military service, for which they were supposed to receive a fair rental rate. Fines for noncompliance were £5. Likewise, settlers were required to allow the army or militia to use their horses, oxen, sleds, and wagons, and in many cases were also required to supply drivers or teamsters, often the younger men of the family.

While acts of resistance against the conscription of property were not limited to members of the historic peace churches, there is considerable documentation of their collective refusal to comply. Quaker archives attest to dogged resistance to the conscription of their person, property, and finances to the point of accepting punishment and forfeiture, and evidence of such resistance by Mennonites and Brethren in Christ is also extant. For example, court records from 1814 show that in the North York region, several Mennonites and at least one Quaker were fined for such actions.[21] On February 18, 1814, David Byer was fined £2 for not rendering his horse, which he insisted was lame. On March 19 of the same year another group, including identifiable members of the historic peace churches, were charged for refusing to allow their horses to be impressed. However, they were acquitted when the constable who had charged them failed to attend.

Some settlers resisted by refusing to sell goods or produce to military forces. For example, Quaker John Doan refused to sell his flour to the military at inflated wartime prices. When approached by a British officer, Doan stated that he would only sell his flour to people who could not afford to pay wartime prices.[22] In this context, settlers in the Markham and Waterloo areas, living on the margins of the conflict, struggled to uphold their religious faith and their hopes for a peaceful life while adjusting to the everyday wartime demands of the governing authorities.

Quakers demonstrated their commitment to principles of nonviolence in various ways.[23] Some chose to flee to the woods to avoid prison, with a few living for more than a year in the wilderness to avoid detection. Some even fled to the United States. In the case of others who either refused or were unable to pay the fine, authorities confiscated their goods and property. For example, from Isaac and Sarah Davis the authorities auctioned the following in lieu of payment: oxen, chains, fanning mill, sled, handsaw, and a clock.[24] Officials seized similar property from Quakers in Niagara.[25] Even those living far from the war zones resisted military demands. Sandra McCann Fuller's work on the Yonge Street Meeting, located in present-day Newmarket, Ontario, demonstrates that even those Quakers living at a distance from battle lived under the close surveillance of the British authorities.[26] Between 1808 and 1810, as a consequence of such resistance, these Quakers endured financial penalties totalling more than £243.[27] Quakers who chose to face prison as a consequence of their convictions risked losing their lives, as was the case with Joseph Roberts who died from exposure in the York prison during a harsh winter.[28]

Although the War of 1812 never reached the Waterloo settlement, it came close; in the fall of 1813 American troops invaded the region to the west and south, crossing at Detroit.[29] With the American conquest of Lake Erie in the summer of 1813 and the advance of troops from Detroit, the British-Native forces began to retreat eastward, eventually arriving at Burlington. Waterloo Mennonites and Brethren, and at least one Mennonite from the Hamilton settlement (Christian Burkholder), were conscripted to haul supplies toward Detroit and to help evacuate the forts and transport the goods of the approximately 7,500 British and Native population stationed in the Western District.[30]

Prior to this massive transport operation some Mennonites resisted officers, who, under the *Billeting Act* (1809), could legally impress their boats, wagons, sleighs, and men to drive them for the journey, which lasted several weeks. When Waterloo Mennonite Cornelius Pannebecker knew an officer was coming for his wagon, for example, he removed the wheels and insisted to the officer that it needed repair. Although the officer left the wagon behind, he commandeered Pannebecker's horse and conscripted his son Henry. The son and horse would return, but a neighbour's wagon was taken by American soldiers who attacked at Moraviantown, near present-day Chatham.[31]

As a result of the Detroit expedition alone the Waterloo group claimed for the loss of two horses, fourteen wagons, and many other items of value to their agricultural work. It was indeed a heavy financial loss for which they would receive scant compensation. They later complained in a letter to the Board of Claims that postwar prices were so high that it actually cost up to three times their original value to replace the goods.[32] Many times the compensation received was only ten per cent of the amount claimed.

Although women in pacifist churches were not subject to military conscription, they also found ways to resist the wartime demands of military officers. In Waterloo, Elizabeth (Gabel) Bechtel was at home alone with her children late in the summer of 1813 when an officer came for her team of oxen. Bechtel had instructed her children to hide the oxen in the woods. She acquiesced to the officer's demands only after he backed her against a cupboard and threatened her life with a sword.[33] Similar to Bechtel's story of courage and resistance, there are other tales of Mennonite women who refused to give in to American soldiers' demands. On two occasions women refused to allow livestock to be taken. Catherine (Hess) Burkholder of Hamilton reportedly scared off American soldiers who were attempting to steal the family's cattle.[34] In another case, Sarah Miller, an eighteen-year-old Mennonite who lived along the Niagara River near Fort Erie, physically blocked American soldiers from stealing their chickens.[35] At gunpoint, after her mother begged her not to risk her life over their chickens, she finally reached into the coop and offered them the smallest one she could find![36]

The consequences of war resistance had a financial impact long after the war, including the difficulties some experienced when seeking compensation for property loss and damage. John Miller, father of Sarah, was suspected of being disloyal to the British and his refusal to serve in the militia complicated his postwar petition for compensation.[37] Indeed, officials made it clear that he would need to prove that he had been loyal during the war. To make his case, Miller secured letters of support offering arguments along the lines of what James Cummings wrote on his behalf in 1824:

> I hereby certify that I never knew John Miller of Bertie guilty of any treasonable act during the late War with the United States of America. Neither did I come to any knowledge that he was in any instance disloyal. I know he professes to be of that denomination of Christians called Menonists and is averse to bearing arms. Further I know not.

To support Miller's case thirteen local residents signed a statement attesting that Miller had not been disloyal and that "he favoured the British cause as far as a Menonist and British subject could conscientiously do."[38]

While most of the resistance to the War of 1812 came from the historic peace churches, there are scattered examples from other denominations in the colony. Two notable examples concern the actions of Methodist ministers who were both military men. Rev. Duncan M'Coll was a trained soldier who served a parish in a border town in southwest New Brunswick. Refusing to allow the war to divide his parish, he formed a committee of leading citizens from both sides of the border and succeeded in brokering a truce when American troops arrived in 1813.[39] In another case, Rev. George Ferguson, an Irish soldier and Methodist itinerant preacher, experienced a conversion to nonresistance while serving with the British army in Upper Canada. His unpublished diary recounts his ethical struggle to remain in the army while living out his religious convictions. This reflection is especially noteworthy since he encountered members of the historic peace churches who were exempt from active service, some of whom were later charged by the British for aiding the occupying enemy.[40] Ferguson proved particularly agitated by those who only partly removed themselves from military involvement:

> I have found some so conscientious and pious that they would not take up arms to defend their property and their families, but who could take four dollars a day to carry arms, ammunition, men, and provisions to assist those whom they supposed were murdering their fellow-men! ... If a man is scrupulous about fighting, from principle, let him carry out that principle in every particular.[41]

Ferguson claims in his journal to have fired only one bullet during the war, which he intentionally shot so as not to hit anyone. Yet he refused to defect because he believed God required that he obey the vow he made to "Caesar." These examples suggest that settlers outside of the historic peace churches also struggled to balance loyalty to the state with religious precepts that emphasized principles of peace and nonviolence.

o o o

These early settlers can be considered "pioneers of peace" for they made a mark on early Canadian history by refusing to march to the beat of the drums of war regardless of the social, financial, and economic costs to their families and communities. To fully understand the development of "national" identity before Confederation, we must acknowledge the actions and ideals of these peace-loving or peace-building people. We must recognize as well that Upper Canada guaranteed such privileges to a sizable religious minority, especially in an era when colonial security was threatened. While remaining loyal in principle to the British Crown, many of these pioneers of peace demonstrated a greater loyalty to their religious principles than to the wartime demands of the governing authorities.

After the War of 1812, anxiety about further invasions led Upper Canada to demand further taxes to support its defence. The historic peace churches jointly advocated for the removal of this burdensome tax, which exempted their bodies but conscripted their pocketbooks. In a further act of lobbying, Mennonites and Brethren in Waterloo circulated a petition, which gained 240 signatures, toward amending the militia tax laws.[42] As a result of steady advocacy by the Quakers, Mennonites, and Brethren in Christ, in 1841 the Assembly agreed to use the historic peace church members' special tax for infrastructure projects instead of contributing to the military budget. In 1849, as a result of further advocacy, the tax was eliminated. This principle remained in place into the twentieth century. For example, during the two world wars, conscientious objectors in Canada could buy peace bonds instead of war bonds so that their money would go toward the alleviation of the suffering from the war instead of directly supporting the military effort. The persistent political lobbying by pacifist churches, resistance to direct support of war efforts through service, money, or conscription of property, and the Upper Canadian recognition of religious freedoms for conscientious objectors are key elements of a tradition of war resistance in Canada.

During the late eighteenth and nineteenth centuries Quaker, Mennonite, and Tunker communities actively campaigned for exemptions from military service. "Quaker meeting house in Wellington" [Prince Edward County]. Archives of Ontario, I0013219, Marsden Kemp fonds, C 130-1-0-27-2, November 10, 1906.

2

A Mixed Blessing

The Pacifist Sects of Upper Canada and Exemption from Militia Duty, 1793–1867

ROSS FAIR

Q UAKER, MENNONITE, AND TUNKER (Brethren in Christ) histories tend to celebrate a congregation or ethnicity. In the late nineteenth and early twentieth centuries such histories promoted the story that these settlers were part of the Loyalist migration specifically invited to settle Upper Canada.[1] This interpretation has left an impression that pacifist beliefs and practices were readily and easily accommodated by the Upper Canadian state. But this was not always the case. Many pacifists were punished for refusing to pay the fines required for militia service exemption. The inability to swear an oath also presented problems of citizenship.[2] To improve their situation, pacifists had to petition the elected politicians of Upper Canada for legislative remedy. As a result their efforts frequently became caught up in the rather dysfunctional governance created by a colonial constitution which, in practice, made for an adversarial relationship between the province's elected House of Assembly and its appointed Legislative Council. The conservative Legislative Council often rejected bills to expand pacifist accommodation that were supported by elected assemblymen, just as it did with most bills aimed at liberalizing colonial society.

Moreover, resistance to war and the struggle for religious accommodation took place in the context of colonial militia service in Upper Canada, which was a fundamental aspect of the colonists' world. The state compelled men between sixteen and sixty to attend an annual militia muster for training, and they constituted the main fighting force for the province in times of invasion or insurrection.[3] While research on pacifism and militia service in Upper Canada[4] is limited by sparse records and a lack of recorded government debates, newspaper notices of petitions, legislative journals and records, and a close examination of the militia laws themselves provide a history of how the state accommodated pacifism during the colonial era, and how the Dominion of Canada incorporated that accommodation into the nation's first militia law.

This chapter provides an overview of colonial militia laws regarding accommodation for those settlers of Upper Canada who were Quaker, Mennonite, or Tunker. By charting the methods by which the colonial government offered militia service exemptions, from a 1793 act to the first militia law passed by the Dominion of Canada in 1868, it emphasizes the long struggle the pacifists undertook to secure such exemptions free of penalty. The chapter identifies moments when the usually apolitical Quakers, Mennonites, and Tunkers protested the terms of exemption under which they suffered and petitioned for better accommodation; demonstrates that accommodations were often a mixed blessing because legal gains secured were regularly accompanied by other unpalatable conditions; and highlights the colonial legacy that informed the federal accommodation of pacifism in the first militia law enacted for the entire Canadian nation after Confederation.

Upper Canada's 1793 *Militia Act* accommodated adult males of the Quaker, Mennonite (or Menonist), and Tunker settlements. Its twenty-second clause stated:

> The persons called Quakers, Menonists, and Tunkers, who from certain scruples of conscience, decline bearing arms, shall not be compelled to serve in the said militia, but every person professing that he is one of [these] people ... and producing a certificate ... signed by any three or more of the people ... shall be excused and exempted from serving in the said militia.

Each adult male between sixteen and sixty who could prove membership in one of the three sects paid an exemption fine to his local militia officer amounting to twenty shillings a year in times of peace and £5 per year during war. A pacifist who did not pay faced penalties similar to those assessed men who did not attend the annual militia muster, including having his goods and chattels seized and sold.[5] Pacifists were also required to attend the annual muster "with such certificates as the law requires"[6] and those who could not produce a certificate were "to be considered as a part of the Militia and subject to attend all Parades and Musters."[7] Thus, the law provided only partial accommodation. While pacifists were not compelled to serve in the militia, they did have to attend the muster in order to register with the local militia officer and to pay him fines that would likely be used for military purposes.

Consequently, Quakers in particular faced a crisis of faith because even paying a fine ran counter to their pacifist beliefs. Those who consistently refused to pay the exemption fine could have their property seized or be imprisoned.[8] In 1808, six Quakers in the jail at York begged Lieutenant Governor Francis Gore for relief of their situation. He remained unmoved, claiming "that he was well disposed to the Quakers in general and sensible of their industrious and peaceable pursuits, but that when the Laws were once made that they must be put in force and that it was a matter of conscience with him not to permit them to be disregarded."[9]

It was a poor time for anyone to be shirking his militia obligations. By 1808 the threat of war between Britain and the United States increased, and the colonial government passed a new militia act that added provisions for a jail term of up to one month for those who did not pay their fines. It also altered the method of paying exemption fines: whereas the initial law required men to attend their local militia muster in order to register and pay fines, they now had to register with the treasurer of their district and pay him the annual fine prior to the first day of December.[10] It is unclear whether this amendment was made in response to protests by the peace sects or was a government decision based on the premise that district treasurers could keep more regular accounts than militia officials.

The changes did not satisfy the pacifist sects. The Mennonites and Tunkers had their own specific problems with the exemption provisions, because they did not square with the practise of their faith with regard to adult baptism and church membership. In 1810, the House of Assembly received several petitions from preachers, elders, and individuals questioning the requirement of a certificate to prove membership when paying the annual fine.[11] Since both sects practised adult baptism, their sons were "not as yet actually considered as Church members, and cannot of course secure the necessary certificates." They requested that their sons might be exempted from militia service "by paying the commutation money until they arrive at the age of twenty-one, or until they be admitted as Church Members." They also asked the government to consider reducing the amounts of the fines, noting "the many difficulties which poor people, with large families, have to labour under in new settlements."[12] This was undoubtedly true, for families with several adult male sons suffered acutely because each was required to pay the annual exemption fine. The petitions did not result in a reduction in fines, but they did spawn a new act that freed the Mennonite and Tunker males between age sixteen and twenty-one from militia duty upon payment of the standard annual fine.[13]

Furthermore, by 1811, with war looming between the United States and Britain, the provincial legislature passed a new bill that reflected the increasing need to maintain a strong militia. It appears that the Upper Canadian government had tired of repeatedly selling the belongings of delinquent Quakers; under the new act, any money raised from the sale of a Quaker's chattels that exceeded the cost of the fine would be paid to the District Treasurer to be kept for that individual's future payments toward his annual exemption.[14] While the act did not identify Mennonites and Tunkers (suggesting they were able to pay their fines in good conscience) the message was clear: nonpayment of militia exemption fines was a serious offence.

When war broke out in June 1812, exemption fines for Mennonite, Quaker, and Tunker males increased automatically to £5 per year. Moreover, provincial officials tried to ensure that pacifist sects conformed to the exemption requirements and each District Treasurer was asked to report the numbers of Quakers, Mennonites, and Tunkers in their district who had claimed exemption from militia service and who had not paid their fines.[15] Difficulty in collecting this information indicates that district treasurers were no better than militia officials in ensuring that every pacifist male paid his militia exemption fine.[16]

In 1814, the wartime government, under increasing pressure to maintain a functioning militia, doubled the exemption fine for pacifists to a staggering £10 per year. Rules for seizing and selling chattels continued to apply, although the government acknowledged the chaos and difficulties that the war was causing. Many pacifists had teams of horses impressed by the military or had crops and livestock raided; some had their entire farm destroyed. The law offered limited relief to those who could not raise the entire fine. In specific cases, a justice of the peace could refer a case of nonpayment to the local militia commander so that a partial payment of the fine would be accepted.[17]

Following the war, the pacifist sects fell silent in their requests for better exemption terms.[18] With peace, the fine was reduced to twenty shillings (or £1), but there was a particular reason for the Mennonites' and Tunkers' silence. As part of the provincial government's concern over resident American aliens, it passed new militia regulations in 1816 that required militia duty only from adult men considered "a natural born subject of his Majesty naturalized by an act of the British parliament, or a subject of his Majesty having become such by the cession of Canada, or a person who has taken the oath of allegiance."[19] Among the Pennsylvania German communities, many men were now exempt because they were not British subjects.[20] Not until the Upper Canadian *Naturalization Act* of 1828 did many of the American aliens become British subjects. At that time, those who became naturalized subjects also became eligible for militia duty and many Mennonite and Tunker men were required once again to pay for exemption. Not surprisingly, in 1829, leaders of the peace sects wrote new petitions seeking the elimination or reduction of the militia exemption fines.

By this point, the Upper Canadian state was increasingly accommodating the peace sects in other ways. The protracted and heated Alien Debates that finally produced the 1828 *Naturalization Act* had spawned a reform movement loosely coalesced around the fight for the rights of American settlers to remain in the province as British subjects, as well as efforts to liberalize various aspects of colonial society and to reform the practices of the tory-dominated provincial administration. As a result, Quakers, Mennonites, and Tunkers benefited from the fight to fully accommodate a wide range of religious groups living in the province. In 1828, the pacifist sects were among a list of religious groups now able to hold church property. A year later, they were able to substitute an affirmation or declaration for an oath to provide evidence in court and by 1833 this substitution was extended to any instance in which the law required a settler to swear an oath.[21]

Elected reformers also took up the pacifists' cause for reforming or eliminating militia service fines during this period. In the 1830 session of the legislature, reformers dominated the House of Assembly for the first time. George Rolph, the reform member from the Halton riding that included the Waterloo Mennonite settlements, introduced a bill to amend the exemption fine provisions of the militia law. Soon after, the House of Assembly received a petition from "Jacob Erb and seventy-eight others (Menonists, and Tunkers) of the Gore District, praying that the amount exacted from them, as exempt money, may be lessened, and that they may be allowed to commute, by working on the roads." After much debate, the assembly approved the bill "to relieve the Quakers, Menonists and Tunkers from the payment of fines, or commutation money, in lieu of the performance of Militia duty, in time of Peace." There exists no record of the debate, but the title of the bill indicates that the reform majority were willing to permit the pacifists to live in Upper Canada unburdened by the annual payment of a fine during peacetime. However, the title also implies that fines during wartime would continue to be imposed. All of this was inconsequential, however, for the Legislative Council refused to support the bill.[22] Whether the upper chamber's decision was a product of its conservative views is unclear, for by that time the Legislative Council was regularly rejecting bills sent to it by the lower house. The influence of reformers in the assembly only made a long-dysfunctional form of colonial government more so, as the appointed tories of the council became increasingly defensive.[23]

Complaints about militia exemption fines generated two legislative initiatives in the session of 1833–34. First, conservative member William Crooks, who represented the Second and Third Ridings of Lincoln where Mennonites and Tunkers resided, presented the House of Assembly with a petition from twenty-eight members of the two pacifist sects requesting relief from the militia exemption fines. The assembly referred the petition to a committee chaired by Crooks and composed of members representing ridings that contained pacifist communities. The committee was given power to report by bill, which it did several weeks later. Meanwhile, reform members Robert Randall and Peter Perry presented the petition of 111 settlers of the Niagara District, "praying that the penal clauses of the *Militia Act* . . . may be suspended or annulled during peace," and subsequently introduced a bill to repeal the existing militia laws. It did not succeed, because Crooks' committee reported with its own bill "for the relief of Quakers, Mennonites, and Tunkers." By mid-February 1834, Crooks' bill had successfully moved to third reading, but in this final phase of debate Perry and Randall attempted to replace the substance of the bill with their own failed measure. Criticizing the cost and poorly managed process of calling out the provincial militia for its annual muster and training, and the mismanagement of the collection of fines for nonattendance and exemptions, they called for an end to all penalties during peacetime for nonattendance and refusal to serve on religious scruples. Though supported by ten reformers, the amendment was lost on division. Instead, the assembly approved Crooks' bill and sent it to the Legislative Council, which provided its support without amendment.[24]

The 1834 *Act for the Relief of Certain Religious Denominations of Persons called Menonists, Tunkers, and Quakers* altered the exemption laws in significant ways. In response to petitions, the bill halved the exemption fine for the pacifist sects to ten shillings during peacetime, but the fine during war remained firm at £5. The most significant changes were that men of the three sects no longer had to present themselves at the annual militia muster and now paid their exemption fines to the local tax collector, who turned the funds over to the District Treasurer. In a period during which the provincial government found it difficult to fund infrastructure improvements, this accommodation was useful for both state and settlers because fines paid would complement local expenditures on "Public Roads, Highways and Bridges."[25]

The pacifist sects remained dissatisfied, however, because they still had to pay a yearly exemption fine. Following provincial elections in 1834, reform member John Phillip Roblin introduced a new bill into the reform-dominated House of Assembly aimed at ending the payment of militia exemption fines during peacetime. The bill was debated, amended, and approved. However, the Legislative Council was not nearly as accommodating and tabled the bill for three months, the standard procedure for simply terminating debate on an unpopular measure.[26] It would do the same when Roblin introduced and shepherded a similar bill through the subsequent session of the legislature.[27] Although the frustrated lower chamber appointed a select committee to ascertain why these bills had not received Legislative Council support the upper chamber remained unmoved.[28]

Elected members did not give up pursuing change. After provincial elections in 1836, reform member David Thorburn introduced his bill for the elimination of militia exemption fines in peacetime. The conservative-dominated House of Assembly supported the measure, but due to broader political issues within the province, tensions between the two chambers of the legislature had become extremely strained, and again the Legislative Council tabled the bill for three months.[29] The political situation boiled over in 1837, culminating in rebellion in early December. During the uprising, the militia was called out to defend the province, and the government, on alert for further unrest, passed a new militia act that eliminated the accommodations secured in 1834.

The 1838 *Militia Act* restored the pre-1834 peacetime exemption fine amounts and the process of collecting them. Once again, Mennonite, Quaker, and Tunker men had to provide proof of membership to the local militia officer and pay a twenty-shilling peacetime exemption fine. The revised law doubled the wartime fine to £10 and included a broadened definition of when such a fine could be imposed, adding "rebellion" to times of "invasion" and "insurrection." The commanding officer was given authority to pursue through military courts those individuals who did not pay their fines.[30]

Understandably, the Mennonites, Quakers, and Tunkers complained about this reversal of government accommodation. In 1840, Quakers attending the Norwich Monthly Meeting petitioned Governor General Charles Poulett Thomson, noting that more than £55 worth of property had been seized during the previous year from twenty-two members of its society. The petitioners requested repeal of the exemption portion of the law as a matter of conscience because the fines they were compelled to pay would be used for military purposes.[31] During the session of 1839–40, both the Legislative Council and the House of Assembly initiated bills to amend Upper Canada's militia act, but the assembly ran out of time to approve the council's bill before dissolution of the final legislature of Upper Canada.[32] Thus, future accommodations for the peace sects would be the responsibility of the new united legislature of the Province of Canada, proclaimed to take effect in February 1841.

The pacifists did not waste time reminding legislators of their displeasure. In the 1841 session, various members presented petitions from pacifist ministers and congregations, requesting that the terms of the 1834 *Militia Act* be restored, or that militia exemption fines be eliminated entirely. A committee considered the requests and recommended amending the militia law of the Upper Canadian portion of the united province.[33] Supported by both chambers without amendment, this 1841 act repealed the terms of the 1838 *Militia Act* relative to pacifist exemptions and restored the 1834 terms, thereby reducing the fine to ten shillings in peacetime and £5 "in time of actual invasion or insurrection, or when any of the Militia ... shall be called out on actual service." Men belonging to pacifist sects were to register with the local tax assessor who would collect the fines, which would be directed to local infrastructure projects. The militia would no longer collect the fines nor have direct contact with the pacifists, though the tax assessor had to report their names to the local militia commander. This legislation also ended outstanding attempts to recover payment from those who had not paid their annual fines.[34]

Governments of the United Canadas in the early 1840s found that in many cases it was practical and expedient to continue with separate legislation for the upper and lower halves of the province. Although this was not a long-term solution for a militia needed to defend the entire province, successive legislatures continued with separate militia acts until 1846. Then, as the Oregon Boundary Dispute threatened conflict with the United States, Attorney General William Henry Draper introduced a bill to consolidate militia laws and provide improvements to the militia's organization.[35] It would include accommodation for pacifists, but the terms would again prove to be a mixed blessing.

Although the new legislation itemized a sizeable list of professions who received automatic free exemption from militia duty in times of peace and war, the government only halved the pacifists' exemption fine to five shillings in peacetime while it quadrupled to £20 the fine during war, invasion, or emergency when the militia was called out for service. Once again, men would pay exemption fines to their local militia captain. They were also compelled to enrol in their local militia company and then claim exemption by presenting an appropriate certificate. Those who did not pay would be subject to prosecution – just as any man would be for failing to perform his militia duty.[36]

These new provisions were not met with enthusiasm. During the next legislative session, William Hamilton Merritt, the Lincoln North MPP, presented a petition from the Municipal Council of the Niagara District praying for an amendment of the previous year's militia act. The assembly took the unusual step of moving into a debate of the whole legislature on the substance of this petition, during which Merritt introduced a motion to expunge the clause that enforced exemption fines for Mennonites, Quakers, and Tunkers. Some rejected this idea out of fear that men would join these sects in order to avoid militia duty. Merritt claimed that "many worthy farmers had left the country rather than pay the fine imposed," but for practical reasons he replaced his motion with two resolutions: that the wartime fine be reduced to £5 and that compulsory militia enrolment be replaced by the collection of fines in a manner that required only the registration of exempted names with the local militia captain. The assembly approved his motions, but the bill that embodied these recommendations died in committee in the Legislative Council with no explanation recorded.[37]

Following the December 1847 elections, a new provincial government received a petition to eliminate exemption fines.[38] The government took action to amend this clause of the provincial *Militia Act* in 1849 when Merritt, speaking on behalf of the government, initiated debate. Coincidentally, debate on this bill was held in the weeks that followed the late April night when an angry mob burnt the parliament buildings in Montreal to the ground. While troops and militia patrolled the city streets, the reform ministry led by Louis LaFontaine and Robert Baldwin and operating under the terms of responsible government approved the new militia bill, which became law in May 1849.[39] This one-paragraph act simply reinstated the provisions of the 1841 *Militia Act*. Again, it was a mixed blessing.[40] The exemption fines remained, and while the exorbitant wartime fine was reduced from £20 to £5, the peacetime fine was doubled to ten shillings. The only consolation was that the peace sects no longer had to enrol in the militia and could pay their increased fines to the local tax assessor for the improvement of local roads and bridges.[41] These terms would be in effect for six years, at which time the provincial government revisited the question.

Reorganization of the colonial militia was one of the most contentious issues that faced provincial ministries of the 1850s and 1860s, and politicians spent hours in hotly contested debates during the 1855 session. In the end, the *Militia Act* of that year provided for an "active militia" of 5,000 volunteers who would enlist for three years, be armed, and be paid for their training.[42] Effectively, this lessened responsibility upon all adult males to defend the province; thus, the matter of free exemption for pacifists was not a point of contention during these debates. The new law provided free exemption for members of the peace sects as well as other denominations, stating:

> All persons bearing Certificates from the Society of Quakers, Mennonists and Tunkers, or any Inhabitant of this Province, of any Religious denomination, otherwise subject to Military duty in time of peace, but who from the doctrines of his Religion, shall be averse to bearing arms, and shall refuse personal Military Service, shall be exempt therefrom.

Free exemption came with the responsibility of registering with the local militia commander. An individual had to submit his claim to the Commanding Officer of the local militia company along with a sworn affidavit.[43] Though the militia laws would be amended in various ways during the 1850s and 1860s, free exemption for pacifists was retained.[44] By 1863, connection to all things military was severed, as exemption claims were to be submitted to the clerk of the local municipality in which the claimant resided.[45]

After the birth of the Dominion of Canada, the federal parliament approved a new militia law in 1868 that extended free exemption for members of pacifist sects. However, it also insisted that claims for religious exemption had to be submitted to the captain of the local militia Company Division, thus re-establishing a direct link between pacifists and militia officers.[46] In 1883, when the federal government consolidated the various militia laws it had enacted since Confederation, the law extended the terms of the 1868 militia law verbatim.[47]

o o o

Across the colonial era, the pacifist beliefs of Quakers, Mennonites, and Tunkers were gradually, but cautiously, accommodated. With regards to exemption from militia service, their accommodation had come at a considerable cost of tens of thousands of pounds paid in yearly exemption fines, plus the large number of chattels seized from Quakers. By paying fines for their exemption, the pacifists also became one of the only groups of settlers in Upper Canada who paid for the improvement of their local infrastructure. While the early accommodations for these pacifist sects fit a wider pattern of increased religious accommodations within the Upper Canadian state and society, free exemption from militia duty took decades to achieve because of the broader political divisions that prevented the two chambers of the provincial legislature from working co-operatively. Moreover, the pacifists' gains were often a mixed blessing. Since the province's defence rested on the dutiful military service of adult males, officials were unwilling to provide exemption without penalty. Only with the creation of an active militia in the mid-1850s did the Province of Canada relax concerns about pacifist exemption, and it would be this colonial legacy that provided the precedent for free exemption from militia service for all pacifists following the birth of the Canadian nation in 1867.

A Try for the Rock [Dead British soldiers], Spioenkop [Spion Kop], January 26, 1900.
Archives New Zealand, Department of Internal Affairs/Te Tari Taiwhenua, ACID 24945
WA250 2/39f.

3

Dissent in Canada against the Anglo-Boer War, 1899–1902

AMY SHAW

In 1899, Great Britain declared war on the South African Boer republics of the Transvaal and the Orange Free State. In a first for the young dominion, Canada followed Britain into the conflict. Many Canadians of the time understood the war to be a righteous one, in support of oppressed expatriate British subjects in South Africa, and of the spread of British civilization more generally. It was the heyday of imperialist fervour in Canada, which meant, for most, enthusiastic and vociferous support of the mother country in this venture. In such an atmosphere, protest against the war was difficult and muted. Some Canadians, however, did speak out against participation in this conflict. They did so by emphasizing the war's actual distance from its apparent motivations and ends as well as the increasingly problematic means by which it was carried out. Because of the strength of imperial ideology in Canada, and an eager colonial atmosphere which made unanimous support of this first overseas war a matter of pride, protest was weaker and more disorganized than in Britain, and, despite the critical efforts of these individuals, they were unable to come together to form a coherent antiwar movement.

The Anglo-Boer War (1899–1902) was the first time significant numbers of Canadians went to fight overseas. The conflict brought forward, often passionately, differing interpretations of the relationship between nationalism and imperialism and exacerbated French-English divisions in the country. It can be seen as something of a dress rehearsal for the First World War. Canada's participation in this conflict, though a matter of vital concern to Canadians of the time is, curiously, not a significant part of our national memory.[1] This seems to stem partly from its uncomfortable fit with the nationalistic lens through which we generally see our war experiences. In helping bring the gold and diamonds of South Africa more firmly into British control, Canada was behaving, arguably, in a way that was both more imperialistic and more colonial than many Canadians today would feel comfortable acknowledging.

Still, bellicose support of the war was not a foregone conclusion. In the years just prior to its outbreak the international peace movement had been making headway. At the end of the nineteenth century there were conventions throughout Europe advocating, if not traditional pacifism, a liberal internationalism that saw war as antithetical to modern economic relations and pushed for the establishment of an international court to solve the problems that could lead to war. At home, the social gospel movement, so popular and widespread in Canada at the turn of the century, also had a strong pacifist component.[2]

At the same time, the close of the nineteenth century marked the high tide of British imperialist spirit. Queen Victoria's Diamond Jubilee of 1897, with its pageantry of empire, was symbolic of the popular attitude. British imperialism was just as popular in Canada as it was overseas. Canadian author Wilfred Campbell's 1904 speech to the Empire Club nicely conveys the imperial feeling, and the sense of responsibilities associated with it:

> It is the duty of Christianity to keep such a great moral force as the British Empire solid and lasting. It is our duty ... to organize and use all the practical means possible.... Present-day Imperialism is more than a mere self-satisfied jingoism, and a desire to emulate the splendours of ancient Rome ... true Imperialism, as it stands today, is more than an opinion; it is a vital force, a sort of necessary phase of human progressiveness, that instead of being the foe to the individual national life, it is the greatest necessary means to that end.[3]

In this atmosphere, Britain's war in South Africa achieved almost general endorsement. As a result, the peace movement in Canada was unable to counter the imperial fervour surrounding the outbreak of the war. Indeed, Thomas Socknat describes it as "more or less paralysed."[4] Both individuals and groups felt almost overcome by the intensity of the war fever. For example, the Dominion Woman's Christian Temperance Union, which opposed the war, found carrying on peace work in such an atmosphere tremendously difficult. "The military craze has been carried to such an extent," it lamented, "that those who did not bow down as hero-worshippers were looked upon as disloyal."[5]

Indeed, those who disagreed with the vast majority of their compatriots about the righteousness of the war faced predictable censure and harassment. Assaults on antiwar activists tended to congregate around specific events, often the British victories. The *Globe* mentioned the shaming of those known to be against the war as part of Toronto's celebration of General Buller's breaking of the siege of Ladysmith.

It was a bad day for the pro-Boer. In one of the west end factories some Boer sympathizers were rounded up, and the employees gave their erring brothers a mock trial and made them kneel on the Union Jack and beg pardon. In another factory the Boer sympathizers were required to stand upon a box and sing "God Save the Queen," much to the amusement of the onlookers. Everywhere the celebration was conducted with the greatest good-humour and to the incessant accompaniment of tooting whistles, cheering crowds and clanging bells.[6]

The jovial mood of attackers, their working-class makeup, and the presentation of the "rounding up" as a spontaneous manifestation of cheerful patriotism, understandable and harmless, all underscore the seemingly untenable position of the war's opponents.

However, some individuals and groups did manage to maintain a principled opposition to the war. This chapter examines these dissenters, who came from a variety of social, religious, and regional backgrounds. They challenged the stated motivations for the war and declaimed against the means by which it was carried out. "Pro-Boers," as they came to be called, were unpopular figures during a conflict that otherwise received broad endorsement, and their stance resulted in sometimes quite significant public censure.

The War in South Africa

The War in South Africa, more properly the Second Anglo-Boer War (known in South Africa as "The War of Freedom") lasted from 1899 to 1902, much longer than anyone expected.[7] It is divided into three phases. In the first, a period of heavy British losses culminated in "Black Week" in December 1899. The second was a period of reorganization and reinforcement ending with the capture of Bloemfontein and Pretoria – the capitals of the Orange Free State and South African Republic (Transvaal). Everyone assumed this would mean the end of the war. There were, however, another two years of fierce guerrilla warfare, during which British frustration with the "bitter enders" led to Lord Roberts' "scorched earth" campaign, in which the farms of those thought to be aiding the commandos were burned, and civilian inhabitants were relocated to "concentration camps," a novelty of the day.[8]

There had been strain and difficulty between the Boers[9] and the British in South Africa for decades before war broke out. While more cynical thinkers pointed to the gold deposits in the Boer territories, the avowed purpose for Britain's declaration of war was to respond to the grievances of the Uitlanders. These were the mainly British non-Boers who had immigrated to the Transvaal upon the discovery of gold in the Witwatersrand in 1886. The Uitlanders faced limitations in terms of franchise and education, high taxes, and other grievances. Britain, according to this argument, had a duty to redress the wrongs done to its subjects.[10] In September 1899, the *Globe* printed an extract from a letter sent by Canadians resident in the Transvaal. It asserted that "the Uitlanders are justly entitled to these rights ... as British subjects and white men."[11] Because of the limitations on the franchise, the motivations for war were themselves explicitly gendered and racialized.

One reason for the war, then, was the protection of British subjects. Another was less often expressed. Britain had assumed that its South African colonies – the Cape Colony and Natal – would eventually engulf the Boer Republics and form a confederation similar to that in Canada. The rapid economic growth of the republics, especially the Transvaal, seemed instead to threaten a republican federation more comparable to the United States and outside of British control.[12] The second reason given for British military intervention was, then, the need to protect imperial interests against an aggressive Transvaal, which wished to displace British paramountcy in South Africa.

If war with the sometimes obstreperous South African republics seemed a chance for an easy victory that would resolve the Boer problem once and for all by incorporating them into a pan-British South Africa, it also offered an opportunity to showcase imperial cohesion. Colonial Secretary Joseph Chamberlain, for whom imperial unity was a high priority, especially the fostering of closer relations between Britain and the settler colonies, wanted an enthusiastic colonial initiative. Neither the War Office nor Chamberlain believed that colonial troops would actually be needed. What the Colonial Office wanted was a clear, symbolic, and official colonial demonstration of support.

Britain wanted Canada to join in the war because it would show how unified the empire was. British subjects in the Transvaal wanted Canadians to go because they were not very happy with their living situation. Demands for a tangible expression of support also came from within Canada. The popular rhetoric of the time saw this as a moral imperative. Newspaper articles argued that Boer leader Paul Kruger's denial of the franchise to the Uitlanders made peaceful change impossible and that his subsequent ultimatum and invasion of the Cape Colony compelled Britain to protect its colony. Many Canadians were also excited at the possibility military involvement offered for proving themselves on the world stage.[13]

Canadians in Khaki, an official account published early in the war, nicely captures the mood of the time. The book included rolls of volunteers and a record of casualties, and opened with a statement of great pride at Canada's reaction to the war:

> One of the most striking features in the history of the present century has been the spontaneous outburst of loyalty shown to the Mother Country.... They [the volunteers] did not stop to ask "is the war just or unjust," or, "why should we fight England's battles in a far country." They simply felt that the dear Motherland, who had done so much for them, had so protected them, had given them such freedom, was in trouble, and even if she did not really need their assistance, they would like to give it; they would like to feel they were doing their share, and to show the world at large "a vaster Empire than has been."[14]

This was a perspective that championed unity and argued that participation in the war was not just a display of British strength, but showcased Canadian abilities to the world. It was not an easy time to disagree with the decision of the majority.

Canadian Opposition to the War

Popular, and loud, support for the war was not a universal Canadian response. As in Britain, there were those in Canada who viewed the war as motivated more clearly by the gold in the Transvaal than by the need to redress the wrongs done to British subjects there. This perception was most prevalent among French Canadians, many of whom found themselves identifying more with the religious, rural Boers, surrounded by expansionist English, than with the rest of the British Empire.[15] Henri Bourassa was the political figure most widely associated with opposition to Canadian participation in the war. A popular and eloquent statesman and editor of the newspaper *Le Devoir*, he resigned his seat to protest the country's decision to send troops to South Africa. There were reactions against the war on a more grassroots level as well, with riots among Montreal university students in March 1900. Indeed, French Canadians tended to interpret the conflict as an imperialist war in which Canada properly had no place.

The Québécois were not the only ones who identified with the Boers, or who saw participation in the war as incompatible with Canada's independence and self-interest. Historian Carman Miller has documented antiwar sentiment in the small-town Canadian press among segments of "farmers, radical labour, protestant clergy, and stout anglophobic Canadians, particularly of Irish and German descent."[16] John Kenneth McInnis, the editor of the Regina *Standard*, drew parallels between the Boers and western Canadian farmers, seeing both groups as God-fearing, industrious, brave, and unyielding. George Wrigley, the editor of *Citizen and Country*, the journal of the Toronto Trades and Labour Council, maintained a consistent antiwar position in his editorials throughout the conflict. Indeed, Thomas Socknat notes that "from its inception in 1898 *Citizen and Country* advocated the Christian socialist position against war and in favour of social, moral, and economic reform."[17] Wrigley maintained a voice for the more radical wing of the social gospel position when other groups backed away.

The Catholic weekly newspaper *The Casket*, published out of Antigonish, Nova Scotia, was passionate and consistent in its opprobrium. Catholics of British, especially Irish, background would likely have been more sensitive to Protestant colonization based on their family histories, and thus to empathize with the Boers. Among all those who protested the war in Canada, a chief issue was disagreement about its necessity and its ostensible provocations. "The formal reason for interference on the part of Great Britain," *The Casket* argued,

> is not the real one. It is not to rectify the franchise of the Transvaal that an army corps is being sent out to the Cape, but to establish British ascendency in South Africa.... But even the establishment of British ascendency is more or less a mask for the financial designs of Mr. Cecil Rhodes. If there were no mines in the Transvaal, the Boers and Uitlanders would probably be left to settle their political differences by themselves. Some centuries ago religion was the great cause of wars; now it is commercial cupidity veiling itself under the pretended mission of the race.[18]

The editor of this paper found the protective sympathies of Canadian popular opinion, roused to protect its expatriate fellows, to be misplaced.

William Marchant, a customs inspector in Victoria, wrote to the Victoria *Times* in a similar vein, arguing that because Britain did not have just cause for going to war, any conflict would be "most diabolical."[19] Journalist and historian Goldwin Smith put forward a similar interpretation:

> The world could hardly be expected to believe that a nation whose own franchise is limited, which has a hereditary House of Lords, which holds in subjection the vast population of Hindostan, and which went to war to uphold Turkish despotism, was so transported with indignation at the restriction of suffrage in the Transvaal, that bursting through the bonds of its solemn and repeated covenants, it flew to arms to redress the wrong.[20]

These observers argued that it was hypocritical of Britain to resort to war over issues that still incurred conflict at home.

Such critics were troubled by the reluctance of Canadians to challenge the presented causes of the war. They argued that the righteous indignation about abuses of Uitlanders was misplaced. Canadians were reacting to the apparent oppression of British-born South Africans, detractors asserted, as though they themselves were paragons of tolerance and political freedom. They argued that Canadians were not truly so concerned with human rights and gave examples of illiberality in this country that should be addressed before Canadians headed overseas to right wrongs there. One letter to the editor cited as examples the "monstrous injustice" to Manitoba Catholics during the schools controversy and the anti-Catholic oath that British monarchs continued to swear at their coronation.[21]

Opponents of the war questioned the jingoism of this apparently kneejerk support of Britain and found the seeming conformity of the Canadian response a source of concern rather than pride. For example, an 1899 editorial in *The Casket* questioned "how far that patriotic unanimity is based upon an intelligent understanding of the real merits of the case, and how far, on the other hand, it is a manifestation of that modern cult which might be termed patriolatry, and whose fundamental tenant [sic] is: 'Our country right or wrong.'"[22] They also attacked as hypocritical the broader argument that the war was a means of promoting British civilization. This was a widely held interpretation. One Canadian newspaper headline hailed the beginning of the war in South Africa with the headline: "Civilization Advances." That Christianity was closely interconnected, in the popular mind, with the benefits of British civilization shaped many Canadians' views of the morality of the war, encouraging support. Ignoring the fact that the Boers were also Christians, many Canadians viewed British soldiers as merely "missionaries togged in khaki, bibles on the end of guns."[23]

Opponents of the war challenged this interpretation. In July 1899, *The Casket* offered the following:

> We are quite sensible of the blessings of stable government and security of life, liberty and property that generally accompany the flag of Great Britain, but ... British trade, not the Christian religion, has been the moving principle in its progress. And if the blessings it bears with it were ten-fold greater than they are, there is a basic law implied in the words *meum* and *tuum* which it may not over-ride even for the purpose of diffusing those blessings. The millionaire may not seize and demolish the dingy hovel of his poor neighbour for the purpose of rearing a marble palace, however well-ordered and beautiful, on its site.

> Doubtless the owner of many flocks would have justified his seizure of the poor man's single ewe lamb on the plea that he could treat the creature so much better than its rightful owner; but no court even pretending to dispense justice would listen to such a plea.[24]

William Marchant wrote, with passionate bitterness, "The British people have a Divine mission to conquer and subdue the earth. If human victims are needed upon the imperial altar, South Africa will furnish them."[25]

Critics equally challenged the righteousness of the war on the grounds of its distance from Christian ideals. Marchant attacked, with acrid sarcasm, the widespread support of the war among ministers, expressed in their sermons. He attacked the clergymen for their "august approval" of the "brave boys" who had left Victoria "to kill, mutilate and butcher the Boers ... the Prince of Peace had been importuned to grant success to the sanguinary contest."[26] His position challenged the popular view of the war as a benevolent crusade and resulted in a public meeting calling for his removal as a school trustee.[27] Similarly, J. Herbert Bainton, a minister in Vancouver, faced an angry reaction that split his congregation and ended with his leaving the country altogether, simply because of his call to prayers "for foe and friend alike."[28]

The imperialistic mindset, especially in wartime, tended toward a patriotic acquiescence and support for a unified response. Those who spoke against the war tried often to rouse a more independent analysis of the situation. Goldwin Smith emphasized that challenging the war did not make one a bad citizen.

> Painful and embarrassing in the highest degree is the situation of a good citizen who believes that his Government is making an unjust war ... the good citizen will pay his war taxes, faithfully perform any duties that may be lawfully required of him, and refrain from thwarting in any way the military operation of his Government. But he is not bound at the dictate of a war party to belie his own convictions or to settle the voice of his own conscience. If he were the world might be given up to the power of violence and rapine.[29]

In an atmosphere that vaunted unity and unquestioned loyalty, critics of the war tried to assert the value of individual conscience. Canadians who opposed the war often drew upon the arguments of like-minded people in Britain, which offered legitimacy for opinions otherwise branded disloyal. They also took advantage of the comparative strength of the movement against the Anglo-Boer War in Britain.

One comprehensive critique of the war that Canadians drew upon was that of British economist and journalist J.A. Hobson, who argued that the real causes of the war were economic.[30] The *Manchester Guardian* sent Hobson to the Transvaal to assess the situation just prior to the outbreak of the war, and he concluded that the conflict could not be justified on humanitarian grounds. He asserted that he could find no evidence of oppression of British citizens in the Transvaal. Instead, he argued for an economic understanding of the war's origins. The Anglo-Boer War was an important inspiration for *Imperialism*, Hobson's classic indictment of imperial motives and policy, which influenced Lenin's theories. In both Canada and Britain this economic interpretation of the war was frequently intertwined with an explicit anti-Semitism. Goldwin Smith wrote "of the outlanders, for whose political rights this war was ostensibly made, and who were styled, for the purpose of aggression, British subjects, a large number and the most influential portion, appear to have been Jews."[31] In a world in which casual racism was accepted, presenting the war as in aid of Jews rather than "Anglo-Saxons" was another means of asserting that Canada's role in it was wrongheaded.

Along with the unfortunate anti-Semitism of some protesters, matters of race in South Africa also begot a certain cynicism. Racial conflict, in the context of the Boer War, generally meant antagonism between English and Dutch. The native people, by far the mass of the population, figure only marginally in the war of words and then in a passive way. British propaganda had maintained that the Boers felt themselves to be racially superior to the Blacks, and thus treated them badly. British control, it was argued, would improve their lot. The "pro-Boers" attempted to disabuse the public of the notion that the war was being fought partly for the protection of the natives, reminding them that Britain's own record in this matter was not noticeably superior. Hobson argued that a major impetus behind the war was the desire by the mine owners to drive down the wages of the Blacks and institute a certain degree of forced labour. Although the pro-Boers criticized both the ideological and economic justifications for imperialism, neither side seemed to consider seriously that South Africa might properly be ruled by Blacks.

The decision to go to war at all was perhaps the most prominent cause of debate. Beyond this was a concern with the means by which it was carried out. And this, in the later years of the war, seemed to become increasingly indefensible. The British had captured Bloemfontein and Pretoria, the capitals of the two Boer Republics, by June of 1900. Many people, in Canada and Britain, assumed the war was all but over. Indeed, there were lavish victory celebrations across the country, and several Canadian histories of the war were written in that year. A complete British victory seemed more or less assured. A number of Boers, however, did not see things that way, and the capture of the capitals did not, in fact, mean the end of the fighting. The guerrilla warfare that shaped this last stage of the war seemed to allow greater space for criticism.

Confronted by this new form of warfare, the leader of British forces in South Africa, Lord Roberts, responded in an increasingly harsh manner. The Boers were now viewed as rebels, not soldiers. His answer was a "scorched earth" campaign and the relocation of their families to concentration camps. These policies were increasingly decried, especially with the wide publicity given to the conditions in the camps by British activist Emily Hobhouse. Due to crowding, unhygienic conditions, and general maladministration, over 20,000 detainees, largely women and children, died.[32]

Britain, while just as jingoistic as Canada, also had a vociferous "pro-Boer" movement which grew over time, gaining support as the war dragged on in uglier ways. It included prominent people like Henry Campbell-Bannerman, leader of the Liberal party and future prime minister, who famously denounced the "methods of barbarism" his country's army was deploying. Canadian dissenters, whose antiwar movement was weaker and less organized, leaned heavily on Britain. Newspapers with an antiwar slant published debates from the British House of Commons and extracts of speeches from prominent pro-Boers in Britain. And in this atmosphere it is perhaps unsurprising that several of those who spoke out against the war were émigrés from Britain including Goldwin Smith, J. Herbert Bainton, and William Marchant.

One aspect that distinguishes the rhetoric of the Canadian antiwar movement from that in Britain, however, was that Canadians, rather curiously, paid comparatively little attention to the last two years of the war. Goldwin Smith was one of the few who drew attention to Canadian participation in the less creditable actions of the war. In an account published the year the war ended, he quotes an unnamed English soldier:

> In ten miles we have burned no fewer than six farm houses; the wife watched from a sick husband's bedside the burning of her home a hundred yards away. It seems as though a kind of domestic murder were being committed. I stood there till late last night and saw the flames lick round each piece of poor furniture – the chairs and tables, the baby's cradle, the chest of drawers containing a world of treasure, and when I saw the poor housewife's face pressed against the window of the neighbouring house my own heart burned with a sense of outrage. The effects on the colonial troops who are gratifying their feelings of hatred and revenge, is very bad.[33]

Outrage against the way the war was fought was a key aspect of anti-war agitation in Britain, but the Canadian response was remarkably muted. Even Smith, introducing the above story of the farm burnings, attempted to distance the Canadians.

> The spirit of adventure fired our valiant youth and hurried them to the field, where many of them earned distinction. That their military merits are independent of the conduct of the politicians and of the justice of the war, it is needless to repeat. But in the course of the war they were set to work from which we are glad to know that some of them recoiled.[34]

This disinclination to pay attention to the less savoury aspects of the war was not solely a contemporary trait. The later years of the war have also received scarce attention from Canadian historians. While military historian Brereton Greenhous admits participation – "The Canadians joined in the fatiguing, mostly fruitless, work of chasing small bands of sharp-shooting, veldt-wise guerrillas in every direction, burning Boer farms as they went" – it is not something that Canadian historians have considered to any real extent.[35] Especially when compared with the soul-searching of British historians, and of American historians about their contemporaneous and ideologically similar Spanish-American War, Canadian historians have not dealt with the darker aspects of the war. Part of this seems to have stemmed from a sense that Canada was not obliged to come to terms with less-than-ideal behaviour because it went into the war as a colony of Britain. Civilians went into concentration camps, in this interpretation, because British commanders said that they should, not as a Canadian decision.[36]

o o o

In Britain, efforts among the "pro-Boers" to consolidate their position and employ more concerted action led to the founding of various active committees. However, in Canada almost no group, religious or political, maintained a united front against the war. Henri Bourassa and Goldwin Smith made a short-lived effort to come together, but the other divisions between them made working together difficult. The inability of Canadians to organize seems to have been partly due to an anxious colonial mentality, eager to prove its worth and loyalty. J. Herbert Bainton, the minister who lost his post for urging his congregation to pray for both sides in the war, felt that it was, perhaps surprisingly, more difficult to maintain an antiwar stance in Canada than in Britain.[37] As well, Canada did not have the same dissenting tradition or established organizations to draw upon.

The muted antiwar voice in Canada, at this time and in our historical memory, also seems to have been due to the absence of leadership and the presence of issues that divided war dissenters. While Goldwin Smith did draw some disparate voices together for a time – that the Roman Catholic newspaper *The Casket* quoted his antiwar arguments approvingly is rather surprising considering Smith's earlier campaign against the Jesuits – he was also a polarizing figure. Carman Miller sees this disunity as key. "On all other public issues they were deeply divided," he notes. "Farm and radical labour interests, for example, were scarcely identical. . . . Goldwin Smith could not have worked long with Anglophobic Irish, radical labour, French Canadians, or indeed anyone else."[38]

Canadians did seem to have a peculiar difficulty in maintaining a critical opposition to the war. However, while the Canadian antiwar movement was weaker than in Britain, the difficulty of maintaining a pacifist stance was not a strictly Canadian phenomenon. Peter Brock has suggested that pacifism was going through a period of change at the turn of the century, moving from something religious and anti-imperial to a more secular, economic-based ideology, and was thus at a rather weak stage.[39]

The success of the dissent is unclear. Obviously these opponents failed to keep Canada out of the war, or to end its commitment before the war ended. But the pacifist movement in Canada strengthened after, and in reaction to, the Boer War. And, while history has judged those who declaimed against the iniquities of an imperial war more gently than did their contemporaries, the angry denunciation of the time also faded fairly quickly. Marchant, deemed too seditious for a school trustee, was mayor of Victoria in the 1920s.[40] The scale of dissent to this conflict might seem muted compared to that against other wars examined in this volume. Individuals expressed their concerns through letters to the editor and speeches; ministers prayed for both sides in the conflict. But the passionate denunciation of these small protests reveals that they were not so minor.

Henri Bourassa, July 1917. Library and Archives Canada, C-009092.

4

With Thought and Faith

Henri Bourassa and the First World War

GEOFF KEELAN

O N AUGUST 4, 1914, CANADA ENTERED the First World War under the auspices of its membership in the British Empire. When Britain declared war against the Central Powers led by Germany, ostensibly in defence of Belgium and France, its colonies and dominions joined the war alongside it. In a few short weeks, soldiers were in battle across Europe and throughout the Middle East, Africa, and Asia. The global conflict stretched on for four years as each side tenuously clung to small victories that were rarely enough to force their opponents to admit defeat.[1]

There were many experiences of the war for Canadians. Soldiers lived and died on the immobile frontlines in France and Belgium amid artillery barrages and gas bombardment.[2] Their successes nurtured a positive postwar memory for English Canadians. Battle performances at places like Ypres in April 1915, Courcelette in September 1916, Vimy Ridge and Passchaendale in 1917, and during the 1918 Hundred Days Offensive that saw the final collapse of the German Army were all counted as national accomplishments. On the home front, Canadians were confronted with passionate rhetoric justifying their participation and sacrifice as they struggled with serious political and social issues intensified by the war. Strengthened federal powers and allegations of corruption, new gender and family roles, and increased racial and cultural tensions all impacted the life of ordinary Canadians. The most pressing political issues often centred on questions about Canadian unity and the scale of its contribution to the Allied war effort, like justifications of the war, conscription, and the supposed apathy of French Canada. These conflicts revealed ethnic divides between English and French Canadians and resentment toward new immigrants from what were now enemy nations. For some the war consisted of a series of Canadian victories, for others it was a story of resistance and rejection, while still others experienced oppression and imprisonment.[3] The diversity of these Canadian war experiences belies the often simplified narratives of our social memory.

Canada's entry into the First World War is popularly remembered by expressions of widespread support. Newspapers across the country trumpeted the national call to arms and championed Canada's chance to serve the empire and defeat German militarism. "Ready, aye ready," were the famous words of Sir Wilfrid Laurier, and most Canadians seemed to agree. Though it is impossible to peer into the minds of ordinary Canadians who did not attend the rallies in urban centres celebrating the outbreak of war, it would appear that most dissenters chose to stay silent. In 1914, only the French-Canadian *nationalistes* were serious opponents to Canada's entry. Few public commentators rejected the war outright. Pacifist J.S. Woodsworth was a lone progressive voice[4] while other opponents, like Ottawa lawyer J.S. Ewart, were voluntarily silent so as to not weaken Canadian unity.[5] Most would stay silent until 1917 when the first real cracks in Canadian society appeared over the issue of conscription. Of those dissidents who did not stay silent, the most vocal, influential, and consistent was Henri Bourassa.

A French-Canadian nationalist, politician, and journalist, Henri Bourassa was the iconoclastic political dissenter of his age. Though his eloquence and passion made him a dominant voice in Canadian and Quebec politics, his arrogance and an absolute certainty in his beliefs did not endear him to his contemporaries. His political career stretched from the 1890s to the Second World War, but its peak was during the First World War from 1914 to 1918. Afterwards, an inward-looking nationalism rose to prominence in Quebec while Bourassa, drained by his wartime experience, became more of an elder statesman than an active participant in the nation's political struggles.[6]

A young Bourassa was inspired by the rising French-Canadian Liberal Wilfrid Laurier, particularly after hearing him speak at a rally decrying the injustice of Métis leader Louis Riel's execution in 1885. Bourassa's admiration only grew as Laurier rose to lead the Liberal party. Laurier described Bourassa as a "castor-rouge." This description combined *castor*, or beaver, the symbol of Ultramontane conservatives, and *rouge*, or red, the colour of liberals and radicals. Ultramontane translates to "over the mountain," referring to their belief in the supreme authority and infallibility of the Papacy above civil authorities – Rome being over the Alps mountain range from France where the term originated. From a young age, Bourassa believed in the primacy of the Church in society[7] and his Ultramontanism infused his writing with moral certainty. Bourassa's religiosity was tempered somewhat by his devotion to a liberal Canadian nationalism. He was attracted to Laurier's cautious liberalism, which moderated its criticism of the Church. The younger man came to believe in Laurier's mixture of individual liberalism, social conservatism, and Canadian nationalism. He joined the Liberals and was elected as a Member of Parliament in 1896. Some believed he would be Laurier's successor for, despite Bourassa's conservative religious beliefs, he embraced the values of British liberalism that Laurier espoused.[8]

However, Bourassa's views soon diverged from his leader. He left the Liberal Party in 1899 after refusing to endorse Canadian participation in the Boer War. To the young politician, that conflict was a question of morality and law. It was immoral to attack the Boer Republics, he believed, and Canada had no legal obligation to join the war as a member of the British Empire.[9] Imperialism forced this European connection on Canada that subverted the long historic and cultural development of French Canadians. French Canadians, he argued at the conclusion of the Boer War, had but one homeland and thus owed allegiance to just one country, Canada.[10] His burgeoning sense of a uniquely Canadian (or perhaps, *Canadien*) nationalism led him to find new compatriots outside the Liberal Party. He could no longer support Laurier's pluralist compromise that seemed to ignore the differences between French and English conceptions of the Canadian nation.[11] Laurier's 1905 Autonomy Bills, which incorporated the provinces of Alberta and Saskatchewan, justified Bourassa's decision. The Prime Minister had bowed to pressure from English Canadians and weakened the protection of French-speaking minority rights in the new provinces. To Bourassa and other French Canadians, it was a grave betrayal.[12]

In 1904, Bourassa helped found the *Ligue nationaliste*, a French-Canadian nationalist movement. Alongside other informed French Canadians, like Olivar Asselin, Armand Lavergne, and Jules Fournier, Bourassa's anti-imperialism coalesced into a coherent political movement that surpassed his political rejection of the Boer War. It advocated greater Canadian autonomy from Britain while also touching on economic, social, and cultural issues.[13] The "social program" its adherents pursued in Quebec owed much to their specific vision of European social Catholicism, where the Church's moral force acted in concert with industrial society, and American Progressivism that resisted corporate influence over society.[14] Over the next decade, Bourassa advocated for French-Canadian rights federally and provincially, founded the Montreal newspaper *Le Devoir*, and helped Conservative Robert Borden become Prime Minister in the 1911 election through his opposition to Laurier. At the

1910 Eucharistic Congress in Montreal, he defended the French language as the best way to protect Catholicism in North America.[15] On the eve of the First World War, then, Bourassa clearly understood his place as a committed defender of Catholic Quebec and a Canadian nation – not a British one. He was a familiar voice in Canadian politics and one of its most dissident voices as well.

Unsurprisingly, Bourassa was one of the few vocal opponents to Canadian participation in the First World War. French- and English-Canadian social memories of the war recall him as a war resister but rarely come to terms with the basis of his resistance. His position was complex. Bourassa's opposition was partly guided by his Catholicism and his belief in a bicultural, bilingual Canadian nation independent from Great Britain. Bourassa argued that, given the social and economic costs of the war, it was in the best interests of Canada (and all nations) to pursue a peaceful resolution to the conflict. His position was also rooted in his criticism of British imperialism. He spurned the dominant English-Canadian narrative of the war, which argued that Canada's involvement was necessary because of its role in the British Empire. In particular, Bourassa believed that fervent war patriotism had led Canadians to accept an imperialist ideology that trumpeted the primacy of its English-speaking peoples over its French ones. Unlike other prewar opponents of imperialism, Bourassa refused to modify his opinion about these political issues under the vastly different circumstances of wartime. The result was an evolving critique of the international and domestic situation during the war informed by his religious and political beliefs.

Bourassa saw the outbreak of the war at first hand. In the summer of 1914, he travelled to Europe to learn more about British opinions on Canadian political issues and explore the state of linguistic and religious minorities of Europe. He visited Wales and Belgium but had to flee through German Alsace-Lorraine in the days before the outbreak of war. He reached Paris where he witnessed the *union sacrée* of France's divided politics. "Royalists, imperialists, republicans, socialists all seemed to be of one heart," he wrote of his time in the deserted capital.[16] The sense of national purpose that bound the French together was palpable, and something Bourassa later lamented was sorely lacking in his native land.

Bourassa understood that the war required a national unity that superseded Canadian political issues. The struggle between imperialists and nationalists over the nature of Canada's imperial ties and policies toward its French minority had defined Canadian politics up to 1914. Canadian imperialists emerged in the late nineteenth century as the young Dominion expanded, and Carl Berger notes that they advocated a form of nationalism unto itself, with its own vision of Canada's national identity.[17] Canadian imperialists believed that Canadian prosperity lay in its involvement with the British Empire. Meanwhile, French-Canadian *nationalistes* believed that Canada should be more bicultural, bilingual, and autonomous. Its national interests deserved to be considered above imperial ones. Previous political clashes, such as ones over Canadian participation in the Boer War, the creation of a Canadian navy, the 1911 election, and debates over provincial linguistic rights, had all hinged in part on the differences between these two views. Historian Sylvie Lacombe divides the English- and French-Canadian political perspectives between "imperial ambition" and "national ambition" respectively and characterizes them not simply as political ideologies but as fundamentally different worldviews.[18] Such competing conceptions of national identity ensured that any wartime compromise would prove difficult.

For a brief moment, though, Bourassa believed that these different worldviews could be amended in favour of a national war effort, like the one he observed in France. In his first written response to the war, he offered a truce to his opponents: make this truly a Canadian war, not an imperial one.[19] His limited support required that French and English Canadian national unity be considered and that the economic obligations demanded of Canada were not too high. Canadian unity, he argued, would be best served by a guarantee that English-Canadian provinces would re-establish French language schooling and language rights while a limited war effort would maintain Canada's economic prosperity. Bourassa further reasoned that the war's unifying potential was only possible if imperialists retreated from their objective of securing Canada's place in the British Empire. The clearest peace offering to extend to the *nationalistes*, Bourassa wrote, echoing his fellow *nationalistes* Armand Lavergne and Omar Héroux, would be for Ontario Premier James Whitney to end the discriminatory legislation of Regulation 17.[20] This legislation had eliminated French language schooling for thousands of Franco-Ontarians in 1912 and remained a sore point for French Canadians, who had seen their rights outside of Quebec repeatedly attacked since Confederation. The abrogation of Regulation 17, Bourassa argued, would be an "act of elemental justice and political intelligence" that would do "more to assure the unity of the Empire and the Canadian nation" than any material or monetary contributions.[21] Why would French Canadians fight for a country that did not even grant them the right to learn their own language? If Canadian imperialists sought to enter the empire's war united with Bourassa and the *nationalistes*, the first step had to be a show of good faith at home.

The demand was largely ignored, except by his critics who included most of the French- and English-Canadian press. Many newspapers treated Bourassa's position as a *nationaliste* polemic denouncing the dangers of Canada's imperial ties rather than as a serious consideration of the problem of wartime unity. To them, he was using the war for his own political advantage. Bourassa perceived the opposite of his critics' claim. He believed that Canadians' support of Britain's war represented support for prewar policies of Canadian imperialism. It was the imperialists who were using the war for their own political advantage. Canadian nationalists could only support the war if it were separated from the political goals of imperialist ideology, which meant no imperial rhetoric should be used in justifying Canadian participation. "All that I asked [of the imperialists]," Bourassa wrote in a letter in 1918, "was to take no advantage of the wave of blind enthusiasm to compromise the issue of interimperial relations. Far from responding to that offer of truce [they] did their best to becloud the real issues of the war, to foster the blind hatred of everything German."[22] If Canada's imperialists and nationalists were to have "one heart" like France's *union sacrée*, the two sides would have to negotiate their understanding of the war's purpose and its consequences. Their inability to do so would quickly sour Bourassa's views on the war and its supporters. As the human and economic costs of the war escalated and Bourassa's voice was ignored, his opposition to the war effort grew.

In September 1914, after Bourassa's initial offer of compromise and tentative support for Canadian participation had been ignored, he wrote a broad analysis of the war. Historian Réné Durocher reasons that Bourassa's early support for the war was purposefully ambivalent and reflected his desire to not contradict the position of Quebec's Catholic Church. Durocher suggests that many members of the clergy privately supported the journalist's views but the devout Bourassa anguished over any perceived conflict with Quebec bishops.[23] Bourassa, who worried about what position the provincial Church hierarchy would take, carefully worded his editorials. His first series of articles examined the British *White Papers*[24] that detailed Britain's diplomatic correspondence from the outbreak of the war. He was impressed by Britain's Foreign Secretary Sir Edward Grey's careful regard for his country's national interests during the July Crisis, and Bourassa urged his fellow Canadians to mirror Grey's policy.[25] Canada's participation should be directed by its national interests rather than by the imperial interests of the Empire. He still did not rule out participation, but he asked that Canadians not support the war unquestioningly. His careful support for the war in August and September alienated some of his former *nationaliste* allies, notably

Jules Fournier, who did not accept Bourassa's distinction that Canada could join the war on Britain's side as a nation, without the strings of imperialism attached.[26]

Bourassa believed that the European conflict required a limited war effort and careful reflection. True national loyalty meant that Canadian interests had to come before those of Great Britain. Thus, he argued that Canada should contribute as much as its economy and resources allowed, but no more.[27] His opponents, whose views of Canada's place in the world demanded that they provide the utmost aid to Great Britain, understandably rejected his view. Nonetheless, he publicly promised to research conscientiously, loyally, and honestly the issues of the war that others did not have the courage to discuss.[28] Unfortunately for the Ultramontane Catholic, the bishops of Quebec released a pastoral letter on 23 September outlining support for Canada's involvement in the war while the Catholic newspaper, *L'Action Social*, published a detailed refutation of Bourassa.[29] Nonplussed, he spent the last months of 1914 deconstructing Canadian war rhetoric by explaining the causes of the conflict and its impact on Canada. Despite his promise to examine the issues of the war openly, few accepted his words at face value.

As 1915 dawned, Bourassa moved further away from his early offer of compromise. In December 1914, he had been accused of treason and nearly caused a riot when he tried to give a speech in Ottawa.[30] For most Canadians, the coming months revealed the bloody reality of the European war. They were forced to confront the Western Front's high casualties in April 1915, when the 1st Canadian Division was attacked in Belgium during the Second Battle of Ypres. The use of poison gas devastated the Canadian forces and many at home were appalled by the number of dead. The sinking of the civilian passenger ship *Lusitania* on May 7 by a German U-Boat was similarly shocking. Taken together these events intensified public support for Canadian efforts to stop Germany by force of arms, yet for Bourassa, the casualties at Ypres were proof that the totality of Canada's commitment had a high cost. The *Lusitania* likewise revealed the dangers awaiting Americans if they entered the war. Bourassa hoped that President Woodrow Wilson was aware of "the terrible consequences that would result from a hasty decision."[31] For the United States, to decide between the "brutalité allemande" behind submarine warfare or the "morgue britannique" of the Western Front was a poor set of options.[32] While other Canadians decried the German actions, Bourassa only saw further proof that he was correct.

Bourassa's opponents grew more committed to winning the war and he grew more certain of the righteousness of his perspective. Like other

Canadians, Bourassa increasingly perceived the war through a moral lens, but as a devout Catholic, he saw Pope Benedict XV as the ultimate moral arbiter. In August, he welcomed the Pope's appeal for peace as evidence that his opposition to the war was in line with his Catholic faith.[33] On New Year's Eve 1915, Bourassa examined peace advocates in light of the war's terrible consequences. Reprinting words from the British socialist newspaper the *Labour Leader*, he noted that its missive was similar to that of the Pope. Both demanded that the people of Europe unite against the suffering of all common people. The nine-point "minimum program" of The Hague's Peace Conference of Neutral Nations from April 1915 also reflected this position, as did the program of Britain's Union of Democratic Control.[34] Those in favour of peace came from an unlikely grouping of Protestant or nonreligious nations (save Catholic Spain) that agreed with the position of the Vatican. Regardless of their source, the Ultramontane Bourassa supported any who offered reasonable opinions aligning with the Vatican.

The first full year of the war had attuned Bourassa to its horrific cost. The war marked the collapse of a political system based on false wisdom, arrogant diplomacy, the thirst for conquest, and the worship of money and force.[35] Perhaps, he suggested, it would eventually bring about the destruction of those systems and re-establish the moral authority of the Pope. That solution was far better than the forces he saw at work in shaping the world in December 1915, be it "German scientific militarism, English mercantile imperialism, the debilitating democracy of the French Revolution, savage mysticism, or the perfidy of panslavism."[36]

The chasm between dissenter and supporter was captured in an interaction between Bourassa and his cousin, Talbot Mercer Papineau, in the summer of 1916. Like Bourassa, Talbot Papineau was descended from Louis-Joseph Papineau, the republican rebel of 1837–38, but he was raised by his American mother after the death his father at a young age. He spoke English and was a Protestant, despite his French name.[37] In August 1914, he joined the Princess Patricia's Canadian Light Infantry and was one of the first Canadians on the battlefield in 1915. His view of the war was shaped by his soldiering experience, and he felt compelled to write to his cousin Bourassa and rally weakening French-Canadian support.

In the spring of 1916, the young Papineau sent a message to his former law partner, Andrew McMaster, asking him to pass a letter on to Bourassa. When Bourassa did not reply, McMaster released the letter to newspapers across the country on July 28. Papineau argued that achievements on the battlefields would create a new Canadian nation after the war, entrenched in a progressive, reformed British Empire and deserving of French Canadians' support.[38] On August 2, 1916, Bourassa published his reply to Papineau's letter in *Le Devoir* and it encapsulated his position against the war's supporters. He doubted that Papineau was even capable of offering the arguments and instead accused McMaster of writing in his name. Bourassa charged that the federal government, the press, and politicians of both parties "applied themselves systematically to obliterate the free character of Canada's intervention." He became opposed to the war when supporting it no longer became a matter of choice, but a matter of "blackmail, intimidation and threats." Bourassa's message was clear: a war of patriots was not a patriotic war. Bourassa did not support the war for he stood by the principles he had first laid out during the Boer War, when he foretold that Canada's involvement in a British war set a precedent that resigned it to future participation in all European wars. Inevitably, Bourassa said a decade earlier, the Old World would dissolve into conflict, and this would lead to Canada's ruin. "All the nations of Europe are the victims of their own mistakes," he explained, as they were all guilty "of the complacent servility with which they submitted to the dominance of all Imperialists and traders in human flesh." Bourassa closed his reply by dismissing his cousin, saying

> most part American, he has inherited, with a few drops of French blood, the most *denationalised* instincts of his French origin. From those he calls his compatriots he is separated by his religious belief and his maternal language.... He was brought up far away from close contact with French-Canadians.[39]

For the *nationaliste* journalist, Papineau did not deserve the attention of French Canada. French Canada's abstention from the war did not result from Bourassa's influence or from his political movement, as his cousin believed, but rather from "hereditary instincts, social and economic conditions, [and] a national tradition of three centuries."[40] Papineau was not offering a new Canadian nationalism, Bourassa argued, but merely a new version of the imperialist appeal to a nonexistent British connection that Bourassa had long ago rejected. If Papineau was so removed from the reality of true Canadian nationalism, Bourassa reasoned, he had little insight to offer about his country's place in the conflict. The public debate between Papineau and Bourassa did little but to highlight the divergent perspectives of the war supporter and the war resister.

Bourassa saw only more proof of the war's disastrous political and moral consequences. In December 1916, a German proposal to enter into peace negotiations was rejected by the Allies. Bourassa framed these international manoeuvres as self-serving acts of diplomacy, ignoring the emotional or moral significance imbued upon them by war rhetoric. To him any chance for peace was worth pursuing, even if it meant defeat. He examined the tense international situation and hoped that the two sides could find some sort of compromise to end the bloody conflict. He reminded Canadians that if the war was not about British civilization or against German militarism and instead furthered Britain's wealth and power, perhaps it was not worth the increasing cost.[41] The Allies' rejection of the German peace offer underlined a disturbing truth. Small nations, including Canada, were victims of the calculated and unscrupulous ambitions inherent in the attempt to preserve Europe's balance of power.[42] It was only through the lens of Canadian national interests that it was possible to properly assess the conflict and thus, according to Bourassa, reject it.

The failure of a diplomatic solution underscored the moral dangers of the war. Reflecting on the December peace note issued by President Wilson,[43] Bourassa repeated the position of Pope Benedict XV: only when nations set aside their self-interests could an acceptable peace be fashioned.[44] Benedict XV had been opposed to the war since his election in September 1914. Bourassa often used his position as the litmus test for other nations. If they agreed with Pope Benedict's desire for peace, then their positions were worthwhile. Sometimes his dissection of international politics slipped into moral lectures informed by Papal dictate. By not accepting Papal moral supremacy on earthly matters, belligerent nations risked catastrophe.[45] Bourassa's fealty to the Church continued to shape the content of his analysis.

In turn, Bourassa's domestic analysis continued to reflect his understanding of the international context as much as his rejection of imperialist arguments. The crisis over conscription and the 1917 election emphasized his dual approach. Prime Minister Robert Borden's promise in 1916 to double the size of the Canadian Army to five hundred thousand, alongside the casualties suffered at the Somme and Vimy Ridge battles and lower enlistment rates, meant that conscription seemed a necessity to the war's supporters and the Canadian government. On May 17, 1917, Borden announced to his Cabinet that he would introduce conscription. The Conservatives approached the Liberals with the offer of a coalition government as it became clear that many English-Canadian Liberals supported conscription. Laurier refused, knowing he could not afford to defy the majority of French Canadians who remained opposed to forced enlistment. Many English-Canadian Liberals spurned their leader and united with Conservatives to form the Unionist Party in support of conscription.[46] The stage was set for an election that December. Effectively a plebiscite on conscription, the election was one of the most vitriolic in Canadian history and perhaps the least democratic, as dirty politics and voter intimidation abounded.[47] One candidate described the election as "essentially a one-party election, one party only in Quebec and one party only in other provinces."[48] The ensuing Unionist victory in December revealed Quebec's national isolation for opposing conscription. Laurier's Liberals would win sixty-two of their total eighty-two seats in the province while the Unionists won only three.

Despite them being former foes, Bourassa supported the Laurier Liberals. He had warned his readers about the danger of conscription since 1915, and when it finally came to pass two years later, he was ready.[49] In an article for the *New York Evening Post*, Bourassa reviewed why Canadians should oppose conscription: Canada had already contributed an impressive amount to the war; any further contribution risked weakening Canada's agricultural production and industry; Canada could not shoulder any more economic cost; it threatened Canada's political independence; and, finally, it would create disunity and strife for the country and the continent.[50] Conscription, Bourassa argued, was not in Canada's national interest, but rather continued to serve British imperial interests. If Canada had an international obligation, it was to strive for a peaceful resolution to the conflict and preserve the international system, not witness its systematic degradation.

Forced military service and the 1917 election were the culminations of everything Bourassa had feared in 1914 as he witnessed Canadians' rampant support for the war. The victory of the largely conservative, Protestant and English-Canadian Unionist Party left little room for Canada's French Catholic minority.[51] As 1917 drew to a close, Bourassa lamented the disastrous consequences of the war and the isolation of French Canada. To his eye, he had stayed loyal to the political principles and religious values with which he had begun his political career nearly twenty years earlier. Despite his loyalty, the war had transformed the Dominion of Canada. The First World War tore apart Canada's two peoples and warped its national spirit, its patriotism, and its moral compass.[52] In the final year of the war, Bourassa grew depressed. Riots throughout Quebec on Easter weekend in April 1918 protested the draft of French Canadians. The journalist was appalled that he may have helped fuel the flames of such disorder and, upon learning that censorship laws would be strengthened, stopped publishing editorials until the war's end in November.[53] The Canadian unity Bourassa had spent his entire career seeking seemed impossible.

○ ○ ○

Bourassa has been remembered by both English Canadians and French Canadians (or later, Quebecois) as the most prominent agitator against the Canadian war effort and the government's wartime policies. The dominant English-Canadian narrative understands Bourassa's opposition against the backdrop of a national myth that heralds the war's creation of a Canadian nation, while the French-Canadian memory casts him in an understandably more positive light as a precursor to its own inward nationalism that developed after the war. Bourassa's presence in these two Canadian experiences of the war is complex. Although he nurtured French-Canadian resentment of English Canada's dominant war narrative, he was not actively involved in shaping it. Moreover, the political details of his resistance, as anti-imperialist, as anti-English Canada, or as championing pro-Canadian interests, often overshadow the persistent moral tone present in his writings. Social memory in English and French Canada recalls Bourassa the *political* war resister but rarely acknowledges Bourassa the *Ultramontane moral* war resister. Each existed in tandem with the other.

It must be better to discard the simplified stories of popular memory since neither English nor French Canada (nor Bourassa himself) was as monolithic as they suggest. Instead, Canadians can remember Bourassa's consistent and rational analyses of the war, though they were sometimes immersed in his religious beliefs. Or they can remember his combative opinions, where his view of the world was the superior one and his "high causes" of Canadian nationalism and Ultramontanism were expressed as absolute certainties rather than personal positions. His opinions made him many enemies, but Bourassa the war resister was so prominent *because* of his confidence about his political and religious beliefs. He believed in his perspective of the war and refused to accept other interpretations. The uniqueness of his opinions, while making him a dissenter, also helped to ensure that he became a caricature in both French-Canadian and English-Canadian war narratives. Bourassa may have failed to fashion the Canada he envisioned, but many of his fears from the Boer War onwards were proven correct. The undeniable legitimacy of his arguments frustrated his contemporaries and assured him a place in both French and English Canadians' memory of the war.

ΑΜΟ INDUSTRIAL BANNER Harvester

Endorsed by Ontario Labor Educational Association and Toronto Trades and Labor Council

26TH YEAR—NO. 27   TORONTO, CANADA, JULY 6, 1917.   PRICE, FIVE CENTS.

THE STATE MUST SAY TO EVERY MAN
"YOUR MONEY   OR   YOUR LIFE!"

REGISTRATION BLANK FOR CONSCRIPTION OF WEALTH	REGISTRATION BLANK FOR CONSCRIPTION OF MEN

IF WE CONSCRIPT OUR YOUTH, WE MUST CONSCRIPT OUR WEALTH

PRESIDENT OF TRADES AND LABOR CONGRESS OF CANADA

DEFINES ATTITUDE OF ORGANIZED LABOR ON THE QUESTION OF CONSCRIPTION

THE GOVERNMENT SYSTEMATICALLY IGNORES LABOR

BUT HOB-NOBS WITH VESTED INTERESTS

THE CO-OPERATION OF THE WORKERS IS NOT APPRECIATED AT OTTAWA

MINE WORKERS OF ONTARIO ARE SPLENDIDLY ORGANIZED

HAVE RECOGNIZED NECESSITY FOR UNITY BOTH INDUSTRIALLY AND POLITICALLY

INDEPENDENT LABOR PARTY OF ONTARIO

PROVINCIAL ORGANIZATION FORMED AND CLEAR CUT PLATFORM ADOPTED

Opposition to conscription took many forms in the First World War, including a campaign for "conscription of wealth" that led to the introduction of the first income tax in Canada. The front page of the *Industrial Banner*, a weekly labour newspaper from Ontario, from July of 1917, shows how the conscription controversy was linked to changes in party politics and public finance that made elections more meaningfully democratic after the war. *Industrial Banner*, front page, July 6, 1917. Library and Archives Canada, The Industrial Banner/AMICUS 8550541/July 6, 1917, p. 1.

5

A Better Truth

The Democratic Legacy of Resistance to Conscription, 1917–1921

DAVID TOUGH

THERE IS A FAMILIAR STORY about Canada and the First World War. It says that young men signed up eagerly to fight in 1914, that they served with bravery on the Western front, and that they played a key role in the Battle of Vimy Ridge; it says that they joined up to defend democracy, and their brave sacrifice on the fields of Belgium and France made Canada a nation.[1] Whatever truth there is to this story, it works as a myth: more than telling us about the war, it tells us what to feel about the war. If we value democracy, it says, we should thank the soldiers who sacrificed themselves defending it against an alien threat. And we should be ready to fight again if another threat looms.[2]

The sacrificial myth of the First World War is very powerful, and growing more powerful. It reflects not only a particular emotional engagement with the war as a memorial artefact, but also a political attitude toward the connection between the military and democracy. The idea of wartime glory is "politically useful in the Harper government's promotion of the military as the crucial Canadian institution," Ian McKay and Jamie Swift say, "with soldiers towering over the rest of us."[3] If we believe that democracy was secured by fighting and dying for it, we will believe that those who fight and die for us deserve our unqualified support, and that, in the case of a trade-off between financing social programs and financing the military, the latter should always win out. However, if we value democracy not as a static object in need of protection from aggressive outsiders but rather as a social process, then it is important that we tell ourselves another, better truth about Canada and the First World War – one that is about the actual lives of common people and their struggles.

To tell a better truth about the war is to underscore the fact that Canada's participation in the war was controversial, and the extent of sacrifice some Canadians were asked or forced to make in the name of the war effort was fiercely contested. The First World War occurred during a time of profound social and civil tension in Canada. Rather than thinking of democracy as something already established that could be defended, it is better to think of democracy in 1914 as struggling to be realized. Women were fighting for the right to participate in electoral democracy, labour was fighting for recognition of their democratic right to organize and – if necessary – to strike, and farmers were fighting for more democratic taxation. At first the war was only incidentally related to these things, but it became more controversial and more central to these democratic struggles as it began to dominate the everyday lives of civilians.

The government's shift toward introducing conscription beginning in 1916 marked an important change in the way the war was understood and experienced. The simple fact of war had been broadly accepted, because it was voluntary, far removed, and irrelevant to anyone who decided not to take an interest in it. But as the demands of the war were increasingly imposed by the federal government on an already exploited population the war became controversial. The unfair apportioning of the burdens of fighting and paying for the war, crystalized in the decision to impose conscription, caused mass alienation and brought existing social tensions to a head. By the war's end, the major political parties were weakened, the economic system they supported was under direct attack, and it had become difficult to separate criticism of the war from criticism of society as a whole. People had organized as farmers and as workers to demand a renegotiation of the burdens placed on various parts of society. This resistance, not the war itself, is the source of the democratic legacy of the First World War.

Opposition to conscription was multifaceted, but this chapter focuses on its economic dimensions. People's lives were affected on a daily basis, and the impact of the war on their survival was a major factor in war resistance. Resistance to the economic conduct of the war resulted in significant changes to Canada's fiscal politics and led directly to changes in the political system that made the country more democratic. In their resistance against the unfair apportioning of the cost of the war, labour unions and farmers created a new politics in which the assigning of the benefits and costs of capitalism could be contested democratically. This is a better truth than the officially sanctioned sacrificial myth, because it tells us about democracy as a social process, as something people lived every day.

o o o

In order to understand how the resistance to conscription changed the country, it is important to recall the political and social conditions of the time. Politically, Canada was not a democracy, in either a technical or a broader social sense.[4] Most people could not vote. Women were expressly barred from voting in provincial and federal elections across the country in 1914. In various places at various times between 1867 and 1914, Aboriginal people and other non-whites could not vote. Together this meant that more than half of the adult population couldn't vote. Elections were the privilege of a white and male minority.[5]

Beyond these formal limitations on political participation, non-whites and non-Christians faced severe and arbitrary limitations on their civil rights. They were legally barred from high-status professions and in many places could not own or even rent property. Status Indians in particular were the object of an aggressive campaign of political marginalization and cultural assimilation, but non-white residents more generally expected the state to treat them as lesser persons, if not as outright threats to white society.[6] Even for those whose gender and race allowed them to participate in elections, the extreme inequalities in Canadian society severely limited the meaningfulness of the political process. Formally and procedurally, electoral democracy functioned much as it does now: bills were debated in Parliament and could only pass into law on the basis of a majority vote by members elected in constituencies from across the country; there were two parties, and it was possible to vote for either one of them. But there was little to distinguish the Liberals and Conservatives in practical terms. Both parties were dedicated to a broad policy of supporting the colonization of the west and the establishment of a national economy, and both saw the role of the federal government as assisting business in this project. As one commentator noted, the parties agreed on what should be done and only differed on who should do it.[7]

The development of the national economy was broadly based on keeping costs low for business by making cheap labour available and eschewing taxes that targeted wealth. The main source of income was the protective tariff, a regressive tax that weighed more heavily on low incomes than high ones. Farmers in the west were particularly affected by the tariff because it raised the prices of imported manufactured goods, including farm machinery and supplies, effectively forcing them to subsidize Canadian industry, most of which was based in Ontario or Montreal. The federal government borrowed against tariff revenues, financing the building of railways and other infrastructure on credit.

Cheap labour was supplied, meanwhile, by a flexible immigration policy that nominally preferred British migrants but relied on migrants from Central and Eastern Europe to do most of the unpleasant work in mining and forestry for low wages.[8]

This economic system was well established by the start of the twentieth century but was approaching a crisis by 1914. In part, this was structural, because the economic model depended on expansion into the west and easy credit. A major depression began in 1913, and the economic system began to collapse: credit dried up, trade contracted, and tariff revenues fell.[9] The collapsing economy hit Winnipeg, as the epicentre of the previously growing west, particularly hard. Mostly it drove home the point that the tariff was a "fair weather friend," in that it worked well when the economy was booming, but was useless when conditions worsened. For the prairie west, this was one reason more than it needed to resent and distrust the tariff. The tariff had, in fact, been a central issue in the 1911 federal election, thanks in part to farmers' agitation against its effects. That election resulted in the election of Robert Borden's Conservatives on a staunchly pro-tariff platform, but it also publicized the farmers' critical perspective on the tariff. A small but growing minority was questioning both the sustainability and the justice of the fiscal system and indeed the economic system as a whole.

More important and widespread than the questioning of the tariff, though, was the suffrage movement, which, in alliance with other reform causes like public health and temperance, was gaining wider and wider acceptance. Attitudes toward sexual inequality were changing rapidly in the early twentieth century. Many commentators believed it was only a matter of time before the government enfranchised women.[10]

Canadian society was thus not particularly democratic in 1914: neither formally nor informally did the majority have anywhere close to a meaningful say in how the country was governed. The young men who rushed to defend Canada in 1914 were, therefore, not defending democracy. The country was arguably in the process of democratizing, and it presented some of the elements out of which it was possible to construct a democratic politics. To a large extent, though, the exploitation and injustice inherent in how Canada was governed were passively accepted in the prewar period as simply normal and expected. The war brought these exploitations into sharp relief and clarified opposition to them. Conscription, in particular, served as a flash point for social tensions because it encapsulated the structural unfairness of Canadian society.

The War Economy and Resistance to Conscription

Canadian society was profoundly unequal in the period between Confederation and the First World War, and the war exaggerated that inequality. Prejudices and exploitations that were understood as normal in 1914 became explicit and extreme, and became the object of direct political struggle. Poverty and economic inequality made life difficult for most Canadians before 1914, and the war made these problems worse. The cost of the war, both in terms of paying for it and carrying it out, was high on the poor and low on the rich. Although there were individual exceptions, the rich benefited overall while the poor struggled. The war exaggerated the existing inequalities between classes and races and turned them into official policy.

Early on, the war was greeted enthusiastically, and it was easy to get men to volunteer to fight. There were a number of reasons for this. One is that Canada was a society of migrants, the majority of whom were from Britain.[11] When Britain entered the war, these migrants signed on quickly. Recent English, Scots, Irish, and Welsh immigrants to Canada made up more than half of the Canadian Expeditionary Force in 1914.[12] Another reason was the pervasive celebration of militarism. Young men who had been raised to revere manly adventurousness welcomed the call to military service as an opportunity to express their masculinity.[13] An additional reason was that the depression left many young men with few other options. Unemployment was high at the outbreak of war, and there was little if any support for those without work or income. Though military service was voluntary in the first years, it is undoubtedly true that "the sting of widespread unemployment and hunger 'conscripted' many."[14] The voluntary principle was key to how the war was understood at the start.

This voluntary spirit was reflected in the economic management of the war. In the first few years, the government was eager to carry on what Ian McKay calls "business as usual."[15] The war economy would be carried out exactly like the prewar economy, with Ottawa acting as an instrument of business. As a strategy, this had the advantage of being easier than developing an entirely novel economic approach. It also dovetailed rhetorically with the conservatism of a war that was about defending an existing way of life.

Business as usual meant continuing to assign war contracts on the basis of party patronage, and for the same, long-standing purpose: generating profits for manufacturers and their creditors. Canada emerged almost immediately as a key manufacturing base for British weapons, ammunition, and materials. Within a few years, this activity had improved economic conditions, reversing the effects of the depression. But this development was double-edged. For one thing it was, like economic development in general in the prewar economy, uneven. Most munitions manufacturing was in Ontario and Quebec; a miniscule amount was in the prairie west.[16] For another, the recovery triggered an increased rate of inflation, which raised the prices of basic commodities. Inflation, unlike economic development, was universal: everyone paid more for basics, even if they still did not have a job. Most Canadians faced a dim outlook and increasing household costs while a minority were getting rich from the war.

The growing gap between the rich and poor created by the expanding industrial economy was exacerbated by the workings of war finance, which were brutally exploitative. The tariff, which had been an unfair but effective means of financing railways and major infrastructure projects, was a poor instrument of war finance yet during the war it was still overwhelmingly the biggest direct source of revenue, generating eighty per cent of federal government revenues.[17] Although the idea of introducing an income tax to pay for the cost of mobilization was raised repeatedly, the "business as usual" stance of the government meant a refusal to move into new areas of taxation – especially ones that primarily affected the rich.[18] Instead, the treasury raised money by issuing bonds. However, the issuing of interest on investments meant that people with money were being invited to profit from the war, a profit paid ultimately out of revenue from the regressive tariff. War finance, therefore, effectively operated as a transfer of income from the poor to the rich.[19]

The combination of increased industrial employment, high inflation, and a steeply regressive system of public finance created the perfect conditions for organizing labour unions. The prewar depression had seen unions weaken and disband, but war development meant a strengthened labour movement, particularly in Ontario.[20] Farmers and labour groups both demanded government action on the rising cost of living and insisted on a revision of the burden of war finance that would see industry and the wealthy pay their relative share. These demands were encapsulated in the increasingly common phrase "conscription of wealth," which captured dovetailing resentment regarding the two major costs of war: lives and dollars. "Conscription of wealth" in turn was increasingly tied to calls for labour and farmers to take action, either through the established political process or by more radical and direct measures, to get their voices heard.[21]

These calls grew more intense as the government began making plans to introduce conscription. Labour and farmer groups that had been critical of war finance and inflation now linked the threat of conscription to demands for a new deal for the people who would be most affected, the first order of which was a revision of war finance. Calls for independent political participation in the form of labour and farmer parties answered the government's threats of conscription. Strikes were threatened, starting in the munitions factories in Ontario where damage to the war effort would be most acutely felt.[22] The spirit of radical independence affected even the Trades and Labour Congress, the moderate labour organization, whose president, James C. Watters, asked locals in an open letter in May 1916 whether "to prevent anything that savours of 'conscription'" they would "use the most effective and almost the only weapon within your reach" – the strike.[23] A year later, in July 1917, he wrote that all wealth should be conscripted, "even if a general strike is necessary to bring it about."[24]

Opposition to conscription also energized farmers. They too were concerned about the inequities of war finance but were more worried about the practical effects of conscription on the farming community. Farm labourers, one of the key groups sought after by immigration officials in the prewar period, were becoming more scarce as part of a general shortage of labour due to enlistments and the lure of better work in war-related factories. While labour's opposition to conscription was political, and in the case of the Trades and Labour Congress arguably strategic, for farmers the issue was practical: who would do the work?

In the spring of 1917, the move toward conscription began in earnest, and the federal government took a number of key steps in short order to try to undermine the opposition to conscription. First, it introduced the Income War Tax, citing concerns about sharing the burdens of war in light of conscription. It wasn't very powerful as income taxes go (it taxed only incomes over $2000, the salary of a senior executive, and the bottom rate was 2%), and was widely greeted as a political gesture. While it did little to bring around opponents of conscription, it arguably played some role in accomplishing the next major task, which was to create a pro-conscription coalition between Conservative members and pro-conscription Liberals. The result of this coalition, the Union government, also disappointed expectations by failing to attract key talents into the fold, but succeeded in at least muddying the issue of how opposition to conscription could be expressed politically.

The final major innovation was designed more directly to undermine the chances of the government being defeated on the question of conscription. The government introduced legislation that disenfranchised enemy aliens and gave the vote to women if they served in the military or were related to someone who was serving. This change, Tarah Brookfield notes, "reconstructed the definition of citizenship," making it contingent on someone else's service to the nation.[25] The government was enfranchising people on the direct basis of their likelihood to support the measure, thus ensuring that it would be re-elected and conscription would become law. On August 29, 1917, the government introduced the *Military Service Act* to revise voting qualifications, and on December 17 the country went to the polls.

The election was not a contest on the question of conscription – a fact the government had arranged carefully. Outside of Quebec, all the major forces in opposition had been sidelined or appeased. The Trades and Labour Congress had arguably never intended to directly oppose conscription and only wanted to use criticism of it as a bargaining instrument to get better terms for labour and war finance. The farmers were more directly appeased. The government responded to their concerns by exempting farm labourers from military service. Lacking a reason to engage with independent parties, voters continued to support the existing parties, one and a half of which had been transformed into the Union government. The Union government won easily, and conscription went into force.

The farmers quickly regretted their decision: in April 1918, the government passed an Order-in-Council that reversed the exemption and made farmers subject to conscription. The political culture changed almost overnight, as farmers abandoned the traditional parties in droves. One farmer opined, "Profiteering urban millionaires have been robbing the farmers of their sons, and robbing them of their representation in Parliament, and they will continue to do so. Isn't it time farmers organized politically?" Membership in the United Farmers of Ontario (UFO) expanded dramatically. During 1918 it more than tripled in membership from eight thousand to twenty-five thousand members.[26]

Labour also developed politically in the aftermath of the conscription issue. A wave of militant strikes stretched across the country, signalling workers' rejection of both the war economy and the moderate strategies and rhetoric of the Trades and Labour Congress. The numbers were staggering. There were 457 strikes in Canada between 1917 and 1920, involving 350,000 workers.[27] In just three months (May, June, and July 1919), there were 210 strikes.[28] After the experience of wartime exploitation, "the country had been saturated with the rhetoric of service and the noble goal of fighting to defend 'democracy,' and workers now bitterly threw these words back at those in power."[29] The state responded with violence and aggressive policies of criminalization. Suspected radicals of European descent were deported, while the leaders who couldn't be deported were tried.[30]

While the fight against conscription served as an important initial rallying point, by the time sustained labour unrest was sweeping the country conscription was no longer a threat because the war was over. However, the widespread alienation from the political and economic system triggered by the fight over conscription resonated with these movements. Where at first that oppositional energy went toward rectifying the injustice of conscription and war finance, in the postwar period it focused on realizing the power of strikes and other political action to challenge the capitalist system and thus build a postwar economy, society, and political system that functioned on entirely different principles. Rather than a sign of desperation, it was the realization of their increased power and their potential role in creating a better world that inspired postwar revolts.[31]

The Democratic Legacy

There is a democratic legacy to the First World War, but it is the resistance to conscription, not the war itself that is its source. To the extent that it was an expression of domestic politics, the war was defensive and conservative, safeguarding the prewar political and economic order. The war was initially conducted in much the same way as the peace had been, but as the federal government moved to implement conscription, the exploitative character of the demand resonated with other forms of exploitation to fuel a prolonged campaign of opposition. In the end, both farmer and labour groups were unwilling or unable to oppose the introduction of conscription directly. Their campaign against conscription did, however, force the government to introduce significant reforms in order to guarantee its re-election. Moreover, it generated an unprecedented wave of independent political action among farmers and labourers that, when the war ended and conscription itself was no longer an issue, created the first viable third party movement outside of Quebec. The reforms introduced to pass conscription and the independent political power wielded by farmer and labour movements constitute together the democratic legacy of the First World War.

In terms of formal democracy, the enfranchisement of women, which at the federal level was explicitly linked to the controversy around conscription, was the key transformation. In 1917, that enfranchisement was partial, dividing women who had been organizing for the franchise into opposing camps. In some ways, partial enfranchisement was a fitting accomplishment for first wave feminism, which often employed rhetoric that positioned women as better citizens than non-British voters who were disenfranchised simultaneously.[32] At the same time, it was bitterly ironic to overcome the exclusion of women as part of a larger plan whose goal was effectively to undermine or negate the democratic will. In any case, female enfranchisement was generalized in 1920 – though other race-based exclusions still applied to women.[33] Despite these exclusions, however, a solid majority of adult Canadians could vote in federal elections for the first time. In formal terms, this is the point from which it is possible to speak of the country as being a democracy.

Another democratic legacy of the resistance to conscription is the widespread challenge to the two-party system it produced. While the Nationalist party was already representing Quebec ridings in the House of Commons before the war, outside Quebec the two-party system held fast until the issue of conscription wedged it open. In part, this was because the Union government weakened partisan political appeals, but the conscription-fuelled growth of labour and farmer organizations and parties had begun before the Union government was formed. As the war ended and the threat of conscription evaporated, a generalized revulsion at the conduct of the war by the established parties sharpened the political focus of voters and led to the provincial and federal election of farmer and labour candidates. In the House of Commons, both the Progressives, boasting fifty-eight elected members in 1921, and the two Independent Labour members owed their victory at least partly to the sense of exploitation and injustice associated with conscription. In Ontario, anti-conscription organizing sparked a demand in the postwar period for "a new political order commensurate with the country's wartime sacrifice," which resulted in the election of a UFO government supported by Labour.[34] None of these victories led directly to any staggering legislative improvements, but these parties opened a third dimension in Canadian politics and are the direct ancestors of the Co-operative Commonwealth Federation (forerunner of the present-day New Democratic Party) founded in the 1930s. Although that party never held power federally, it did provincially – playing a key role in establishing universal healthcare. This permanent challenge to the old parties influenced the direction of social policies to help the aged, the unemployed, and the sick for decades after the First World War.

Just as important as the appearance of third parties was the development of the state's capacity to generate revenue and intervene in the economy, which was minimal before the introduction of direct taxes – in particular, the Income War Tax of 1917. The tax was specifically framed as a response to public criticism of the inequalities of war service as encapsulated in the phrase "conscription of wealth." But it also reflected an existing critique of the tariff, particularly among western farmers, as exploitative and undemocratic. A regressive tax, the tariff was also grossly inefficient, because part of its intended effect was to force consumers to buy more expensive products, effectively taxing them for private gain. In the early years of the war, the government's reliance on voluntary financing meant that wealthy Canadians invested in the war and were paid interest on their investment from tax revenue collected by the tariff, effectively transferring income from poor people to rich people. War finance clarified the exploitative nature of the prewar political and economic system by exaggerating its inequalities. Calls for "conscription of wealth" arose from the belief that war finance had to weigh more heavily on the rich. A graduated income tax, which taxed higher incomes more heavily, was thought a fairer way to pay for the war.

The income tax, from this perspective, was supposed to "hurt" the rich, and the Income War Tax, by all accounts, disappointed those expectations.[35] Workers and farmers wanted it to ease the effects of other taxes, particularly the tariff, but mostly they saw it as an instrument of justice rather economics. In practical terms, of course, they were right: income taxation played almost no role in actually financing the war. But in the longer term, progressive income taxation created the possibility of a vastly expanded state capacity. Unlike the tariff, income taxation could influence more than consumption choices. It could, in theory, raise vast sums without weighing exorbitantly on those without the means to pay. Those vast sums of money could perhaps be transferred between regions, provinces, or even people. Whereas with the tariff the treasury had to borrow against its future income to build railways, after 1917, in theory, billions could be spent on war or peace. There was, therefore, a range of actions a government could take, and thus a range of actions a party platform could promise to voters. In combination with the development of third parties, the sudden expansion in the state's potential for action made for a much more meaningful electoral democracy.

o o o

Canada was undoubtedly more democratic in the aftermath of the First World War than it had been when it went to war. The war was fought to protect the political and economic system that had been built since Confederation – a system that, though it had parties and elections and the rule of law, was not particularly democratic. Thanks to the way the government tried to impose the war on the people, the fundamentally exploitative nature of the system was revealed in particularly stark terms and, when set against the threat of forced military service, cried out for transformation.

By the end of the war, the controversy over conscription led to a fundamentally more democratic public culture. For the first time, the majority of people could vote. More important than this, perhaps, was the fact that, because the state had the capacity to raise unprecedented revenue and to target its taxing powers with unprecedented precision, the outcome of the vote could change the lives of ordinary people for the better. Some of these changes were introduced by the government, but others were produced by the actions of a public brought to fresh awareness of their political condition by the sacrifices the war demanded of them economically and personally, and the benefit it gave others. The resistance to conscription under conditions of economic exploitation led to fundamental changes in the way people experienced electoral democracy and, through further efforts, on a day-to-day basis as well.

The stories we tell ourselves about war are important. The sacrificial myth of the First World War clearly resonates with some members of the public, but the ideological work it does in shielding militarism from critique is very dangerous. The point is not to deny that war service itself was heroic, or claim that the decision to enlist was not a courageous one. There are, however, better truths about the war that need to be remembered. The war was organized in profoundly unequal ways that reduced people to machines. It was a major contributor to inequality, which in itself is undemocratic. Resistance to the war took many forms, but one of the most common was economic. Strikes and other forms of agitation against war taxation and conscription stretched into the postwar period, ultimately broadening into a critique of the structural inequality of the war as well as economic and social conditions under peace. This resistance and the vision of a new political order it articulated was important in shaping a postwar world that was significantly more democratic.

Does this mean we should worship war resisters the way that the dominant interpretation demands we worship soldiers? Probably not. If we value democracy, it is arguably counter-productive to hold anyone or anything up as exemplary. We should perhaps ask instead that people memorialize the struggle for democracy by participating in it, taking responsibility for the world simply as an expectation of themselves, and not worship anyone as a "hero." We do justice to the legacy of a movement that sought to multiply human freedom not by worshipping it but by multiplying freedom in our own time and place as far as is in our power. Telling stories about the past that give us the insight and tools to do that is a good first step.

Children were frequently depicted in uniform in wartime propaganda, symbolic reminders of "what we are fighting for," present and future. *Everywoman's World*, July 1917, cover. www.canadiana.org.

6

Challenging Strathcona

The Cadet Training Controversy in English Canada, 1920–1950

CYNTHIA COMACCHIO

IN MARCH 1909, WHEN THE LAURIER GOVERNMENT announced that the British High Commissioner to Canada, Sir Donald Gordon Smith, Lord Strathcona, had endowed half a million dollars to a self-named trust "For the Encouragement of Physical and Military Training in Public Schools," public approval rang clear.[1] "With half a million rifles in the hands of a young Canada that could hit the bull's-eye three times out of five," the *Globe* trumpeted, "the Dominion would be safe from invasion even if there were only one or two generals at Ottawa."[2]

Despite the chorus of patriotic hurrahs, a number of Canadians quickly challenged the beneficence, and benefits, of compulsory military drill for schoolboys. Their opposition was a crucial component of the peace movement during the interwar years, abating with the exigencies of the Second World War, and reviving in the anxious early Cold War years. This chapter explores the controversy over school-based cadet training for English-Canadian boys as it manifested among parents, educators, and "ordinary" citizens, focusing on Ontario, the most "militarist" of the provinces. With remarkable consistency, public debates considered the meanings of militarism, manliness, patriotism, civic duty, public schooling, "fitness," and democracy itself. Such discourses reflected and reinforced ongoing negotiations about gender, citizenship, and national identity and how they should be defined for a modern Canada.

Setting the Scene: "The Militarist Moment"

The practice of military drill as "physical culture" for boys in the public school system predated Confederation and was well established in Ontario schools by 1900. The South African War (1899–1902) that spurred the period's "nationalist imperialism" encouraged the "moment of militarism" necessary to its institutionalization across the young Dominion.[3] By 1904, thanks to provincial legislation promoting the training of both teachers and boys in military drill, 132 cadet corps, mostly in Ontario and Quebec, were operating in the predominantly male secondary schools. In 1908, Minister of the Militia Sir Frederick Borden, an officer and committed supporter of cadet training, formalized an agreement with his home province of Nova Scotia to inaugurate school cadet corps directed by Militia-trained teachers. The training emphasized drill and rifle shooting; the Militia also provided arms, manuals, and a bonus for participating teachers. In short order, Borden's Nova Scotia arrangement became the model for cadet training programs under the aegis of the Strathcona Trust.[4]

Although its scope and influence are perhaps exaggerated, militarism was fairly established in schools and communities by the time the Strathcona Trust was announced. Children in most provinces celebrated Empire Day, an Ontario-initiated, annual, school-based, nationalist-imperialist celebration preceding Queen Victoria's late May birthday. In many locations, the day's highlight was a cadet drill and parade. Moreover, in view of concerns about the physically and morally degrading nature of modern urban life and the potentially feminizing propensities of modernity, the emergent "boy problem" demanded organized extracurricular activities to train boys to attain exemplary male citizenship. The most influential of these, the proto-military international Boy Scouts movement initiated by the hero of the South African War, Sir Robert Baden-Powell, took enthusiastic root in Canada in 1909 – the very same year that Strathcona's endowment was announced. That pivotal year also gave rise to the Canadian Defence League, whose mandate was military expansion and the promotion of cadet training in schools.[5]

Where cadet training is concerned, the crowning achievement came when Borden shared his enthusiasm for military drill with Lord Strathcona at the 1909 Imperial Conference, from which was born the Strathcona Trust. Administered by the Ministry of the Militia, its funds were distributed to provincial education departments for allocation to any high school that could bring together at least twenty boys to perform curriculum-based military exercises. Although its patron encouraged physical training and elementary drill for boys and girls alike, the Trust's stated purpose was "to bring up the boys to patriotism and to a realisation that the first duty of a free citizen is to be prepared to defend his country." In varying degrees of enthusiasm, and despite protests from labour, farmer, pacifist, educational, and women's groups, each province agreed to make cadet training an integral part of the regular boys' physical education curriculum in high schools. The number of cadets enrolled under the Trust nearly doubled between 1910 and the outbreak of war in 1914, reaching approximately 40,000.[6]

The First World War was the formative generational experience for the Dominion's youth, a national "coming of age" coinciding with their own. The Canadian commitment "at Britain's side" made calls for military recruitment constant refrains in political, educational, associational, and media circles, giving impetus to the Strathcona mission. Ironically, the war itself initially constrained its goals: a significant number of the male teachers were among the early recruits, as were the Militia officers who trained them. Physical education programs were often left to female teachers who were neither specifically trained in military drill nor particularly enthused about the military aspects of the curriculum. But the 1915 annual report of the Ontario Department of Education remarked that "it is manifest everywhere that the boys for the first time feel that military drill is worthwhile, and that it may have for them and their country a momentous value."[7] Despite the challenges involved in training and recruitment, the latter culminating in the explosive conscription crisis of 1917, the number of cadet corps across the land continued to grow, even as the war ended.[8]

The "New Day": Manliness, Modernity, and Anti-Militarism after the First World War

For many contemporaries, in this "new day" wrought by cataclysm, neither "tradition" nor "progress" could be counted upon to deliver the best conceivable results for humanity. If Canada might play a critical role in the new Commonwealth and the new League of Nations, the First World War turned attention to the tragic potential of militarist ideologies, and consequently to their place in the socialization of children. In sombre preparation for the first postwar Empire Day celebration, the Ontario Department of Education entreated that, if the "next generation" failed to learn the war's lessons, "the world of the future will be little better than was the world before 1914." Thus, children needed "the best lesson that the schools can teach – preparation for effective citizenship!"[9] The interwar peace organizations saw "the education of children for war" as the basis of militarism, the root cause of all conflict.[10]

Meanwhile, the tremendous expansion of secondary education in the early 1920s was transforming the high school into "the school of the common people." An unprecedented number of young men and women, representing an equally unprecedented class, religious, and "racial" mix, would spend more of their adolescence in classrooms than ever before. High schools thus presented a tremendous opportunity for citizenship training at what was considered the ideal life stage for such formative socialization.[11] But which ideas about citizenship, war, and peace would determine the nature, method, and purpose of such training?

For the organized peace movement, the war's lessons hinged on the elimination of militarist texts and cadet training in the schools. Canadian branches of the Fellowship of Reconciliation, the Society of Friends (Quakers), and the Women's International League for Peace and Freedom (WILPF) resolutely monitored textbooks for signs of militarism and actively campaigned against cadet training through the interwar years. As a 1924 letter to the *Toronto Star*, signed simply "A MOTHER," expressed, school texts were "the gravest hindrances to the teaching of ideals necessary to bring world peace and justice," while government funding that supported cadet training permitted "the germs of militarism [to be] planted in the childish mind." Tolerance of "educational policies so inconsistent with the need of the times" signified a wilfully blind society denying the urgency of acting against the possibility of war.[12]

If the anti-cadet campaign must be situated within this larger postwar "moment of anti-militarism," the controversy also highlights divergent ideas about gender and modernity. In this "new day" when sociocultural change might permit some redefinition of gender roles, and despite the wartime enfranchisement of women, the manly ideal intrinsic to cadet training was far more traditional than modern. Anxieties about girls were common, given the ominous break with tradition that "the flapper" represented; anxieties about boys, which were already circulating in prewar discussions, abated somewhat as boys became the principal resource of war. However, public concern about "the boy problem" resumed in the swirl of the seemingly "dangerous" youth culture that the new day entailed, signalling a rising preoccupation with "the problem of modern youth." For some, cadet training was an invaluable form of structured, purposeful recreation which made boys into men rather than juvenile delinquents and future reprobates.[13]

In 1920, the Strathcona Trust reiterated its military objectives by announcing that no high school without a cadet corps would receive financial support for physical education. For education budgets straitened by the need for rapid expansion, the subsidy, while small, was still important; most municipal school boards continued with the Strathcona program, even in view of growing protest against "inappropriate" use of school time and facilities to promote the kind of militarism that had so recently led to catastrophe. The federal government proposal to allocate $390,000 of the military budget to cadet training stirred some opposition about what one parliamentarian termed "excellent amusements" that "possibly had a tendency to develop the mind of the boy in a better direction" but were largely unjustified in both economic and educational terms. In and outside the House of Commons, the various provincial farm and labour groups under the Progressive banner formally expressed their "absolute opposition." The Trades and Labour Congress passed similar resolutions throughout the decade.[14]

The conflicted nature of the subject was reflected even among the churches. At the Methodist Church convention held in Windsor, Ontario, in 1924, a Wardsville clergyman called for a "pronouncement" on whether cadet training "tended toward militarism or not and whether the conference should give the movement encouragement." The "awkward question" led to the postponement of discussion in favour of striking a dedicated committee for further study. Similarly, although the United Church's General Council "went unanimously on record as declaring the Church's will for peace," its special committee reported in Winnipeg in 1928 that its efforts had not uncovered anything contrary to "the Christian conscience" in school-based cadet training.[15]

The nervous peace of the interwar years thus kept the cadet training controversy alive, especially in Ontario, historically the most supportive of the provinces and home to the nation's largest school board, that of Toronto.[16] Newspapers regularly detailed the debates among trustees, school administrators, parents, and representatives of anti-militarist groups. Discussions about this "now vexed problem" rose to a crescendo late in 1924 over a speaking engagement by the inimitable Agnes Macphail, Grey County Member of Parliament for the United Farmers of Ontario. Macphail had initiated a number of unsuccessful motions to abolish cadet training in the schools, each inspiring vehement public reaction on both sides. The situation became inflamed when the Toronto WILPF arranged for her to speak at an evening rally at the Central Technical High School. The board's management committee granted the permit but, faced with public outrage, argued that trustees had not realized that Macphail was "set to denounce the school cadet system" on school property. The six voting members at the emergency board meeting to consider cancellation were deadlocked. Although he had never heard her speak on the matter, one trustee declared Macphail's views on cadet training "absolutely perverted." The two others who favoured cancellation conceded, "nobody wants boys trained for soldiers, but if the evil day of war should come again, we should be prepared." The board's labour representative likened this line of reasoning to "carrying a revolver for an emergency."[17]

In the end, an anonymous telephone message to the board office forced resolution. Identifying himself as a veteran, the caller threatened, "A lot of us will go there and smash up the meeting ... we are not going to stand for that." Extensive newspaper coverage, including letters from angry readers and reports of heated exchanges among trustees and also in Parliament – where a Nova Scotia Liberal member told Macphail to "go back to Russia" – indicate how the subject aroused vehement, and conflicted, public emotion. Macphail continued to "score" what she termed "tinpan jingoism" at every opportunity, thereby serving as the nation's foremost anti-cadet campaigner.[18]

Similar discussions, with varying outcomes, took place across Canada throughout the 1920s. Many local boards opted for a compromise measure like that in Edmonton, Alberta, where it was decided in 1927 to continue cadet training only with parental approval and with the provision of alternative physical instruction for the sons of parents who objected.[19] While adults debated, the number of cadets in Canada reached 112,000, nearly tripling between 1913 and 1926. Their participation suggests that the boys themselves, regardless of adult opinion, remained keen to don uniforms and take up drill, yet their agency in this regard is necessarily speculative. With more boys in high schools for longer periods, and school-based cadet training still largely in place, how much adolescent agency could these rising numbers actually signify? Whatever they felt about cadet training, few Canadian high school boys could have avoided it entirely during the 1920s.

Even in schools that allowed for a non-military option in boys' physical training, there were allegations about coercion. These were supported by the Toronto WILPF's education committee, which issued a formal report in 1927, when amendments to both the *Militia Act* and the provincial *High School Act* loosened the compulsory aspects.[20] Some testified to a subtle but forceful pressure from school authorities to "encourage" their voluntary participation. A former York Township student who spent five years on the school cadet corps related how, each spring, cadet instructors quietly "took aside" prospective school team members to inform them that they would not be playing in the fall unless they joined the corps: "Any students who refused to join were put to endless trouble. . . . Whether they wished to or not they were forced to take rifle and military drill of various kinds in the gym periods." A concerned father testified that one of his sons, a rugby player, had been bullied into participation by these means, unbeknownst at the time to either himself or the boy's mother – who very much opposed cadet training. But even coercive measures only went so far among recalcitrant adolescents, who subverted the training's purpose by making their own choices: some "went to the trouble" of procuring medical certificates in order to be excused, while others took to "skipping" the gym classes in which the hated drill took place.[21] However, support still rang strong among some participants. An Oshawa cadet believed that his training constituted "one of the finest types of preparatory work which can be given to a boy," in that he was learning "discretion, neatness, moral training and to be independent." With four years of cadet training, another young proponent also echoed the language of his elders: "If a boy is raised a 'mamma's pet,' afraid of hot sun and drizzling rain, what good is he in peace or war to his country?"[22]

The Great Depression: "Milk and Boots Instead of Uniforms"

The Great Depression fixed the discussion on the "value" of school-based cadet training not only in terms of its actual cost to taxpayers but also in the less tangible public "investment" for citizenship purposes. In its "annual memorandum" to Cabinet in 1931, the Trades and Labour Congress insisted that schools should "confine the training of our boys along lines that will inculcate ideas of peace not of war." The Toronto District Labour Council "condemned" educational authorities for continuing cadet training "contrary to the tenets of the League of Nations." Organized labour now strengthened its opposition by pointing out how "many children are not receiving sufficient food to keep their bodies nourished as they should be, and all the military training in the world will not make up for lack of wholesome food." Others also called for "milk and boots instead of uniforms."[23] Finances ultimately proved reason enough for state action: the Bennett government's cost-cutting measures eliminated federal grants to school-based cadet corps in spring 1931. In Toronto, this translated to a shortfall of more than $12,000 for the following school year. The Strathcona Trust's meagre subsidies could not sustain school-based training, especially when provincial and municipal budgets could stretch no further. As the *Globe and Mail* warned that cadet training remained "of prime importance to the future manhood of the nation," public commitment kept school-based training alive in some measure for some school boards throughout the Depression.[24]

In view of the federal cuts and negative reports about its "value" from ten of twelve collegiate principals as well as the Toronto Board of Education's physical education director, the city's Chief Inspector of Schools ruled for abolition of school-based cadet training at the end of 1932.[25]

But the matter was not laid to rest by budget cuts, efficiency arguments, or even the near-consensus of the education authorities. Such supporters as the Reverend F.C. Ward-Whale of the city's St. Alban's Cathedral (Anglican) declared the ruling "a concession to the pacifist tendencies of a few fussy women." The board's own Chair, Dr. J.W. Russell, intensified the manly militarist-imperialist thrust of such arguments in his blunt statement that "when a man does wrong you may talk him out of it, but a crack on the jaw will often settle matters quicker. So it is with nations. Where would we be today if it were not for conquests?"[26] The Orange Lodge officially censured those trustees who, as fellow Orangemen, "allowed themselves to be swerved from their plain path of duty by the propaganda of a few effeminate and pacifist organizations at a time when patriotic training is needed to offset the propaganda of various disloyal agencies."[27] The predominantly male supporters of cadet training were committed to fixed definitions of the ideal citizen: not only male but "manly," as denoted by the physical and moral discipline required to take up arms and "stand on guard" for nation and empire. Opponents were "feminized" in stereotypical ways that dismissed their views as those of "the weaker sex" or of "unmanly" men, all of them cowardly, unpatriotic, possibly treasonous. And the overall scent of "bolshevism," another common denunciation, marked them as transgressors against all "Canadian" values.[28]

Ultimately, opposing arguments probably gained most force in the wake of the deteriorating European situation, as fascist governments took hold in Germany, Italy, and Spain and made more aggressive forays in Japan. Views that school-based cadet training simply ensured a ready source of cannon fodder intensified even among those not formally affiliated with peace movements. A First World War veteran from Hamilton, Ontario, identifying himself as "not a conscript" but one who had signed up in August 1914, sought to warn parents about their sons' cadet training in order to "avoid their future destruction in bloody warfare." With "every far seeing public-spirited citizen . . . bending every effort to preach international peace and goodwill," he asked, "then why all the wooden guns, khaki uniforms, squad drill and military training for children, in a so-called democratic country?"[29]

All such strains of the public debate about cadet training did not so much determine the outcome as confirm what was already in process in the early Depression years. In London, the cadet corps had unofficially ceased to exist at high schools because they were out of uniforms and no longer received adequate funding; the city's school inspector also contended that "for the most part, people today don't want it . . . the uniform is a glorification of the military viewpoint and a nullification of peace propaganda."[30] British Columbia schools dropped the Trust's training syllabus in favour of a more "progressive" approach to physical education without military drill. With federal funding gone and education budgets seriously constrained by Depression exigencies, with declining enrolment due to its now optional nature in many schools, and in view of determined antimilitarist campaigns, the Strathcona Trust's glory days were past.[31] In view of the budget cuts and increasingly negative public opinion, the military personnel in charge of training teachers revealed a certain ambivalence about the "preparedness" aspects of such physical education. As an address to teachers at an Ottawa training session in 1933 asserted, "The time may come when we can do without armies, but it is not thought that the time will ever come when we shall be able to do without the military virtues of courage, loyalty, qualities of leadership, and the spirit of sacrifice and fair play ... all of which are taught to Cadets." The language continued to make "military virtues" synonymous with those of manliness and citizenship, but opponents scored a significant victory by decentring the historic argument linking "preparedness" and patriotism. If the peace movement retreated during the latter half of the 1930s, it had managed to achieve its goal of eliminating compulsory cadet training in the schools – at least until Canadians became involved in a second "war to end wars" in little more than a generation.[32]

The Second World War: Reviving the School Cadet Corps

The arguments for "preparedness" quickly resurged as the world again headed toward war, but so too did antimilitarist views that were especially resonant in view of the fascist tyranny that threatened. When Brigadier General C.H. Mitchell, Dean of Engineering at the University of Toronto, publically deplored "the wave of sentiment that swept over Canada some years ago against cadet training in the schools," one school board trustee responded that "'the time has not yet come when we have to imitate Mussolini's method of putting seven-year-olds in uniform and marching them up and down with dummy guns in their hands." Yet, by spring 1939, a sound majority voted to revive the program in city schools.[33] Within days of Canada's declaration of war against Germany, Winnipeg petitioners were also pleading for its reinstatement. Calling it a matter of "self-preservation," the school board approved the establishment of cadet training corps for junior and high school students under the direction of its Military District commanders, who would train the teachers in co-operation with the physical education director, despite his own misgivings about creating "military machines." In the context of world war, there could be no downplaying the cadet corps' military purposes.[34]

As more school boards across Canada reinstituted cadet training, organized labour reiterated its historic "solid" opposition to "bring[ing] back the toy army idea"; some protestors argued that such training was simply "a back door method of recruiting."[35] The "moral panic" over juvenile delinquency occasioned by the wartime employment of mothers and service of fathers again made cadet training the foremost means to encourage manly responsibility. Supporters quickly asserted that "certain effects of the training" were manifesting in improvements in manners and the "slouchiness of bearing" that boys had evidently developed in the absence of cadet training. Its revival, they argued, had "'made over' the lives of tens of thousands of young men" by encouraging "physical fitness, scholastic progress, character building, and the ability to work successfully with others." "Good cadets" made "good citizens."[36] "Without drill or [physical] culture, the first thing that we will be seeing in Canada will be afternoon classes for boys in crochet work and knitting," warned a supporter, again correlating military training with the inculcation of manly ideals.[37]

Because "doing your bit" was also revived by the war, women were again called upon to contribute to the cause. The Second World War occasioned a historic first by turning attention to military training "in some form" for high school girls. While this initiative disrupted the exclusively male nature of the cadet corps, "girl cadets" were mainly designated to auxiliary roles, contributing to the war effort by supporting their male counterparts. When they did participate in military activities, their femininity was emphasized in the very "quaintness" of their doings. They were sometimes awkwardly called "cadet-ettes" to accentuate or "protect" their femininity. An *Ottawa Evening Citizen* report on the Lisgar Girls' Rifle Club, established in 1941 at the city's Lisgar Collegiate as an unofficial adjunct to the school cadet corps, coyly described its members' "girliness" despite their manly endeavours: the "comely young misses," instructed by "a lady teacher," devoted their Friday lunch hour "to lend their feminine charms to the firing of the cadet corps' BSAs at targets some 20 yards away."[38] Similar undertakings, usually at the girls' initiative, took place across the nation. Female naval cadets were organized in Hamilton in 1942. At Kitchener-Waterloo Collegiate, some 100 girls signed up for the "Airettes" corps before the war's end. Vancouver's Magee High School organized young women in air cadet corps in 1942; a senior male cadet trained the girls, who were "trying their best . . . to bring their standards up to those that the boys have set." On the national scene, the Canadian Auxiliary Service Corps established a cadet corps for girls 12 years old and over in 1943, popularly referred to as "Army-ette Cadets."[39] For girls, the activities that made cadet training a worthy "manly" endeavour were exceptional, temporary, and even "cute."

As the war wound to its end, supporters argued that cadet training was "as important in peacetime as it was in war." The Dominion Inter-Service Cadet Committee, specially constituted for Reconstruction purposes, found enough support among provincial governments to recommend its continuation in the high school curriculum. In view of its postwar spending priorities, however, the federal government rescinded its order of compulsory school-based cadet training in late 1944.[40]

The Resurgence of Anti-Militarism: Cadets in Cold War Canada

In the new Atomic Age, Canadian peace activists had much with which to occupy themselves. While their unequivocal goal was nuclear disarmament, domestic issues such as cadet training retained primacy in their campaign to prevent a war that would leave no survivors. Opponents saw the stakes as never higher; even proponents downplayed the military aspects and emphasized its invaluable training in democratic citizenship. Yet only the Ontario Ministry of Education was eager to continue the federal government's wartime plan for "100 percent cadet training" in the schools, at both junior and senior levels. When provincial representatives petitioned defence minister Brooke Claxton to that end, he responded that his ministry had "no disposition whatever" to change its earlier decision. As he concluded, "I do not think there is any desire on the part of the country that we should."[41]

Because cadet training continued to predominate in high school physical education courses for boys, George Drew's Ontario Conservative government became the target of a major campaign by peace activists, including the Fellowship of Reconciliation and labour groups. Members of the Co-operative Commonwealth Federation youth wing contended that Drew was effectively "glamourizing war" in this "insidious" manner. Terming the "Drew cadets" the "first step to fascism," they called for immediate termination of compulsory training.[42]

The "citizenship" argument appeared especially offensive to many in the aftermath of war and in the context of the current "battle" against communist tyranny. Compulsory cadet training was fundamentally undemocratic. It encouraged "blind obedience to command" and

"a willingness to subscribe to military direction [as] absolutely necessary under a dictator." If Canadians upheld "the ideal of a democracy of
free men," the young needed training in "ready response to moral inspiration instead of force."[43] Nor did arguments for "preparedness" in this
Cold War world justify compulsory cadet training. One opponent
related the story of an instructor who told his cadets "you're the fellows
who are going to have to fight Russia." In her view, "no one could fail to
see the broader implications of educating our children in the belief that
Russia is their enemy, and thus sowing the seeds of hatred and mistrust
which will jeopardize relationships with that country for many years to
come." Parents should work to abolish cadet training in order to "help
to defend the much-lauded 'freedom of the individual.'" "We must
guard against narrow nationalism," protested another; "brass bands
and bright uniforms" would not advance "the brotherhood of man."[44]

Yet, in one of the ubiquitous Gallup Polls, published in virtually every
Canadian newspaper in June 1947, 56 per cent of voters who were asked
"Do you think all boys should be obliged to take cadet training at
school?" responded positively; only 8 per cent wanted it abolished outright.[45] The nation had endured two world wars and a prolonged economic crisis, had attained sovereignty, and had committed to the League
of Nations and the United Nations, but the issue of cadet training in the
public schools continued to polarize Canadians. As it happened, shortly
after the Gallup Poll's report, on the eve of the new school year in late
summer 1947, the Drew government abruptly capitulated. As most provinces had already done, Ontario replaced compulsory cadet training with
a mandatory citizenship course. Although national and regional veterans'
groups urged its reinstatement over the next several years, compulsory
school-based cadet training was effectively finished across Canada.[46]

○ ○ ○

The cadet training controversy that unfolded between the First World
War and mid-century reflected the anxieties of a society trying to come
to terms with national commitment to military preparedness and possible international entanglements on behalf of the Commonwealth, the
League of Nations, and later the United Nations. The debate's gendered
language is also striking. Supporters emphasized its presumed lessons in
"manliness" as much as in military skills. Opponents generally agreed
about what constituted worthy manly traits, but contended that exemplary male citizens were more effectively honed by developing the
strength of character that eschews aggression and war in favour of diplo-

macy and peace. If boys were exposed early to these ideals – as were their sisters, socialized in complementary "feminine" traits – the extent to which they were internalized as "the militarist spirit" is open to question. The tenacious debates among their parents, teachers, and other adults reveal that children and youth were also subjected to, and involved in, antimilitarist messages and activities during these years. Although the most subordinate of citizens, boys (and girls) did not simply ingest militarist concepts on an unimpeded path to adult warrior-citizen status, even if they participated in cadet training in its voluntary or compulsory forms. Like protesting adults, they, too, found ways to challenge Strathcona. Most important, the persistent public discourses over compulsory cadet training and their eventual outcome in its abolition constitute an overlooked, but nonetheless significant, element of the multifaceted crusade against war in early twentieth-century Canada.

Fourteen conscientious objectors building the Tote Road along the Miette River in Jasper National Park near Camp Giekie, ca. 1942. Mennonite Heritage Centre, Peter Unger photo collection 600:3.

7

Jane Jiang

"This Thing Is in Our Blood for 400 Years"

Conscientious Objection in the Canadian Historic Peace Churches during the Second World War

CONRAD STOESZ

"War will exist until that distant day when the conscientious objector enjoys the same reputation and prestige that the warrior does today."
— *John F. Kennedy*[1]

S HE THREW HER HEAD BACK, LAUGHING, and said, "Oh no one wants to talk about that – next question." It was 2012, and I was attending a history conference presentation analyzing a Canadian-operated Second World War prisoner of war camp. I knew that in the same vicinity there was also a conscientious objector camp, and I had suggested that the two sites should be compared. I sat there feeling embarrassed because I had evidently asked a "dumb" question and angry because it was not taken seriously.

The experience of Canada's conscientious objectors in the Second World War is a fascinating and complex part of our history that is often (conveniently) overlooked. Annual days of commemoration, tributes at sporting events, documentaries, and museums all emphasize the centrality of military activity to Canadian identity. However, the experience of men who objected to war on the basis of conscience does not fit this selective national narrative. Such political priorities are reflected in the less than rigorous collection of documents by the nation's archive about the conscientious objectors (COs) and their experiences. Indeed, not even a list of the over 10,000 COs who served in the Second World War has survived.[2]

This chapter examines conscientious objection during the Second World War by members of the historic peace churches (Mennonites, Hutterites, Brethren in Christ, and Quakers), with a particular focus on the Mennonite experience. While struggling to stay true to their convictions, COs performed alternative service in areas deemed essential by the Canadian government. They provided food and hospital care, protection of natural resources, and industrial and agricultural labour. However, just as important as the experience of COs in wartime is the lasting legacy of their experience for the country, their communities, and their self-understanding.[3] The pages that follow explore the political decisions that structured CO experiences during the war, the process by which men applied for CO status, and the varied forms of alternative service they undertook during the war. The chapter concludes by highlighting the long-term impact of their wartime experiences for themselves, their communities, and the country.

Background

The historic peace churches, founded during or immediately after the European Reformation, hold the biblical New Testament, and specifically the life and teachings of Jesus, as their greatest moral authority. In the life of Jesus, they saw a person who taught and lived a life that stood up to the political powers of the day in a nonviolent way.[4] For Anabaptist groups like Mennonites, their primary allegiance was to Jesus and not the state. Such groups, facing significant persecution, migrated throughout Europe and to North America seeking an opportunity to live according to their principles. Often leaders of these groups negotiated with heads of state and governments before immigrating to ensure exemption from military service. Success, in their eyes, came through being faithful to Jesus and his example, not preservation of a country or even of one's self. Some pacifist groups advocated separation from the larger society while others were more integrationist in outlook. They all found themselves in conflict with mainstream public opinion concerning Canada's role in the Second World War.[5]

As 1939 dawned and the winds of war again began to blow, members of the historic peace churches pondered the future. Not far from their musings were recollections of disenfranchisement (losing the right to vote), imprisonment of some of their young men, and human suffering during the First World War. Now, as Europe was again teetering on the edge of war, what should their response be? Leaders of the historic peace churches held meetings in the United States and Canada, hoping that a unified position would increase their leverage with state authorities.

Yet even among the Mennonites, the largest of the peace churches, there was disagreement regarding how the church should respond. In

Canada, those who settled in Manitoba from Russia in the mid- to late 1870s adamantly pointed to the 1873 Order-in-Council that promised complete military exemption. Conversely, those who had come from the United States in the late 1780s and settled in Upper Canada were open to alternative service provided it was not under military control. The most "liberal" view came from those who arrived from Russia after the First World War. Having experienced alternative service in forestry units and as medics under military control near the front during that conflict, they now advocated a similar arrangement.[6] From these competing viewpoints, two positions developed. Those willing to offer some kind of service formed the Conference of Historic Peace Churches.[7] Those expecting the government to live up to its promise of complete exemption formed the Elders' committee (*Aeltestenkomitee*) which remained active, but marginalized, throughout the war.[8]

The Government's Response

The Conference of Historic Peace Churches created an eight-member Military Problems Committee, which quickly sought an audience with the Canadian government to express concerns about the war and to offer an alternative to military service.[9] Initial meetings with Prime Minister Mackenzie King in June 1940 seemed positive.[10] However, supplementary meetings with two deputy ministers for war services, T.C. Davis and Major General L.R. Lafleche, proved disappointing. Delegates proposed a plan that would see young men active in relief, reconstruction, and public health projects under the direction of the historic peace churches. The government ministers dismissed this proposal, wanting noncombatant service under military control. This was quickly rejected by the church leaders. At one point, with frustration mounting, Major General Lafleche, a veteran of the First World War asked, "What will you do if we shoot you?" In outrage, Rev. Jacob H. Janzen of Kitchener, Ontario, replied, "Listen general, I want to tell you something. You can't scare us like that. I've looked down too many rifle barrels in my time to be scared in that way. This thing is in our blood for 400 years and you can't take it away from us like you'd crack a piece of kindling over your knee. I was before a firing squad twice. We believe in this."[11]

After heated discussion, Lafleche assured the delegates that he would present their case to James C. Gardiner, Minister of National War Services. The delegates were apprehensive with this arrangement and secured the help of MP W.H. Moore, who arranged a meeting with Gardiner that same afternoon. Gardiner, who enjoyed a good relationship with the Brethren in Christ and Mennonite communities during his youth in Ontario and while he was Premier of Saskatchewan, assured the delegation that "there's one hundred and one things that you fellows can do without fighting; we'll see that you get them."[12] On December 24, 1940, the federal cabinet amended the National War Service Regulations to permit alternative service.[13] Six months later, the government authorized the establishment of work camps, the first available form of alternative service.[14]

Once called for military duty, men could apply for CO status. Provincial mobilization boards reviewed their applications and in most regions each applicant had to make their case before a judge, usually without legal representation. If successful they would be sent to serve under civilian control for four months – the same amount of time as basic training. Each CO was given fifty cents a day, with the remainder of their wages sent to the Red Cross for relief work.[15] This agreement became the basis for an alternative service program for all Canadians, for the Second World War marked the first time conscientious objection was open to all people and not based on affiliation with a particular group or religion.[16] However, historian John A. Toews notes that men who did not have affiliations with historic peace groups had a more difficult time proving their convictions and securing CO status.[17]

Moreover, judgments made by the mobilization boards differed greatly from province to province. In Ontario, for example, an agreement was reached between the historic peace churches and the mobilization board that made the process easy. In fact, there was no need for a hearing if the applicant was from a historic peace church.[18] A contrasting situation arose in Manitoba with Judge Adamson, who chaired the Winnipeg Mobilization Board. He had a harsh, "pro-British demeanor" and was personally opposed to conscientious objection. Indeed, he used various tactics to entice, shame, and scare men into the armed services. As Kenneth Reddig notes, Adamson was keen to dissuade "as many Mennonites as possible from claiming conscientious objector status."[19] Some of Adamson's views and arguments became more widely known when he, together with his good friend and Mobilization Board Medical Advisor, Herbert Wadge, published *Should a Christian Fight?*[20] The book, sent to several COs, was designed to give "the correct answers" to biblical passages COs used to justify their stance.[21] COs in Saskatchewan faced a similar plight when they appeared before Judge Embury, a decorated war veteran. He and Adamson were dismayed by the "dominating influence" of community leaders such as Bishop David Toews.[22]

Assessments of CO applications thus varied widely. In October 1942,

Mennonite leader B.B. Janz wrote to the Prime Minister complaining that while men from Ontario, Alberta, and BC had a relatively easy time securing CO status, those in Manitoba and Saskatchewan "are being sent to jail for not being willing to deny the faith of their fathers."[23] Indeed, some COs were counselled to travel to other jurisdictions so they could circumvent people like Adamson and Embury.[24] Conscientious objection thus frequently necessitated awkward and uncomfortable formal hearings.

Before the Court and Community

In coming before mobilization boards, many young men felt ill prepared to give an account of their peace stance. Not surprisingly, many felt unable to clearly articulate and defend their beliefs in a courtroom. For some this task was further complicated by the fact that they were expected to converse in English, while their main language was German. For Henry Funk of Rosenfeld, Manitoba, the experience was daunting:

> It was a large room and each judge had his own bench about 30 feet from each other. Both faced the room where the rest of us sat watching the proceedings. The judges dealt with the applicants one at a time, each working separately, but simultaneously. Formally we were called up one at a time to be interrogated by one or the other. They were gruff and authoritative men. At least to us timid farm boys they seemed that way. Each bench was raised a bit and from it this robed authority figure looked down at the applicant who in turn had to look up to the judge. If this arrangement was deliberate and if intimidation was the object, it worked. It worked out that way psychologically. Most of us were insecure farm boys who had perhaps been out in the field the day before.[25]

John C. Klassen of Morden, Manitoba, summarizes a similar experience:

> I was summoned to appear before Judge Bowman in Altona, for a court hearing, and to be accompanied by my father and represented by a clergy. I do not know how many 21 year olds appeared before the judge that day, but I know that my school classmate who was much more involved in church life than I, and had practically memorized the Bible in preparation for this hearing, was given a rough interrogation and finally rejected CO status. This discouraged me and I thought I could never make it. When my name was called, my knees were knocking enough to almost shatter the windows, as I stood before Judge Bowman. But all I did was answer a few basic questions and was then told to go home and wait for a contact from the Selective Service.[26]

While men like Klassen worried about articulating their faith, the hearing focused primarily upon whether they lived according to their beliefs.

Most historic peace church applicants were accepted, but in some cases their application was denied and they were given the option of military duty or prison. It was usually a mystery to the men as to why they were denied CO status. Judge Adamson singled out one CO, who recalled the judge's aggressive tone: "I was asked if I were a church member, whether I smoked and drank or went to dances. 'What would I do if the Germans won the war and took away my possessions?' These questions and many others were not asked in a civil tone, but yelled as though Mr. Adamson were raging mad." The CO repeated that he didn't think war was right. Finally, Judge Adamson had had enough. If the CO wouldn't join the army, the judge said, he would have to go to jail. "The RCMP picked me up at home," the CO recalled, and "[I] was ... locked up one week ... before being sentenced" to six months hard labour.[27] In summary, the process was uneven and unfair. Men were treated harshly and challenged outright for their beliefs.[28]

The men applying for CO status came from many walks of life: thirty-three ethnic backgrounds and over twenty religious denominations from Prince Edward Island to British Columbia. The majority came from Ontario and the West, drawing from the Mennonite, Hutterite, Doukhobor, and Quaker communities. In the Mennonite community, about 60 per cent (7,534) of the men who were called for military service chose alternative service – a reminder that even within this pacifist group opinion on military participation was divided.[29] The percentage was much higher in other communities. Among the Doukhobors, 95 per cent of the men claimed CO status.[30]

The men serving away from home left a hole in the families they left behind. Other family members had to step into the breach. As Marlene Epp notes, women in the communities supported the CO position by writing letters and sending care packages containing home baking, clothing, writing paper, and sometimes notes on the latest sermon in church. Some younger women uprooted themselves to live near their husbands while others managed the farm.[31]

Having survived the trauma of mobilization board hearings many COs then felt the weight of public disapproval for their choice.[32] Some faced persecution in the form of vigilante attacks on individuals, homes, and churches.[33] Some imprisoned COs faced beatings and the denial of some of the essentials of life.[34] Sam Martin of Dutchess, Alberta, was placed in solitary confinement and rotationally on a bread and water diet for refusing to put on a military uniform. Authorities kept his cell window open during the cool spring while he persevered in his underwear. Finally, taking advantage of his weakened state, the authorities forcibly dressed him in the uniform. Once he was alone again Martin removed it.[35] In a letter to Bishop David Toews, one of the most influential and active Mennonite ministers in Western Canada, Jacob Gerbrandt expressed deep concern about the public mood toward Mennonites and other peace groups:

> It seems possible now to desecrate our churches, forcibly close our schools and indulge in all kinds of insolent activities, and still be identified as heroic. It also seems that regardless of how right we are, we lose out in the police investigations.... As to the attack upon our Bible School, Br. E. Schroeder will have informed you, and you yourself were personally threatened.[36]

Given this situation, the decision to claim CO status was not a simple one. Henry Funk recalled that, "at that time I was definitely not ready to make such a profound decision. Society decreed that I was old enough to kill and to die – even though I was not deemed old enough to vote.... The choice was upon me, and it was mine to make."[37]

How did men render these decisions? They weighed several factors. Many felt blessed to live in a country like Canada and wanted to be good citizens. Private Leslie Neufeld, a Saskatchewan Mennonite, enlisted and wrote shortly before he died in battle, "The time has come for that long-awaited invasion of France.... If anything should happen to me do not feel burdened by it, but take the attitude, 'he served his country to his utmost.' ... And let it be known that the town of Nipawin, [SK] did its share to win the war."[38] Others felt the tug of civic duty but prioritized pacifism.

It was a clash not only of values but also of cultures. A 1941 article in the *Prince Albert Daily Herald* highlighted this tension:

> The average Canadian, like the British, is reared in the tradition of national and Empire heroes. He is taught to look up to and admire the men who sacrificed everything, including life, for their country and their country's cause. On the other hand, the Doukhobors have been raised in the tradition of martyrs and taught to revere those who suffered persecutions for their pacifist ideals. They wish to be Christ-like and they remember that Christ was persecuted for His beliefs.[39]

This deviation from the larger societal norm produced a clash of values that was evident among Doukhobors and other groups such as Mennonites and Hutterites.

Not only were young men faced with the choice of being a good Canadian or a good pacifist, but the situation also created a gender identity crisis. Canadian society equated masculinity with strength and military might. Men who did not take up arms when their country called were labelled cowards.[40] In addition, men were supposed to be providers for their families. In many cases the men entering CO service were the oldest in the family, carrying a heavy load of responsibilities on the family farm, or newly married, leaving a wife with babe in arms. Choosing conscientious objection, and thus alternative service, placed their manhood in question. In this context some COs asked judges to specifically assign them to positions of danger, such as the Friends Ambulance units in Britain, in order to demonstrate that they were not cowards.[41]

Alternative Service

T.C. Davis, Associate Deputy Minister of National War Services, was in charge of finding work for the COs. As the architect of the Depression-era work program at the national parks, he saw these remote areas as ideal locations for alternative service because they already had the required infrastructure, kept the COs out of the public eye, and did not appear to contribute directly to the war effort. The first COs arrived at Clear Lake, Riding Mountain National Park, Manitoba in June 1941.[42] Soon others began to arrive at Montreal River near Sudbury, Ontario, or Prince Albert National Park, Saskatchewan.

When the men arrived they filled bags with straw for mattresses to help furnish their new living quarters – a tent or, if they were lucky, a cabin. They worked at road building, dam construction, logging, surveying, and cutting brush. Sometimes their camp bosses banned the German language. At Prince Albert National Park, superintendent Herbert Knight made it difficult for the religious ministers to visit and encouraged the COs to abandon their principles and embrace military service.[43]

The young men were homesick and eagerly awaited letters from loved ones. Henry Sawatzky of Halbstadt, Manitoba, wrote sixty-nine letters during his four-month stay at Clear Lake.[44] Noah Bearinger of Ontario was stationed at Montreal River and remembers that "we sat on . . . bunks reading the letters real slow to let the meaning of each word soak in like the warm rays of an April sun. We exchanged letters and re-read them."[45] Hoping to recreate a sense of community, the COs established a newsletter, the *Beacon*, which was first published at Montreal River. Edited by Wes Brown of the United Church of Canada, it helped the men and their families remain connected.[46]

In March 1942, the Canadian government declared that the COs were now required to remain in alternative service for the duration of the war. More work camps were set up with a concentration on Vancouver Island and the nearby mainland. Here many COs participated in cutting cordwood to alleviate the fuel shortage in Vancouver, fighting forest fires, and planting trees.[47] Over fifty camps were now in operation.[48] The reforestation program on Vancouver Island facilitated the replanting of the large Sayward Forest area that had been devastated by fire in 1938. First the area needed to be cleared of snags, or charred tree trunks still standing.[49] Then, with the Douglas Fir seedlings on their backs, the COs formed a line of fifteen men spaced six feet apart. In a rhythmic cadence they chopped a slit into the ground with a heavy tool called a mattock, bent down, inserted a seedling, removed the pick, stepped near the seedling to pack it into place and then did the routine over again. Each man could plant a thousand trees a day.[50]

The majority of the alternative service workers abided by the laws that governed their activities – though they were never given the same respect as those who entered the armed forces. Like the important contributions pacifists made to the colonial infrastructure in an earlier era, conscientious objectors in these camps were able to provide non-military service to the country. The national parks benefited greatly from their cheap labour, and park officials fought to maintain access to this labour force through the war. As people flocked to the parks to find peace and quiet after the war they benefited directly from wartime CO labour. As Bill Waiser notes, "The image of Canada's national parks as sanctuaries of peace thus reflected a double – if somewhat ironic – meaning."[51]

At times the culture of the camps could mimic mainstream masculine ideals. Camp officials learned from their experience with the Depression-era workers that men needed to be kept busy in their off hours as well. Horseshoes, baseball equipment, and even boxing gloves were provided, encouraging competitive games and rivalries.[52] More telling, perhaps, was the *Beacon*'s triumphant report on the inhabitants' arboreal labour. "The zero hour had come," it announced. "Everyone rushed to their posts and at the close of the first half day, no less than 64,000 trees were pulled, tied and heeled in, before the murderous onslaught. Due to the imminent danger of the attack being blunted, reinforcements were summoned."[53] And yet for some COs, the challenges of camp life proved either unacceptable or insufficient. Some men abandoned the alternative service camps for the military because they believed that, earning fifty cents a day, they could not adequately provide for their families. Others joined the military because they felt that the work they were doing was not of high enough importance. In total some 243 Mennonites left the camps for military service.[54]

On at least one occasion, government duplicity ensured that COs unknowingly contributed directly to military endeavours – in the form of support for a bizarre top-secret war machine dubbed the Habakkuk project. With German U-boats intercepting ships travelling the North Atlantic, political leaders at the highest level in Britain, the United States, and Canada entered into a partnership to test English inventor Geoffrey Pyke's concept of a floating aircraft carrier made of ice mixed with wood pulp. It would be unsinkable and unstoppable, or so they hoped. Conscientious objectors produced a 1:50 scale prototype at Lake Patricia in Jasper National Park. They cut blocks of ice out of the lake and tarred them together. Cooling pipes were installed to keep the boat frozen during the summer and a roof was placed on it to disguise it as a boathouse. The COs were not told what they were working on. Some found out only fifty years later that they were working on a weapon of war.[55]

And yet, on a more positive note, alternative service could also lead to new friendships and postwar opportunities. For example, while some COs had their teaching certificates revoked for their pacifist beliefs,[56] others were sent to educate displaced Japanese Canadians.[57] For Wilson Hunsberger this began a lifelong friendship with his Japanese-Canadian students. COs also worked as teachers in Native communities in Northern Manitoba. This experience later led Henry Gerbrandt to establish, through his church, a long-term presence in some of Manitoba's northern communities in what became known as the Mennonite Pioneer Mission.[58]

In April 1943, facing an acute labour shortage, the Canadian government acquiesced to mounting pressure from business leaders, the public, politicians, and some COs themselves and began to transfer the COs out of remote camps into other essential industries, hospitals, and farms with the aim of matching their skills to the nation's specific social and economic needs. Many in the historic peace church community approved of this move and hoped it would increase the perceived validity of alternative service.[59] COs were now also allowed to enter restricted enlistment and serve as medics in the military without taking weapons training.[60] By 1945, over ten thousand COs participated in alternative service. Table 1 summarizes how they were allocated in 1945.

One new area of service was hospitals and mental institutions. At least eighty men worked in three mental hospitals in Manitoba. Incorporated into the nursing staff on the male wards, they took on a wide variety of tasks including feeding, bathing, diapering, digging graves, night

Table 1

Alternative Service	Number of COs
Agriculture	6,655
Miscellaneous essential industries	1,412
Sawmills, logging, and timbering	542
Packing and food-processing plants	469
Construction	269
Hospitals	86
Coal mining	63
Grain handling	15
Alternative service camps	170
Serving jail sentences	14
In hands of or being prepared for Enforcement Division	34
In hands of RCMP or agencies to locate whereabouts	201
Under review	921
Total	10,851

Source: Regehr, *Mennonites in Canada*, 53.

guarding, preparing bodies for autopsy, and dispensing medications. Some COs relished the fact that they were young healthy men placed in charge of others, including violent offenders. At times, physical force was used to carry out their duties on the ward. These experiences helped support their masculine identity. The work in the hospitals improved the quality of life for the patients and helped restart research programs. Their work was highly valued by their superiors, and some received job offers after the war.[61]

For many of the young men, this was their first time away from home for any extended period and thus an opportunity to mix with people of different religious and ethnic backgrounds. This was most evident in the camps and especially in the hospitals. As historian John Toews argues,

> It taught those, who because of previous isolated church life held the members of another denomination in narrow esteem, to respect and love their brothers. Through discussion and observation these men had a wonderful opportunity to free themselves of denominational bigotry. By the same means, they arrived at destinations in their spiritual development in which they experienced in a broader way what their religious leaders and teachers at home had often only hinted at and some had in vain attempted to instill.[62]

In this way, through their experience, engrained prejudices were challenged.

CO service profoundly impacted the young men themselves in other ways. After the war, they returned home to discover that farming had been transformed: increased mechanization reduced the need for farm labour, and larger farms pushed smaller operators off the land. Yet the COs came home with new self-confidence, new networks of friends, and new skills to re-establish themselves. Many saw their CO service as life altering. Many found a new direction in life; others found new employment. "It was a tremendous experience for me especially in the hospital work. It changed the direction of my life," said David F. Friesen of Altona, Manitoba, who would later serve as minister in the Altona Bergthaler Mennonite Church.[63]

o o o

Canada benefited significantly from alternative service arrangements during the war including manpower contributions in essential industries such as farming, forest fire fighting and hospitals, the $2.2 million sent to the Red Cross from CO wages, the development of its national parks, and a renewed forest on Vancouver Island that was worth $1.7 billion in 1995.[64] Indeed, some officials were keen to champion alternative service tasks as an important part of the war effort. This helps explain Parks Director R.A. Gibson's observation that "the first line of defense lies in the soul of a people ... and is anchored deeply in the land."[65] For members of the historic peace churches, these contributions were at times awkward, challenging, and dangerous, and they occurred amid a political culture that frequently denounced them for their beliefs in nonviolence.

Moreover, the experience of the conscientious objectors was also significant for the individual COs and their communities. Some separational pacifists felt the government had not lived up to its promise of complete military exemption. This was one of the factors that pushed some Mennonites to immigrate to Paraguay in 1948. Yet many others became convinced that integrational pacifism was the new standard and drew upon the legacy of wartime service to create relief and social service organizations after the war.[66] CO service also pushed young men into forming new relationships across denominational and ethnic boundaries. When they returned home, many men were soon ready for community leadership and this set the stage for a new level of interdenominational cooperation.

While COs were at times ridiculed for their stance, some of their wartime contributions softened the attitudes of others, including camp officials impressed by their good behaviour, attitude, and work ethic.[67] At the veterans' memorial dedication in Winkler, Manitoba in 2011, Brian Minnaker shared his father's experience. "Dad was a D-Day Veteran . . . he had choice words for conscientious objectors. How could the God of justice possibly be with the likes of them? That was his opinion until some of his buddies began to have mental troubles. . . . Who was it that went into institutions like that and found deplorable conditions [but COs]. . . . Dad would realize that yes God was truly with the group of people that gave up so much to improve the medical and psychiatric care in our country."[68]

While the value of conscientious objection may be contested, the experience of Canadian COs is an important part of Canadian history that deserves to be added to Canada's war narratives, especially in our primary and secondary schools. This has been recognized in part through the Canadian War Museum's 2013 display, "Peace – the Exhibition," which includes the story of conscientious objectors.[69] However, much more work needs to be done. The CO story is an important element of Canadian history and its legacy continues to shape our lives. As such, it cannot be dismissed with a haughty laugh and an assertion that it is time to move on to the "next question."

Rev. J.E. Purdie, Principal of the Pentecostal Bible College in Winnipeg 1925–50. Pentecostal Assemblies of Canada Archives, Mississauga, Ontario.

8

Principal Purdie Objects

Canadian Pentecostal Students and Conscription during the Second World War

LINDA M. AMBROSE

IN APRIL 1944, THE REVEREND J.E. PURDIE, principal of the Western Bible College in Winnipeg, wrote to the Pentecostal Assemblies of Canada head office in Toronto urging his colleagues to lobby on behalf of one of his most promising students who was being called up for active service.[1] "Please move every force in the country to save him for the Church," Purdie pleaded. "We need him in the church so much from every angle. I believe Ottawa could free him for the Ministry."[2] The correspondence around this intervention, which met with limited success, illustrates how one Pentecostal church leader attempted to prevent or postpone the conscription of the young men attending his Bible College during the Second World War.[3] Purdie had already made several attempts in connection with this student including going "to the Court and plead[ing] for him." However, his efforts had been to no avail because "the Judge held his ground and refused." Undaunted, Purdie continued to lobby, describing the student in question as "one of the finest chaps we have ever had in College. From a spiritual viewpoint, as preacher, student, culture and fine appearance, we lose, if he goes, a most promising Minister." What makes these acts of war resistance all the more intriguing is the fact that Purdie was not a pacifist. Nor was the student in question a conscientious objector. Exploring the response of the Pentecostal Assemblies of Canada to conscription during the Second World War demonstrates that war resistance took a variety of forms among religious leaders and that when they called for exemptions from military service, the rationale was often more complex than it first appeared.

"Conscription if necessary, but not necessarily conscription," is a phrase that every undergraduate student of wartime Canadian history can recite

because it encapsulates the political posturing for which Prime Minister Mackenzie King is so famously remembered. The controversies about mandatory service were heightened as the war progressed, and King sought to fulfil his obligations to the allied forces while maintaining a fragile unity at home. The story of Canada in wartime is most often told with French-English conflict as the central tension. The government's 1944 reversal on the promise not to conscript Canadians to serve overseas demanded great rhetorical finesse and, as Thomas Socknat has argued, resistance to overseas service was widespread, "especially but not exclusively, in Quebec."[4]

Beyond the domestic politics of French-English relations, religion is another arena where themes of war resistance in Canada can usefully be explored. As Conrad Stoesz reminds readers in this volume, the historic peace churches in Canada took a strong stance for conscientious objection and chose alternative service to avoid bearing arms. Resistance by Canadian Christians with roots in the historic peace churches included Quakers, Mennonites, and Hutterites, but they were not alone. Others took a stand to resist the war because of liberal Protestant and humanitarian reform traditions that emphasized Jesus as a pacifist, war as irrational, and universal brotherhood as common sense. When pressures mounted, and the King government reversed its decision not to send conscripts overseas, tensions increased and those who resisted war service were challenged about how they could best maintain their stance.

This chapter considers the case of Rev. Purdie during the 1940s and his attempts to negotiate the call for mandatory service for his students. Canadian Pentecostalism is a particularly rich site for exploring the complexity of religious expressions of war resistance in this period. Because the Pentecostal movement represented individuals drawn from a variety of backgrounds, their resistance took a variety of forms. Hence, the story of Pentecostals who tried (successfully or not) to avoid the call to service is complex. To understand why a Canadian Pentecostal might have expressed hesitation about going to war one must consider several factors. These include the heterogeneous nature of the Pentecostal movement itself, the specific context of marginal religious groups in Canada at the time, and the process of acculturation that was underway among Pentecostals as their movement evolved from a marginal to a more mainstream expression of Christianity in Canada.

Pentecostalism in Canada

It is useful to establish what comprised Pentecostal belief and practice in the 1940s. The defining characteristics of this movement include an emphasis on the work of the Holy Spirit, manifested by reports of miraculous healings and the occurrence of glossolalia (speaking in tongues, either of known or unknown languages). Converts to Pentecostalism reported personal episodes of "spirit baptism" which resulted in these supernatural experiences; indeed such personal encounters typically initiated followers into the movement and marked the point from which they began to self-identify as Pentecostals. The second defining feature of Pentecostal beliefs in the first half of the twentieth century was an overt sense of eschatological urgency. Pentecostals were convinced that the second coming of Christ was imminent, and that conviction translated into an urgent campaign to evangelize the world, and consequently to be less engaged with the culture around them or issues of social justice.

Michael Wilkinson, a leading scholar of Canadian Pentecostalism, explains the complexity of tracking Pentecostalism, pointing out "in Canada there are thirteen older or 'classical' Pentecostal denominations" as well as "numerous independent Pentecostal congregations that have no affiliation with these denominations." In addition, there are individual believers "who have had a Pentecostal or charismatic experience but stayed within their established, historic, mainline denominations like the Anglican Church of Canada or the United Church of Canada." The Pentecostal Assemblies of Canada (PAOC) is but one of the thirteen denominations Wilkinson points to, but it is the largest, having experienced what he called "phenomenal growth" in the second half of the twentieth century, going "from 45,000 members and adherents [in 1951] to 232,000, with 1,000 congregations and approximately 3,000 credential holders [in 2001]."[5] Given that expanding presence in Canada, it is worthwhile exploring the attitudes of PAOC leaders such as Purdie during the Second World War, just as that growth was beginning.[6]

According to the 1941 census, Pentecostals were still very much on the edge of Canadian society during the war with approximately fifty-eight thousand adherents in all the various Pentecostal groups among the total Canadian population of eleven million people. The majority of those were likely affiliated with the PAOC given that ten years later, according to Wilkinson, that denomination claimed forty-five thousand followers. Remarkably, census data suggests that just five hundred Canadians identified as adherents of all forms of Pentecostalism in 1911. Yet even with that growth rate Pentecostals at mid-century were only starting to register attention on the national consciousness.[7] Thomas William Miller, the official historian of the Pentecostal Assemblies of Canada, explains that, "The Pentecostal awakening of the early 20th century began in such obscurity that it was virtually unknown to leaders of the established denominations." Moreover, Miller notes, "Those of the mainline denominations who bothered to notice the religious upstart usually condemned it as a fanatical sect."[8]

By the 1940s, then, Pentecostalism in Canada had been in existence for just over thirty years, and its followers were full of optimism about the growth trajectory they were on and their potential impact on Canadian society. By 1943, the PAOC boasted 849 Canadian missionaries, ministers, and licensed workers serving approximately 420 congregations across the country.[9] The war years proved to be a testing ground as the fledgling movement flexed its developing muscles through interactions with the Canadian state, trying to define its place in society at large through its response to conscription.

Pentecostalism is an expression of Protestant Christianity that draws upon its roots in evangelical, revivalist traditions.[10] The classic version of North American Pentecostal history traces the origin to the so-called "Azuza Street revival" which took place in Los Angeles in 1906, but recent Canadian studies complicate that interpretation with simultaneous stories of origin in other locations, including the Hebden Mission on Queen Street East in Toronto, Ontario, where founder Ellen Hebden reported her own testimony of having been baptized in the Holy Spirit and speaking in tongues in the same year.[11] Adherents to the new movement were mostly converts from a surprisingly wide range of Protestant churches including Methodists, Presbyterians, Anglicans, United Church, and the Salvation Army.

Given that Pentecostals were a group drawn from mixed sources, it is not surprising that their views on war covered a whole spectrum spanning from pacifism and conscientious objection to loyal participation and even promotion of war. As Amy Shaw and Thomas P. Socknat have documented, there were several cases of Pentecostals who were subjected to shocking treatment at the hands of Canadian military officials for their firm stance as conscientious objectors during the First World War.[12] However, other Pentecostals served their country with pride and were commended for doing so, with reports of their exploits appearing in the denomination's publications.[13] A survey of the PAOC's official magazine, the *Pentecostal Testimony* (*PT*), which began publication in 1920, reinforces the fact that Pentecostal views about war varied because in its pages leaders of the movement expressed a wide range of opinions in the years leading up to the Second World War. For example, in the early 1920s, Pentecostal evangelists like Zelma Argue took a decidedly apocalyptic view, expressing the idea that while war was inevitable, it was not an issue that should distract Pentecostals because the second coming of Christ was imminent. Argue and others like her believed that "wars and rumours of wars" were only further proof that the prophecies predicting Christ's return were about to be fulfilled and true believers should be busy preaching the gospel, not becoming entangled in worldly affairs.[14]

In 1935–36, George A. Chambers, a Pentecostal preacher from Peterborough who had served as the first General Superintendent of the PAOC from 1919 to 1934, published a four-part series of articles in answer to the question "Should Christians Go to War?" Chambers' emphatic answer was "No." His was a classic expression of conscientious objection, arguing that "there is no such thing as a holy war," that Jesus forbade his disciples to use violence as a means of defending him in the Garden of Gethsemane, and that there were no references in the Book of Acts to the Church ever "taking up arms or returning evil for evil." Moreover, Chambers maintained that while the Apostle Paul taught believers to be "good soldiers of Jesus Christ," he also told them that a Christian should not "entangle himself in the affairs of this world."[15] Chambers' position was no surprise, given that he came into the Pentecostal movement from his background as a minister in the Mennonite Brethren in Christ Church.[16]

Despite such objections during the interwar years, by the 1940s *PT* regularly featured articles in support of going to war including "articles of special interest to military men and women."[17] In September 1941 Rev. D.N. Buntain, the PAOC General Superintendent, wrote an article entitled "If I Were Caught in the Draft." Buntain, who was ordained as a Methodist minister in 1918 and had become a Pentecostal in 1925,[18] addressed the tricky question of what stance Pentecostals should take on conscription. While Buntain did acknowledge that some Pentecostals were conscientious objectors, his main argument was that military service would present Pentecostals with a unique opportunity for making converts among their comrades. Subtitled "Words of Encouragement to our Young Men Who are Answering the Call to the Army," Buntain's article pointed to a model recruit who was serving as a petty officer in the Royal Canadian Navy, saying that this young Pentecostal "sings, testifies, and prays before and with the men with a holy joy and finds many opportunities to lift up Christ where there is no one else to do so."[19] Buntain exhorted readers that "if I were caught in the draft, I would put myself afresh into the hands of God and say, 'Lord, thy will be done. Keep me true, that in and through the experiences that lie ahead, I may like Joseph and Daniel rise to a place of useful service in thy kingdom.'"[20]

Purdie and Western Bible College

Other Pentecostal leaders were not convinced that such willing compliance was the best course of action. James Eustace Purdie, principal of Western Bible College in Winnipeg, went to great lengths to help his students avoid serving when they were called up to enlist, yet by his own admission, Purdie clearly was not a pacifist. Ordained as a priest with the Anglican Church of Canada, Purdie had trained at Wycliffe College in Toronto before he personally experienced the "Pentecostal blessing" in 1919, including an experience of glossolalia, and became affiliated with the Pentecostal Assemblies of Canada. A loyal supporter of the British Empire, Purdie was the founding principal of the Winnipeg school, and he occupied that role for twenty-five years, until its closure in 1950. Describing his views about war, Purdie declared, "This College and the members of the Faculty are 100% behind the Allied Cause to fight the demon of Hitlerism."[21]

Yet if Purdie and his faculty were so loyal to the cause of war, why did he try to prevent his students from serving? Purdie counselled many students, instructing them on how best to avoid serving when the recruiters came calling. The earliest evidence of his efforts to intervene in decisions about whether his students would be called up for military service dates from 1941 when he wrote to ask that a senior student be excused from military service since he was set to graduate, become ordained, and be appointed to pastor a church.[22] Because members of the clergy could be exempted from service this was a completely reasonable request, and C.D. McPherson, the Divisional Registrar of the Department of National War Services, replied to Purdie asking for "more particulars as to the status and standing of the Western Bible College and the denomination which it represents."[23] It was a routine request, and once the authorities were convinced that the student would soon join the ranks of a recognized church as a member of the clergy, his exemption would be granted.

Other students wrote directly to Purdie asking for his advice about how they should respond to the call for military service. One student from small-town Manitoba wrote to say that he had complied with the required medical examination and had assumed that given a previous injury, he would not have to serve. Yet it turned out that he was called up in the summer of 1942 and he wrote to ask Purdie whether he should also tell the authorities that he was a student at the Bible College because he wondered if that would help his case or "would it be best to leave all as it is?"[24] Principal Purdie did write to the authorities, arguing that this student's theological training was a higher priority than his recruitment.[25] A third case involved a young farmer from northwestern Ontario who wrote to Purdie in the summer of 1942 to explain that when he appeared before the army officials in Port Arthur, Ontario, he had been given a choice to declare himself a conscientious objector or be "'frozen' to the farm for eight months of each year." As he explained to Purdie, "I chose the farm."[26] Purdie responded to assure the student that he had made a wise choice because this would still allow him to spend his free months off the farm at school continuing his training for the ministry.[27]

These grounds for exemption (clergy status, medical limitations, and essential farm work) were quite standard, but in other cases Purdie tried to push the authorities further by making a case that Pentecostals should no longer be regarded as a group on the margins of Canadian society, but rather as loyal Canadians who, like other Christians, were central to the public life of the country. Given the immediate context of the 1940s, it was important for Pentecostals like Purdie to be able to articulate very clearly and fully the nature of their hesitation to serve or allow their ministerial students to serve in the war. As a marginal religious group, it was important to assert the group's loyalty to the cause and compliance with the state because other religious groups were capturing headlines and finding their liberties curtailed. The most well known example is the Jehovah's Witnesses, who were legally banned in Canada under the Defence of Canada Regulations from 1940 to 1943. Witnesses refused to salute the flag and were firmly opposed to war as a "work of the devil."[28] Banned from meeting and from circulating their publications, the Witnesses served as a cautionary tale for other groups who might dare to defy wartime regulations on the basis that their allegiance was to a higher authority than the state.

While the Pentecostals were not so homogenously committed to resisting participation in the war as Jehovah's Witnesses were, it was important for Purdie, given the context of the times, to articulate carefully why he was reluctant to let his students serve. Historian James Penton argues that the wartime curtailment of the Witnesses' activity actually served to increase public sympathy for the movement because they came to be perceived as martyrs who were being persecuted for their beliefs by a wartime government that was heavy-handed in its reaction to religious convictions. Although Pentecostals did not experience anywhere near the same level of regulation that Jehovah's Witnesses did, it seems Purdie was capitalizing on a similar argument, trying to establish that if Pentecostals were treated differently from the mainline churches, then the state was somehow guilty of discrimination. Despite Pentecostals' reputation for being misunderstood by mainstream society, Purdie was requesting from government officials that they be treated the same as more longstanding Christian groups. Recent controversy over the Jehovah's Witnesses no doubt served to frame the way that Purdie shaped his rhetoric and the way that officials responded to him.

As mandatory enlistment came into force, and having established that he and his college were firmly behind the war effort, Purdie argued that given the high calling on the lives of theological students to serve the country as clergy, all Bible College students (not just Pentecostals) should be exempt from war service. Purdie was convinced that when the war ended, the country would need the moral influence that clergymen would bring and military authorities should recognize that as a legitimate way to serve the country and plan for the postwar period. This argument is similar to that made by postsecondary educators across the country, who asserted that Canadian postwar society would demand an educated class of leaders in all sectors. Significantly, though, the Pentecostal principal made his case using the logic of social justice. He argued that Pentecostals were facing discrimination because his Winnipeg Bible College students were not being recognized in the same way as other Christians. He bluntly pointed to the special status of other faith groups. "The Church of Rome," Purdie reminded the authorities, "has exemption for her young men studying for the Priesthood and many of our Protestant leaders feel to be fair we ought to have exemption also for our Theological students."[29] In fact, that discrepancy between Catholics training for the priesthood and Protestant seminarians was already being redressed and by October 1942 media reports revealed that a new class of "persons exempt from compulsory service" had recently been created, comprising "bona fide candidate[s] or students for the ministry of a religious denomination eligible to supply chaplains to the armed forces."[30]

Unfortunately, that announcement would not help Pentecostals very much, and Purdie knew it. The problem was that Pentecostals were limited in their ability "to supply chaplains to the armed forces" because of their marginal status in Canadian society.[31] In an attempt to learn from the lessons of the First World War, by 1939 the Canadian armed forces had established that chaplains would be appointed according to the following formula: one Protestant chaplain for every 1,000 conscripts and one Roman Catholic chaplain for every 500 Catholics enlisted, based on the logic that Catholic priests would be more occupied with administering the sacraments and hearing confessions, and would therefore require more manpower than Protestant clergymen in the same role. Enlistment statistics indicate that Pentecostals were simply not numerous enough among armed forces personnel to meet the statistical quota that would necessitate the appointment of very many of their chaplains.

When other efforts to have his students excused from active service failed, Purdie decided to press the authorities to allow Pentecostals in the forces to serve as chaplains rather than in combat roles even though their numbers did not warrant such appointments. He was convinced that numbers were not the real reason Pentecostals were not being accepted; in his mind, this was a case of discrimination based on widespread misperceptions about Pentecostalism. Indeed, Purdie invoked arguments using the rhetoric of equity and inclusiveness. It was unfair, he insisted, that Pentecostal clergy or soon-to-be-clergy, loyal to the country and the empire, should be excluded from serving as chaplains because their movement was not as widely recognized as other Protestant denominations.

Moreover, he argued, there were anomalies with the enlistment records of the Canadian military. Because Pentecostalism was a religious expression that was still not completely familiar to recruitment station personnel, recruiters freely applied the code "O.D." for "other denomination" when they were not certain about a conscript's religion. Similarly, as Albert Fowler, historian of the Protestant Military Chaplains reveals, "it was commonly believed that, upon enrolment, if a soldier hesitated when asked his religion, he would be recorded as either Church of England or Roman Catholic."[32] Purdie highlighted these irregularities to question whether Pentecostals were being fairly represented. In effect, Purdie's argument, and the liberal sentiment behind it, called upon state authorities to recognize a relatively new expression of evangelical Christianity and give it the same respect afforded to the older, more established churches.

o o o

In the end, the student whose case was cited at the beginning of this chapter did serve in the armed forces, though only for a few months because Purdie arranged for him to receive an early ordination and placement as co-pastor in a local church near the Bible College. Although the student had not completed his college training, he was granted a release from service under a clergy exemption.[33] His case, then, did not prompt the military establishment to make changes to their existing policies. Even so, the story of Principal Purdie and the Western Bible College offers three valuable lessons about the relationship between war resistance and religion during the Second World War.

First, the nature of Pentecostalism in Canada meant that this group was a hybrid of several existing religious traditions, representing a variety of views about war; for some of those believers, past affiliations with religious traditions that emphasized pacifism and conscientious objection carried over directly into how they responded to war even though they had converted to Pentecostalism. For others who came into Pentecostal circles from state churches with a proud military past, ideas about war were reframed in light of the new eschatological urgency they had embraced as Pentecostals. Second, given the regulatory measures that the Canadian government adopted during the 1940s, marginalized religious groups needed to tread carefully as they articulated their hesitations about war participation. The case of Canadian Jehovah's Witnesses made that very clear. As a result, Purdie continuously declared allegiance to the state, even as he put conditions on his Pentecostal students' willingness to serve. Third, some leaders among Canadian Pentecostals ironically hoped that by qualifying their participation in Canada's war effort they would gain wider acceptance for their movement; inadvertently, they were speeding the acculturation of this marginal group by appealing to liberal sentiments about equity and justice. Refusing to be sidelined as a "fanatical sect," Purdie pushed Canadian officials to take Pentecostals seriously and to treat them in exactly the same manner as more traditional Christian denominations.

For Purdie and the Pentecostals associated with the Western Bible College, efforts to resist military service were a complex mix of pragmatism and apocalyptic convictions, together with self-preservation and social justice. First and foremost, Purdie wanted his students exempted from serving because he wanted to "save them for the church." Like all Pentecostals at the time, he was motivated by an eschatological urgency to spread the gospel message before the imminent return of Christ. At the same time, he was pragmatic enough to make clear that he and his college students were sympathetic to the war effort because he did not want to run the risk of being associated with groups like the Jehovah's Witnesses, whose refusal to salute the flag meant they were criminalized under wartime regulations. When he realized that he could not successfully prevent the conscription of his students, Purdie lobbied instead for them to serve as military chaplains, even though it was clear that their numbers did not warrant such appointments under the established system. Despite their small numbers, Purdie invoked the rhetoric of social justice by arguing that failing to treat Pentecostals the same way that the older state churches were treated amounted to discrimination. Purdie's shifting arguments demonstrate that it is impossible to arrive at a simple answer to the question of Pentecostals' position on war resistance. But this only serves to illustrate that sorting out the nuanced motivations of religious war resisters is a complex task that must consider the competing demands and ambiguities facing religious leaders in particular historical contexts.

Delegates to the World Congress of Women, tree planting, Moscow, 1963. Margaret Russell in the forefront. Swarthmore College Peace Collections, Women Strike for Peace Records, Acc. 94A-32, file: WSP demonstrations, 1960–1969.

9

Margaret Ells Russell, Women Strike for Peace, and the Global Politics of "Intelligent Compassion," 1961–1965

IAN McKAY

O N NOVEMBER 1, 1961, IN WASHINGTON, DC, an unusual march – made up of some 750 "school girls, government workers, mothers and grandmothers, together with a score of children, half a dozen men, and a Collie named Candy" – made its way from the grounds of the Washington Monument to the White House. Their placards read: "End Arms Race, Not the Human Race"; "Use Nuclear Power for Peace"; "Negotiation is Not Appeasement," and "Please, no more strontium 90" – this one carried by the Collie. One bore a quotation from U.S. President John F. Kennedy, who was watching the demonstration from his window: "Mankind must put an end to war, or war will put an end to mankind."

Received at the door by the White House guard, the protestors dropped off a petition urging Jacqueline Kennedy to "think what hope would gladden the world if women everywhere would rise to claim the right to life for their children and for generations yet unborn." Then one contingent of the protestors went to the Soviet Embassy, where they delivered an identical petition addressed to Nina Khrushchev. "We had a perfectly charming time; the Russian women are as anxious for peace as we are," was their verdict. Later that day came the news that thousands of women in scores of U.S. cities had taken part in what became known as the "Women Strike for Peace" (WSP). These "extremely earnest" protestors impressed President Kennedy. Both of the "First Ladies" wrote responses indicating the wholehearted support of their respective husbands. And the world gradually took notice of a new force against nuclear war.[1]

WSP has been analyzed as a forerunner of radical separatist feminism in the U.S., a continuation of conventional "motherist ideology," a movement that fatally weakened McCarthyism, a vintage example of the spontaneity of "the Sixties," an early version of environmental activism, and a moment in the career of Congresswoman Bella Abzug – all interpretations that shed some light on its history. To date, it has almost always been placed in a U.S. framework. This national framing minimizes the extent to which WSP was one part of a *world* peace movement, the fact that many of its leaders attached overwhelming significance to internationalism, and the perils and potential of combining grassroots spontaneity with international diplomacy.

WSP exemplified what Catia Cecilia Confortini calls "Intelligent Compassion," a "theory of agency, such that deliberative inquiry, skeptical scrutiny, and guiding criteria in concert can promote emancipatory social change."[2] Guided by this critical theory, key WSP members moved beyond liberal internationalism – an outlook that maintained that wars could be prevented through fairer and freer trade among nations, the scientific study of international relations, the diffusion of liberal political systems, complete disarmament, and international humanitarianism,[3] as exemplified by such contemporary figures as Lester Pearson and John F. Kennedy and such institutions as the United Nations – toward something that might be called transnational radical humanism. This entailed a position of critical, compassionate identification with those presently or potentially damaged by militarism, a conviction that both liberal and communist states were complicit in human suffering, an emphasis on face-to-face meetings between non-state actors, and an increasingly oppositional stance toward Western governments perpetrating acts of genocide. This chapter traces this evolution through the activism and writings of Margaret Ells Russell, the Nova Scotian who planned and managed that important Washington demonstration in 1961 and who in 1963 became one of the first Western women to engage directly with the women of Vietnam and bring word of their suffering back to North America.[4]

o o o

WSP began – so the story goes – one September evening in 1961. Six women and two men came together in Washington, D.C., to share their fears about nuclear annihilation.[5] Margaret was one of them. She was born in 1909 in Malden, Massachusetts, but both sides of her family were descended from eighteenth-century settlers in Nova Scotia. Her childhood was spent in the Annapolis Valley, which Margaret romanticized as a premodern refuge from "the hurried existence of the twentieth century."[6] At Dalhousie University, she excelled in English and history, and after she had received her M.A., she secured an Imperial Order Daughters of the Empire scholarship to study in England, where she sought unsuccessfully to obtain a doctorate in history.

Upon her return to Halifax in 1932, she served for thirteen years as an archivist and historian at the Public Archives of Nova Scotia. Her numerous contributions to scholarship tended to adopt an unusually sceptical tone with respect to people in power, especially the patronage-keen Loyalists. Over the course of the 1930s, Margaret moved from a quite conservative politics[7] to one that supported social equality and an expanded state, even the social-democratic Co-operative Commonwealth Federation.[8] In the 1940s, she was an activist in the Halifax Co-operative Society, an experiment in alternative retailing that promoted grassroots liberal democracy.[9] She also adopted an increasingly critical, antiwar view of international affairs, one sharpened by an around-the-world tour (with a special emphasis on Asia) in 1936 and 1937.[10] Margaret's book-length manuscript about her trip contains, in addition to many Orientalist passages about picturesque places and stabs at humour à la P.G. Wodehouse, critical analyses of Chinese politics and compassionate memories of interactions with locals on train trips.[11]

In 1955, after a short stint as a teacher, Margaret married Ralph Russell, a distant relative and civil servant at the U.S. Department of the Interior, and at the age of forty-six settled into a new life in suburban Washington.[12] Over the next decade, alongside her close friend and fellow WSP leader Dagmar Wilson, whose upper-class British accent bespoke her British childhood and youth and whose partner Christopher worked at the British Embassy, Margaret enjoyed sufficient security in her relationship with Russell to pursue a full-time career as an antiwar activist.[13]

She was joining the world of women's peace activism at an interesting moment. The most storied institution in this world was the Women's International League for Peace and Freedom (WILPF), constituted in 1919 at the high tide of Wilsonian idealism, which still retained quasi-observer status (although not much power) in the post-1945 world of international diplomacy.[14] WILPF was a transnational movement from its inception, and most of its supporters, certainly in Canada, were not "isolationists" but supporters of such bodies as the League of Nations and, after 1945, the United Nations.[15] Among post-1945 WILPF supporters, writes Confortini, one found some feminists and some pacifists – but a predominating number of ardent "liberal internationalists" who sought the improvement, through more rational international relations, of the existing international system.[16] Many WSPers who claimed to break with WILPF were often subtly influenced by its philosophy.[17]

Margaret was initially involved with the National Committee for a Sane Nuclear Policy (SANE), which exemplified this liberal paradigm. She served on its Washington local executive but broke with the organization in August 1960 as the national group began to implement a screening procedure to weed out supposed communists. She, along with three other future WSPers, condemned the way in which the policy had been imposed: "Why," they asked, "are some people who so glibly talk about democracy really so afraid of it?"[18] Coming from a mainland Nova Scotia milieu little touched by the rivalries between communists and social democrats, and sympathetic to co-operation as an ideal as well as a practice, Margaret never made anti-communism the lodestar of her life.

The women in Washington were picking up and adapting antiwar philosophies and tactics circulating throughout the Western world and were particularly attuned to developments in Great Britain and Canada. In Britain, the Campaign for Nuclear Disarmament (CND), formed in 1957, conducted its Aldermaston March every Easter between 1959 and 1965 and made both the slogan "Ban the Bomb" and its symbol known throughout the world.[19] In Canada, Lotta Dempsey's columns in the *Toronto Daily Star* responding to a sudden worsening of U.S.-Soviet relations prompted the organization in 1960 of the Women's Committee for Peace; it soon became the two thousand-member strong Voice of Women /La Voix des femmes (VOW) and an important collaborator with WSP in mounting parades at the U.N. Plaza to mark Demand Disarmament Day.[20]

Sharing the insight that women had both an incentive and an obligation to resist war, each of the three movements had its particular approach to adapting this insight to its own country. In the early 1960s, all three campaigns emphasized similar themes: the perils of atmospheric testing, especially toxic implications of fallout for public health; the false promise of building shelters instead of achieving disarmament; the impoverishing hold of Cold War paradigms; and the urgent need to demonstrate mass opposition to the bomb.

Yet there were also subtle differences among them. The British, strongly influenced by supporters of the Labour Party, had a highly centralized organization, pushed hard for unilateral disarmament, and viewed spontaneous actions with reservation. VOW supporters in Canada sought international linkages from the beginning. Its members tended to argue that both superpowers were responsible for the Cold War and aspired to hold Liberal leader and Prime Minister Lester Pearson to his avowedly peace-loving principles. In the U.S., the initial two precipitating causes of the formation of WSP – a crusade against communists in

SANE and the resumption of the atmospheric testing of atomic weapons – served to highlight the issue of communism throughout the organization's early career. Many WSPers and peace activists were predisposed to draw a moral distinction between Kennedy's government, seen to be more or less peace loving, and the bellicose Soviets, whose ramped-up atmospheric tests had imperilled humanity.

On that September evening when Margaret and her friends gathered to talk, they were particularly concerned about these tests. Nobody kept minutes. Some say the idea for a "Women's Strike" was the brainchild of Lawrence Scott, one of the two men present.[21] What we know for certain is that out of the meeting emerged a remarkable letter. "Democracy and Communism have deep basic conflicts," the letter observed, but the same applied to "Democrats and Republicans, husbands and wives, parents and children." They all had ways of working out their differences. So why should such feats of reconciliation be impossible on a world scale? Unless *people* survived, all freedom would perish. Why didn't people demand that their own elected government understand that human survival came before such empty gamesmanship? Their plan was for a WOMEN'S STRIKE FOR PEACE – emphatic capitalization in the original. Women were to go "on strike" – the phrase is placed in scare quotes – from "domestic and business duties. Husbands or babysitters take over the home front. Bosses or substitutes take over the jobs." There were to be big demonstrations. There were to be mass visitations of congressmen, mayors, and city councillors. There was to be a media blitz. "Get on the phone," the letter urged the women of the U.S. "Write your friends elsewhere (no matter if they hear from several people). Make up your own leaflets." There was no time to be lost.[22]

It was all, like so many sixties schemes, so very last minute, so very amateurish. And it worked. Women across the U.S. responded to the call on the first of November. Margaret, the key organizer in Washington, was delighted by the nationwide response. "The typical reaction, here and everywhere," she noted, "is Thank Heaven! At last there is something I can do to speak out for humanity!"[23] The spontaneous strike-born "non-organization" with no hierarchy, headquarters, official members, program, or explicit philosophy made quite a splash. Here was a *happening* more than just an event. If it had one core idea, it was that self-activated, autonomously organized women could make a big difference to all of humanity. Beyond that, much was open to interpretation. The "strike" at WSP's very heart was polysemic. Was WSP drawing upon the strike traditions associated with the working class? If so, against whom were the women striking? The very husbands whose support (perhaps in an after-strike barbecue) they solicited?[24] What services were women withdrawing? Or did "strike" mean – as the Washington circle evidently assumed – a sudden, effective action, rather like "striking a match"?[25] "Telephone ... Telegraph ... TELEWOMAN!" was the slogan of WSP's *Washington Newsletter*. It worked with – but surely transformed – the sexist stereotype of the idly chatting housewife with time on her hands: now this often-disparaged woman had communities to mobilize and a world to transform.[26]

The very "innocence" and improbability of the strike made it appealing, at a time when male leaders menaced each other over often arcane yet life-threatening issues. These women – "appalled at our own audacity, for we are just ordinary people, not experts," explained the letter of 1961[27] – were both modest and unusually candid about the limitations of their knowledge. If this was "leftism," it was operating without the authoritarian bravado of the central committees of yesteryear. It recalled much more closely the communitarian and co-operative movements that had inspired Margaret in Nova Scotia.[28]

Very much like VOW, then, WSP emerged almost spontaneously as an antiwar movement among women responding to a specific moment. Both movements involved a contradictory "performance of gender," in which women consciously worked with existing stereotypes of ladylike dress and deportment to challenge the warriors.[29] WSP's most calculated and famous performance occurred before the much-feared House Un-American Activities Committee (HUAC) shortly after the November strike. The Wise Men of the Peace Movement thought it madness for WSP to challenge the legitimacy of HUAC.[30] They underestimated WSP. The WSPers – self-effacing, beautifully dressed, often with children in tow and armed with bundles and bundles of flowers – arrived *en masse*. As historian Catharine Stimpson remarks, "Women jammed the committee room, rose in support when witnesses were called, applauded the performance of these witnesses, wore flowers and gave out bouquets, and dandled babies."[31] Observing the scene for his readers in the Toronto *Globe and Mail*, George Bain reflected that HUAC had been frustrated in its "familiar task of sticking the brand of Communism into the faces of witnesses to see if they will blink" by the women's sheer amiability.[32]

In contrast with its British and Canadian counterparts, WSP was "loose-knit" to the point of structurelessness – there was no official membership. It adapted the transnational idea that the self-activating women of the world could rise up spontaneously for peace to the specific circumstances of a still-McCarthyite America. So what if some red-baiter found an Old Leftist handing out WSP pamphlets? WSP placed no restrictions on any woman – whether Communist or Conservative, Republican or Democrat – who could wholeheartedly commit herself to peace. By 1965, WSP did boast annual conferences, a central clearing-house, and a policy statement, whose major planks consisted of the banning of all nuclear tests and the end of the arms race, the strengthening of the U.N., and the nonviolent negotiated resolution of disputes.[33] Yet, to the frustration of red-baiters, it had militants but no members; a clearing-house but no politburo; a policy statement but no program.[34] Such structurelessness was, in this context, not merely "subjectively" satisfying but "objectively" useful. Although both the FBI and CIA infiltrated WSP, such spies were often reduced to working long, fruitless hours on the telephone, doing the work of the movement.[35]

A further reason why HUAC proved a launching pad rather than a tomb for WSP could be found in the red-baiters' poor timing. They launched their attack before the Strike-as-happening had been transformed into "the Strike" as a unified and coherent tendency. Like CND and VOW, after the signing of the Nuclear Test Ban Treaty in early October 1963,[36] WSP could no longer mobilize women on the menace of strontium-90, and a decrease in tensions between the U.S. and USSR convinced some that the arms race no longer posed an imminent danger to human survival. What next? Once a large network of women – much of it based on "telephone-trees" that helped middle-class housewives organize everything from PTAs to bridge clubs – had been established, it seemed unthinkable to throw it all away.[37] But the minimum program – resistance to atmospheric nuclear testing – had seemingly been achieved.

A more daunting prospect of antiwar unity based on the politics of intelligent compassion beckoned in the form of Vietnam. Any such transnational turn raised inevitable questions about the group's 100 per cent Americanism. In the wake of their famous Strike, WSP's leading figures received invitations from around the world.[38] Many raised the prospect of making the group's transnational identity – already plain in the thinking and biographies of its prominent leaders – controversially obvious. Any transposition of the spontaneity and energy of the 1961 Strike as a "moment" into the Strike as a "movement" also demanded more structure. One could not show up in Geneva, Moscow, or London without some prior planning, some notion of a program, and some spokespeople.[39] Once it entered international politics, WSP was obliged to play by some of the same rules of the Hobbesian realism hegemonic in that sphere – ones that tended to reify each country as a unified, coherent player among other equally self-contained and self-interested players, all of them competing in an anarchic jungle.[40]

For Margaret, who brought decades of historical research and reflection on patterns of empire, grassroots democracy, and the turmoils of war to this assignment, WSP had no other option.[41] Isolationism of the type common in the U.S. and appealing to some WSPers was profoundly foreign to her. For her, Wilson, and most of the Washington and Berkeley WSP circles, WSP had *never* been just the "U.S. Women Strike for Peace." It was the *Women's International Strike for Peace*.[42] They attempted to make this the accepted name of the entire organization. For them, WSP was *not* in essence a U.S.-defined organization. It was the voice of the entire world's women for peace, as it could be made to reverberate in the United States.

"If they had so much as thought of it," complains Amy Swerdlow, the leading historian of WSP, who is channelling some of the numerous contemporary critics of a move rightly associated with Margaret's Washington crowd, "they would have insisted that an international association was so far beyond their dreams, their capabilities, and their resources as to be out of the question."[43] But Margaret *did* think long and hard about it. Like many peace activists in Canada, but arguably unlike many of her American sisters, isolationism for her held no attraction. She was neither thoughtless nor an innocent but rather a seasoned political historian long fascinated with empire, democracy, and grassroots mobilization.

For Margaret, the 1961 Strike she had brought to the gates of the White House lived on as a glowing inspiration, yet in one sense it had been merely a fleeting "moment" in the antiwar struggle. If it was to become a "moment" in a deeper sense – a phase or element within a larger process of enlightenment and becoming – it had to lead on to something beyond itself.[44] From this perspective, it seemed possible (her *Washington Newsletter* explained) to combine structure with spontaneity – "To remain a movement, not an organization." In Washington, the "National Information Clearing House," which was to have no executive staff, and a volunteer-run office, would receive all proposals for *national* co-ordinated action, leaving intact autonomy for all *local* actions.[45] As a pivotal figure in that Clearing House, Russell would play an indispensable co-ordinating role, one that encompassed liaising with other women's peace groups in the Northeast.[46]

o o o

. There were many perils to going beyond local happenings to national events and then on to international diplomacy. Rank-and-filers like Shirley Lens in Chicago, zealous to maintain WSP's "active neutrality" with respect to the superpowers, demanded that WSP put unilateral demands to Russia.[47] WSP had, after all, constituted for many a critique of the Kremlin's nuclear testing. Margaret was also sceptical of the Soviets.[48] But did that mean that WSP should reject Eastern Bloc invitations and restrict its message of hope and emancipation to a much smaller U.S. crowd? The issue arose in 1963, when WSP received an invitation to send as many as thirty delegates to a Women's International Democratic Federation event in Moscow. The Federation, though headed by a French non-communist and drawing women of various political and religious hues, was widely considered to be communist-leaning.[49] Should U.S. women accept Russian hospitality? Under what conditions could a WSPer "represent" her fellow militants? Russell was plainly in favour of participating, but she also thought that any WSP "observer" – not delegate – "should be equipped with a statement greeting the conference and setting forth the policies of our movement." Then she could speak authoritatively, but only in general terms, and in ways that directly echoed WSP principles.[50] It fell to Margaret as the "Head of the U.S. Delegation" to worry about the considerable complexities – airline bookings, accommodation details, even smallpox vaccinations – entailed in participating in the Congress.[51]

The World Congress of Women in June 1963 marked a turning point in Margaret's activism. It incorporated, she noted, four main topics of discussion: "winning, defending and implementing of women's rights as mothers, working women and citizens"; "the contribution of women to the struggle for a world at peace"; the "role of women in achieving the political and economic independence of all countries"; and the "role of women to protect children and youth and ensure that they are educated in the spirit of peace and friendship."[52] However, it was the address of the delegates from North and South Vietnam to the whole Congress on the "barbaric war" afflicting their country that galvanized her.

Margaret vividly described the testimony of Madam Ma Thi Chu, "a beautiful young woman," who "spoke with deep emotion of the truly terrible conditions where, since 1959, 500,000 have been killed, about 600,000 bombed, beaten or tortured, 350,000 imprisoned." She spoke of the shooting of Buddhists, the indiscriminate spraying of chemicals, and the water poisoning that had killed women, children, and animals. Once they heard the report, Margaret and the other delegates secured a face-to-face meeting with the Vietnamese women, who assured her there was no chance of the "U.S.-Diem" forces winning the war and that it was up to the American delegates "to urge our government to withdraw from Vietnam." "They urged us, especially as mothers and women of the U.S., to use our best efforts to bring to an end the 'US war of aggression in South Vietnam,'" she explained.[53] John F. Kennedy had a few more weeks to live, but in Margaret's eyes his liberal peace credentials were already dead.

Drawing on her years of experience as an archivist-historian, she helped draw up a comprehensive information kit, heavy with citations of the Congressional Record and newspaper sources, about the war.[54] Charged with co-ordinating the "Committee on Viet Nam" Margaret proposed an ambitious program for WSP. She felt compelled to share her insights into the chemical attacks, the poisoned water, the concentration camps ("strategic hamlets"), torture, and murder in Vietnam with as wide an audience as possible.[55] Telling Congressmen about the Vietnam tragedy was a priority.[56] The following November, the "Appeal to Reason" campaign – on which WSP collaborated with six other peace groups[57] – generated an advertisement carrying six hundred signatures in the *Washington Post*. Margaret wanted to take the campaign across the country.[58]

WSP was at a Rubicon. Both in Britain and Canada, antiwar movements focused on the abolition of nuclear weapons confronted the challenge of responding to the new reality of an accelerating war in Vietnam, one that forced them to redefine their objectives and potentially narrow their constituencies. The dangers in such a challenge were graver in the United States, where taking a stance against the war meant declaring one's opposition to a program launched by one's own country, in the name of the "free world," by such liberals as Presidents Kennedy and Johnson. "Vietnam is the only place in which our armed forces are actually engaged," Margaret noted:

> We therefore feel a special responsibility to inform ourselves and others on the dangers and horrors of this particular situation. As we have alerted the public of our country to the dangers of radiation, so we must now alert it to the possibility that this undeclared war may escalate into nuclear conflict and to the specific ways in which basic human morality is being violated by attacks on civilian population – women and children.[59]

By connecting the earlier issues with Vietnam, Margaret was plainly attempting to help WSPers make the transition to a new, more transnational, politics.

Much of the U.S. left initially could not do it – even the Students for a Democratic Society half-heartedly supported Johnson in 1964. Perhaps because it was so influenced by women who were transnational – by many definitions, its "American" Washington sparkplugs were in fact British and Canadian – WSP was made of sterner stuff. "The committee has no official position on the Vietnam question," Margaret diplomatically explained in a November 1963 *Information Bulletin* – but she demanded that it took one. Suffused with the politics of intelligent compassion, combining a realist reconnaissance of the chances of U.S. military success with a vivid appreciation of the human suffering arising from the war, she presented her U.S. friends in February 1964 with a portrait of a losing cause:

> The war in Vietnam goes from bad to worse, our newspapers shriek that we are going to carry it into N. Vietnam – and thence into WWIII. We are at the beginning of a real crisis and time of decision. Even Saigon, though protected by thousands of Vietnamese and American soldiers and police, is the scene of terroristic bombings – snipers are daring enough to fire from ambush at the city's airport. Morale, alike in military and government circles, is very low. There is talk, firmly denied, of sending home 1800 dependents of American personnel. The U.S. is forced to change its policies, one way or the other, or lose by default.[60]

The culmination of Margaret's Vietnam War activism came with her return, after twenty-eight years, to Indonesia, where in July 1965 she participated in a Jakarta conference attended by nine women from Vietnam.[61] A younger Margaret had experienced Indonesia during her world tour in the 1930s as a realm of innocence and a validation of her liberal, middle-class values.[62] Her outlook had changed.

Once again, in this bid to build peace through a face-to-face sharing of insights, WSP was developing a path that many others would follow.[63] Margaret reported back to WSP that a supposed halt to the U.S. bombing of Vietnam had never happened. "We heard the other side of the story," she observed, "tales of anguish ... heart-rending personal tragedies."[64] Bringing the war home to the U.S. became one of Margaret's central objectives. She helped make WSP into one of the first groups in the U.S. to engage in mass protests against the war.[65]

So, if Margaret's writings of 1964 and 1965 suggest a continued emphasis on established mainstream techniques of liberal internationalism – "Write Your Congressman!" – she was also implicitly pushing against liberalism's limits. She came to a position of critical, compassionate identification with the women of Vietnam, as they told her of hiding from U.S. bombs and struggling to protect their children. Did it matter that some of her interlocutors were communist? Were the Vietnamese not entitled to work out their political futures without the threat of death from the skies? Was there not a link between the genocide in Indochina and the arms manufacturers flourishing under free enterprise? Although it would stretch the evidence to say that her politics had become those of revolutionary solidarity, it would be accurate to describe her as an advocate of solidarity with women revolutionaries. Once, WSP had been ever so diplomatic and even-handed in its approach to Kennedy and Khrushchev, understandably aware of the penalties a liberal order could exact were it to stray too far into subversion. Now, the term "genocide" came to assume a place in the WSP's lexicon – and it was applied to the servants of the U.S. government.

o o o

Although she was only in her mid-fifties, Russell's health was declining – she may have already started suffering from the Alzheimer's that later incapacitated her – and her activist years were drawing to a close.[66] In April 1967, when thousands of people came to Washington as part of the Spring Mobilization against the War in Vietnam, there were few memories of the complicated Canadian who, six years earlier, had helped break the Cold War consensus by bringing antiwar women to the doors of the White House. But the marchers of 1967 were following in her footsteps. Perhaps even more than as a forerunner of a new wave of feminist activism or as the nemesis of HUAC, WSP's most striking accomplishment was to awaken many North Americans to the liberal genocide taking place in Southeast Asia.

In many respects, Margaret's record runs counter to influential interpretations of women's activism between 1945 and the consolidation of second wave feminism in the late 1960s. Of course, for some of today's inheritors of the HUAC tradition, Margaret was a "useful idiot" of red dictatorship,[67] one more bleeding heart who blocked a U.S. victory in Vietnam. For their part, many second wave feminists have tended to look back on 1945–65 as a desolate era of gender conformity and repression. From this perspective, what stands out about WSP was its women-centred "separatism" – its partial realization that women and men were engaged, in essence and perhaps forever, in a "battle of the sexes."[68]

Yet both critiques largely miss the mark – in Margaret's case and that of the WSP more generally. There is no evidence that Margaret wavered in her life-long reverence for liberal rights and freedoms. What she had come to realize, however, was that self-declared liberals themselves imperilled the survival of such rights and freedoms. Liberalism as a doctrine of freedom had come to be an apology for empire. Nor is there strong evidence that Margaret was a consistent apostle of an "ideology of motherism." The rights of women and mothers were often emphasized in WSP discourse. However, strictly "maternalist" arguments – ones that claimed authority because their author was a mother or argued that the "mothers of the nation" were the bearers of its destiny – were rather uncommon.[69] When Margaret invoked images of the bombed-out women of Vietnam, her purpose was not the sentimental essentialization of motherhood but the arousal of humanitarian outrage about the suffering of other human beings.[70] Moreover, from its foundational Strike onwards, WSP always solicited the support of men and never separated itself from – indeed its supporters often also joined – the many other groups made up of men and women struggling for peace. Working within a wider North American peace culture of Quakers, WILPF advocates, VOW, and many Old Leftists,[71] Margaret understood that a multitude of voices might be orchestrated into one great antiwar chorus, with each voice retaining its autonomy and none drowning out the others.

Instead, Margaret's engagement with the world suggests a third, quite different way of seeing this moment of postwar history. It would focus on her awakening to a world of napalm, Agent Orange, and double-talking liberals, politicians who preached diplomacy and practised genocide. It still demanded a good-humoured, enthusiastic outlook, and even a sense of fun – despair for Margaret was not a useful option. But it also called upon life-long liberals, as they struggled to speak truth to power, to re-examine their world with more intelligent, compassionate, and critical eyes.

In November 1964, the *Woman Strike for Peace Newsletter, Greater Washington Area* published an unsigned poem that commemorated the achievements and legacy of the Women's Strike for Peace. Everything about it suggests the spirit – both defiant and ironic at the same time – of Margaret Ells Russell:

Of Women and Walking

November, 1961 – the world's not at war,
But peace hasn't really begun.
Problems abound, fears by the score –
Fallout, radiation, and the Cold War.

"Is peace for our children to be left to luck?"
"Nonsense," says Dagmar, "it's time women struck!"
Across the nation from coast to coast,
Women march to protect what they care for most –
Families, children, the world at peace –
"Protect Us from Fallout!" "Testing Must Cease!"

Put an end to all the fruitless talking.
If men won't do something we'll keep on walking.
(At least all this walking and milk that's been skimmed
Has kept us in shape, and our shape's neatly trimmed).

And then a breakthrough – success at last!
The Test Ban Treaty has finally passed.
We breathe in air that's a little clearer.
The issues are sharper, peace is nearer.

Next – MLF.[72] And then there's Viet Nam!
The world's still in a mess, but we do give a damn!
We have three years behind us and more to go,
Maybe six, maybe ten, or a dozen, who knows?
So take out your shoes – [and] check your sole
We're gonna keep walking till we reach our goal![73]

Twenty-eight VOW delegates for the International Cooperation Year (ICY) Travel Mission, Malton (now Pearson) Airport, headed to the USSR and Europe, June 10, 1963. Helen Tucker, Chairman of the Women's International Liaison Committee for International Cooperation Year and first VOW National President (1960–62), front row, fifth from right. Library and Archives Canada, MG28, I218, Voice of Women fonds, vol. 7, file 19, VOW National Newsletter 29 & 30, November 1963, "International Cooperation Year ICY Travel Mission," p. 13.

10

Bridging and Breaching Cold War Divides

Transnational Peace Building, State Surveillance, and the Voice of Women

MARIE HAMMOND-CALLAGHAN

T HE FOUNDING OF THE VOICE OF WOMEN (VOW) Canada in Toronto on July 28, 1960 mobilized thousands of women against the threat of nuclear war in the cause of a universal motherhood. However, the group was soon treading a minefield of Cold War peace politics, crossing enemy lines and transgressing a rigid gender order.[1] Less than five years later in 1965, their third National President, Kay Macpherson, penned an open letter urging the VOW membership to resist the "communist smear." Her message defied the Cold War ideologies and institutions that would divide women:

> Our work for peace, human rights, whatever it is, will be attacked by smear tactics because there is no reasonable argument for war, for social injustice or against peace, human rights, international coopera-tion. . . . We must refuse to be drawn into this "guilt by association" process. . . . What if there are communists among us? It is for us to ask, "Is she working for peace and international cooperation, against war and the threat of war," not "Is she a communist, anarchist or anything else." . . . We have got to learn to work with everyone for our common goal, no matter how much we diverge on other matters, religious, social, philosophical.[2]

Like many other peace and disarmament groups at this time, VOW Canada was suffering the effects of the Cold War paradigm – a binary of Free West versus Soviet Iron Curtain with opposing versions of peace. The battle for peace was embedded in the ideological warfare of secu-rity regimes on both sides of the Cold War, rendering political dissent an enemy act. Cynical of Soviet policies of peaceful coexistence, peace became a dirty word for Cold Warriors who "relied on rearmament and alliance after the war." For the Royal Canadian Mounted Police (RCMP), peace activists fit the catch-all category of subversion devoid of social context, focusing "almost exclusively on the left" and on individuals deemed "to initiate discontent." Subsequently, VOW Canada's nonpartisan, nonaligned approach to global peace was in itself cause for Cold Warrior suspicions of communism and subversion.[3]

This chapter locates VOW Canada within a postwar transnational women's peace movement that created critical cultural and political spaces for female antinuclear campaigns across Cold War frontiers.[4] Linking international and domestic peace, VOW entered a long rhetorical tradition of employing "motherist arguments" against global militarism.[5] In keeping with other transnational Cold War activists, VOW's "mother-citizens" developed and utilized the discourse of motherhood and peace as a political tool to "secure a public hearing for their views."[6] VOW's early political engagements with Soviet, European, and American women, little examined to date, reflect a nexus of New Left and feminist origins within the postwar arena of international social movements. The New Left in Canada was strongly rooted in a national antinuclear movement – especially the Combined Universities Campaign for Nuclear Disarmament (CUCND) – with which VOW soon became engaged.[7] However, a transnational women's peace movement born of Cold War anxieties in the late 1940s was critical in shaping the New Left tendencies of VOW. As with other recent scholarship on Canada in the 1960s, this chapter challenges the stereotypical sixties narrative that the New Left was comprised largely of white male university students and professors.[8] Employing a global gender lens that decentres a Western paradigm in histories of the Cold War and the sixties, it shows how middle-class women, donning ladylike attire of hats and gloves, and calling for universal disarmament on behalf of the human family, played a significant role in the formation of the New Left.

By 1962, VOW Canada was forging global alliances with communist, progressive, and non-communist women in their work for nuclear disarmament. They participated in conferences organized by the Women's International Democratic Federation (WIDF), co-ordinated travel exchanges with the Soviet Women's Committee, and opposed nuclear proliferation under NATO (North Atlantic Treaty Organization) and NORAD (North American Aerospace Defence Command), alongside their American "sister organization," Women Strike for Peace (WSP).[9] The WIDF was established in 1945 by the Soviet Women's Anti-fascist Committee and the Union des femmes françaises (UFF) to promote "antifascism, lasting peace, the rights of women, and better conditions for children." Although communist-smeared by the early 1950s, the WIDF was arguably the most relevant transnational women's movement for women's peace activism in the postwar context – uniting progressive (left feminist, anti-fascist, pro-communist and autonomous) women's organizations globally, from Western countries to Africa and Asia. The WIDF so effectively wielded maternalist strategies against nuclear weapons, testing, and the arms race that its motherhood for peace campaigns garnered unprecedented support across racialized, ideological, class, and Cold War boundaries.[10] Perhaps the WIDF's successful appeal to such a broad array of Canadian women lay at the root of Canadian Cold Warrior security fears.

From VOW's founding, the RCMP were concerned that its peace work exposed them to communists – either through infiltration at home or at international conferences. Regardless of whether they saw VOW as communist-influenced, they certainly considered VOW a potential threat to the resolve of the Western alliance. Even in their earliest reports, when RCMP spies portrayed the VOW as a "legitimate pacifist organization," they also regarded them as stumbling toward communist dupe-dom.[11] Was the RCMP's fixation on communist subversion a consequence of their entrapment in an Old Left paradigm which did not allow them to understand the somewhat eclectic and progressive framework of the New Left,[12] a force to which the VOW was becoming increasingly attuned? As the sixties unfolded, VOW Canada matured politically under the progressive leadership of Thérèse Casgrain and Kay Macpherson and became increasingly well connected to transnational global disarmament and antiwar movements, women's organizations in China and Eastern Bloc nations, and nonaligned groups within the United Nations.[13]

The Voice of Women, Canada, the Cold War Panopticon, and Gender Deviance

The early leaders of the Voice of Women were well aware of the dangers awaiting their movement in a repressive Cold War climate. The massive influx of Canadian women into VOW comprised an eclectic mix of Old Left, social gospel, interwar peace activists, the politically inexperienced, and women engaged in professional, community, and church associations. From the outset, VOW carefully guarded an image of middle-class feminine respectability and political moderation so as not to draw allegations of communist influence and alienate potential members. To this end, the founding executive attempted to limit the involvement of members with any past or present communist affiliations, as well as those whose husbands had communist associations. From 1960 to 1962, VOW President Helen Tucker and Vice President Josephine Davis steered the organization toward nonpolitical approaches to disarmament and nuclear war.[14] Confronting the nuclear bomb shelter controversy and the question of nuclear weapons on Canadian soil, VOW's early leaders argued that such political decisions must be left to "the highest statesmanship." Hence, they emphasized VOW's feminine and maternal – rather than feminist – attributes in exerting influence on governments in order to foster a new global political climate.[15]

In a Cold War panopticon,[16] gender and peace politics were inextricably linked. For anti-communist forces, a conservative sexual order constituted the postwar lens of gender norms and gender deviance.[17] Because of their supposed emotionality and political instability, women were generally viewed as more susceptible to communist plots.[18] Cold Warrior masculinity was evident in one RCMP report that characterized a speech by VOW President Helen Tucker in 1961 as "an appeal to the emotions and compassion of women rather than to any intelligent thinking" which, in the author's view, caused VOW to "play right into Communist hands and expound their propaganda."[19] For Canada's Cold Warriors, VOW's susceptibility to communism also made them vulnerable to sexual deviance. Remarking on the attendance of VOW members – including Thérèse Casgrain – at the 1962 WIDF World Congress of Women in Vienna, former RCMP undercover agent Pat Walsh expressed concern that "our three Voice of Women delegates" would be among "the kind of women" who had a legacy of advocating free love.[20] Walsh's comment underscored Western perceptions of communist or leftist women with loose morals, deviant in terms of both their politics and their gender.

VOW's growing popularity, media savvy, and political influence, both nationally and internationally, convinced Canadian security officials to continue close surveillance throughout the early 1960s. With a membership of five thousand by the autumn of 1961, VOW branches were established in every Canadian province and constituencies launched internationally in the United States, Australia, New Zealand, Sri Lanka, India, Japan, Yugoslavia, and Austria.[21] In addition, VOW had enlisted the heavyweight support of six female senators and two wives of opposition leaders as honorary VOW sponsors – including Senator Muriel Fergusson, Senator Nancy Hodges, Senator Elsie Inman, Senator Olive Irvine, Senator Marianna Jodoin, Senator Jose Quart, Mrs. Hazen Argue and Mrs. Lester B. Pearson.[22] RCMP and Canadian military officials in 1962 assessed VOW Canada's successes in terms of "very effective publicity" and access to senior government officials such as Prime Minister Diefenbaker and External Affairs Minister Howard Green. "Although not too great in numbers, the VOW attempts wherever possible to exert considerable pressure on Government," one report noted. "It has not necessarily been responsible for any major policy changes, but very likely its influence is being felt."[23] Indeed, Howard Green later attributed the Progressive Conservative government's decision during the Cuban Missile Crisis to "delay putting the Royal Canadian Air Force (RCAF) on NORAD alert requested by the United States" to the "vigorous lobbying led by VOW."[24]

VOW's New "Militants": The Presidencies of Thérèse Casgrain (1962–63) and Kay Macpherson (1963–67)

In the aftermath of crises in Berlin (1961) and Cuba (1962), and perhaps also emboldened by the success of the Partial Test Ban Treaty (1963), VOW Canada contested government policy and masculine authority both at home and abroad.[25] New activist models furnished by Women Strike for Peace[26] and the elections of Thérèse Casgrain and Kay Macpherson as VOW's next national presidents signalled a shift toward progressive, feminist, and New Left politics within the organization.

Since the early twentieth century Thérèse Casgrain had been championing women's issues while also working to establish a Quebec constituency for the Co-operative Commonwealth Federation (CCF), later the New Democratic Party (NDP). As the first Quebec VOW President in 1961, Casgrain's class privilege and political networks offered VOW resources and respectability. However, her close ties to the NDP and her demands for the autonomy of the Quebec VOW branch founded in January 1961 were a cause for deep concern within National VOW.[27] Under Casgrain's provincial leadership, La Voix des femmes Quebec publicly opposed nuclear weapons for Canada and independently endorsed the peace petition of the Canadian Committee for the Control of Radiation Hazards (CCCRH), much to the consternation of the early National VOW executive who preferred a more "ladylike" approach to government and rejected protest politics at that time.[28] From 1960 to 1962, the early VOW executive, President Helen Tucker and Vice President Josephine Davis, tried to steer the organization away from taking political positions on disarmament. Two contentious national debates threatened to divide VOW at this time: the nuclear bomb shelter controversy and the question of Canada accepting nuclear weapons under NATO/NORAD obligations.[29] The VOW Organizing Committee declared it was not VOW's role to oppose the government on these issues because, in their view, disarmament could only be determined by "the highest statesmanship." Instead, they urged VOW to help foster a new global political climate through education and internationalism. Distinguishing VOW from contemporary "ban the bomb" groups, early VOW leaders wished to portray a conventional female image emphasizing VOW's "feminine," as opposed to "feminist," attributes of co-operation, preservation of life, and maternal instinct.[30] However, as VOW began to challenge government policy and develop protest tactics they subverted Cold War gender norms and faced growing public scrutiny.

As VOW's second National President, Thérèse Casgrain led a Peace Train protest in the aftermath of the Cuban Crisis to demand that the Diefenbaker government take a concrete stand on the nuclear question. With a dozen or so children in tow and a strongly worded brief in hand, approximately two hundred VOW members travelled by train from Montreal to Parliament Hill on November 1, 1962.[31] The *Globe and Mail* reported on VOW's "hardened stand" and noted that it signalled a new direction for VOW under Casgrain's leadership: "The VOW came to Parliament Hill ... with a couple of brass knuckles under its velvet glove, demanding no nuclear arms for Canada or Canadians at any time or any place."[32] Uncomfortable with this assertiveness, former VOW Vice-President Jo Davis fired an unorthodox missive at the entire membership urging them to "stay the middle course" somewhere between militant organizations and study groups: "Don't we, as women, know that gentle persuasion is more effective than nagging?" she queried.[33] However, the tide had already turned within the group. Continuing their campaign against nuclear arms with the Pearson administration, VOW lost some notable Liberal members, including Maryon Pearson,[34] and gained a reputation for militancy among both internal and external critics. To the RCMP, VOW's campaigns represented "a turn to the left in VOW policy" and a triumph for the "militant wing of VOW."[35]

When Kay Macpherson took the helm as National VOW President after Casgrain resigned to run for the NDP in 1963, she was well aware that she was "considered very radical."[36] Macpherson described herself as "left of the CCF" and was married to internationally renowned Marxist scholar C.B. Macpherson. They shared many friends, including communists, on the Canadian left.[37] Under Macpherson's presidency, VOW's transnational women's peace network was further strengthened through relationships with women in the WIDF and Soviet Women's Committee launched through a series of international conferences, specifically the World Congress of Women in Vienna (March 1962), the World Congress for Peace and Disarmament in Moscow (July 1962), and VOW's very own

Conference of Women for International Cooperation Year in Montreal (September 1962).

The Montreal conference boasted "up to 500 participants, including 61 women from 17 countries, east, west and non-aligned."[38] This event inspired the formation of the Women's International Liaison Committee (WILC) for International Cooperation Year (ICY) chaired by former VOW President Helen Tucker and comprised of VOW members and representatives from the USSR, Czechoslovakia, Poland, the U.S., Norway, England, Nigeria, and India. In the end, VOW was influential in getting a resolution put forward at the U.N. General Assembly on December 19, 1962, to establish International Cooperation Year in 1965.[39] Although VOW's founding executive initially campaigned for the United Nations to declare a "World Peace Year," they soon heeded the warning of the federal Minister of Citizenship and Immigration, Ellen L. Fairclough, about the dangers of using communist slogans such as the word "peace."[40]

Between 1963 and 1968, VOW/WILC launched a series of travel exchanges with the USSR, Eastern Europe, and China. On the first exchange, in June and July 1963, VOW/WILC sent twenty-nine delegates to the USSR who also visited a number of European countries including the Netherlands, Denmark, Norway, Sweden, Poland, East and West Germany, Czechoslovakia, Hungary, and France.[41] The VOW/WILC group were among an estimated 2,000 delegates from 110 countries at the WIDF organized World Congress of Women in Moscow.[42] A second, smaller VOW delegation of six members headed by Thérèse Casgrain visited the USSR for three weeks in October of the same year at the invitation of the Soviet Women's Committee, who wished to reciprocate the hospitality shown by their Canadian hosts during the Quebec conference in 1962. "Les Six" included VOW members from across the country: Beatrice Brigden, National Vice President of VOW, from Winnipeg, who had a strong background in the western labour and social reform movement as well as in the CCF and NDP; Marta Friesen, of Vancouver, who had been born in Czechoslovakia and spoke five languages; Nancy Pocock of Toronto; Helen Howse of Prince Albert; and Jeanne Duval of Montreal.[43] Upon their return, VOW delegates highlighted the common concerns they shared with Russian women, from "radiation hazards" and their children's health to education and housing. As one VOW member recalled humorously, for women "there was little difference between washing a communist diaper and a capitalist one."[44]

In the autumn of 1964, VOW arranged a cross-Canada tour for four female Soviet visitors, most of whom were communist party officials. Two years later, in 1966, the Soviet Women's Committee in Moscow hosted another six-member VOW delegation, this time led by Kay Macpherson.[45] The 1964 visit comprised a formidable group: Zoya V. Nironova (the head of the delegation and a member of the Soviet Women's Executive Committee); Ludmilla Doilnitsyn (a chemical engineer and former deputy USSR representative at the U.N. but now Deputy Chief of the Second European Department of the Ministry of Foreign Affairs); Marina M. Baneskina (a doctor working in neurological research); and Natalie Sladkevich (an engineer, economist, and teacher). Although VOW Canada had been sending representatives to WIDF conferences since 1962, Cold Warriors viewed VOW's growing association with Soviet women and the WIDF under Macpherson as solid evidence of communist infiltration:

> You are aware of the targeting of the VOW by the communists and as a "peace" group it was ready made for infiltration and for cooperation with communist infiltrated peace organizations. Our suspicions have been borne out and not only has there been evidence of these two factors but VOW appears to be one of the foremost "pressure" groups in Canada today.[46]

A shrill-sounding January 1965 RCMP report revealed the presence of an informer who relayed their impressions of the Ontario VOW Day of Study: "From meeting to meeting there is evidence that the extreme left is taking this organization over. The numbers of known communists are increasing – their conduct is becoming more overt and the discussions more along the communist line. Even those who are not known communists display a warm intimacy with the known communists that cannot be disregarded.... Maybe they are keeping well-known communists fairly well off the executive but every chance they get they give the floor to communists to explain a point."[47] Whether it was VOW's increasing engagement with Soviet or communist women internationally or their attempt to uphold a non-partisan position and reject the communist smear, security officials' suspicions that VOW was fast becoming a communist front were compounded by VOW's participation in a transnational women's campaign to oppose NATO.

VOW, Canada, and the NATO Women's Peace Force, 1964

In mid-May 1964, a series of RCMP communications disclosed that VOW Canada was protesting at The Hague where the NATO Ministerial Council was considering an American proposal to create a Multi-Lateral Nuclear Force (MLF) of twenty-five ships, each bearing eight Polaris ballistic nuclear missiles, manned by American and West German naval personnel.[48] Eleven VOW delegates were among fifteen hundred women from fourteen NATO nations that Women Strike for Peace (WSP) had gathered together at The Hague for a conference and protest to call for "a complete test ban treaty, military cutbacks, a nonaggression pact, and a nuclear free zone for central Europe." On the day before the conference, VOW President Kay Macpherson and several VOW members, along with hundreds of other delegates, had been temporarily banned from entering the Netherlands due to Dutch officials' anxieties that they would not be able to manage the women's protest. Consequently, WSP, VOW, and other foreign delegates of the "NATO Women's Peace Force" were forced to ask their embassies to intervene on their behalf.[49] Criticizing the police handling of eight hundred foreign "peace-loving women" at the Dutch border, one reporter remarked: "They want to discuss something as threatening as peace, while NATO has its ministerial meeting at the Hague ... maybe even sit down in front of the place of the meeting to demonstrate against a common nuclear force for NATO." As he noted wryly, "Such things make a bad impression – lower the nuclear weapon-morale, so to speak."[50] Dubbed the "NATO Women's Peace Force," hundreds of women walked "silently in a cold drizzle in single file" to the Juliana Barracks where the NATO meetings were being held on May 13. Led by Dagmar Wilson of WSP, each woman wore an armband designating her home country and carried "paper sunflowers bearing their children's pictures" and "a tulip to symbolize the fragility of life." British delegate Judith Cook relayed her impressions of this procession: "The sight of the serried ranks of soldiers, military police, civil police, mounted police, and police with dogs set against 14 women in summer dresses, their arms filled with tulips, was one I shall not forget."[51]

Following The Hague demonstration, VOW Canada met with Secretary of State for External Affairs Paul Martin Sr. and Ambassador George Ignatieff, Canada's Permanent Delegate to NATO, who were attending the NATO meetings along with Prime Minister Pearson. Macpherson proudly reported that the Canadian delegation met with much "higher ranked officials" than the U.S. and U.K. groups, "who were only successful in seeing minor officials." At their meeting with Ambassador Ignatieff VOW presented an anti-MLF petition bearing over 2,500 signatures, which he agreed to forward to the Canadian government. They also discussed VOW's broader strategy for universal disarmament, including nuclear-free zones, an end to Canadian participation in NATO, and an expanded Canadian role within the United Nations "for peace-keeping and international co-operation."[52] An RCMP report recorded that VOW's request was well received and "took place in a friendly and pleasant atmosphere." However, an anonymous handwritten note at the end of the account expressed frustration with VOW's foray into the arena of global security: "I don't know why these women don't stay home and tend their kitchen."[53]

In the months following the NATO Women's Peace Protest at The Hague, VOW's continued anti-MLF campaign incurred both setbacks and success.[54] In mid-November, a VOW delegation including Kay Macpherson, Ghislaine Laurendeau, and Ann Gertler secured a meeting with both Minister Martin and Prime Minister Pearson. However, on December 15, 1964, Kay Macpherson and Thérèse Casgrain were arrested at the NATO Headquarters in Paris along with at least thirteen other women for, as Macpherson put it, "daring to deliver a letter to the Secretary-General of NATO." All the "peace-loving offenders" were searched and jailed for about five hours with little but "a small flask of scotch" to warm them. Evidently their Paris arrest made headlines back in Canada. While Casgrain was "fêted" upon her return to Quebec, Macpherson recorded that she was interrogated by "a mini-inquisition of Voices" who deemed her behaviour unbecoming of a VOW President and expressed concerns that she was "consorting with communists."[55] Some resignations of Ontario VOW members followed.[56] Such a contrast between public receptions of Casgrain and Macpherson may be best understood in the context of significant cultural and political differences between English Canada and the Quebecois. The Quiet Revolution and the sixties in Quebec were characterized by radical, vigorous forms of dissent. In keeping with these tendencies, La Voix des femmes Quebec – uniquely comprised of French and English Canadians, including a sizeable contingent of Jewish women – reflected a progressive stance quite independent of the National VOW on the nuclear disarmament issue.[57]

In the end, the "NATO Women's Peace Force" emerged victorious as the U.S. Pentagon decided not to deploy the MLF. Macpherson noted in her memoir, "We will take credit for some of that decision, although it was probably due to all kinds of other reasons."[58] In a similar vein, WSP activist Amy Swerdlow recounted that while the "WSP chalked up the MLF campaign as another victory for the house-wife brigade," there were other political forces also at work stemming from deep concerns about the rearming of West Germany, a mere twenty years after the Second World War and the Nazi holocaust.[59] Like WSP, VOW may have ultimately "strengthened the hand" of those in government who favoured a reduction rather than expansion of nuclear weapons.[60]

○ ○ ○

Against the backdrop of Cold War peace politics, the VOW in Canada became part of a transnational women's peace movement campaigning for global nuclear disarmament. As VOW members worked with women across the Cold War divide, their political consciousness evolved toward a critique of global militarism and national security. Indeed, the postwar transnational women's peace movement may have been the cradle for VOW's New Left tendencies. Under the progressive national leadership of Thérèse Casgrain and Kay Macpherson, the organization embraced New Left political protest alongside the more traditional tactics of lobbying and education to bring about change. Although La Voix des femmes Quebec may have led the charge in radicalizing the group's strategies, transnational engagement with progressive, leftist, and non-aligned women's groups was critical in shaping VOW's formative identity in the 1960s.

However, VOW Canada's politicization had consequences both inside and out. Members who were opposed to challenging the government on security issues, or who feared being smeared as communists, left the group. For Canadian Cold Warriors, VOW not only threatened to undermine the resolve of the Western Alliance but also contested deeply embedded gendered political and social orders. RCMP surveillance showed that they were especially concerned that VOW might influence the Diefenbaker and Pearson administrations on disarmament and foreign policy. For VOW, the Cold War divide among women peace builders could only be bridged by the breaching of a Cold Warrior paradigm that posed a greater threat to global security.

"Anti-War Toy Campaign Poster," 1962. Library and Archives Canada, Voice of Women fonds, MG28 I218, vol. 7, file 2.

11

Fighting the War at Home

Voice of Women and War Toy Activism in Postwar Canada

BRADEN HUTCHINSON

O NE OF THE MOST MEMORABLE moments from Kay Macpherson's time as Executive Director of Voice of Women (VOW) occurred during a meeting of the organization's War Toy Committee.[1] A VOW member reportedly ran into the convenor's living room and announced: "One of our kids was playing with a war toy and he scratched his ear."[2] The host was quick to identify the opportunity inherent in this incident for VOW's new campaign: "Wounded by a war toy! What a headline! Quick, smear ketchup on his face and take a picture – we'll rush it to the press!"[3]

The joke, recounted by Macpherson, highlights the importance VOW and other peace organizations placed on their ability to mobilize popular support for their efforts. Realizing that many people might not be stirred by formal resolutions and high-level meetings with politicians, VOW embraced tangible concerns about childhood consumption and leisure to mobilize support for their initiatives. In a world where tensions between the Soviet Union and the United States were at an all-time high thanks to the 1960 U2 spy plane incident and the 1962 Cuban Missile Crisis, war toys offered VOW a promising way to bring home the dangers of the Cold War to everyday families in the hope of influencing the political beliefs of Canadians.[4]

The years between 1960 and 1979 witnessed a rising tide of activism across Canada. Anti-colonial liberation movements, feminism's so-called "second wave," Quebec nationalism, and gay liberation all fostered uncertainty and a radical counter-culture.[5] As part of this phenomenon, peace activism inserted itself into the social and cultural life of Canadians in new and diffuse ways. The growing emphasis on peace as a state of social and personal security, rather than merely the absence of war, meant that activists' efforts increasingly focused on producing the conditions for peace as much as preventing war. In this context, war toys became a focal point for a wide variety of activist groups, including the Voice of Women.

This chapter documents antiwar toy activism by VOW and others during the 1960s and 1970s. It demonstrates the extent to which war resistance campaigns waged by organizations such as VOW were shaped by, and helped shape, North America's burgeoning culture of consumption. Moreover, by focusing on the changing nature of antiwar toy activism after 1960, it highlights how ongoing debates about ideal masculinity and children's proper psychological development informed these campaigns. While the campaigns' impact on war toy sales is difficult to determine, they clearly underscore how VOW embraced the possibilities of popular culture and the mass media to keep their war resistance goals in front of a broad, mainstream audience.

Background

Anti-war toy activism was not new in 1960. Beginning in the nineteenth century several groups, including women's and pacifist organizations, became actively involved in opposing toy guns in Canada for their potential to cause bodily harm to their users and targets.[6] Their use was thought to promote warfare and juvenile delinquency among boys. During the opening decades of the twentieth century, peace groups actively discouraged Canadian parents from purchasing war toys.[7] Organizations like the Women's International League for Peace and Freedom (WILPF) were particularly active in efforts centred on educating parents and children on the dangers of violent playthings.[8] This campaign paralleled the growing concern about and subsequent regulation of firearms during the same period.[9] During the interwar years, these efforts enjoyed the support of a number of child experts across North America, who eagerly pointed out the negative developmental effects of war toys.[10] The connection between peace and child development was captured succinctly by one mother's letter to the *Globe* in 1936: "Every parent knows that a child's play is real life to him, and whether we are advocates of peace or believers in the inevitability of war, surely the child in our midst should be protected from ideas of death and destruction until his reason matures."[11]

Following the Second World War, WILPF and other peace and women's organizations continued to stress the danger posed by war toys to international co-operation and children's growth and development. In 1948, the Vancouver chapter of WILPF allied itself with the city police department to demand a ban on toy guns in response to their rising use in the commission of crimes.[12] Similarly, the National Council of Women forwarded a resolution to Prime Minister Louis St. Laurent in 1957 asking for a ban on war toys, describing them as "dangerous weapons ... which serve no useful purpose whatsoever."[13]

Despite such initiatives, antiwar toy activists suffered a setback in the immediate postwar period as their former allies in the burgeoning field of child psychology changed their tune. William Blatz, a prominent psychology professor at the University of Toronto, and others within the child study movement in Canada began to regard war toys as potentially beneficial for children, rather than a danger to their normal development.[14] These generally positive, or neutral, assessments of war toys were indicative of a wider rejection of mass produced and mass marketed toys. Blatz and others emphasized a traditionalist return to "play materials" like paste, paper and scissors in order to place psychological emphasis on what children did with the objects, not what the objects looked like. Under this rubric, the important thing was *that* the child was playing, not what the toy in question was.

A number of factors would combine to expand the scope of antiwar toy activism in the 1960s and 1970s. First, the period after 1960 was characterized by persistent and steady increases in toy consumption in Canada,[15] which is not surprising given that the end of the Second World War heralded an expansion of Canadian consumer society and a population explosion with over six million children born between 1945 and 1961. This expansion in itself partly accounts for the growing interest in, and public debate about, children's consumer culture, including war toys.

Second, as noted above, Cold War concerns and anxiety about nuclear warfare raised the stakes in this public debate for Canadian families. Family life and children in particular became potent symbols during this period for the threat posed by the Soviet Union and nuclear annihilation.[16] The United States, Canada, and other nations used children to promote fear of the Soviet Union and rally public support for Cold War armament. This fear was mirrored by growing anxieties about long guns and attempts by the federal government to regulate their use during the 1960s and 1970s.[17]

Third, antiwar toy activities would be influenced by, and gain credibility from, a new turn in child psychology. The idealization of a psychologically "normal" childhood in postwar Canada by experts like William Blatz and Samuel Laycock emphasized the importance of toy purchases for parents.[18] Toys were increasingly invested with the potential to support or undermine a child's normal development.[19] Under an earlier formulation toys did not make children normal or abnormal, they simply opened or closed different pathways of development. Beginning in the late 1950s, experiments underway at Stanford University's Psychology

Department under the purview of Canadian-born psychologist Albert Bandura helped to shift the meaning and importance of toys for child development. Bandurian social learning theory emphasized the importance of modelling and the observation of authority figures for childhood cognitive and social development.[20] Bandura provided a pivotal link between behaviourism and social psychology. He situated the roots of normal and abnormal development in the great expanse of "the social." By effectively moving the corrective efforts centred on the developing child out of the laboratory and the research preschool and into the lived social world, Bandurian social learning theory merged anxieties about the socialization of the conditioned child with the focus on normal development. This would ultimately prove particularly useful for critics of war toys after 1960. Now war toys' actual materiality mattered just as much as their eventual use. In fact, the materiality of the toy partially dictated how it would be used under this psychological paradigm because of its connection to wider social structures. Social learning theory offered war toy critics a new conceptual tool in their attempt to dissuade parents from purchasing the purportedly offensive toys.

The VOW Campaign

Women's peace organizations were particularly active in antiwar toy campaigns for two reasons. First, many of their members were mothers and the historic effectiveness of maternal feminist discourse in securing suffrage and other political gains allowed them to speak with greater authority on issues pertaining to children, including war toys, than on issues still largely considered to fall under male purview. Second, they were well situated to challenge the growing supervision and regulation of women's parenting efforts by male child experts, including psychologists, medical doctors, and educators.[21]

In order to fully appreciate the logic of the Voice of Women war toy campaign in the 1960s, however, it is essential to recognize how their organizational structure shaped their understanding of peace building and violence. Unlike established organizations such as WILPF, VOW was a new Canadian peace organization. Founded in 1960 in response to journalist Lotta Dempsey's call for women to work for international peace in the face of rising concerns about nuclear war, effective grassroots organizing and modest membership fees helped to swell the ranks of the group and it quickly became one of the largest peace organizations in Canada.[22] As a moderate left wing peace group, VOW attracted a heterogeneous membership of committed feminist and peace activists as well as less overtly political homemakers and professional women from across the country. Among its founding members were Opposition Leader Lester B. Pearson's wife, Maryon Pearson, and Thérèse Casgrain, a prominent feminist activist in Quebec and active politician for the Liberal Party and CCF. They were joined by individuals like Kay Macpherson, Peggy Hope-Simpson, and Muriel Duckworth, peace and women's rights activists whose professional activities centred on civil society organizing.

As Marie Hammond-Callaghan points out in this collection, VOW worked to build lasting peace through the mobilization of women across Canada and the world. In 1960 VOW chartered a peace train to Ottawa to protest the militarization of the Canadian north and to lobby the Canadian government to declare Canada a nuclear-free nation.[23] It also organized and hosted an international peace conference and sent delegates to Europe and Moscow to promote nuclear disarmament.[24] In many instances, VOW leveraged the status of women and children as the present and future victims of war and nuclear proliferation to press their cause with politicians in a similar fashion to other women's peace organizations across North America.[25] For instance, they used an analysis of strontium-90 levels in baby teeth to highlight the need for a ban on nuclear testing.[26] When the U.S. Congress passed the Gulf of Tonkin resolution, VOW began knitting baby clothes in dark colours to raise awareness about American bombings of civilians and to help Vietnamese children remain unseen.[27] These simple activities established VOW's maternal feminist credentials to act on behalf of children as surrogate, potential, or actual mothers and effectively drew media attention to their causes and solidified widespread public support for nuclear disarmament and world peace.[28]

However, VOW's early history was not without its challenges. Lester B. Pearson's acceptance of the Bomarc missiles on Canadian soil necessitated Maryon Pearson's resignation from VOW. According to Macpherson, Casgrain and the more moderate wing of the organization came into conflict with more "radical" elements led by Macpherson and Duckworth. In the end, the "radicals" took over the organization's executive in 1964. The reality of VOW's internal politics shaped their response to the Cold War peace movement. VOW opted for forms of activism that could effectively mobilize members and the wider public through everyday activities that required only limited ideological conformity among the membership. Similar to their efforts around the Vietnam War and baby teeth, politicizing the consumption of war toys was considered an effective way to raise awareness and engage Canadians in efforts to promote an end to conventional and nuclear war.

Hence the antiwar toy campaign. Initiated in 1964, it asked members to boycott war toys for children, especially boys. VOW claimed that war toys would lead to a future dominated by violence and destruction. The antiwar toy campaign was designed to parallel lobbying efforts for disarmament and provide the organization's grass roots with an opportunity to participate directly in efforts to promote world peace. In the press release announcing the launch of the campaign in time for Christmas 1964, VOW justified their actions on the grounds that war toys were more realistic than in the past and that the offending toys made "war seem inevitable and acceptable."[29] Along with boycotting the purchase of toys, VOW encouraged women to tear out the pages of catalogues featuring war toys and to mail them back to retailers.[30]

War Toy Committee Chair Marjorie Lawrence argued that the advertising scripts, images, and physical construction of G.I. Joe, in particular, expounded militaristic values. According to Lawrence, G.I. Joe was Barbie's counterpart, evoking the exciting fantasies of warfare in place of conspicuous consumption, domesticity, and marriage. She argued that toys like "exploding mine road" and guerrilla weapons and uniforms brought children too close to the adult realities of the Cold War:

> When the arms race and the toy race become synonymous, what does this mean for countries that protest to the world that they stand for peace? Are we paying lip service to one principle, while we carefully and psychologically prepare our children for the inevitability and acceptability of nuclear war?[31]

VOW's provocative stance garnered widespread media interest. In October 1964, the War Toy Committee reported that their publicity efforts had resulted in over seven hours of television and radio coverage.[32] Some stations even contacted the famed childrearing expert Dr. Benjamin Spock and Hasbro, makers of G.I. Joe, for commentary. Spock and Hasbro initially dismissed concerns about war toys, citing a lack of clinical evidence and the catharsis theory that war toys constituted a healthy outlet for violence.[33] However, VOW had their own expert, citing the claim of Judd Marmor, clinical psychologist and Professor of Psychiatry at the University of Southern California, that war toys "prepare the soil for the psychological acceptance of war and violence."[34] Marmor's arguments rested on many of the same assumptions that underpinned Bandurian social learning theory: exposure to the "value system" inherent in the war toy would generate abnormal psychosocial development in children.[35] Eventually, Spock's position on war toys became more critical as part of his personal opposition to the war in Vietnam.[36]

The committee also distributed free of charge a list of addresses for companies known to produce war toys, encouraging mothers to express their concerns directly to toymakers. In British Columbia, the Society of Friends (Quakers), the Pre-School Association, and the Unitarian Church all permitted the VOW to deliver their antiwar toy message at local meetings.[37] In 1966, VOW protested the Canadian Toy Manufacturers Association Annual Toy Fair in Montreal to highlight their antiwar toy message.[38]

In writing up their campaign material, VOW drew directly upon the new language, and authority, of psychological studies. According to one leaflet, "toys are the tools with which children learn to behave as adults." The form letter distributed by VOW for mailings to toy companies argued that "these 'playthings' can make war seem acceptable to children ... these toys can also harden children to the idea of violence." In a mailing to 172 schools in 1965, VOW asked principals to promote their message by distributing a short article titled "A Psychiatrist on War Toys," which highlighted Judd Marmor's ideas. Only one principal reportedly refused.[39] Posters distributed in schools, charitable organizations, and city libraries highlighted the simple but effective messaging of the campaign.

Boys' Play and Consumption

Masculinity and boyhood formed the main points of discursive tension during the campaign. The emphasis on being constructive highlighted psychological concepts of the developing child and the need for positive environments. However, the binaries of construction and destruction also implied a tension within traditional definitions of masculinity and boyhood. VOW celebrated the physical and productive labour associated with a modern definition of masculinity that idealized the male adult as a breadwinner and caretaker of the family, while simultaneously deploring traditional martial virtues indicative of earlier forms of boyhood and manhood.[40]

The concern about war toys dovetailed with shifting ideas about the relationship between doll play and masculinity. By the 1960s, advice about the use of dolls by boys was increasingly moving in a more accepting direction. Manufacturer and self-proclaimed toy expert Arnold Arnold claimed in 1968 that the prohibition against the use of dolls by boys was "an absurd prejudice." He invoked recent psychological writing to support his case. Yet Arnold tied this positive endorsement of boys' doll play to a condemnation of the present selection of dolls for boys as "almost exclusively military [or] 'character dolls' that represent the folk heroes of comic book, movie and TV land, accessorized with all the hostile hardware of destruction."[41]

In a 1975 column in the *Toronto Star*, antiwar toy activist Lotta Dempsey neatly tied together concerns about girls' dolls and war toys. According to Dempsey, Barbie was problematic because of her devotion to accessories and the rampant commercialism associated with the doll. However, Dempsey applauded Mattel for its "Big Jim" doll targeted at boys, including its interchangeability with Barbie accessories. Dempsey noted that Barbie and Big Jim could use each other's accessories, opening up play possibilities for boys and girls beyond traditional gender dichotomies.[42] Dempsey implied that playing house with Big Jim or sending Barbie on a secret mission could form the basis for women's liberation and a reconfiguration of gender relations.

Concerns about boys playing with dolls, like concerns about war toys, were indicative of a conflict over the meaning of masculinity. As Chris Dummitt has argued, the "manly modern" emerged in postwar Canada as a way to reinforce patriarchal authority while celebrating the achievements of a technocratic industrialized society.[43] Under this formulation men were celebrated as the sacrificial victims of modernity who had given up their primal power and authority in order to improve the lot of their dependants. It supported the continuation of patriarchal dominance while authorizing male resistance to modernity in numerous forms including alienation and irresponsibility.

The "updated patriarchy" that thrived in Canada during this period also touched on boys as well, licensing them to explore their martial urges for violence and domination and bestowing upon them a privileged position within the family, all while simultaneously suggesting that their masculinity must eventually be tamed for the good of others. The ascendant manly modern described by Dummitt brought breadwinner definitions of masculinity into tension with those that relied on an idealization of separate spheres and martial virtues. Boys constituted a visible and important battleground in this conflict.

When it came to toys, boys' relationship to dolls and war toys was constructed as either evidence of a rising modern masculinity or as the degeneration of traditional masculine virtues, with clear homophobic overtones. In this context, boy consumers were frequently understood by organizations like VOW and their opponents to possess an inborn tendency toward violence that contributed to patriarchal domination and global conflict. VOW sought to celebrate the breadwinner definition of the manly modern and deplore the use of war toys in order to guard against stimulating the violent tendencies of men by socializing them into a culture of militarism. Consequently, war toys acted as an important symbolic battleground for peace activists, as well as in the growing debate over masculine culture in Canada.

Assessing the VOW Campaign

In launching the antiwar toy campaign, VOW was adding its voice to an ongoing public debate. By 1961, for instance, military toys were prevalent but facing increased consumer criticism. Though they remained top sellers in some quarters, the U2 Spy Plane incident and the Cuban Missile Crisis meant that a growing number of Canadians did not "want toy A-bombs, soldiers and guided missiles under the Christmas Tree."[44] A letter in the *Ottawa Citizen* from resident Muriel Nickel highlighted the need to steer boys away from war toys.[45] In 1965, the *Vancouver Sun* declared that war toys had "been put out to pasture" and replaced by "farm animals and other toys."[46]

However, from the VOW's perspective, the war toy campaign wasn't just about banning toys. It was designed to mobilize their large and diverse membership base and draw public and political attention to Cold War peace initiatives. This is not to question the sincerity of their concerns, but rather to point out that an attachment to broader political issues sustained the antiwar toy campaign regardless of changes in toy consumption patterns. The fight against war toys was about publicity and policy. Armed with evidence from psychologists and other authorities that toys could improve or damage children's development, the war toy campaign was something of an insurance policy for future peace. It kept alive the possibility that women from across the country would continue to push for peace and disarmament through their consumption, and perhaps their votes, even as politicians disregarded their demands to exclude Bomarc and Cruise missiles from Canadian soil. Even if the struggle in the present seemed daunting, by targeting future citizens, especially boys, they hoped to ensure that women's rights and world peace would be respected. Thus, the futurism of the campaign sustained the overall peace efforts by creating the sense that eliminating war toys was achievable even in the face of present setbacks.

VOW continued to press their case with the media over the course of the decade and into the early 1970s. They prepared speaking points on war toys, circulated copies of newspaper articles by psychologists condemning war toys, and distributed other material to support their stance.[47] VOW's efforts also inspired other groups to enter the debate.

Rev. A. Gordon Baker's November 1964 article in the Anglican Church of Canada's magazine, *Canadian Churchman*, declared war toys "symbols of hell" because of their capacity for "ingraining in children the fantasy-glory of war."[48] In 1966, Grant Munro directed *Toys*, a film for the National Film Board focused on the perils of war toys. The film begins with children enthusiastically examining a display of toys. However, they soon become silent and mesmerized by a selection of war toys that begin violently to slaughter one another and the other toys in the display.[49] The implication was clear: war toys should be understood as a threat to children's proper growth and development. In 1971, the National Organization for Women met with toy manufacturers to extend the fight for women's liberation to the toy box by discouraging war toys for boys.[50] San Francisco Women for Peace took inspiration from VOW, launching their own antiwar toy campaign in 1965.[51] Indeed, the intersection of concerns about war toys with those about America's role in the Vietnam War meant that antiwar toy efforts took on an even greater urgency in the United States.[52]

Negative assessments of war toys led manufacturers and marketers to respond in a myriad of ways. American toy firm Lionel began an antiwar toy advertising campaign across North America in the hope of capitalizing on a growing market. The most famous of these, a microscope advertisement, reminded the reader, "No one ever held up a store with one of these. Or learned to make war with a Lionel train. Or played like a dagger-bearing monster with a Lionel-Porter science set. Lionel makes nice toys only. They are good for thrills and fantasies, but the healthy kind."[53]

Other companies pursued a more defensive and antagonistic response toward VOW's position. *Toronto Star* journalist Sidney Katz reported that one toy company executive in Toronto claimed that war toy critics wanted "a race of namby-pambys" and concluded that war toys were essential for boys: "[If you] give your boy a machine gun for Christmas ... he won't turn into a homosexual."[54] "Guns," according to the toy company executive, helped to "promote leadership and strength."[55] The politics of heterosexual masculinity were not lost on toy manufacturers. Rather than seeking to change the frame of the debate, they accepted the basic premise of critics like VOW that this was a conflict about boyhood. Clearly some manufacturers were disdainful of the liberal masculinity promoted by VOW and other groups, preferring a more martial definition of boyhood.

It is hard to determine the extent to which VOW's efforts affected the sale of war toys. There are no tracking numbers on war toy sales, in part because definitions of what constituted a war toy varied widely. Some activists and campaign supporters included only those toys with explicit military themes, whereas others thought all violent themed toys should be considered war toys. Furthermore, the qualitative evidence highlights the rather mixed outcomes of the campaign. In 1966, for instance, despite VOW store pickets, retailers reported robust sales of war toys.[56] Newspapers remained positively hostile toward both VOW and their war toy campaign, declaring that it "fell flat" and that the organization had "produced little tangible result."[57] Yet by the end of the decade it was clear that public opinion was shifting against the now infamous playthings. In 1967, the *Montreal Gazette* reported that the Hula-Hoop was replacing many male children's interest in war toys.[58] Simpsons-Sears ceased carrying war toys in 1968, purportedly in response to the Robert Kennedy assassination.[59] In 1970, the Canadian Toy Testing Council (CTTC) ceased testing and reporting on war toys altogether and suggested that parents "buy more constructive toys than destructive."[60] CTTC member Dorothy Morrison publicly expressed her disgust at the continued availability of war toys, which were "conducive to unwholesome fantasies."[61] In Scarborough, Ontario, two towers with replica machine guns were declared a health hazard in 1977 and removed, partially out of racially charged psychological worries that the guns would "turn children into hijackers."[62] The efforts of VOW and other groups across the globe appeared to have an effect in other countries as well. In 1972, the California Legislature banned the sale of realistic war toys and torture toys in response to concerns about crime and warfare.[63] In 1977, G.I. Joe, now going by the less militaristic moniker Super Joe, was temporarily retired by Hasbro after exchanging military fatigues for scuba suits for most of the 1970s.[64]

Though the war toy debate would reach a fevered pitch again in the 1980s in response to the re-launch of G.I. Joe, a growing antifeminist backlash, and Cold War rearmament under the Reagan administration, by the end of the 1970s it was clear that war toys were no longer an unquestioned part of Canadian boys' toy boxes.[65] The antiwar toy campaign undertaken by VOW and others mobilized anxieties about masculinity, violence, and child development to attract attention to their efforts to build a peaceful future for Canadian families.

o o o

Historically, toys have been used as a "way in" to mobilize Canadians' support for conflicting sides of numerous political issues, including warfare and world peace.[66] Toys and other children's commodities helped to forge a link between children's wellbeing and everyday acts of consumption. By emphasizing the dire developmental consequences of war toys for boys, VOW hoped to attract widespread public support to their lobbying efforts for disarmament. While perhaps a contributing factor to the initial decline of war toys in the mid-1960s, in the end VOW's efforts were more broadly focused on raising serious questions about the symbolic violence these consumer goods encouraged. The subsequent debate over the relationship of gender, child development, and consumer culture to war and peace collapsed the boundaries between the economic, political, and intimate spheres of postwar Canadian life. The antiwar toy campaign demonstrates that peace and consumer activism share a common focus on security. The rising importance of consumer and popular culture as points of conflict in debates over war and peace was indicative of a broader shift among doves and hawks to frame their contrasting visions of international relations in terms of producing security, rather than the prevention of war or protection through war.

The cost of VOW's antiwar toy campaign was the stigmatization of certain play behaviours undertaken by male children and the consumer choices of their parents. It placed play under political and public scrutiny and formed yet one more axis along which the parenting efforts of women might be stigmatized and regulated, in this instance by other women. Yet it also highlighted the role of consumer industries like toy companies in promoting the values of militarism and violence among children and others, expanding the definition and field of action for peace activists. Thus, VOW worked to shape Canadian political culture by mobilizing consumption practices. Consequently, the consumption of war toys was influenced by persistent global political issues and in turn helped to shape the outcome of those political struggles. In order to accomplish their objectives, activists drew on emerging psychological models, particularly that of Bandurian social learning theory. From the standpoint of groups like VOW, resisting war through the politics of consumption was inescapable in a postwar popular culture dominated by a masculine culture of violence. In a contemporary world increasingly dominated by consumer-focused activism, the VOW war toy campaign of the 1960s raises important questions about the possibilities, limits, and broader implications of awareness campaigns for contributing to lasting social change and building more secure communities.

"Sitting down in front of the barrier and waiting." (La Macaza). *Sanity* (July 1964, p. 8). Permission courtesy of Dimitrios Roussopoulos. William Ready Division of Archives and Research, McMaster University Library.

12

Project La Macaza

A Study of Two Canadian Peace Protests in the 1960s

BRUCE DOUVILLE

I N JUNE 1964, OVER ONE HUNDRED peace activists made their way to La Macaza, Quebec, a rural community situated in the Laurentians, 175 kilometres north of Montreal, and the site of a Canadian military base. The activists were there to protest Canada's decision to allow American nuclear weapons on Canadian soil. Their week-long vigil culminated in an act of civil disobedience, in which seventeen demonstrators sat down and blocked the road to the base and were repeatedly dragged to the ditch by military police. A similar follow-up protest took place at La Macaza three months later over Labour Day weekend. During this second protest, nearly sixty participants sat down to block the road.[1]

These two events were significant for several reasons. Never before had a substantial number of Canadian peace activists employed civil disobedience in a collective protest. In addition, Project La Macaza, as it became known, brought together a broad cross-section of activists: French-Canadian separatists, English-Canadian peace activists, and members of the Student Christian Movement. Furthermore, these demonstrations marked a shift in activist strategy to a new kind of confrontational protest that would characterize the activities of the New Left during the sixties, and an analytical shift from a single focus (such as nuclear disarmament) to an understanding of the interconnectedness of social concerns.

While historians have written about Project La Macaza in the broader contexts of Canadian peace activism and the Canadian New Left in the 1960s, no in-depth examination of these two protests exists.[2] This chapter explores the rationale, organization, execution, and historical importance of these protests – including the role of religion in these demonstrations. As the first large-scale exercises in civil disobedience at a Canadian military base, they were bridging events between older forms

161

of peace activism and a newer, more radical youth activism; consequently, these protests deserve a more prominent place in the historical narratives of the Canadian peace movement, and of Canada's New Left.

Setting the Stage: Missiles and Movements

While Project La Macaza was not officially connected with any single peace organization, much of the leadership for the protests came from members of the Canadian Combined Universities Campaign for Nuclear Disarmament (CUCND).[3] Though it would radicalize by the mid-sixties and address a broader range of social issues, CUCND began as a single-issue peace group in October 1959. The immediate impetus for its formation was Prime Minister Diefenbaker's decision to acquire Bomarc missiles from the United States. That was the spark for the creation of a Canadian student peace organization, and within several months chapters of CUCND could be found at campuses across Canada.[4]

In the fall of 1961, faced with a concerted campaign by peace activists from CUCND, the Canadian Campaign for Nuclear Disarmament (CCND), and the Voice of Women, Diefenbaker backtracked on his decision, and although Canada acquired the missile delivery system and bases were established for the missiles, his government decided that it would not accept American nuclear warheads.[5] But antinuclear activists in CUCND were frustrated in January 1963 when Liberal opposition leader Lester Pearson publicly stated that Canada should fulfil its international obligations and accept nuclear weapons – a reversal of his earlier position.[6] In the election that followed in April 1963, Canadians elected a minority Liberal government and Prime Minister Pearson lived up to his election promise; by January 1964 the government had installed American nuclear missiles at Canadian military bases in North Bay, Ontario, and at La Macaza, Quebec.[7]

These developments radicalized the Canadian student peace movement. Like their American counterparts in Students for a Democratic Society, young Canadian activists became disillusioned with conventional parliamentary politics and began to look at the wider social and economic structural issues that led to nuclear bases being established in Canadian communities. What was required, they now believed, was for oppressed peoples to insert themselves into the democratic process and take decision-making power from the social, political, and economic elites. For that to happen, activists would have to engage in acts of consciousness-raising and community organizing, to foster what students in the American New Left called "participatory democracy."[8] One way to raise consciousness, and hopefully spark a groundswell of active involvement, was through collective acts of civil disobedience.

The Rationale for Civil Disobedience at La Macaza

Civil disobedience occurs when people directly challenge a law, or a power structure supported by law, because they believe it to be unjust and seek to bring about positive social change.[9] It is inherently radical, because it relies on "people power" rather than the mechanisms of the state, and it places conscience above law. Social justice activists in the sixties drew their inspiration regarding the philosophy and practice of civil disobedience from Henry David Thoreau, Mahatma Gandhi and the movement for Indian independence, and Martin Luther King, Jr. and the American civil rights movement.[10] In particular, participants in the peace and civil rights movements regarded nonviolence as an essential component of civil disobedience. They reflected the influence of Gandhian philosophy and practice, channelled through American radical pacifists such as Bayard Rustin of the War Resisters' League and A.J. Muste of the Fellowship of Reconciliation.[11] Proponents of nonviolent direct action emphasized an organic relationship between means and ends: if one's goal concerns peace, then one should achieve that goal through peaceful means. It was a rationale that reflected the influence of the Society of Friends (Quakers) on the peace movement.[12] As we shall see, this rationale was central to the purpose of the protests at La Macaza, which had their genesis at the Montreal Peace Centre.

The Montreal Peace Centre was a focal point for activists from several peace groups, and it was also home to two leading publications of the Canadian peace movement: *Sanity*, and *Our Generation Against Nuclear War*, a quarterly journal associated with CUCND.[13] Dimitri Roussopoulos not only edited both of these publications but was also a principal organizer of Project La Macaza. Along with Roussopoulos, two other figures played key roles in the original planning of the first protest: Dan Daniels, a forty-two-year-old playwright and former Communist Party member who had been an organizer with the Seafarers' Union before becoming active in the peace movement, and twenty-four-year-old André Cardinal, a French-Canadian separatist and secretary of Quebec Socialist Youth.[14]

The protest, as originally conceived by Roussopoulos, Daniels, and Cardinal, had a dual rationale. First, the organizers opposed nuclear arms in Canada and demanded that the government close the base.[15] But the second purpose was equally important to the organizers. As the three explained in an initial letter sent out to other peace activists, "it will be

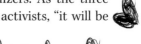

an attempt to influence the sense of social, economic and political injustice that separatists and other Quebecers feel and to show them that violence is not the way." It would thus demonstrate that nonviolent direct action "is a concrete expression of the principle of moral approximation of the ends and means relationship, and that it can be regarded as the most unique contribution to the philosophy and technique of revolution in our time."[16] The political context for this is important: in the early 1960s Quebec separatist sentiment was on the rise, and many young separatists in the radical left sympathized with the actions of groups such as the Front de libération du Québec (FLQ), which championed the violent overthrow of English Canadian colonial rule.[17] Both separatists and more moderate Quebec nationalists had expressed their opposition to the presence of missiles at the La Macaza base (and, indeed, their opposition to the presence of the base itself).[18] As Dimitri Roussopoulos explained in an interview,

> The way La Macaza was presented in our literature and argumentation was that it was yet another imposition on Quebec from the outside. It was the federal government, building this military base, which was bad enough. And not only building this military base, but bringing in these American missiles. And not only bringing in the Bomarc-B missiles, but on top of that, putting nuclear warheads on these missiles. So it was an affront on an affront on an affront. Therefore, we said, this is such a serious affront that we should use the best strategies of the radical pacifist tradition, of the civil rights tradition, and block La Macaza with our bodies as a form of protest.[19]

It is no accident that Project La Macaza was known initially as "Operation St. Jean Baptiste," and that the protesters commenced their act of civil disobedience on June 21, one day before the three-day festival that culminated in St. Jean Baptiste Day, a celebration infused with Quebec nationalism.[20] In their manifesto, published in the June 1964 issue of *Sanity*, the organizers drew a clear connection between the upcoming protest and Quebec nationalism. "We believe," read the manifesto, "that the people of Quebec as a nation ... have the right to determine for themselves their own affairs and destiny." It called for "the renunciation of the satellite status of every nation" and "the overthrow of forces within every country which live on an armament economy and fear." More importantly, it argued that nonviolent resistance was rooted in the history of French Canadian protest against militarism.[21] There was a concerted effort made to encourage French-Canadian participation in the protest, with invitations sent out to prominent radicals such as labour leader Michel Chartrand and journalist Jacques Larue-Langlois.[22]

At the same time, the organizers worked hard to secure the participation of anglophone peace activists from inside and outside Quebec.[23] However, several peace activists in Ontario were less than enthusiastic about the proposed June demonstration. Indeed, there appears to have been significant tension between organizers in Montreal and some CUCND members outside Quebec.[24] Some activists from outside Quebec questioned the wisdom of civil disobedience and were not convinced that the protests would remain nonviolent.[25] They expressed concerns over the philosophical basis of the protest, the content of the manifesto, and the planning of the event itself ("with the unilateral initiative coming from Montreal").[26] Nevertheless, many activists from outside Quebec ended up participating in the June protest, including CUCND federal chairman Art Pape. Roussopoulos recalls:

> Art was instrumental in convincing the Ontario people ... that this attempt to create a new way of organizing a movement, a movement of ideas and of people in Quebec ... which blended with a nuclear disarmament and anti-militarist approach, was legitimate. And if people from Ontario went to La Macaza to work with the Montreal group to say no to a nuclear missile base in Quebec, no to an imperial or colonial imposition in Quebec, then there would be much more of a bridge, of a relationship, with sympathetic and understanding people outside of Quebec in Canada with which to work. So all of that was worked into the way he looked at it [and] the way we looked at it.[27]

Some of the activists from outside Quebec may well have come to share Roussopoulos' perspective on the June demonstration. However, for many other anglophone participants in the June or September protests, the most important goal was not to teach French-Canadian nationalists the value of nonviolent resistance, but more broadly to confront militarism, raise consciousness, and demonstrate for *all* Canadians the value of nonviolent resistance. In the bulletins of Project La Macaza, protesters explained their rationale for committing civil disobedience in terms of moral or religious duty to challenge unjust laws and the desire to bring about a nonviolent society.[28] What they shared in common was their opposition to nuclear arms on Canadian soil and a commitment to nonviolent civil disobedience.

The Two Protests: Organization and Execution

The first demonstration began on June 13, 1964, when participants arrived at La Macaza from the Montreal Peace Centre. Organizers had secured a cottage about eight miles from the base, and this primitive dwelling ("which looks and feels as if it will collapse any minute," one participant wrote at the time) served as base camp for the activists.[29] At 3:15 p.m., six protesters stationed themselves along the road into the military base and commenced a week-long vigil.[30] Their numbers grew throughout the week, and by June 21, at least one hundred protesters lined the road.[31] During this time, the three leading French-Canadian participants in the protest (André Cardinal, Michel Boyer, and Christian Sivrel) attempted to reach out to the surrounding communities and explain the reason for the protests.[32] While *Sanity* and the *Project La Macaza Bulletin* reported that there was ample community support for the protesters,[33] two participants distinctly recalled a hostile encounter with local residents.[34] Despite the apparent contradiction, it is likely that both accounts are correct. The military base was a source of resentment for the locals, since few of them actually worked on it, but the sudden presence of a hundred protesters in the community might well have provoked an equally strong sense of resentment.

Of the one hundred present for the vigil by June 21, seventeen had chosen to take part in civil disobedience by blocking the gate. While the bulletins do not provide much information on the crowd of vigil participants, they are very informative on the smaller group. Of these seventeen, only two were women, and only three were French-Canadian. Eight were from Montreal and the remainder from Toronto, Vancouver, or Kingston. Most were in their early twenties; Dan Daniels was significantly older than the others.[35] For many of these "CD'ers," (as practitioners of civil disobedience called themselves) this was their first time engaging in nonviolent direct action, and they prepared for it with the assistance of Robert Gore, an American civil rights activist from the Congress of Racial Equality (CORE).[36] On the morning of June 21, they rehearsed their approach to the base and engaged in role-playing of civil disobedience strategies.[37] Then at 2:30 p.m., the seventeen "CD'ers" approached the gate to the base, singing "We Shall Overcome," a key anthem of the civil rights movement south of the border. Their plan was to seek entry to the base and if denied, sit down on the road and block the entrance. Not surprisingly, they were denied entry; they sat down in front of the gate, where they remained for the next seventeen hours.[38] They spent the night singing peace songs, talking with each other and with the soldiers on the other side of the fence, and reading aloud from the Bible and books by Bertrand Russell.[39] With the arrival of the first military vehicle the following morning, the officer in charge ordered that normal traffic into the base be resumed. Guards began dragging the protesters into the ditch, and the protesters responded by promptly returning to block the road – sometimes at great personal risk.[40] One participant recalled that Peter Light – a peace activist from British Columbia – scrambled up from the ditch and threw himself in front of a moving truck to prevent it from entering the base.[41] This process was repeated approximately thirty times, for upwards of two hours, until "the guards lined up along the side of the road outside the barrier, and confined the demonstrators to the ditch area."[42] The blockade of the road had ended.

This final stage of the protest – when the guards dragged demonstrators to the ditch – was the most confrontational and stressful part of the ten-day event, not only for the seventeen protesters but also for the vigil participants who witnessed the conflict and for base personnel. Lucia Kowaluk, a social worker active in the Montreal Peace Centre, recalls seeing vigil participants cry as they watched the airmen dragging the protesters.[43] Eilert Frerichs, a twenty-four-year-old United Church minister and one of the seventeen directly involved in the blockade, recalls that the guards "hated dragging us around":

> At one point, we had reached an agreement with [the guards] that all they had to do was to reach and touch us and we would go into the ditch . . . everybody had to be non-violent, including them. And I think, in that process, they became really human. They were no longer air force police, but they were normal men, forced to do something that they didn't want to do. And the whole mood of that event changed. It made it possible for me to reach out to the guy on the other side of the fence. . . . We were no longer enemies.[44]

Early in the afternoon of June 22, the protest concluded with what *Maclean's* correspondent David Lewis Stein called "probably the strangest devotional meeting ever held at a Canadian military installation":

> The peaceniks formed a semi-circle on one side of a barbed-wire fence; the airforce police lined the other side . . . Frerichs, still wearing his torn clerical collar, read the Sermon on the Mount and led the peaceniks in the Lord's Prayer. Only one airman seemed to be praying along with the peaceniks. But when the group joined hands to sing, for the last time, *We Shall Overcome*, and Frerichs thrust his hand over the barbed wire, one of the airmen took it.[45]

The presence of these overtly Christian elements reflected the fact that a substantial number of participants in both protests were members of the Student Christian Movement, which emphasized the connection between faith and social justice. Members of Canada's Student Christian Movement had engaged in peace activism since the 1920s, and in the early 1960s they were instrumental in forming chapters of CUCND across Canada.[46] It also shows the willingness of the "peaceniks" to make space for public expressions of faith, even though many of those present were not Christian.[47] The demonstration was a performance for the Canadian public (thanks to ample media coverage), and non-Christian peace activists likely recognized that religious symbols lent their protest an aura of righteousness and respectability. Furthermore, these Christian elements (e.g., prayers, singing, and the presence of clergy) reinforced the protesters' sense of identification with the civil rights struggle in the American South, which was permeated with the spirituality of the black churches.[48]

Project La Macaza organizers had hoped that the June protest would spark a mass movement of nonviolent resistance at Canadian military bases.[49] Consequently, in consultation with Toronto CUCND members, it was decided to hold a larger protest at La Macaza at the beginning of September.[50] In many ways, the second protest mirrored the first: it began with a vigil on August 31 and ended with a prolonged sit-in on the road in front of the base entrance.[51] This time, however, the number of participants was larger: about one hundred fifty took part in the vigil, and over fifty demonstrators engaged in civil disobedience.[52] Furthermore, the "CD'ers" had more training, and the civil disobedience lasted longer – forty-eight hours, from the morning of September 7 to the morning of September 9.[53] Moreover, the demonstrators who blocked the road in September were more diverse than their June counterparts. Of the fifty-nine participants listed in the *Project La Macaza Bulletin*, thirteen were from Montreal, seventeen from Toronto, and the remainder from across Canada and, to a lesser extent, the United States. At least fifteen were female. Most participants were in their twenties, but at least seven were thirty or over, and more than a third of the protesters were teenagers, the youngest being thirteen. The group included students, teachers, clergy, housewives, artists, and blue-collar workers.[54]

The September demonstration differed from the first protest in another important way – the attitude and behaviour of the military servicemen. The participants went out of their way at both the June and September demonstrations to relate to the military police as human beings and, when possible, to engage in friendly debate with them. In

June, even in spite of the two hours of "ditch-dragging" on Monday morning, there was a curiously friendly rapport between the protesters and the base personnel. In an article for *Maclean's*, David Lewis Stein noted that the protesters shared cigarettes with the guards, talked with them, and shook hands with them, and that base personnel took part in the devotional service that followed the protest.[55] In essence, the protesters invited the military personnel to behave as human beings, and not simply as cogs in the machinery of power. By September, however, the military personnel on the front lines of the protest had been fortified against this kind of humanizing experience. According to the account of the September protest in *Sanity*, the Commanding Officer of the base "shouted orders to his men not to listen and forbid them to speak to the demonstrators." The same article reported that on "the previous occasion the men were not conditioned in any way against the pacifists. This time they were told that the CDers were communists or were led by communists, and a general attempt was made to place the peacemakers outside the pale and make 'its' of them instead of human beings."[56] And this time, the military police tried different tactics, including playing Beatles music at ear-splitting levels.[57] According to *Sanity*, the military police were considerably rougher in how they handled protesters in September – so much so that NDP members of parliament raised the matter in Question Period.[58]

Assessing the Success and Significance of Project La Macaza

It would be easy to dismiss the demonstrations at La Macaza as neither successful nor historically significant. They were not unexpected; one year previous, large numbers of protesters had descended on La Macaza, and while they didn't employ civil disobedience strategies that year, they informed the police that they might do so in the future.[59] Nor were they unprecedented; for several years, British and American peace protesters had engaged in civil disobedience at military sites housing nuclear weapons.[60] For example, a demonstration at a missile site in Rome, New York, in the summer of 1963 was almost identical to the protests at La Macaza one year later.[61] Furthermore, judging by the subsequent actions of the FLQ, many radical separatists in Quebec remained unconvinced of the efficacy of nonviolent direct action. While Project La Macaza secured the support and participation of some Quebecois radicals, it was predominantly an anglophone endeavour. Original planning meetings took place in English, and only a minority of participants in either protest were French-Canadian.[62] Finally, if the peace activists' primary goal was the removal of nuclear weapons from Canada, they were not successful, at least not in the short term. It was not until 1971 that the Trudeau government announced its intention to return the Bomarc missiles and nuclear warheads to the United States. And it was not until 1972 that the missiles and warheads were removed, and CFB La Macaza was closed.[63] What, then, makes these protests so significant? And what did they accomplish?

First, they were significant because they were the first large-scale exercises in civil disobedience at a Canadian military base. Project La Macaza gave many young protesters from across Canada their first taste of nonviolent direct action. For those that already had some background in peace or civil rights activism in the United States or Great Britain, this was their first experience of civil disobedience in Canada. In the process, they generated favourable media coverage – making front-page news in the *Globe and Mail*, *La Patrie*, and *Maclean's* – and consequently drew the nation's attention to the seriousness of their cause and the power of nonviolent protest.[64]

Second, these demonstrations were significant because they occurred at a critical time in the history of youth activism, both in Canada and abroad. In 1964, American student radicals became more deeply disillusioned with the "liberal" political establishment and more confrontational in their dealings with power structures.[65] This was the year of Freedom Summer in Mississippi and the Free Speech Movement at Berkeley.[66] By protesting at La Macaza, young Canadian activists demonstrated that, like their American counterparts, they were becoming more radical in their analysis (moving beyond single-issue politics and recognizing that peace was interconnected with other issues such as Quebec's colonial status within Canada) and more confrontational in their strategies. Though these protests were peaceful, they were undeniably radical in their critique of state power. (This may be the reason that the RCMP gathered a substantial amount of information on the La Macaza protesters.)[67] And they were harbingers of further radicalization. By the end of 1964, the young activists had transformed CUCND from a single-issue peace group into Student Union for Peace Action (SUPA), a nationwide New Left organization.[68]

Finally, while Project La Macaza did not trigger an immediate wave of mass peace protests, it did lay the groundwork for subsequent civil disobedience actions. Protests at the military base in Comox, British Columbia (the site of nuclear-armed interceptor jets) in the summer of 1965 were directly inspired by the actions at La Macaza. Peter Light, an active participant in La Macaza, was the organizing force for the Comox protests.[69] Furthermore, in the spring of 1965, SUPA organized a highly successful week of sit-ins in front of the American Consulate in Toronto to protest the brutal police crackdown on civil rights marchers in Selma, Alabama.[70] SUPA also organized an anti-Vietnam War demonstration on Parliament Hill in the spring of 1966, which resulted in mass arrests.[71] Participants in all three of these protest actions had been present at La Macaza in the summer of 1964. In essence, Project La Macaza prepared the way for further endeavours in civil disobedience, and some of these subsequent protests – particularly that in Comox – may have paved the way for Canadian peace and environmental activism into the 1980s or beyond.[72] Indeed, it is important to recognize that today, a half-century after the civil rights and peace activism of the sixties, nonviolent civil disobedience continues to be a relevant and principled means of challenging oppression and injustice.

SUPA Anti-Draft Programme office, Toronto, August 1967. (Photo by John F. Phillips, creative commons attribution, shareAlike 3.0 unported, creativecommons.org/licenses/by-sa/3.0/deed.en).

13

"A Very Major Wheel That Helped Grind the War Down"

The Canadian Anti-Draft Movement, 1966–1973

JESSICA SQUIRES

T HE CANADIAN ANTI-DRAFT MOVEMENT was a network of groups in Canadian cities that actively supported the immigration of war resisters – including "draft dodgers" and "deserters" – during the American War on Vietnam, and was active from 1966 to 1973.[1] The ebbs and flows in its activity and effectiveness ran roughly parallel to the broader antiwar movement, whose peak was arguably the massive antiwar protests of early 1970. Following events at Kent State University in May of that year, demonstrations in Canada and around the world complemented massive student protests across the U.S. that denounced the U.S. war and the actions of its government. The anti-draft movement also shared terrain with movements for women's and Black liberation and formed international networks. It used ideas associated with a growing left-wing or "new" nationalism to convince the public and politicians of the value of allowing American war resisters into Canada.[2]

The activism and organization of the Canadian anti-draft movement took a specific form that was not yet prevalent in the late 1960s. It was the precursor of the movement that in the late twentieth and early twenty-first centuries grew to support war resisters escaping the American wars on Iraq and Afghanistan. As a movement supporting immigrants, and whose practice featured some form of casework, it also shares a lineage with present-day organizations whose specific purpose is to enable immigration and provide casework style support to individuals and families upon their arrival.

The impetus for its development, of course, was the American war in Vietnam. The United States' Selective Service System drafted young men into the U.S. military and sent them overseas. The resistance to this war by the Vietnamese people and by Americans, coupled with an upsurge in movements against racism and colonialism more globally, was a key feature of the period. In this context, between 1965 and 1973, a small but dedicated movement in Canada supported American war resisters who came to Canada to escape the draft and the war. Forming a network, in an era long before the Internet, these groups worked together, overcame differences, and supported the goals of war resisters in cities across the country.

Many people today remember a war resister who was close to their family, or that their parents had a war resister as a lodger. The impact of this comparatively small part of the movement against the Vietnam War has a lasting place in the psyche of Canadians; Canada, it is often believed, welcomed the "draft dodgers" with open arms. Many remember that Prime Minister Pierre Trudeau asserted a view in accordance with this welcoming stance. What is less known is that the initial position of Canada on draft dodgers and deserters – on war resisters in general – was mixed at best, and at times decidedly antagonistic, although the government did not openly acknowledge their ambivalent position until forced to do so in 1969. This ambivalence translated into RCMP and police surveillance, and sometimes actions viewed by many as harassment, of anti-draft movement activists and resisters themselves.[3] Further, the differences between draft dodgers and deserters were, for the most part, lost on the general public, which brought its own advantages and disadvantages for those seeking to help them arrive and settle north of the border.[4]

Roots

In early 1966, Hans Sinn, the editor of *Sanity* magazine, a leading North American peace newspaper based in Montreal, began receiving letters from young American men looking for advice on how to come to Canada to escape the draft.[5] "I oppose American policy in Vietnam and am thinking seriously about moving to Canada to escape from the draft," wrote one resister.[6] This man and hundreds of others like him, along with their parents, friends, lovers, and wives, were the beginning of a phenomenon the effects of which are still felt today in Canada. At first the number of resisters in Canada was a trickle, and most were actually avoiding the draft rather than deserting the military. As the war progressed, however, more and more young men deserted and fled to Canada. Women were not generally counted as part of this group, although many of the American immigrants motivated to journey north were women.

Some had been referred to *Sanity* by conscientious objector organizations in the U.S., likely based on the newspaper's opposition to the war and perhaps on personal connections with Sinn through pacifist circles.[7] Sinn contacted U.S. pacifist groups for any information they had on the draft for the purposes of properly responding to the letters.[8] As the letters increased, Sinn enlisted the help of Virginia and Lowell Naeve, immigrants from the U.S., who had settled in the Eastern Townships. "I am delighted I made contact with you. The need is great for help," wrote Virginia Naeve to Sinn in March 1966. The Naeves had also been receiving letters, some referred to them by the War Resisters League, an American secular pacifist organization formed in 1923, and Virginia identified a need to line up job and school opportunities as well as housing. Since she had connections with many U.S.-based antiwar and pacifist groups, her involvement was crucial.[9] Sinn developed a media release, a format he was familiar with as a journalist, to outline Canada's immigration rules.[10] This missive was later developed into a fact sheet and would eventually be published as a broadsheet for mass distribution. In time, this group became the Montreal Council to Aid War Resisters (MCAWR).

Meanwhile, activists in Vancouver and Toronto were taking similar action. In Toronto, the Student Union for Peace Action (SUPA) became aware of the need for a support group in part through war resisters Tom Hathaway and Mark Satin.[11] They decided to form a working group on the issue, which would become the Toronto Anti-Draft Programme (TADP) and continue on after SUPA wound down in 1967. On the Pacific Coast, the Vancouver Committee to Aid American War Objectors (VCAAWO) received dozens of letters as well.[12] Communication between Sinn and activists in other cities was soon established, but co-ordination, which Sinn thought essential, took longer.[13]

By early 1967, more frequent communication was established with the Toronto and Vancouver committees. Benson and Meg Brown in Vancouver and Tom Hathaway and Nancy Pocock in Toronto exchanged correspondence with Sinn, and they visited each other during holidays. In January 1967 Sinn and the nascent Montreal committee, which enjoyed the participation of some American war resisters, adopted the Vancouver fact sheet in place of its own.[14] By 1968 Calgary, Edmonton, Vancouver, Victoria, Winnipeg, Fredericton, Moncton, Sackville, Newfoundland (likely St. John's), Guelph, Hamilton, Kingston, Kitchener-Waterloo, London, Oshawa, Ottawa, Peterborough, Port Arthur-Fort William, Toronto, Windsor, Charlottetown, Montreal, Regina, and Saskatoon all had committees or contact people.[15] These contacts were publicized on the Vancouver information sheet and, importantly, in the

Toronto Anti-Draft Programme's *Manual for Draft-Age Immigrants to Canada* (the *Manual*).

In addition to the network of organizations that focused on immigration information and support work, American refugee groups formed, comprised solely of American deserters whose identity often centred on their opposition to American foreign policy. One such group was the Toronto American Deserters Committee; another was the Yankee Refugee group, based in British Columbia, which established an American Deserters Committee Program in 1969.[16] These groups coexisted uneasily with the support committees, and at times tactical debates over the best way to oppose the war exploded in the pages of movement publications.

The various groups in the network of anti-draft groups (although less commonly for the refugee groups) developed similar practices rooted in three different sources. One key source was pacifist casework as practised by anti-draft and conscientious objector movements in the U.S. and often typified by the involvement of the historic peace church communities. Among the organizers of the TADP were Nancy and Jack Pocock. The Pococks had training in pacifist traditions; both were Quakers, and Nancy was very involved in the Canadian Friends Service Committee's Peace Centre on Grindstone Island.[17] The files of the TADP contained manuals for anti-draft counselling from such groups as the Central Committee for Conscientious Objectors (CCCO) Military and Draft Counseling Center of Buffalo. Hans Sinn was a central figure in Grindstone Island as well.[18] In Ottawa, where a group was formed under the name Ottawa AID: Assistance with Immigration and the Draft, some of the central activists were of Mennonite backgrounds. In addition to pursuing aims similar to the TADP, by 1969 Mennonites Bob Janzen and his wife had established a coffeehouse in a francophone United church in central Ottawa where resisters and their supporters, and other elements of the Ottawa scene, likely congregated.[19] Frank Epp, another Mennonite, donated office space to the cause.[20] Official support from churches, including the United Church and church networks such as the Canadian Council of Churches, was also a main feature of the movement to support war resisters, although this support did not become entrenched until comparatively late.[21]

The second key feature of the anti-draft groups' perspective was that war resistance, more than simply being a pacifist, anti-violent principle put into practice, was an active opposition to war. As Bill Spira, a central activist with the TADP explained, "A lot of people have asked me, why are you doing it for Americans? My answer always is I'm not doing it for

Americans. I'm doing it for the Vietnamese."[22] Joan Wilcox, an Ottawa AID organizer, shared Spira's antiwar spirit: "I'd like to think we were one cog on a very major wheel that helped grind the war down, maybe not as soon as we would have liked, but sooner than it would have otherwise."[23] A concern for ensuring that chosen tactics were indeed leading to effective opposition to the war led to debates on both sides of the border about the wisdom of emigrating from the U.S. to Canada in comparison to enlisting and opposing the war from inside the military or going underground; but these debates were rather muted in Canada.

Finally, the ideas of the New Left were also influential. The precursor organization to the Toronto Anti-Draft Programme, Student Union for Peace Action (SUPA), was closely identified with New Left ideas and was one of the few Canadian organizations that can be clearly identified as New Left. Heather Dean, author of a section in the *Manual* about Canada's political system, was a key figure in the Canadian New Left, and especially in SUPA.[24] Mark Satin, editor of the *Manual* in its first editions, was a former American New Left activist.[25] A Pan-Canadian Conference of U.S. War Resisters, held in Montreal in 1970, featured guests Carl Oglesby and Tom Hayden of the American New Left organization Students for a Democratic Society. As early as the summer of 1963, the *War Resisters League News* carried an article covering a joint conference of the U.S. and Canadian peace movements in New York State that enjoyed the participation of Tom Hayden and Canadian New Left figure Dimitrios Roussopoulos.[26]

Not only was this movement pan-Canadian; it was also international. The Canadian anti-draft movement was in constant contact with American draft counselling networks and New Left activists. Further, it was a multigenerational movement with influences from multiple sources – peace churches, pacifist traditions, and the crucible of radical ideas of the sixties.

Methods

In a time when even the fax machine was still a rarity, anti-draft movement communications relied on letters and phone calls. Many of the groups kept extensive files of letters to and from potential immigrants and Canadian and American support groups. Groups rapidly developed template-style responses and letterhead, which both enabled a more rapid and efficient response and allowed for the systematization and uniformity of casework.[27]

In many cases, permanent offices were established, and in some, staff were hired.[28] Staff and volunteer activists were in constant contact with each other between cities and each group developed a sense of its history. Groups and staff developed a great deal of specialized expertise on immigration rules, stratagems for crossing the border, and rules about the Selective Service Program.[29] Montreal issued a broadsheet-style flyer outlining the basics; the Toronto Anti-Draft Programme published a book, the *Manual for Draft-Age Immigrants to Canada*, which was widely distributed in the U.S. and Canada. Working closely with groups south of the border, it distributed copies of literature far and wide. TADP records showed an average of 450 bulk sales per month in 1969, escalating to several thousand issued to dozens of American groups and some individual counsellors as well as to Canadian groups between January and June of 1970.[30]

The *Manual* was published six times between 1968 and 1971. The first three editions had a combined print run of thirty-five thousand copies. The fourth edition had to be printed twice. Later editions moved away from national symbolism in cover art and content. University of Toronto historians J.M.S. Careless, Elliott Rose, and Kenneth McNaught helped with the general text of the manual and the sections on war resisters' immigration history. In these historical sections, the authors cited Canada's history of providing sanctuary to various kinds of war resisters. The introductory section, titled "Words from Canadians," contained short messages from lawyers and church officials. Contributors represented a cross-section of antiwar and New Left circles in Toronto, where anti-draft activity was most pronounced. Each new edition of the manual provided updated group listings and changes in immigration procedures.[31]

Alternative journalism and movement literature was centrally important in broadening and deepening the reach of the movement into the U.S. The importance of *AMEX* magazine, originally titled *The American Expatriate in Canada*, and other publications cannot be underestimated. *AMEX* in particular became a site for information sharing and debate among Canadian and American activists and war resisters.[32] The movement learned to use the mainstream media as well. Hardy Scott, a draft dodger who arrived in 1967, was interviewed for articles in *Ladies' Home Journal*. He agreed to those interviews on the condition that the magazine would also print the Vancouver committee's address. As a result, the committee received a boost in inquiries.[33]

The movement also made use of the mainstream media to good effect in its campaign to open the border to deserters in 1969. As Bill Spira recalled in a 1970 interview:

When the border was closed by MacEachen we at that point decided to take the wraps off deserters. . . . The first thing we did was to start a publicity campaign showing deserters to the press; in other words, meet your local deserter and see he doesn't have horns. That made big news and the stories the guys had to tell made big news. . . . A lot of human interest came out. That really was the first of our campaign, to let the Canadians see deserters and meet deserters and have them on TV and on radio shows.[34]

Some groups, especially in Toronto and Vancouver, developed the idea that they were playing a central leadership role in the network and that others should follow their lead. This attitude did not always play well outside these centres. Further, tensions emerged, at first centred on tactical questions about supporting resisters and later on deeper philosophical differences about the war and capitalism.

That said, each group developed a particular role in the network. Ottawa AID was central in lobbying the federal government and thus an essential part of the network's advocacy efforts to shift official border policy and regulations. The TADP gained the reputation of being the authority on the rules in the U.S. and Canada. Others played key roles in locating jobs and housing. The network, which at first made contact for the purpose of information sharing and improving resources, grew into a more formalized structure, especially when it began receiving regular funding from churches in early 1970.[35] It also availed itself of legal advice. Indeed, lawyers played a key role in the campaign to open the border in 1969.[36]

Advocacy

The network not only allowed for better casework but also facilitated co-ordinated action to force policy change. On several occasions between 1967 and 1973, the anti-draft groups, in more or less co-ordinated fashion, attempted, sometimes successfully, to influence public policy on immigration. The first such effort took place in 1967, when the Vancouver group developed a brief entitled "A Note on the Handling of Draft-Age Americans Who Apply for Entry into Canada," aimed at pressuring the government to address informal discrimination against war resisters by border officials.[37] Unbeknownst to the movement, Immigration was about to issue a secret memo to its border officials encouraging them to discriminate and exclude deserters.[38]

While the efforts in 1967 were not successful, they did lay the groundwork for the most significant campaign of the movement's history: the campaign to open the border to deserters in early 1969. Between mid-1968 and May of 1969, the government ordered border agents to ban deserters on the grounds that they had legal, moral, or contractual obligations in their country of origin. The order was secret until it was exposed in early 1969. The increasing numbers of deserters and their needs encouraged the movement to take action to bring about a change in policy.

In late 1968, anti-draft groups became aware of a growing problem of deserters being turned away by immigration officials. While some war resisters had already experienced a high degree of scrutiny and, anecdotally at least, some discrimination, it seemed to the groups that there had been a qualitative shift in how war resisters were treated at the border. After they had compared notes, the groups determined that immigration officials might have been issued instructions to turn away deserters in particular.

The campaign to open the border was the most ambitious and co-ordinated campaign undertaken by the anti-draft movement to date. While it is unclear to what extent the campaign was centrally planned, the breadth of the campaign and its common features across various aspects show a great degree of co-ordination. The network certainly had a degree of self-awareness of itself as a network, engaged in a common struggle.

In Toronto, deserters had become a matter of some concern by late 1968. Their status was murky as they were bona fide law-breakers in the U.S. Bill Spira of the TADP, whose responsibility it was to offer programming for deserters in Toronto, summarized the situation:

> The committees themselves thought from the very beginning that this desertion was illegal.... To our surprise we found that there was absolutely nothing in the [Immigration] Act to prevent people who had unfulfilled obligations in the army....
>
> When we found that out then we acted accordingly.... We started counselling deserters to immigrate.... Some of the early ones we [had] had to put ... underground ... all kinds of cloak and dagger.[39]

These efforts began to lose effect after the secret instruction was issued to border personnel.

In response to opposition questions about an apparently secret (but leaked) memo ordering border guards to discriminate on the basis of military service, anti-draft networks across the country were activated. Dozens and then hundreds of letters poured into immigration offices. After the issue began to garner media attention, letters in support of excluding resisters were also received, but at their height the numbers were a fraction of those received in support of war resisters.[40]

In early 1969, two Committees for a Fair Immigration Policy were formed: one in Toronto and one in Ottawa. These committees featured well-known intellectuals, journalists, and writers, such as June Callwood, Pauline Jewett, and Mel Watkins. Anti-draft groups arranged for a sample of war resisters to tell their stories to a lawyer. From that, a brief was drafted. The committees sought and secured meetings with MPs to present the brief.[41]

The letters and telegrams, as well as a petition circulated by Voice of Women, carried some common arguments. The demands of the brief were re-stated again and again. Criticism of the government policy centred on the supposed pacifist tradition in Canada of welcoming refugees from war, the need for foreign policy independent of the U.S., and the need for democratic discussion of policies, as opposed to secrecy.

In early February, five Glendon College students staged a media stunt to expose the border policy. They crossed the border using their Canadian identification, and then attempted to return Canada, this time each posing as a deserter, William John Heinzelman. The five had slightly different experiences at each border point, but all experienced discrimination. The results of the attempt became widespread news, and the questions in the House of Commons increased. The Department of Immigration attempted damage control by issuing a statement on March 5 to emphasize that desertion was merely one factor among others to be considered in the border official's exercise of discretion.[42] However, the damage had been done. The public eye was on the border situation for war resisters. The following days saw open letters from university professors and church officials pronouncing in favour of an open border. The Heinzelman stunt was crucial for the eventual success of the campaign.

Debates

Perhaps inevitably, tensions arose when the movement faced disparate aspirations on the part of the resisters themselves, and when strategic and tactical debates presented obstacles to united approaches. The superior attitude of some, like Bill Spira, likely did not help matters. But the tensions really centred on age-old questions about long-term strategy. Some on the Canadian left saw the American presence as needing containment and control, encouraging assimilation over the more radical associations of American resisters' groups. Among the more active Americans, many maintained their sense of self as Americans, even internalizing the idea, held by some on the left, that they were agents of American imperialism, but the vast majority of resisters either assimilated directly into Canadian culture or eventually returned to the U.S. under the amnesty programs offered under presidents Ford and Carter.[43] A third category of resisters made the decision to act as Americans in opposition to U.S. policy, forming groups of American war resisters who sought more radical forms of action and a more radical perspective on the act of desertion. This form of organizing eventually led to the creation of a plethora of American Refugee groups that became part of the movement landscape and, to a greater or lesser extent, also participated in both casework and political campaigns.

In May of 1970, a pan-Canadian conference was organized in Montreal. Its purpose was to bring together the different groups in the movement to discuss next steps following the success of the 1969 campaign, and to try to develop common positions on how best to oppose the war while supporting war resisters in their desire to move to Canada. Attended by most of the groups in Canada and with participation from the peace movement, the women's movement, and American groups, the result was a remarkable consensus on how to continue to support resisters while encouraging them to consider all of their options, including remaining in the U.S. to resist the war at home.[44]

Remobilizing

After the success of the 1969 campaign, the intensified debates, and the Montreal conference, the movement settled into a routine similar to that pre-dating the secret government immigration memo. But in early 1972, the government began revising its approach to immigration in general. Back in 1967, it had introduced section 34 of the immigration regulations, which allowed visitors to Canada to apply to be "landed" both at the border and at immigration offices inside Canada. The result had been an influx of visitors seeking to take advantage of the system and who, for one reason or another, had not yet applied to be landed, or whose application had been denied. The appeals process in place from 1967 to 1972 also encouraged growth in the number of visitors to Canada with no formal immigration status. The result was an enormous appeals backlog.

To address this situation, Bryce Mackasey, Minister of Immigration, repealed section 34 in June 1972. Under the new Administrative Measures, anyone who was waiting for an appeal had the opportunity to have their appeal fast-tracked under relaxed rules, and officers were given greater discretion and allowed to consider humanitarian concerns in assessing applications. However, the government was intent on eliminating section 34 altogether. After that date, an application to immigrate from within Canada's borders would no longer be possible.

Not surprisingly, this new policy resulted in a rapid increase in the number of applications to immigrate from visitors already on Canadian soil. By September 1972, the department had received a record-breaking forty-four thousand applications; it was expected that this number could come close to doubling before December 31. Immigration offices were hard-pressed to manage the demand. Nevertheless, the government moved ahead with its plans to revoke section 34.

During the implementation of the Administrative Measures program, anti-draft movement activity was largely limited to spreading the word as quickly as possible. Eventually, groups began to co-ordinate to pressure the government to do something for those potential immigrants who had arrived between the June deadline to apply under the Administrative Measures and the revocation in November of section 34. There were also hundreds who had not applied because they feared deportation. The predicament also drew the attention of journalists. Anti-draft activists and their supporters lobbied for a solution.[45] Mackasey's successor, Robert Andras, then introduced penalties for visitors who remained in Canada longer than three months without registering their continued presence with immigration officials. The government's move essentially drove underground thousands of visitors who had already been in Canada for a long time, since to present themselves to immigration officials would result in punishment.

Ultimately, after some internal discussion at Department of Immigration offices, Andras established a second grace period to deal with the problem of illegal visitors. Called the Adjustment of Status Program, the grace period of one month's duration would theoretically allow thousands of now illegal visitors to land under relaxed rules. Touted as an amnesty, it eventually resulted in many more visitors, now illegally in Canada, securing landed status. This success was partly due to the active promotion of the program by the anti-draft movement. The groups joined forces once again in this effort, this time not to oppose a government policy but to promote it. For the purpose of co-ordinating efforts, both to influence the shape and scope of the programs and to encourage resisters to take advantage of them, defunct groups re-activated, new ones formed, and a coalition rapidly emerged. The speed with which this coalition was formed showed how much this movement had learned from the years of development between 1966 and 1971.[46]

The operation was marked by a co-ordinated media campaign. Groups placed ads in local and regional newspapers, using slogans such as "It's Now or Never," encouraging war resisters to use their counselling services before approaching immigration officials, since to do so without preparation could result in an immediate deportation order.[47] The groups even bought a bus, painted it with the slogan "Last Chance to Get Landed," and sent it on a tour of rural towns. The efforts bore fruit; in the end, thousands of immigrants won landed status during the program's brief duration, and the anti-draft movement found itself counselling not only Americans but immigrants from many other nations as well.[48]

o o o

The story of draft dodgers and deserters in Canada in the Vietnam War era is one that shows how transnational movements can have an impact beyond their apparent scope. From its beginnings in 1966 until its actions in 1972 and 1973, this social movement developed from a scattered array of more-or-less networked individuals to a robust, if small, movement capable of rapid and effective action, displaying an understanding of the interaction between the media, mobilization, public opinion, and politics. The various organizations in this movement developed extensive knowledge of immigration and border crossing regulations, job and housing information, and the legal consequences of resisting the draft or deserting the military. Though responses to the needs of resisters differed somewhat by region and local expertise, the movement used this knowledge to advocate on behalf of resisters and to challenge federal government policy on immigration. In late 1973 the movement transitioned to become a more American-centred, American-driven movement calling for an amnesty to allow Americans to return to the U.S. following the end of the war. But during its existence, it contributed to and shaped both Canada's self-image as a peacekeeping nation and a haven for refugees and the immigration policy that remained, essentially unchanged, until the twenty-first century.

Claire Culhane poses during her second hunger strike, Ottawa, December 24, 1969 – January 12, 1970. Permission courtesy of Dara Culhane. William Ready Division of Archives and Research, McMaster University Library.

14

The Fasting Granny vs. the Trudeau Government

Demanding an End to the Canadian Presence in Vietnam

TARAH BROOKFIELD

PARLIAMENTARY RECORDS FROM MAY 4, 1971 contain a cryptic note indicating that there was "an interruption from the gallery" during a House of Commons debate on Canada-U.S. relations.[1] What the records do not state is the fact that this "interruption" was a planned protest by Claire Culhane, who, upon chaining herself to a chair in the select visitors' gallery, tossed antiwar pamphlets down onto the House floor.[2] In a loud voice, she demanded Minister of External Affairs Mitchell Sharp answer for Canada's complicity in the Vietnam War. Culhane was well known to Sharp as "the fasting granny," the fifty-three-year-old former aid worker and long-time activist renowned for her two hunger strikes on Parliament Hill. In response, Sharp did what he usually did when confronted by Culhane: he ignored her. While police officers cut away Culhane's chains and escorted her off the premises, the House debate continued. The only official acknowledgement from the floor came from NDP MP Tommy Douglas, who joked about his familiarity with being interrupted by a woman because he had "been married for a long time," an oddly sexist comment from an MP who had previously been supportive of Culhane's aims.[3]

The dismissal of Culhane's presence and demands by political enemies and allies alike was emblematic of the indifferent and often condescending attitude radiating from Ottawa toward Culhane from the time she began her antiwar crusade in the spring of 1968 to the Trudeau government's first and only official condemnation of the Vietnam War in January 1973. Although more muted than her previous public demonstrations, the Commons disruption was the first to result in Culhane's arrest. When she stood trial a month later on charges of disturbing the peace, Culhane explained to the court, "I went before Parliament to object to a crime, not to commit a crime."[4]

The crime Culhane referred to in her testimony was twofold. She was certainly referencing the Vietnam War as a crime against humanity. By the early 1970s polls show that the majority of Canadians shared Culhane's opposition to the war and expressed both sorrow and anger over the tragic loss of life, a nightmarish refugee crisis, and environmental destruction.[5] The United States, often viewed as an imperialistic interloper in Vietnam, was usually the focal point of this blame. However, Culhane's use of the term "crime" also referenced Canada's culpability in the war. In her opinion, Canada, as a neutral nation, acted appallingly in Vietnam as "the butcher's helper," for Canada's assistance and allegiance to the U.S. came at the expense of the Vietnamese people.[6] This accusation was based on Culhane's long held socialist ideology and her recent experiences working as an administrator at a Canadian anti-tuberculosis clinic in South Vietnam, through which she claimed to have witnessed numerous examples of how Canada's presence in Vietnam was prolonging the war and doing the exact opposite of its stated humanitarian goals. Therefore, Culhane dedicated the next five years to getting Prime Minister Trudeau, Sharp, and the Canadian International Development Agency (CIDA) to reclaim Canada's neutrality and help end the war. The provocative and sacrificial nature of her activism, combined with press and public fascination with her grandmother persona, made Culhane the most recognizable antiwar figure of the era, something that often gets overlooked in a historiography that emphasizes mass mobilization over singular efforts.[7] Although Culhane's activism did not ultimately change the government's policies, she should be credited for her perseverance and creativity in directing the public to condemn Canada's transgressions in Vietnam.

Canadian Involvement in Vietnam

Canada's presence in Vietnam was informed by the Cold War mentality influencing international relations since the end of the Second World War and by Canada's increasingly intertwined, yet strained, political and economic relationship with the United States. Officially Canada had been involved in Vietnam since 1954 when it agreed to join Poland and India as the United Nations International Commission for Supervision and Control (ICSC). The ICSC was to monitor the ceasefire from the First Indochina War between France and Vietnam, organize elections, and work toward a truce between the northern and southern governments. Ostensibly ICSC members were neutral observers, yet the selection of countries to sit on the ICSC ensured that they represented, or rather appeased, a triad of Cold War interests: communist, non-communist, and non-aligned. From the outset, then, Canada was expected to consider Vietnam's future alongside the interests of the non-communist Cold War alliance to which it belonged, presumably in the hope that Vietnam would elect a pro-Western government.[8]

Regardless, there was not much opportunity for ICSC members to mediate; in 1955 the ceasefire dissolved into a war between the northern-based communist Democratic Republic of Vietnam, supported by the Soviet Union and China, and the American-fronted Republic of Vietnam in the South. During the late 1950s and 1960s, the United States' role in the conflict increased dramatically with the massive deployment of American military personnel in the South and aerial bombings of the North. Canada remained in Vietnam on the ICSC throughout the war, resigning only after the American withdrawal in 1973.[9]

Beyond Canada's ICSC role, the Canadian government had no formal policy on Vietnam. Lester B. Pearson, whose tenure as Prime Minister coincided with the American escalation of the war, encouraged the Americans' anti-communist vision for South East Asia. Nevertheless, Pearson considered the U.S. military escalation in Vietnam to be "a threat to world peace."[10] Both privately and publicly, he urged President Lyndon Johnson to withdraw American troops from Vietnam, stop bombing the North, and seek peace through diplomatic channels. Yet as historian Andrew Preston points out, Canada never presented an alternative diplomatic solution and, even if it had, it is doubtful that Canada had the political clout to convince its more powerful ally – and key trading partner – to negotiate rather than fight.[11] So although Canada urged an American withdrawal, the Pearson government never came out directly against the war, and instead preferred to allow what Robert Bothwell characterizes as having "its anti-war inclination ... understood rather than explicitly stated."[12] This was not good enough for the growing number of antiwar protesters in Canada. "By keeping quiet," one activist claimed, "Ottawa is agreeing with the war, agreeing with the U.S."[13]

Prompted by the escalation of American military personnel in Vietnam, anti-Vietnam War activism gained considerable momentum across the United States in the early to mid-1960s. College campuses held regular protests, teach-ins, and vigils while major American cities saw mass demonstrations ranging from fifteen thousand to three hundred thousand people between 1965 and 1967.[14] In Canada, proportionate antiwar activities were organized by university students, Quakers and other pacifists, New Left intellectuals, labour, and women's peace groups. As in the U.S., this activism was bolstered by the already organized and engaged portion of the citizenry who were active in civil rights, student, antiestablishment, or disarmament movements. Pre-existing peace groups turned their attention from banning the bomb to Vietnam, and new organizations such as the Canadian Committee to End the War in Vietnam organized at the local, provincial, and national level. Several aspects of Canada's war resistance were distinct from the activism south of the border. Emanating from Quebec was a unique strain of anti-imperialism among French-Canadian nationalists who found kinship in the Vietnamese resistance.[15] Canadian antiwar activism was also shaped by the migration of approximately twenty-five thousand American draft dodgers and a smaller number of deserters who sought refuge in Canada between 1964 and 1973.[16] Peace groups took advantage of Canada's official neutrality to offer their nation as a safe meeting space to bring together the war's participants. This allowed the Voice of Women/La Voix des femmes (VOW) and the Quaker-run Grindstone Peace Institute to host conferences and workshops bringing together diplomats, civilians, and former combatants from North Vietnam, South Vietnam, and the United States to discuss their wartime experience and possibilities for resolution.[17] Canada's neutrality also allowed two nongovernmental foreign aid agencies, Canadian Aid for Vietnam Civilians and Quebec Medical Aid for Vietnam, to send aid to civilians living in the North and South.[18] By the time Culhane began her activism in 1968, Canada's anti-Vietnam war resistance was fully entrenched among the traditional radical crowd and spreading to newly engaged Canadians.

Culhane's Encounter with Vietnam

Culhane was a veteran of left politics who was freshly inspired by the Vietnam War. As Mick Lowe describes in his biography of Culhane (née Elgin), she was born in Montreal to Russian-Jewish immigrant parents in 1918 and grew up during the Great Depression. Social justice causes had captured her attention at a young age. In high school, Culhane was inflamed over the lack of voting rights for Quebec women; her peers named British suffragette and hunger striker Emmeline Pankhurst as Culhane's prototype in the high school yearbook. This interest also prompted a teenage Culhane to interview Quebec women's rights activist Thérèse Casgrain, who would later become a fellow anti-Vietnam war activist.[19] In the 1930s, Culhane joined the Young Communist League and volunteered for the Friends of the Mackenzie-Papineau Battalion dedicated to preserving democracy in Spain. The *Foreign Enlistment Act* would prevent Culhane from travelling to Spain herself, but she spent the next two decades engaged in leftist causes. When the Communist Party was made illegal in 1940, Culhane and her future husband Garry Culhane, also a Communist Party member, went underground for almost two years until the party was made legal again. After her separation from her husband in 1955, Culhane took a break from politics to prioritize her family needs and provide for her two school-aged daughters. Having two years of nursing school in addition to years of secretarial work, Culhane found work in the medical records department of Montreal Neurological Institute.[20]

It was not until the spring of 1967 that Culhane experienced a political reawakening while reading a *Weekend Magazine* article about a five-person Canadian medical team testing and treating Vietnamese civilians in the tuberculosis ward of the Quang Ngai Provincial Hospital in South Vietnam. The cover featured a photo of Quebec nurse Louise Piché holding a Vietnamese baby among a long line of children awaiting immunization. The article was representative of the typical human interest story commonly featured in the Canadian press about the suffering of the Vietnamese and the war-torn nation's endless need for assistance. Tuberculosis, endemic in rural Vietnam, was exacerbated by wartime conditions such as overcrowding, lack of access to health care, healthy food, clean water, or shelter, the inhalation of smoke from wood fires, and lack of opportunities for bed rest.[21] The article celebrated the work of Canadian physician Dr. Alje Vennema, who had successfully petitioned the Canadian government to open a specialized anti-tuberculosis clinic in the region. Culhane applied to work at the clinic through the Department of External Aid (renamed CIDA the following year). After interviews and reference checks, she was offered the position of Hospital Administrative Assistant. Strangely her background check did not reveal the extensive Royal Canadian Mounted Police file detailing her past membership in the Communist Party.[22]

In October 1967 Culhane arrived in the coastal province of Quang Ngai, known to be a stronghold of the National Liberation Front (NLF), the political organization operating as a military unit in South Vietnam against the South Vietnamese government and the United States.[23] The NLF presence meant the province was frequently a target of the U.S. military and the Army of the Republic of Vietnam (ARVN). It was also the site of three documented mass murders of Vietnamese citizens, including the infamous My Lai Massacre in 1968.[24] Vennema, who had been working in Quang Ngai for three years, had voiced opposition to the American intervention in the war and was known among locals to be sympathetic to the NLF. His reputation was thought to extend protection to the other Canadians working in Quang Ngai.[25] Culhane found a political ally in Vennema, but he left soon after her arrival for postgraduate studies in England. She divided her time between working at the provincial hospital and getting the new tuberculosis clinic open, where she witnessed the misery caused by the war on a daily basis. Culhane reported that approximately 80 per cent of the patients were women and children suffering the consequences of war, be it injury, illness, rape, or malnutrition. "In the Emergency Ward, one became dazed with shock," she recalled, "[of] lifting a baby out of a pool of its own blood, a young girl with her breasts sliced off and a broken bottle rammed up her vagina, a child with a hole in its back large enough to put one's fist into, a dead mother with an infant still sucking at her breast, and an old man with only the top of his face left."[26]

Prior to travelling to Quang Ngai, Culhane had clarified with CIDA that "apart from having to accept American logistics for transportation, communication and supplies, in some cases, I would be part of a 100% humanitarian, Canadian, independent medical team."[27] She began to question these assurances almost immediately upon arriving in South Vietnam where she observed that "Canada's every action and every statement throughout the war in Indochina, has been first and foremost to defend the U.S. position and to make it more palatable to world opinion."[28] Culhane's 1972 book *Why is Canada in Vietnam? The Truth About Our Foreign Aid* details dozens of examples of how the Canadian medical team lacked independence in Quang Ngai. What she found more troubling was that American intelligence and military needs were being prioritized over the wellbeing of her Vietnamese patients.

In particular, Culhane was appalled at the behaviour of the anti-tuberculosis hospital's new physician, Dr. Michel Jutras. Two chapters in her book are devoted to her reconstruction of Jutras's misconducts: his indifference toward patients, his refusal to assist emergency arrivals of non-tubercular patients, his reduced office hours, his arming of the hospital and Canadian residence, his suspected misappropriation of supplies and funds to sell on the black market, and, most alarming, his sharing of patient records with American embassy personnel.[29] All of these issues were accentuated during the Tet Offensive, the NLF surprise attack during Vietnamese New Year in early 1968. In the first few days of the attack, before Culhane was evacuated with the rest of the Canadians, she witnessed the clinic being told to evacuate patients so it could be used as an ARVN military base. As the head of the clinic, Jutras had no objections to Canadian property being used for military purposes. Although Culhane was disgusted by Jutras's actions as a doctor, it was clear to her that his behaviour was perfectly aligned with Canada's unofficial mission to help the Americans win the war.

Culhane only had to look up to the sky to see more Canadian hypocrisy. The Americans flew Canadian-made warplanes full of Canadian-made military supplies, products of the 1958 U.S.-Canada Defence Production Sharing Agreement. As part of this trade agreement, Canada sold an estimated $2.47 billion worth of military goods produced by American-owned firms operating in Canada or Canadian Crown – or Canadian-owned – corporations between 1965 and 1973. The majority of these goods ended up in Vietnam, including military equipment, vehicles, uniforms, weapons, ammunition, grenades, napalm, TNT, and Agent Orange.[30] Culhane "found it impossible to accept the posture of one government department [the Department of Defence] selling military hardware to the U.S. while another department [CIDA] strikes the humanitarian posture of easing the sufferings of the same people it is helping destroy."[31] She was also perturbed by the lackadaisical attitude of the head of Canada's ICSC delegation, Ormond Dier, who once told her after a tour of the anti-tuberculosis clinic that "it didn't matter if we didn't see a single patient, all that mattered was that the hospital was there."[32] Culhane interpreted this comment as meaning it only had to look like Canada was doing something. The medical aid was merely a way to help the Vietnamese "smell a little sweeter before they died."[33] Refusing to associate herself with such a compromised aid program, Culhane resigned after five months.

Culhane's Antiwar Activism

When she returned to Canada, Culhane met with CIDA president Maurice Strong and vigorously demanded the withdrawal of the Canadian medical team and an investigation into Jutras's conduct. Her reasoning was framed in both ethical and economic terms, explaining that the clinic was a waste of taxpayers' dollars if it was not truly a humanitarian effort. Following this meeting, she submitted to CIDA a detailed sixteen-page report listing the problems she observed in Quang Ngai. CIDA staff promised to investigate her "serious" claims, but after a series of letters resulted in no follow-up Culhane began to copy Sharp and Trudeau on all her communications with CIDA. Initially Culhane hoped Trudeau, who was elected Prime Minister two months after she returned from Vietnam, would re-evaluate Canada's position on Vietnam and personally respond to her report. In a letter to Vennema in August of 1968, Culhane wrote, "Trudeau has shown courage in cutting down Canada's NATO commitments.... Nothing else new re China or VN [Vietnam], but maybe! maybe! he will do right there too."[34] Yet despite his reputation as the counterculture Prime Minister, Trudeau had even less to say than Pearson when it came to Vietnam. Having a hands-off policy on the war was a more politically expedient route when negotiating Canada's increasingly volatile relationship with the U.S. under President Nixon. As Ivan Head observed, neither Trudeau nor his ministers were "driven by any ambition to be architects of peace" and, given his tumultuous relationship with Nixon, Trudeau seemed aware there would be "no effective third party influence" regarding Vietnam.[35] Trudeau did permit American draft resisters entry into Canada, a symbolic act which "allowed the Canadian government to demonstrate its independence from the United States and its opposition to the war."[36]

While waiting for an answer from CIDA, Culhane decided more radical action was needed. Having previously sent copies of her CIDA report to every member of parliament, Culhane found sympathetic ears across party lines from MPs such as Liberal Warren Allmand, NDP members Tommy Douglas, Ed Broadbent, and Grace MacInnis, and Conservative David MacDonald; the latter two unsuccessfully presented a private member's bill to Parliament requesting Culhane's CIDA report be released and investigated.[37] Culhane was also welcomed into Montreal's antiwar community and became a frequent speaker and participant in vigils and marches. Reuniting with Casgrain, an active VOW member, Culhane joined the women's peace organization and was invited to speak about Quang Ngai at local and out of province VOW meetings. Following a VOW protest at the Suffield Army Base in Alberta, Culhane proposed holding a ten-day hunger strike in the fall of 1968. Hoping to create a spectacle guaranteed to get the media's attention and shame the government on its doorstep, Culhane planned to stage the fast on Parliament Hill where she would sleep outside under the East Block Portico and subsist on water, orange juice, and vitamins.

Self-starvation as a nonviolent expression of political discontent was a feature of key social movements around the globe in the twentieth century.[38] Hunger strikes are usually employed to demonstrate the gravity of a cause represented by the striker's willingness to deny themselves the sustenance they need to survive, sometimes to the point of death or severe malnutrition. Culhane's fasts represent both her militant commitment to the peace cause and a strategy to embody the suffering caused by war. The use of fasting to protest the Vietnam War was not widespread, and Culhane's is the only documented case in Canada.[39] By striking, Culhane was also following her heroine Emmeline Pankhurst, who along with her fellow jailed British suffragettes and American counterparts starved themselves to protest the lack of women's political representation and their treatment by authorities.[40] Given the surveillance and policing of women's bodies, hunger strikes by female activists contain the added symbolism of women defying approved uses of their bodies. As feminist sociologist Cynthia Cockburn observes, "putting your body on the line for politics is an effective, if perilous, strategy. But for women, because of the way women are often reduced to the body and routinely sexualized, putting the body in play has a special meaning."[41] Given these gendered dimensions it is not surprising that the media paid close attention to Culhane's body, consistently referencing her age, grey hair, and status as a grandmother. These features set her aside from the image of the stereotypical antiwar protester, often envisioned in this era as young (student) and male (draft dodger), and made Culhane a distinct and often sympathetic figure in the press.[42]

A rotating vigil of VOW members acting as her honour guard, fellow fasters, and public relations liaisons joined Culhane day and night on Parliament Hill between September 20 and October 9, 1968.[43] Dressed in Vietnamese style pyjamas and carrying a placard proclaiming "Ten Day Vietnam Fast," Culhane received mixed reactions from the public and politicians ranging from acclamations and donations to dismissals and accusations of treason. Five women senators debated issues with Culhane, though all but Muriel Ferguson were highly critical of antiwar activism and felt that victory in Vietnam was the key objective. Postmaster General Eric Kierans disclosed that unlike most of the cabinet, he supported U.N. Secretary General U Thant's proposal for the U.S. to stop all bombing of the north during the ongoing Paris peace talks, one of his many disagreements with Trudeau. During Minister of Manpower Jean Marchand's visit, he insisted it was impossible to pull out of the Defence Production Sharing Agreement with the United States without suffering great job losses for Canadians.[44] Sharp stopped by to reiterate that Canada would call for a "balanced response" regarding Vietnam, but nothing more at an upcoming U.N. meeting.[45] Just before Culhane broke her fast, Trudeau invited her and Casgrain into his office for a brief meeting where he expressed respect for their convictions, but refused to engage in a political discussion about Vietnam.[46] For Culhane, the fast was a triumph. Her fifteen-pound weight loss had been worth the publicity garnered by her strike. The fact that the fast did not achieve a shift in the government's position on Vietnam, she explained, meant that further action was desperately needed.[47]

Culhane's urge to do more was reinforced when CIDA reported in

November 1968 that ICSC representatives visited the clinic and determined the program in Quang Ngai was "meeting a real need" and being "efficiently administered."[48] It also dismissed Culhane's accusations toward Jutras as "preposterous and malicious," the result of a personal vendetta because he did not allow her the same free administrative reign over the hospital as Vennema.[49] Unless Culhane could provide concrete evidence of wrongdoing, CIDA considered the matter closed. Coming from a program managed by External Affairs, CIDA's response represents not so much a refutation of the evidence Culhane presented, but a different interpretation of why Canada belonged in Vietnam. From the perspective of External Affairs, tasked with balancing the delicacies of diplomacy on a global scale, maintaining Canada's relationship with the United States, and bolstering Canada's new image as a friendly peace-focused middle power, supporting relief programs in Quang Ngai accomplished all of these. To withdraw, as Culhane recommended, would be a statement against the war that the government was not willing to make.

Yet the attempts to ignore Culhane's opinion and evidence went beyond diplomacy. Even before her past in the Communist Party was discovered or her protests positioned her as an objectionable ally, Culhane's gender, age, and clerical position left her outside the typical male and university-educated circle of foreign policy experts. If her radical grandmother persona had made her a cause célèbre in the press, it limited the impression Culhane made within the government. Despite Culhane having been on the ground in South Vietnam during a period of escalated warfare, CIDA denounced her claim to be an "expert."[50] According to Culhane, Sharp referred to her as only a "casual observer."[51] Gordon Longmuir, the new head of the ICSC delegation, claimed that Culhane was "highly emotional and erratic."[52] In the press and privately, other External Affairs cohorts referred to her as "insatiable," "unscrupulous," bizarre," "naïve," and "confused."[53] Even if these adjectives were an accurate description of Culhane, they were applied through a gendered lens that predetermined her opinions as less worthy than those of the male diplomats.[54] In comparison Vennema, who openly shared much of Culhane's politics, was referred to "as a man of unquestionable integrity" and was inducted into the Order of Canada in 1967 for his Vietnam service.[55] Considering her report to be slander, CIDA refused to make it public because the state's legal advisors worried it left them open to a libel suit from Jutras. The same advisors encouraged each involved government department that "a curtain of silence would be the best way to handle this matter."[56] Specifically External Affairs recommended that Culhane never receive a response directly from Trudeau because "there is no telling what unscrupulous use she might make of a letter from the Prime Minister."[57]

The silence only served to incite Culhane further. She inundated Sharp and Trudeau with almost weekly letters, and spent the rest of 1968 and much of 1969 giving speaking engagements for Canadian antiwar groups and international peace conferences. In one letter to Trudeau, Culhane admits her "seemingly endless tirade" must appear "foolhardy" to some; however, she found "it impossible to desist, since if I were to do so, I would – at that moment – be joining the ranks of those who are either responsible for these injustices, or those who are content to stand by and remain silent although a partner in the project."[58] When news about a 1968 massacre of hundreds of civilians in My Lai was made public in November 1969, Culhane redoubled her efforts and held a second hunger strike on the grounds of an Anglican Church across from Parliament Hill for nineteen days in the middle of winter between Christmas Eve 1969 and January 12, 1970. The fast was organized under the theme of "Enough/Assez" in reference to "Enough Killing in Vietnam" and "Enough Canadian Support for this Endless War." This time Culhane was joined by Michael Rubbo, National Film Board director of *Sad Song of Yellow Skin*, a documentary about the war's effects on Saigon civilians. The "Enough" fast received considerable press coverage and interaction with the public and politicians, though with the location being adjacent to, rather than on the Hill, combined with the holidays and cold weather, it did not allow for as much pedestrian traffic as the 1968 strike. The 1971 fast concluded with an impromptu meeting between Culhane and Trudeau captured on film by a news team. The transcript from the recording reveals an initially warm Trudeau turning flippant and chilly as he suggests the war in Vietnam was "the [U.S.] president's problem," needing an American solution. All Canada can do is "wait," Trudeau explained. "If we had a solution, believe me the war would be ended tomorrow but we don't have a solution to the Vietnamese war and I don't believe you have."[59]

o o o

This final face-to-face encounter represents the impasse Culhane found herself in with the Trudeau government. From the government's perspective, there was nothing tangible Canada could do to stop the war or change the American position. Shaming the Americans into pulling out of Vietnam would accomplish nothing and likely damage the profitable but dependent economic relationship Canada had with the U.S. In the meantime CIDA continued to fund the Quang Ngai clinic and other aid projects in South Vietnam because it was a gesture that Canada was doing something to aid civilians. It was not until 1973 when Trudeau was in a minority government position that he spoke out against the U.S. bombing of Hanoi, a measure to score points with the antiwar NDP whose support he needed to remain in power. This action forced Trudeau to explain to a reportedly furious Nixon that his condemnation arose from "domestic considerations."[60] To Culhane and other war resisters, political expediency was an unforgiveable excuse. Vietnam was a moral choice, not a political issue. Culhane believed that, with so many lives lost and still at stake, Canada should have risked everything, as she had in her fasts and arrest, to act as the "butcher's conscience" or at the very least not profit in blood money. Undeterred, Culhane continued her activism until the American withdrawal from Vietnam, when she transferred most of her efforts into campaigns for Canadian prison reform and prisoners' rights. Within the broader anti-Vietnam war movement, Culhane's unique persona as a witness to the war, as an older woman, and as someone willing to relentlessly punish her body as a symbol of her commitment in desperate times made her oft standalone and spectacular protests as relevant and influential as the massive protests drawing hundreds of thousands of people.

Vietnam War demonstrations, parade to Toronto city hall, *Toronto Telegram*, June 1, 1970. York University Libraries, Clara Thomas Archives and Special Collections, *Toronto Telegram* fonds, ASC04980, 1974-002/285.

15

"A Good Teacher Is a Revolutionary"

Alternative War Perspectives in Toronto Classrooms from the 1960s to the 1990s

ROSE FINE-MEYER

THE SOCIAL ACTIVISM OF THE 1960s laid the groundwork for educational change within Ontario classrooms. Influenced by the political upheaval of the period, many young teachers soaked in the ideas of, and were active participants in, peace movements, protests against the Vietnam War, the emerging women's movement, and labour union activism. Public activism affected curriculum development, the work of teachers in classrooms, and the kinds of resources teachers could access, and it facilitated partnerships with parent groups. Curriculum change was the result of dedicated and purposeful work carried out by teachers who believed that changes within the education system were essential components of broader social amelioration and fundamental principles of equity, respect, and peace.[1]

The history and social science teachers whose oral testimonies were used for this study were also influenced by the new social history emerging at the time, which placed greater emphasis on the history of ordinary people and events, traditionally marginalized in nationalist narratives found in textbooks. Some Toronto teachers brought their activist perspectives and new social history methods into the classroom. When interviewed, one teacher noted that the "history curriculum, so heavily focused on wars, provided opportunities to question death and destruction. I regularly asked my students 'why do we continue to participate in wars, and what are some of the alternatives to war?'"[2] The efforts to change the content delivered to students in history classrooms remained a constant and passionate focus for many teachers throughout the 1970s and 1980s. As one teacher recalled, "Peace keeping was the message."[3]

This chapter examines the experiences of history and social science teachers who incorporated antiwar narratives into their classes in Toronto schools between the 1960s and the 1990s.[4] It explores how they were influenced by the antiwar sentiment of the Vietnam War era and the political and social activism of the period more generally. It also examines the way in which the former Toronto Board of Education[5] and parent groups equally took up the cause for peace, providing teachers with the necessary intellectual space and teaching materials. While bringing antiwar perspectives into the classroom remained a personal choice, teachers in Ontario could take advantage of their considerable independence in curriculum delivery. By the 1980s, teachers had a broad array of peace-oriented materials to draw upon and many had begun to conceive of social justice activism as part of their mandate as educators.[6]

School Reform

The political activism of the period provided a stimulating environment as the school system itself was undergoing radical change. The provincial government's 1968 *Living and Learning* (or "Hall-Dennis") report embraced the belief that systems of education should revolve around individual student needs and resonated with many parents and educators. Schools, the report stated, "should be built for human beings interested in learning" and "viewed as a place of personal growth and development based on a learning process of self-discovery."[7] The report recommended individualized programs of instruction and a de-emphasis on competition in the classroom and rote learning. Curricula were to provide a greater variety of learning opportunities for students.

Similarly, the Ontario Association for Curriculum Development Conference report of 1968 argued that the role of curriculum in education needed to better reflect changes taking place in society. One conference working group concluded that "authoritarian methods in education are harmful and undesirable," adding that "a good teacher is a revolutionary" as "he [sic] can build critical awareness only by example. He must be ready to question established values, the system and himself."[8] A decade later a 1978 Federation of Women Teachers' Association of Ontario (FWTAO) publication reflected the continuing pedagogical shifts taking place, noting that "teachers were soul-searching about the inadequacies of their methods.... Nothing was sacred: everything was to be questioned."[9]

In this context, many history and social science teachers regularly incorporated current events into their classroom and sought to "bring the outside in." Educational publishers incorporated current event issues into supplementary books that brought critical thinking into course work.[10] It was common and accepted practice, then, for history teachers during the 1970s and 1980s to incorporate alternative resources and pedagogical strategies. These practices occurred amid public discussions about greater flexibility in schools in terms of eliminating grades or creating "open concept" classrooms.

Within the broader public sphere, concerned parents, activists, educational reformers, political leaders, and women's history organizations contributed ideas about how history curricula should take shape in Toronto schools. The *Toronto Community Schools Newspaper*, for example, published between 1971 and 1974 by the "Community School Workshop of Toronto," represented the voices of activist parents, students, teachers, and concerned citizens from across the city.[11] The Community School movement sought fundamental changes in schools, including a greater dispersal of power and an increase in community-based social responsibility, which translated into ideas of "de-schooling" or "free" or "liberated" schools, where students, parents, and teachers shared educational decisions. A number of new alternative schools emerged in Toronto during this period. Their names spoke directly to the ways in which their supporters hoped to challenge traditional learning environments. They included SEED (Shared Experience Exploration and Discovery), ALPHA (A Lot of People Hoping for an Alternative), Inglenook Community School, and MAGU (Multi-Aged Group Unit).

Teachers were also radicalizing through their labour unions. During the 1970s, teachers in Ontario were extremely involved in teacher unions, which grew in size and influence.[12] Each school had teachers who served as union representatives. It was a period of widespread job activism: work stoppages, work-to-rule, strikes, and lockouts. The FWTAO, the Ontario Secondary School Teachers' Federation (OSSTF), and the Elementary Teachers' Federation of Ontario (ETFO) all lobbied for change at school board meetings, through posters, pamphlets and conferences, and through a wide range of publications and networking initiatives.

Educators and parents demanded a more inclusive curriculum that better reflected the changing demographics and growing population of Toronto. As a result the school board faced major expectations from city teachers, parents, and educators who demanded that schools reflect greater diversity in programming and curricula to address immigrant and "inner-city" children's needs and incorporate peace and environmental education. Many teachers were thus well situated within political environments that provided opportunities to engage in activism or access new and innovative course resource materials as part of their pedagogy. The school and union meetings provided a space for common work-related and community concerns. Toronto teachers, then, were acclimatized to challenging work-related issues through union work and protests.[13]

Different groups provided new materials and resources for teachers. Toronto was a key centre for the dissemination of New Left ideas, many of which focused on educational concerns. *This Magazine Is about Schools*, a local community paper, advocated that schools reflect the city's growth and diversity. Later known as *This Magazine*, it was one of a number of new periodicals that emerged between 1965 and 1975 that reflected an interest in new approaches to Canadian social and cultural life such as Canadian studies, Native Studies, and Women's Studies. According to John Wadland, *This Magazine* provided a "radical interdisciplinary critique of contemporary social mores."[14] Similarly, Toronto's Hogtown Press had its origins in the student movement of the 1960s. As Russell Hann, a member of its editorial collective, explains, "The goal initially was to create as broad a political spectrum as you could on the independent Left."[15] A number of Toronto teachers in this study used Hogtown Press materials, which focused on social and labour history, women's liberation, and peace activism.[16] Women's peace activism was connected to larger struggles for women's equality. Frieda Forman, an antiwar activist, feminist and educator who came to Toronto from New York in 1970, argues that "the antiwar movement was a training ground for the feminist movement ... what was true for the antiwar movement, what was true for the New Left, was also true for the women's movement." She added, "It was a period of such co-operation. Everyone provided support."[17]

New materials also came out of social protest groups in interesting ways, further illuminating the link between peace, war resistance, women's activism, and education. Historian Barbara Todd, an early member of the Vancouver Women's Caucus, recalled organizing a conference in 1971 to bring a delegation of Vietnamese women to Canada to share their accounts of the impact of the war on their families and communities.[18] These women emphasized the need for unity in the antiwar movement. Members of the Canadian Voice of Women (VOW) and the American group Women Strike for Peace, along with other Canadian and American human rights activist groups, also attended. Public rallies and marches to protest the war followed their presentation.

Some of the women involved in that conference were part of the Vancouver Corrective Collective which, along with the B.C. Teachers' Federation, developed and published *She Named It Canada*, which became an important history resource for classrooms across the country.[19] The Collective also published *Never Done: Three Centuries of Women's Work in Canada.* Todd notes that the success of the first book prompted the Collective to continue producing materials for educational purposes.[20] These books and others illuminate the way social history was altering history education in the 1970s, particularly in terms of decreasing the emphasis on industrial and military discourses. Labour movement histories, which examined working conditions and worker activism, provided additional opportunities to explore equity issues more broadly. Although the study of war in schools had predominantly focused on celebratory military victory narratives, these books, and others that followed, allowed students, as Todd notes, "to see the world as a world of families and women and children."[21] They provided important new conceptual frameworks for the teaching of history and, in particular, for examining the broader implications of state policies. In a pre-Internet world, publications such as these provided an important medium in which larger groups of people could access new ideas and support peace advocates, who looked for ways to press for government action against war. Many of these publications ended up in the hands of teachers. The focus on social history, the demands for a greater integration of diverse perspectives into course studies, and the initiatives of feminists and peace activists resulted in an influx of new resource materials into the classroom.

The Influence of the Vietnam War on Toronto Teachers

Toronto was a major reception area for Vietnam War resisters and a hotbed of peace activism. By the early 1970s, there were more than 20,000 American war resisters living in the city.[22] Many of the first to arrive settled in the Annex community around the University of Toronto, an area occupied by a number of academics and teachers. That area soon became known as "the American ghetto" and "provided a focus point for the relationships, politics, and daily life of the growing exile community and its organized resistance activities."[23] Churches such as Trinity–St. Paul's United played an important role in offering support by allowing space for gatherings, workshops, and networking. Connected through multiple networks, a number of teachers became linked in some capacity to this community.

Teachers were also exposed to ideas of antimilitarism in their workplace. A number of Toronto teachers who lived in the Annex and who knew war resisters or were involved in peace activism within the community were also connected with community groups that advocated alternative education. One teacher noted, "Some of the Americans I knew were involved in alternative schools and the alternative schools movement either as teachers or parents."[24] Teachers working in alternative schools provided a welcoming atmosphere for Toronto's growing New Left community. Myra Novogrodsky, a prominent educator in the city, worked in an alternative school at that time and acknowledged what many alternative teachers believed:

> It was easy for me, working in an alternative high school, to bring this topic into the curriculum. Every year at City School we taught an interdisciplinary course and one year it was on War and Peace. We did a lot in this course on the war in Vietnam and on war resistance. Parent Nomi Wall, a former employee of the Toronto Anti-Draft Program, was one of the speakers in this course.[25]

Educator Margaret Wells offered a similar view:

> Since at that time I was teaching in an alternative school there was a lot of anti-war activism among staff and students, participation and general work on the issues such as peace marches, committees etc. In addition we brought speakers into the school; I remember one group of young people around the world who were affected by war who did a cross-country tour. I believe that they were called "Young People for Peace and Social Justice."[26]

Unionism also brought teachers into direct contact with antiwar activists. One teacher made the links between social activism and unions when he explained,

> It was common to meet American draft dodgers at OSSTF meetings. Many teachers themselves were activists – some were involved with the teachers' unions, and some part of labour unions. They were into Federation work – in District 15 – and some were even on the Council.[27]

Teachers also became more aware and engaged in social movement activism through their participation at demonstrations throughout the city. Margaret Wells recalled that she participated "in some peace marches" and was also involved with a group of teachers promoting the teaching of "antiwar" perspectives. "We actually called ourselves Educators for Social Responsibility and were based entirely in the Toronto Board of Education," she recalled.[28] John Pendergrast, a teacher and co-founder of Educators for Social Responsibility, offered the following recollection:

I consider myself a pacifist. You didn't have to be one to oppose the Vietnam War, but I was and am one. During my time as a teacher Vietnam was over, but the nuclear arms race was alive and well, with cruise missile testing in Canada a big issue. That's where I wanted to put my energy. I was also involved with being trained in and teaching the *Facing History and Ourselves* curriculum on (mainly) the Holocaust of World War Two. The focus of that curriculum is the need to oppose discrimination and warmongering in the early stages – the connection to opposing nuclear weapons is pretty obvious.[29]

In general, activism that focused initially against the Vietnam War was later channelled into the nuclear disarmament and peace movements. Some teachers noted how their activist network improved their access to resources, others how it shaped the approach they took to course pedagogy, still others how it encouraged them to adopt new approaches to student course work. Teachers reflected on individual pedagogical choices, which were also influenced and supported by like-minded colleagues, using materials they accessed from workshops or from each other.[30] "I really think that teachers acted independently" one teacher recalled, "but I was fortunate to work in a department where there were good teachers . . . it was a dynamic sharing environment."[31]

Educator John Waksmundski voiced what many were feeling when he argued in the November 1974 edition of the *Social Studies Journal* that teachers should include a Vietnam War examination in their history or social studies course work. Recognizing that the Vietnam conflict had "dominated the headlines as well as the evening news," he urged social studies teachers to "get something going" by asking students to engage in class discussions. To facilitate this initiative he recommended resources and guest speakers.[32] Teachers responded in different ways. One teacher noted that he liked to play Phil Ochs and Bob Dylan antiwar and civil rights songs for his class. This teacher used the lyrics of the songs to engage students in the political activism of the time and "to look at issues from a social view, something not present in textbooks."[33] Many teachers similarly sought out resources that encouraged students to think critically about current and past issues.

Another teacher recalled using resources produced by Educators for Social Responsibility. "The focus was on examining many perspectives," she explained, and "slowing down students' responses so that they really engaged in critical thinking and reflection."[34] As a whole, these teachers tried to "push the boundaries" by stretching the required curriculum to ensure that it was relevant and meaningful to students and reflective of societal concerns. It was a period in which many parts of society were re-examined and questioned, and teachers with a strong sense of social justice felt compelled to reform the system from within. As one teacher added, "I'm interested in social and political movements that are outside the mainstream. I looked for material that I could bring into the classroom to help [students] with that."[35] Teachers submitted that teaching history provided opportunities to give their students a deeper understanding of the ways in which the past linked to contemporary issues. One teacher recalled that he assigned antiwar readings in his study of the Vietnam War. He asked students to analyze the materials and report on how the antiwar movement might have affected political decisions. Teachers thus taught about the ways in which the antiwar movement illustrated how the power of people could be mobilized against government military activities.[36]

Many teachers accessed their own resources and developed their own course studies. According to one educator who offered a "stand-alone" locally developed course,

> The students did action projects: collecting materials from newspapers, helping in a shelter – it was a hotbed of feminism consciousness and all in the media. And marches – we went on marches and the kids really got into it, even though the kids came from very traditional families.[37]

The decision to incorporate antiwar narratives within course studies in schools remained an individual choice for teachers. Activist educators keen to address issues such as environmental conservation, civil rights, women's rights, eradicating poverty, and nuclear disarmament felt that students needed to be engaged with these concerns.

The Toronto Board of Education and Parent Groups: Supporting Teachers

In the pursuit of their aims, activist teachers introduced supplementary materials that presented alternative narratives. Many principals who delegated the responsibility of ordering textbooks to the heads of subject departments did not intervene when supplementary resources that did not have official approval were used in individual classrooms. Other teachers found that they had the explicit support of their administrators and school board. As one teacher explained,

> Once I wanted this Toronto teacher, a self-defined member of the Communist Party, to speak to my class about communism. I asked my Principal and he said go ahead, in fact he was surprised that I had

asked. The textbook only provided so much – we needed to bring in our own resources and we had the support to do this.[38]

Other teachers emphasized the importance of allowing students to draw upon their family histories, some of which were steeped in personal war experiences. Another teacher added, "I was able to bring critical war narratives into my classroom. I had no problems with the department head. In the Canadian and American history courses we examined the bomb, antiwar protesting, and nuclear testing."[39] Such examples reflect the ways some school administrators supported teachers' initiatives as well as the extent to which many teachers were sensitive to their students' needs.

The Toronto Board of Education also supported teachers' initiatives to bring alternative perspectives into the classroom. The majority of trustees were left leaning, and a large number were women.[40] The Board provided meeting space for, and partnered with, a number of peace organizations including the Voice of Women, Educators for Social Responsibility, and Parents for Peace. In 1983, the Board established the "Thinking and Deciding in a Nuclear Age" advisory committee with a budget for "in-service training" for teachers and for "handling controversial issues" in the classroom through visiting speakers and additional resources.[41] The Board's Continuing Education department offered a ten-week course on "Nuclear War and Peace." Teachers were offered in-service programs that exposed them to new ideas, with speakers such as David Suzuki.[42] As one teacher stated, "The Toronto Board was ahead of its time." It was well-funded and provided support for teachers interested in delivering alternative narratives. The committee, she noted, boasted a number of "left-leaning teachers," including what she termed "Old Stalinists," and was keen "to address a number of issues related to the prevention of war."[43]

Committee and group newsletters reflected the work taking place to promote peace education at this time. "Peace festivals" were held at the Toronto Islands and events throughout the city included antiwar films and peace activist speakers. Some of the events were held in schools.[44] As a result, teachers secured multiple opportunities to explore how best to address antiwar issues in their classrooms. The Board provided meeting space, materials, and support for Professional Development. It also allowed one teacher from each secondary school to attend a five-day retreat in the early 1980s to support peace education strategies through interactive workshops. Overall, the Board boasted progressive administrators and an extensive resource library, which facilitated the examination of controversial and important social issues.[45]

Parents also provided support for peace initiatives. "Parents for Peace" worked closely with the School Board, teachers, schools, and parents in the community and published a newsletter that promoted their activities.[46] The group pursued a number of initiatives throughout the city including conferences, workshops, discussions, film nights, and curriculum development. They also had a representative on the "Thinking and Deciding in the Nuclear Age" committee. Its "Peace Curriculum" included Remembrance Day units, information about social events, films, and speakers' names for K-13 teachers.

The solidification of peace education in school curricula by the mid-1980s stemmed from the work already taking place in schools throughout the 1970s. It was clear to the teachers engaged in peace education that their students should develop understanding and respect for different perspectives. Topics such as global issues, participatory citizenship, and Canadian studies incorporated issues of multiculturalism, world poverty, and global conflicts, while providing a space for family and community research. A survey of peace education in Canada, published in 1986, noted the wide range of teacher initiatives. Ontario teachers' federations, such as FWTAO and OSSTF, had published official peace education policy statements that included nuclear awareness, the arms race, world hunger and poverty, racial inequality, and ecology, and had developed curriculum materials for use in classrooms. Government-supported programs, such as films produced by the National Film Board, were widely used in schools. Journals such as *Canadian Dimension, This Magazine Is about Schools*, the *Forum*, and the *History and Social Science Teacher* – to name only a few – contained suggested resources. A wide range of organizations also offered advice on accessing resources and how to lobby governments.[47]

The networking between parents, teachers, and communities to bring antiwar narratives and peace education into the classroom was central to the Toronto scene. Concerned parents, activists, educational reformers, political leaders, and women's history organizations predominantly within the centre core of the city lent their voices to ideas about how curricula should take shape in Toronto schools. They shared a belief with other community groups in Toronto that the school and community-based approach would enhance their ability to pursue systemic change throughout the broader society.

The Canadian Peace Educators' Directory, published in 1990, reflects this activism. It contains a staggering list of 350 Canadian and international organizations concerned with education about peace and global issues, with resources and contacts for teachers.[48] Teachers for Peace, Teachers for Social Justice, Educators for Social Responsibility, the Ontario Teachers' Federation, and teachers' colleges all worked with educators. Organizations such as Canadian University Service Overseas, the Canadian Coalition for Nuclear Responsibility, Greenpeace, and UNESCO supplemented the valuable resources and support found at the Toronto Board of Education Resource Centre.

o o o

The teachers examined in this chapter began their professional lives at a time when the Vietnam War dominated public debate. Many felt the war's impact both within their schools and in their communities. Anti-war actions taking place in the city and across the globe shaped their curriculum delivery. Despite the fact that nonviolence education was not explicitly required in the provincial curricula at that time, interested teachers incorporated peace education topics into their lessons. Activist teachers in Toronto in the 1970s and early 1980s were committed to challenging traditional war narratives within curricular documents through their collaboration with a wide range of personal and professional communities. Their efforts were facilitated by their own peace activist positions and through the support of the Toronto School Board and independent publishers.

An ideological shift among the trustees at the Toronto Board of Education in the late 1980s resulted in what some teachers interpreted as an attack on critical pedagogy about war.[49] It challenged "bringing controversy" into the classroom and resulted in an educational climate that resonates today when the need to critically reflect and debate issues related to war seems all the more pressing. Historian Sharon Cook argues that by the 1990s, Conservative provincial governments transformed peace education "almost exclusively into conflict management and resolution, in aid of citizenship skills," thus altering the former focus on human and environmental rights and equity issues established in the 1970s.[50] In *Warrior Nation: Rebranding Canada in an Age of Anxiety*, Ian McKay and Jamie Swift expose the "toxic rebranding of our country" and the current public focus and celebration of military achievements propagated by the current Conservative government.[51] They argue that the government has shifted the focus away from "peaceful accommodation" to present Canada as a nation "created by wars, defended by soldiers, and kept free by patriotic support of its military virtues."[52]

The Conservative government's emphasis on military commemoration in the past few years highlights the continued need to bring alternative views about war into the classroom. The government is financially and publicly supporting war narratives through a number of new awards and initiatives. For example, in 2013 the government announced it would double funding to the "Memory Project" to "allow for more veterans and serving soldiers [to interact] with students in the classroom" and thus "help promote Canadian history."[53] The government focus on "service and sacrifice" has influenced what is taking place in classrooms across the country, with a growing interest in championing battlefield commemorations and increasing educational partnerships that support study tours for teachers and students to Canadian battlefields and memorials in Belgium and France.[54]

Current state support for the militarization of Canadian history in schools has placed teachers in a position of perpetuating or challenging dominant narratives of military heroism. To counter this and provide a broader study of war, teachers might turn to the retired teachers in this study as role models. These teachers sought out alternative narratives and resources for their course studies through their involvement with a variety of communities, both professional and personal, and through the inclusion of supplementary materials from independent organizations and publishers. Mainstream textbooks and websites are still fuelled by corporate and state interests and stories of war heroism have an impact on how students perceive military conflict. The commonplace pedagogical approach to the teaching of war is quite narrow and greatly limits students' opportunities to explore the broader implications and consequences of war. Like today, classroom resources and textbooks in the 1970s and 1980s focused predominantly on military campaigns in the study of war. Despite this emphasis, interested teachers in Toronto chose not to separate their ideological beliefs from their teaching. Educator Frieda Forman encapsulates this best: "we were who we were."

Teachers need to seek out antiwar narratives in order to provide a more balanced portrayal of war. Scholars have argued for a stronger focus on employing a social justice lens when teaching lessons about war, by focusing on the human and environmental costs and by encouraging students to be agents of peace.[55] A focus on women and families, like that promoted in the 1970s by Barbara Todd and other social historians, might allow for a deeper examination of the ways war directly affects a nation's citizens. The world is still engaged in wars, and educators have a responsibility to ensure they employ a critical lens when studying war in the classroom, one that allows opportunities for students to engage with pacifism and antiwar critiques.

War Resistance Walk. Picture taken September 13, 2008. Photo credit: Tim and Selena Middleton. www.flickr.com/photos/tim_and_selena/2859058910/.

16

Rewriting History

Iraq War Resisters' Struggle for Asylum in Canada and the Mythology of Vietnam

LUKE STEWART

> We're not talking about draft dodgers, we're not talking about resisters....
> We're talking about people who volunteer to serve in the armed forces of a
> democratic country and simply change their mind to desert.
> — *Jason Kenney, Minister of Citizenship and Immigration, January 2009*

> If Canada's going to convince you, if your Government's going to convince you
> that the war that's coming is right for you ... people like us that can remind
> you of the things that just happened cannot be here.
> — *Anonymous Iraq war resister speaking in Toronto, September 2012*

SINCE 2004, FIFTY UNITED STATES SOLDIERS have sought refugee status in Canada after refusing orders to (re-)deploy to the Iraq and Afghanistan wars. While estimates vary, it is believed two hundred soldiers went absent without leave (AWOL) in Canada at the height of the wars in Iraq and Afghanistan.[1] Soldiers who are AWOL for more than thirty days are considered by the U.S. armed forces to be deserters. The vast majority of these soldiers cited the Iraq War's illegality under international law and the fact that war crimes and crimes against humanity were being committed by U.S. troops against the civilian population as their primary motivation for deserting. Despite Canada's historical role as a sanctuary for draft dodgers and military deserters during the Vietnam War, both Liberal and Conservative governments have intervened in the Immigration and Refugee Board cases to argue that the war's legality was "irrelevant" to its proceedings.[2]

Not one of these soldiers has received refugee status in Canada, and at least five Iraq War resisters who sought sanctuary in Canada have been tried and convicted by the U.S. military court-martial system. Whether they were deported or returned voluntarily, they have been made examples of for refusing to participate in the war on Iraq. The punishment for desertion during war theoretically remains death; while no current war resisters have been executed, they have been punished with dishonourable or bad conduct discharges, confinement, loss of pay, and reduction of rank. Moreover, a soldier receiving a dishonourable discharge obtains a felony conviction and thus forfeits substantial civil and political rights: disenfranchisement in certain states, ineligibility for housing grants and student loans, and an inability to travel back to Canada. Thus, the decision to leave the military and come to Canada will affect the resisters for the rest of their lives.[3]

While 94 per cent of deserters in the U.S. military are administratively discharged, the five soldiers who came to Canada have received relatively lengthy jail sentences. The first, Robin Long, was arrested by Canadian authorities and deported in July 2008. He received fifteen months in military prison for desertion and a dishonourable discharge. The evidence submitted in his court-martial included statements he made in Canada against the war on Iraq. Cliff Cornell, who voluntarily returned to the U.S in 2009 after exhausting his legal options, received twelve months in military prison. The most severe sentence was handed down to Patrick Hart in April 2011. Hart voluntarily returned to the U.S. but received a twenty-five month prison term. In March 2013 Justin Colby received nine months in military prison, reduction to the rank of Private, loss of all pay and forfeitures, and a bad conduct discharge. Most recently, in April 2013, Iraq War resister Kimberly Rivera secured a pre-trial plea deal and received ten months in a military prison and a bad conduct discharge. At Rivera's court-martial, the military prosecutor told the judge that they needed to "give a harsh sentence to send a message to the war resisters in Canada."[4]

With the beginning of the U.S.-led "war on terror," much soul-searching among U.S. military personnel led to confrontations with their conscience. The creation of Iraq Veterans Against the War (IVAW) in 2004 and the doubling of the AWOL, desertion, and missing movement rate between 2004 and 2010[5] demonstrate that the wars being waged in the name of fighting terrorism brought important questions about war and peace to the forefront of soldiers' moral conscience. Do soldiers who volunteered for military service have a right to refuse unlawful commands? What recourse do soldiers who are not pacifists or traditional conscientious objectors opposed "to participation in war in any form" have in the face of unlawful orders? Are soldiers able to invoke Nuremberg Principle IV (1950), which states that the "fact that a person acted pursuant to order of his Government or of a superior does not relieve him from responsibility under international law, provided a moral choice was in fact possible to him"?[6] Most importantly, can these soldiers claim refugee status for fear of being persecuted for refusing illegal orders?

These U.S. soldiers have not only the right but also the moral and legal duty to refuse unlawful commands under the Nuremberg Principles of 1950, the United Nations Charter of 1945, and U.S. civilian and military laws such as the Constitution and the U.S. Army Field Manual. But because the U.S. Department of Defense has not taken these post-1945 developments in international law into consideration in its legal definition of conscientious objector status, soldiers who are not pacifists and thus opposed "to participation in war in any form," face an untenable situation. Having gone AWOL and sought refugee status in Canada after refusing to participate in an illegal war or war crimes, they argue that they will be persecuted if returned to the United States.

Moreover, while American war resisters wait in Canada in a state of legal limbo, politicians and the mainstream media offer pervasive but inaccurate arguments delegitimizing their claims for refugee status. The pages that follow refute the two most prevalent arguments against granting refugee status to U.S. war resisters in the twenty-first century. The first is the claim that, unlike the Vietnam War when there was a draft, these soldiers volunteered for service in the U.S. armed forces. They thus should have known what they signed up for and should accept the consequences for deserting. The second assertion is that these soldiers are, in the words of the former Minister of Citizenship and Immigration Canada, Jason Kenney, "bogus refugee claimants" who clog up the system for legitimate refugees. Oftentimes, these two widespread arguments intersect and play off each other. In doing so, they have formed a formidable obstacle for U.S. soldiers who refused to participate in Iraq or Afghanistan. It is time to set the record straight.

U.S. War Resisters in Canada: Refusing to Participate in an Illegal War, 2004–2008

In March 2003, Canada refused to participate overtly in the U.S.-led invasion and occupation of Iraq. Prime Minister Jean Chrétien, who faced a growing Canadian antiwar movement and a divided cabinet, stated in Parliament that "without a second UN resolution, Canada will not participate." Chrétien publicly argued that international law under the United Nations Charter set boundaries on Canada's participation. The U.N. Charter, the pre-eminent treaty governing world order and the international use of force, prohibits nation-states from resorting to armed conflict except in cases of self-defence against an armed attack which *has* occurred and cases where the U.N. Security Council sanctions the use of force.[7]

The Bush administration failed to secure the required Security Council resolution authorizing the use of military force in Iraq and illegally launched its massive "shock and awe" bombing campaign on March 20, 2003. On September 14, 2004, eighteen months after the invasion and occupation, U.N. Secretary-General Kofi Annan told the BBC World Service that the war on Iraq "was not in conformity with the U.N. Charter. From our point of view and from the charter point of view it was illegal."[8] Under international law, a war fought outside of the strict confines of the U.N. Charter is a war of aggression.[9] According to the Nuremberg Principles, formulated during the trials of Nazi party members after the Second World War, a war of aggression "is the supreme international crime differing only from other war crimes in that it contains within itself the accumulated evil of the whole."[10] Under the ruling at Nuremberg, the war crimes and crimes against humanity committed in Iraq are derivative of the supreme international crime of waging war in the first place.

While each case is unique, the major arguments in the refugee applications submitted by roughly fifty American war resisters in Canada have emphasized that the war on Iraq was illegal, that war crimes and crimes against humanity were being committed by U.S. forces, and that soldiers refusing (re-)deployment faced persecution in the U.S. military justice system for following their conscience and obeying international law. Under the 1951 Convention Relating to the Status of Refugees and the 1967 Protocol Relating to the Status of Refugees, a refugee is a person who "owing to well-founded fear of being persecuted for reasons of race, religion, nationality, membership of a particular social group or political opinion, is outside the country of his nationality and is unable or, owing to such fear, is unwilling to avail himself of the protection of that country."[11] The Office of the United Nations High Commissioner for Refugees (UNHCR) states that:

> Not every conviction, genuine though it may be, will constitute a sufficient reason for claiming refugee status after desertion or draft-evasion. It is not enough for a person to be in disagreement with his government regarding the political justification for a particular military action. *Where, however, the type of military action, with which an individual does not wish to be associated, is condemned by the international community as contrary to basic rules of human conduct, punishment for desertion or draft-evasion could, in the light of all other requirements of the definition, in itself be regarded as persecution.*[12]

Under this definition, there is good reason for military deserters to apply for refugee status.

But despite Canada's honourable history of offering sanctuary to Vietnam War resisters, not one U.S. soldier has received refugee status in the twenty-first century despite the war on Iraq being certified illegal by U.N. Secretary-General Kofi Annan. The primary legal strategy for war resisters in their Immigration and Refugee Board (IRB) hearings and in subsequent Federal Court appeals was to cite the war's illegality. The War Resisters Support Campaign (WRSC) placed international law and the Nuremberg Principles at the centre of these cases, arguing that:

> The struggle to achieve political refugee status for U.S. war resisters in Canada can be seen as one of many efforts worldwide to defend the primacy of international law. The Geneva Conventions on War and the Nuremberg Principles make clear that soldiers have not only the right, but also the *responsibility to refuse to participate in war crimes*. Such war crimes include illegal wars of aggression, indiscriminate or purposeful killing and wounding of civilians, and torture and abuse of prisoners.[13]

Despite the legitimacy of such claims, and the fact that Prime Minister Chrétien cited the legal necessity for a second U.N. Security Council Resolution condoning the use of military force in Iraq, the Liberal Government that succeeded Chrétien under Paul Martin intervened early in the first IRB hearing of Pfc. Jeremy Hinzman who came to Canada in January 2004. Government lawyers argued that the legality of the war in Iraq and evidence of war crimes were "irrelevant."[14]

We now know, thanks to U.S. Army whistleblower Chelsea Manning, that on the same day Prime Minister Chrétien announced that Canada would not participate in the Iraq war without a Security Council resolution, Canadian officials were meeting with their American and British counterparts at the Department of Foreign Affairs to discuss how Canada could "be discreetly useful to the military effort" and were "prepared to be as helpful as possible in the military margins." U.S. officials reported back to the State Department that "while for domestic political reasons and out of a deep-seated Canadian commitment to multilateralism the [Government of Canada] has decided not to join in a U.S. coalition of the willing, they will refrain from criticism of our actions, express understanding, and focus their public comments on the real culprit, Iraq."[15] This assurance on the part of the Chrétien government squares with the Liberal government's subsequent efforts to undermine the soldiers' refugee applications. Canada did not want to be seen supporting the argument that the U.S.-led war on Iraq was an illegal war of aggression.

Unfortunately, both Immigration and Refugee Board officials and Federal Court judges concurred with the position that questions about the legality of the war on Iraq and the means with which the war was fought were irrelevant to the question of whether the soldiers deserted the military and therefore violated the Uniform Code of Military Justice. Central to the legitimacy of a refugee claim is whether the applicant has the proper judicial protections of their country. After Jeremy Hinzman's refugee application was denied by the IRB, he appealed to the Federal Court. In a remarkable ruling, Justice Anne Mactavish argued that "the ordinary foot-soldier such as Mr. Hinzman is not expected to make his or her own personal assessment as to the legality of a conflict in which he or she may be called upon to fight." Moreover, she claimed "the illegality of a particular military action will not make mere foot-soldiers participating in the conflict complicit in crimes against peace." Justice Mactavish concluded that when assessing the refugee claim of a war resister, one must assess "the 'on the ground' conduct of the soldier in question, and not to the legality of the war itself."[16]

This disturbing ruling completely misread the applicability of international law and the Nuremberg Principles to the case at hand. While the Government of Canada, the Federal Courts, and some international legal scholars have argued that ordinary soldiers cannot utilize the Nuremberg Principles in order to refuse participation in an illegal war,[17] since the Vietnam War a movement of antiwar activists, intellectuals, active-duty GIs, veterans, international lawyers, and legal scholars have maintained that soldiers have the moral and legal responsibility to refuse orders which are unlawful.[18]

Since 2006, the Conservative government of Prime Minister Stephen Harper has pursued U.S. war resisters more forcefully. Despite the fact that, by 2008, 82 per cent of Canadians opposed the invasion of Iraq and 64 per cent favoured granting resisters sanctuary in Canada,[19] the Conservative government embarked on a campaign to criminalize and deport war resisters.[20] Canada's persecution of U.S. soldiers appears to be a policy reversal from the Vietnam War when, popular memory tells us, the country opened its borders to Vietnam resisters. However, a politically expedient draft dodger myth has been used to refuse sanctuary to current resisters because they are labelled military deserters instead of draft resisters.[21] This myth distorts the history of what happened during the Vietnam War and undermines the central tenets of post-1945 developments in international law.

Vietnam Draft Dodgers vs. Military Deserters: Unpacking the Draft Dodger Myth

A central stumbling block in the struggle for contemporary U.S. war resisters seeking refugee status in Canada is the pervasive myth that Canada only offered sanctuary to draft dodgers during the Vietnam War. For instance, when it became clear that a growing number of Iraq war resisters were claiming refugee status in Canada, a memorandum to Minister of Immigration Joe Volpe noted: "Some of these persons have made refugee protection claims in Canada, citing conscientious objection to the 'illegal' war and the risk of being imprisoned in the U.S. for their desertion. This is in contrast to the 'draft-dodgers' of 1965–1973, who faced compulsory military service."[22]

The media reinforced the information being shared within the government. Before the ruling on the refugee application of Pfc. Jeremy Hinzman, the *Globe and Mail* editorialized that:

> Canada opened its border to tens of thousands of draft dodgers *and more than a few deserters* during the Vietnam War in the late 1960s and early 70s. The difference is that the U.S. draft still existed then, making military service compulsory and an assignment in the war zone a distinct possibility. The draft dodgers also were not true refugees, but there were good humanitarian reasons behind the political decision to allow them to remain in Canada.
>
> By contrast, Mr. Hinzman volunteered for military duty, to cover the costs of a university education. He did not appear to harbour any pacifist tendencies at the time of his enlistment. Otherwise, why would he have volunteered to train as a paratrooper?[23]

Hinzman was in the elite 82nd Airborne and came to Canada in January 2004 on the eve of his deployment to Iraq. Hinzman and his family claimed refugee status in Canada because the war on Iraq was an illegal war fought outside the confines of international law; violations of international humanitarian law (war crimes and crimes against humanity) were taking place; and his conscientious objector application was denied. The *Globe and Mail* invoked an idealized form of draft resistance during the Vietnam War to justify the current deportation of Iraq war resisters because they are understood as volunteers rather than legitimate draft dodgers. Unfortunately, not much has been done to set the record straight.

During the Vietnam War, an estimated 20,000 to 26,000 draft dodgers and *at least* 4,000 to 10,000 military deserters came to Canada, representing more than just "a few deserters."[24] Indeed, the numbers should encourage us to do away with the narrowly defined "draft dodger" as a means of explaining the totality of the resistance during the Vietnam War. Not only does the substantial number of Vietnam deserters who came to Canada challenge our understanding of that war resistance, but also the treatment of those deserters closely corresponds to the treatment of U.S. war resisters in Canada today.

The governments of Lester Pearson and Pierre Trudeau understood that both draft dodgers and military deserters were entering Canada and attempted to distinguish between them in their official policy. The government categorized draft dodgers as those who had been drafted or feared being drafted by the Selective Service System and military deserters as people who had already been inducted and were serving in the military. Politicians and civil servants in the Department of Manpower and Immigration categorized draft dodgers separately from military deserters, and officials directed all Canadian border officials to refuse admission to military deserters from the United States because they were viewed as a political liability.[25]

This distinction is most clearly seen in a covert ministerial directive, Operational Memorandum 117, issued by Tom Kent, Deputy Minister of Immigration. Between January 1966 and May 1969, various iterations of the Memorandum distinguished between draft dodgers and deserters.[26] J.C. Morrison, Director of Immigration, clarified the Government's position on military deserters in January 1967 through a letter to the regional director of immigration. Quoting OM 117, he wrote "permanent admission to Canada is not to be granted to military deserters" and emphasized that "the Department's view is, as firmly as ever, that we do not want deserters as immigrants."[27] As Jessica Squires demonstrates in this collection, the issue would come to a head due to the work of war resister aid groups exposing this fundamental duplicity on the part of the Canadian government and their treatment of deserters and draft dodgers at the border in early 1969.

There is a second, perhaps more insidious, premise to the draft dodger myth that must be clarified: that all those who came to Canada were resisting the draft or fleeing a military that had drafted them. The Selective Service System did draft American men between the ages of eighteen and twenty-six, but in response to the massive draft resistance movement, President Richard Nixon instituted the draft lottery in 1969 and replaced conscription with the All-Volunteer Force in 1973.[28] Draft dodgers were no doubt evading the draft, but military deserters were not necessarily fleeing simply because they were drafted into the military.

Indeed, the evidence suggests that about half of those military deserters who fled to Canada during the Vietnam War *voluntarily enlisted* into the armed forces. This is a crucial distinction to make because it undermines the key arguments against current Iraq and Afghanistan war resisters seeking sanctuary.

The U.S. military witnessed an unprecedented desertion rate during the Vietnam War, 500,000 in total.[29] The most conclusive data on the method of entry into the armed forces for the deserters who came to Canada can be derived from information collected from the two clemency programs established by presidents Gerald Ford and Jimmy Carter between 1974 and 1977. A 1979 study shows that President Ford's program received 4,317 Army deserter applications and of these 12 per cent fled to a foreign country. Of those in exile, 59 per cent volunteered for military service while 41 per cent were draftees. President Carter's program received 643 Army deserter applications and of these 81 per cent fled the United States. Of those in exile, 40 per cent volunteered and 60 per cent were draftees.[30] Such figures are consistent with Renée Kasinsky's classic study *Refugees from Militarism: Draft-Age Americans in Canada*. Of the hundreds of deserters Kasinksy interviewed in British Columbia, the majority (three-quarters) voluntarily enlisted. Of those who enlisted, 20 per cent fled during basic training, 40 per cent fled after four to eleven months, and the other 40 per cent served one to three years in the military. Of all those she interviewed, 9 per cent were Vietnam veterans.[31]

Given the political climate in Canada, a rightward shift in immigration policy, and the use of the draft dodger myth by politicians, the media, and even progressives, making the above distinctions helps clarify the actual experiences of Vietnam War resisters and demolishes a dangerous impediment facing current U.S. war resisters. Indeed, the only difference between a "draft dodger" and a "deserter" is that the latter made their decision after actual experience in the military or combat. Current day deserters, like nearly half their counterparts during the Vietnam era, were enlistees who refused to participate any longer in wars they considered immoral, unjust, and illegal.

The "War On Terror": U.S. War Resisters, Refugee Status, and International Law

U.S. war resisters in the twenty-first century are applying for refugee status in Canada because of changes in Canadian immigration policy. During the Vietnam War, draft dodgers and military deserters did not apply for refugee status. Between 1966 and 1972, resisters could simply apply for permanent resident status at the border. Since changes to Canadian immigration law in 1972, all potential immigrants applying for permanent resident status have to do so from outside of Canada and must prove they have warranted job skills and financial resources. Moreover, those applying have to wait up to two years to receive a decision. Because they did not have the time to become permanent residents, contemporary war resisters began applying for refugee status, citing the illegality of the war and their inability to qualify for conscientious objector status under American military regulations.[32]

While nowhere near the size of the desertion crisis during the Vietnam War, in March 2006 the Pentagon reported that roughly eight thousand soldiers deserted in the three years since the invasion of Iraq.[33] The nature of the All-Volunteer Force (instead of the draft) and heavy reliance on activating the National Guard and the Reserves caused many to speculate that the U.S. armed forces were entering a period of crisis. The military quickly responded by cracking down on deserters who left the military (such as Camilo Mejia, Kevin Benderman, Stephen Funk, and Ehren Watada) because they argued that the war in Iraq was illegal.[34] Many of the soldiers who deserted to Canada after the 2003 invasion of Iraq did so during their two week R&R (so-called rest and relaxation) in the United States.[35] Before the implementation of the Western Hemisphere Travel Initiative (which made passports mandatory at the U.S.-Canada border), U.S. soldiers were simply able to come as visitors using their driver's licenses. As dissatisfaction with the military or the wars in Iraq and Afghanistan increased, more soldiers began going AWOL (and eventually deserting) in Canada.

In January 2009, the inconsistency between an official policy of not committing Canadian troops to Iraq and at the same time deporting war resisters from that same conflict came to a head when the newly appointed Minister of Citizenship and Immigration, Jason Kenney, openly called Iraq war resisters "bogus refugee claimants." In making this claim, Kenney employed the draft dodger myth, arguing that: "We're not talking about draft dodgers, we're not talking about resisters.... We're talking about people who volunteer to serve in the armed forces of a democratic country and simply change their mind to desert. And that's fine, that's the decision they have made, but they are not refugees."[36]

In an unprecedented move a year and a half later in July 2010, Kenney issued Operational Bulletin (OB) 202, which specifically sought to bar U.S. soldiers from seeking refugee status in Canada. Identifying the current deserters as "primarily members of the United States armed forces," OB

202 directs border guards to immediately inform their Regional Program Adviser concerning those applying for permanent residency and, in the case of those applying for refugee status, to immediately contact their Case Management Branch.[37] Hence, what Canadian officials covertly accomplished between 1966 and 1969 during the Vietnam War with Operational Memorandum 117 has now been normalized and endorsed as official government policy. It is clear that the Canadian government does not welcome U.S. military deserters.

In the aftermath of OB 202, Alex Neve, Secretary General of Amnesty International Canada, asked Kenney to repeal the Bulletin because "military desertion for reasons of conscience is in fact clearly recognized as a legitimate ground for refugee protection, including by the United Nations High Commissioner for Refugees." Neve outlined the fact that conscientious objection is recognized under the Universal Declaration of Human Rights of 1948 and the International Covenant on Civil and Political Rights of 1976.[38] Canada's treatment of U.S. war resisters clearly gave short shrift to such recognition.

The draft dodger myth serves as the basis of the unfounded accusations launched against U.S. war resisters seeking sanctuary in Canada. While those U.S. soldiers seeking refugee status volunteered for service, the argument that draft resisters are more legitimate than deserters is irrelevant in light of international legal developments after 1945. In fact, with the end of compulsory conscription in the United States, volunteer soldiers in the military have even greater responsibility to follow their conscience and the dictates of international law in the face of the United States' imperial overstretch after the Vietnam War. These soldiers are, in essence, the new conscientious objectors who rely on international law instead of religious principles as the basis of their war resistance. However, U.S. military regulations do not consider applications for conscientious objector status from soldiers who are not opposed "to participation in war in any form."[39] Moreover, there is no regulation that forces soldiers' commanders to inform them of their right to conscientious objector status. Soldiers in the U.S. military have little recourse other than going AWOL.

In December 2013, the United Nations High Commissioner on Refugees (UNHCR) released long anticipated guidelines on military personnel claiming refugee status.[40] The guidelines bear directly on the cases of U.S. war resisters claiming refugee status in Canada because they do not start from the basis of those who are opposed "to participation in war in any form." In other words, these guidelines help clarify the options for soldiers who are not pacifists. For instance, the resisters who came to Canada between 2004 and 2008 argued in their refugee claims that they refused to participate in the war on Iraq because it was illegal under international law. The UNHCR states unequivocally that:

> Where an armed conflict is considered to be unlawful as a matter of international law [in violation of *jus ad bellum*], it is not necessary that the applicant be at risk of incurring individual criminal responsibility if he or she were to participate in the conflict in question, rather the applicant would need to establish that his or her objection is genuine, and that because of his or her objection, there is a risk of persecution. Individual responsibility for a crime of aggression only arises under international law for persons who were in a position of authority in the State in question. *Soldiers who enlisted prior to or during the conflict in question may also object as their knowledge of or views concerning the illegality of the use of force evolve.*[41]

While the UNHCR guidelines reaffirm the international laws on the use of armed force and the guidelines for refugee protection already in existence, the experience of U.S. war resisters with the Canadian Immigration and Refugee Board and the Federal Courts between 2004 and 2008 has been fraught with challenges to these international standards.

o o o

The December 2013 United Nations High Commissioner on Refugees' guidelines affirming that soldiers have a right to claim refugee status for refusing to participate in an illegal war should help put to rest the long struggle for U.S. war resisters seeking sanctuary in Canada. The fact that U.S. military personnel have been disproportionately punished for publicly refusing orders and that U.S. military prosecutors specifically argued that a strong message needed to be sent to the remaining war resisters in Canada should demonstrate unequivocally that these soldiers of conscience are being persecuted.

Various Canadian governments – both Liberal and Conservative – took the rare step of intervening in the refugee hearings to argue that U.S. war resisters do not face persecution in the United States because the war's legality is irrelevant to the question of whether there are enough state protections for the dissenting soldiers. Despite the Canadian government's position and the inability of a single war resister to secure refugee status, we must continue to insist that the war resisters are legitimate refugees and conscientious objectors in light of post-1945 developments in international law. To date, the Canadian government, the Immigration and Refugee Board, and the Federal Courts between 2004 and 2008 have failed war resisters. The struggle continues, however, as the War Resisters Support Campaign seeks the repeal of the discriminatory Operational Bulletin 202 and a parliamentary motion granting permanent residency status for these U.S. soldiers.

Springfield, New Brunswick, became decidedly less "friendly" in January 2009 when a dispute over the singing of "O Canada" at the local elementary school made national headlines. Photos by C. Gidney.

17

"There Is Nothing More Inclusive Than O Canada"

New Brunswick's Elementary School Anthem Debate and the Shadow of Afghanistan

MICHAEL DAWSON AND CATHERINE GIDNEY

IN JANUARY 2009, A CONTROVERSY erupted at Belleisle Elementary School in Springfield, New Brunswick, a small, rural town approximately sixty kilometres southeast of Fredericton.[1] The "Belleisle Brouhaha"[2] involved a dispute over the playing of the national anthem and produced what the *Globe and Mail* described as "a coast-to-coast fury of patriotic indignation."[3] The controversy subsided several months later but not without the resignation of the school principal, the provincial government scrambling to revise the *Education Act*, the criminal conviction of one parent for uttering threats, MPs offering nationalistic rhetorical flourishes in the House of Commons, and a flurry of radio call-in, online, and newspaper editorial debate.

The previous chapters in this collection highlight Canada's long and diverse history of war resistance. Among the many lessons they impart is the fact that opponents of war often faced hostility. Waging peace frequently meant steeling oneself in the face of insult, ridicule, and physical threats from a dominant culture that understood warfare to be necessary and, in some cases, desirable. In this chapter we explore Canada's contemporary orientation as a "warrior nation" by examining the political, cultural, and social significance of the Belleisle school anthem debate.[4] The chapter underscores how acts of war resistance can focus on seemingly prosaic and quotidian practices and demonstrates the very real consequences facing those who dare to challenge contemporary commonsense notions of Canadian patriotism – especially when Internet access and a 24-hour news cycle can be leveraged in invasive and harmful ways. While war resisters once faced white feather campaigns or stern lectures from judges determining their conscientious objection status, in 2009 those identified with a pacifist cause, or who criticized war policies, faced not only physical intimidation and public shaming on a local level but also the prospect of cyber bullying and a near total erosion of their privacy as media outlets transformed a local dispute into a national event.

We focus primarily upon the rhetoric that infused the debate, highlighting in particular the contested attitudes toward patriotism, minority rights, and understandings of freedom and democracy. More briefly, we examine the very real consequences of the dispute for the school community, educational administrators, and authorities. We argue that playing the Canadian national anthem is far from a benign and inclusive ritual. Indeed, controversy erupted in this community largely because the daily singing of the anthem, tied to a particular conservative and militaristic vision of the nation, clashed with the principal's desire to champion the individual rights of children and families who did not wish to participate in this communal practice. While there was no evidence to suggest that the children in question were recent immigrants, many opponents of the principal's position assumed otherwise and voiced their displeasure at the prospect of outsiders challenging an established practice of patriotic observance.

"At the End of A Bayonet": Political, Public, and Institutional Reaction to the Principal's Decision

The controversy at Belleisle Elementary School erupted after the principal, Eric Millett, altered the school's practice from broadcasting "O Canada" every day to having students sing the anthem once a month at school assemblies. He made the switch in September 2007 in order to accommodate two families who did not wish to have their children participate in the ritual.[5] Prior to the change, one child sat outside the classroom during the playing of the anthem.[6] While playing the anthem at assemblies and special events was more common in the francophone than anglophone system, even within Millett's own school district, at least one other elementary school, Macdonald Consolidated, followed that same practice.[7] The school's new anthem regimen might well have continued, unnoticed and unchallenged, but for the actions of Susan Boyd, whose two daughters attended the school. Having complained to the principal with no result, in January 2009 Boyd took her concerns to the media. She was motivated to see the daily singing of the national anthem reinstated after learning that one of her daughters felt the need to practise the anthem prior to a Canada Day performance in 2008 because she could not remember all of the words. For Boyd, the daily singing of the anthem was also an act of patriotism and a sign of respect for military servicemen and women, issues personally poignant to her due to the death of her nephew, Pte. David Greenslade, in Kandahar in April 2007.[8]

In light of Susan Boyd's complaint, the *Saint John Telegraph-Journal* approached Principal Millett for his side of the story. For privacy reasons, Millett would not delve into the specifics of the case. But he explained that he had made his decision on the basis of the need "to protect the minority rights as well as the majority rights"; that singing the anthem once a month would actually enhance students' patriotic experience; and that eliminating daily singing of the anthem would make the start of the school day more productive.[9]

With the media attuned to the issue, Boyd received the immediate and vociferous support of her MP, Conservative Greg Thompson, who was also the Federal Veteran Affairs Minister. "First and foremost," Thompson explained in a television interview, "this gentleman is a principal and he has an obligation not only to his students, but to the community.... I suggest he admit his mistake and restore the tradition."[10] Thompson's colleagues picked up the story the next day in the House of Commons, decrying what they described – inaccurately – as the banning of the anthem.[11]

The comments in the House fanned the flames of what was becoming a national story. The end of January witnessed a flurry of opinion pieces, letters to editors, and online commentary across the country. Much of the early media coverage of the controversy lambasted the principal for his decision.[12] Indeed, in a matter of days, both Millett and his superintendent, Zoë Watson, had received hundreds of irate e-mails and phone calls.[13] Just two weeks after the controversy broke, Millett noted that "I received probably over 2,000 e-mails, most of them hurling abuse at me, saying everything that I should be at the end of a bayonet, I should be shipped out of the country, I should be put on the front lines with the Taliban."[14] Several online critics upped the ante by circulating Millett's personal phone number and e-mail address. Millett also experienced direct confrontations with outraged parents. Bradley Howland, whose child attended Belleisle Elementary, met with Millett on January 31. During the meeting, Millett claimed, Howland boasted that if the principal's secretary had not been there he would have dragged Millett into the parking lot and beaten him senseless. Howland was later charged and ultimately found guilty of uttering threats.[15]

A contributing factor to the controversy may well have been Millett's previous, and highly public, peace activism. Millett had twice run for office as a federal Green Party candidate and in 2006 attended a community debate in St. Stephen, N.B. wearing what the *Telegraph-Journal* reported as "his nuke protestor get-up complete with white jump suit and gas mask." In addition to denouncing the refurbishment of the nearby Point Lepreau nuclear power plant, Millett criticized Stephen Harper's support for the U.S. invasion of Iraq by taunting his Conservative opponent – the same Greg Thompson who would be so quick to vociferously support Susan Boyd's campaign – with "a list of potential jobs his kids could get in Iraq and a box of garbage bags ... for their body parts."[16] A *National Post* report in the midst of the controversy suggested that Millett's activism had indeed factored into the public's response. "Some critics" had "questioned whether the principal's decision was ideological," the newspaper reported, noting that the Green Party's website described him as "actively involved in the peace movement."[17] Global News emphasized that Millett was "on record as opposing the war in Afghanistan" – "a touchy subject," reporter Ross Lord added.[18]

Not long after going to the media, Boyd started an online petition to reinstate the daily singing of the anthem and to secure legislation mandating the practice throughout the province. Education Minister Kelly Lamrock quickly took up Boyd's cause. He called upon school superintendents to ensure that students were singing the anthem throughout New Brunswick.[19] Two days later Superintendent Watson overruled Millett's decision and reinstated daily singing of the anthem at the school.[20]

By February 4, Millett had taken medical leave. The face-to-face confrontation with the parent, along with the general level of anger in the community, led the principal to request police protection at the school door – a request denied by the superintendent. Millett's leave then necessitated removing vice-principal Heather Wilson from her classroom so that she could attend to the principal's duties.[21] Millett's girlfriend, who taught French at the school, also took leave from the classroom.[22] Kelly Cooper, vice-chair of the school's Parent School Support Committee noted, "In one week, with one issue, we are left today with a school without a principal to lead it, and a community divided."[23]

In the months after the initial controversy, Education Minister Lamrock endeavoured to institute regulations mandating the singing of "O Canada." At the time, Education Department policy simply stated "A teacher *may* provide for the singing of the national anthem at the beginning of each day."[24] While the revised regulations mandated daily broadcasting of the anthem, they empowered District Education Councils –

the New Brunswick equivalent of school boards – to release a principal from the anthem-playing obligation so long as he or she proposed "another activity that promotes the spirit of patriotism."[25] Moreover, pupils or their parents could apply for student exemptions from both the anthem and the alternative patriotic activity. Many of the province's schools, particularly those in the francophone system, immediately began requesting exemptions.[26] The Education Department now championed daily anthem singing more fully than before, and the onus was now more squarely on principals and parents to justify student exemptions.

Militarism and Majority Rule: The Contested Meanings of Politicized Patriotism

The swift response from media outlets, school administrators, and politicians underscores the fact that this local controversy clearly touched a nerve. But on what grounds did observers feel obliged to respond and how did the frequency with which the anthem was sung in a small, rural school come to be imbued with such meaning? Two interrelated issues repeatedly structured the debate: respect for Canada's military past and present, and the necessity of protecting majority interests from minority rights.

From the start of the controversy, proponents of the daily singing of the anthem linked that practice to patriotism, which was, in turn, linked to respect and support for military servicemen and women. The *Fredericton Daily Gleaner* reported that Susan Boyd believed that the anthem was "a key part of children's knowledge of the country's history" that "honours soldiers killed on duty." "If our troops hadn't died for our country," she argued, "we wouldn't be discussing this. We wouldn't be singing a national anthem because our country wouldn't be free."[27] Boyd's logic was wobbly, of course. Historically, nations as diverse as the Soviet Union and South Africa have boasted national anthems while strictly limiting personal freedoms. But her sentiment that the singing of the anthem was an effective and appropriate way of paying tribute to military personnel enjoyed a good deal of support. "We have soldiers in Afghanistan on a continuous basis rotating in and out and the least we can do is show pride for our country and our flag," opined Keith Ashfield, Conservative MP for Fredericton.[28] The Dominion Institute released a forceful statement very much in the same vein. "Singing the national anthem is an important way of showing our pride in our country," explained the organization's executive director, Marc Chalifoux. "We believe that our schools are an ideal place to help instill this pride in the next generation of citizens." For the Institute, that pride was directly connected to military service. Indeed, the Institute offered to "work with the school in order to send a delegation of Canadian veterans to talk with the principal and staff about the importance of the national anthem and what it means to Canadian military service men and women." A Dominion Institute news release offered a concrete example of the kind of didactic voice Belleisle students could expect to hear:

> Sid Gladstone is an Air Force veteran of the Second World War who speaks with thousands of young people each year as part of the Memory Project, Canada's largest speakers' bureau. "As a veteran, I believe it is important that every young person across Canada recognize what a privilege it is to live in this country," said Mr. Gladstone. "Reciting the national anthem is the least we can do to honour the service and sacrifice of our soldiers, both young and old."[29]

Many letters and commentaries similarly connected singing the anthem with support and respect for past and current servicemen and women.[30]

The pairing of the anthem with patriotism and loyalty overlapped with an attitude of conformity to majority rule. This was certainly clear in the comments made by New Brunswick Conservative MPs in the House of Commons. Mike Allen, MP for Tobique-Mactaquac, for example, offered the following lament:

> This is political correctness run wild. There is nothing more inclusive than O Canada. It is a song that belongs to each and every Canadian. The singing of O Canada is an expression of our collective pride in being citizens of one of the most prosperous and peaceful nations the world has ever known. I hope that we can come together to convince the principal to reverse his decision and give O Canada back to the students in his school. This will demonstrate the importance of our national anthem as a symbol of our respect for this great country and the people who helped to build it.[31]

Keith Ashfield reiterated those sentiments. "Canada is an inclusive country and we take tremendous pride in our national anthem," he argued. "It is a song that is sung from coast to coast and it unites us as Canadians." Tilly O'Neill-Gordon, the Conservative MP for Miramichi, employed a more autobiographical trope while reinforcing her colleagues' position:

> Mr. Speaker, as everyone knows, I am a retired teacher. One of the most important moments of each day was watching my students rise every morning for the singing of O Canada. Seeing our future generations show pride in their country means a lot to me. I was very saddened to

> hear that the principal of a New Brunswick school has banned the singing of O Canada because he apparently believes it is not inclusive enough.[32]

Setting aside the occasional inaccuracy – the principal did not "ban" the anthem but, instead, reduced the frequency with which students were expected to sing it – the rhetoric of the three Conservative MPs is instructive not only for its consistency but for its emphasis on the notion that political correctness in the name of minority rights was preventing children from participating in a nationally inclusive ritual.

While the politicians were forceful in their condemnation of the principal's decision, they were astute enough to express these views in the politically correct language expected of a parliamentarian. Other critics of the principal were not nearly so restrained. Indeed, letters to newspaper editorial departments seethed with outrage. Some suggested that if the principal or the families in question opposed the singing of the anthem they could leave the country.[33] Keith Tindale of Shediac, N.B., questioned the principal's manhood. "It is time that we the silent majority stood-up, spoke-up and told the highly vocal minority groups to shut-up!" he wrote in a letter to the *Times & Transcript*. "And if that namby-pamby school principal hasn't got the intestinal fortitude to stand up to a small group of malcontents and speak out for what is best for the majority of his students, then maybe it is time for the school board to find a replacement!"[34] An editorial in the *Calgary Herald* offered similar advice:

> Those families who don't want their children "exposed to" the national anthem of the country in which they are citizens can pack their bags for elsewhere. Millions of people living lives of utter hopelessness under tin-pot Third World regimes would happily trade places with these families of "different beliefs" in a minute and they'd be proud to have their children sing the anthem of a country that abounds with the richness of freedom and democracy.

The principal's "argument was that he had to respect the minority as well as the majority," the newspaper lamented. "The minority, however, did not deserve respect in this instance," it argued. "In a democracy, the majority rules – and the majority of Canadians are upset about this incident, as witnessed by the outrage expressed by groups on MySpace and Facebook and comments posted online to news stories."[35] Moreover, some online commentary very specifically targeted immigrants. As one participant stated, "We should all be supporting each other by banding together, to keep our Canadian Traditions [sic] and beliefs. If people have their own beliefs and religions fine, but don't come to Canada and try to take away ours!!"[36]

While such sentiments reverberated widely, they did not go unchallenged. T.J. Lightfoot, a young First Nations woman from New Brunswick, boldly suggested that the anthem should be taught at home and not played in schools at all. "I believe this is all stolen land," she explained in reference to wars and episodes of imperial expansion that are *not* generally reflected in Remembrance Day ceremonies. "When you present children with the idea of Canada," she explained, "you aren't acknowledging the proper history or that this land was taken from First Nations people."[37] Judith Doyle, a sociology professor at Mount Allison University, expressed concerns about unrestrained expressions of national identity and argued that the anthem should be sung only on special occasions. Daily singing, she suggested, "devalues the national anthem and at the same time . . . raises a reactionary type of nationalism where you just have to sing the song and love it, and you can't criticize the country and you can't be critical or thoughtful about your nationalism." She also offered a comparative perspective by noting that at one time singing the song "half-heartedly in a classroom with someone just playing it recorded over the PA system" was considered disrespectful.[38] One student at Montgomery Street Elementary School in Fredericton reiterated Millett's position that daily singing of the anthem took time away from the start of the school day.[39]

Observers from outside New Brunswick also took issue with the call to reinstate daily playing of the anthem. Michael Payton of the Canadian Secular Alliance staunchly defended Principal Millett's decision. "I love our national anthem," he emphasized. "But for those who are non-religious, the mention of God gives them the feeling that they are less Canadian, that they are not part of the country."[40] For Payton, mandatory singing of the anthem was problematic precisely because the lyrics were not inclusive. One of the more outspoken critics of the federal government's response to the situation was retired history professor Michael Bliss, who joined with others in contrasting the political furor over the national anthem at a single elementary school to politicians' silence in the face of a report critical of the lack of Canadian history courses in the schools. Bliss suggested that the Conservative MPs' campaign against the principal's decision was "the worst kind of token symbolism." "The real problem is curricular content," he argued, "not getting up and forcing reluctant kids to mouth some words every morning. To take that seriously – as opposed to the much greater issue of the solid education of students – is to get your priorities all wrong."[41]

Singing, Symbolism, and Citizenship

The calls for Belleisle Elementary School to provide opportunities for children to demonstrate patriotic sentiment, of course, have tangible historical precedents. Historians have illuminated the ways in which, in the late nineteenth century and through much of the first half of the twentieth century, schools aimed to instil a particular type of citizenship marked by duty to the nation, including military service. Indeed, schools included a variety of militaristic elements such as cadet training, the celebration of Empire Day, and a curriculum that often glorified war.[42] However, the anthem itself, a staple of classroom experiences for many (but not all!) children, has not been the subject of much study.[43]

At a basic level, the purpose of anthems is to illustrate loyalty and devotion to one's nation. Yet this happens in a very particular way. As American musicologist Carlos Abril explains, "The meaning of an anthem – or any other musical work – does not reside within the work alone; its meaning also exists within a sociocultural field of human actions and perceptions."[44] Anthems appear to be unifying because people join in the singing together, and thus contribute to a shared experience. This is reinforced by the lyrics, which in the Canadian context include collective references such as "*Our* home" and "*we* stand." The music can evoke an emotional reaction – a stirring of the heart for one's homeland that is not bound to the period in which it was created.[45] In this way, an anthem acts as a unifying and timeless symbol denoting loyalty and patriotism to one's country.

Musicologists in the United States have commented on the lack of music education accompanying the singing of the American anthem. We tend to take anthems for granted, they note, and in schools they are often sung without reflection. Anthems, like all rituals or cultural artifacts, are created within a particular historical moment, yet children are rarely taught to analyze them as texts or encouraged to discuss them as historical documents. For example, there is little knowledge, Abril argues, that *The Star Spangled Banner* was first "adopted as a symbol for the Union during the Civil War" and that John Philip Sousa and others actively opposed its adoption in 1931 as the official U.S. anthem in part because they saw it as a symbol of division.[46] According to sociologist Joel Westheimer, unreflective regular singing of the anthem, or reciting the Pledge of Allegiance, encourages an authoritarian patriotism rather than a democratic form based on critical thinking and reflection.[47] Could the same not be said of educational regimes that command children to recite "O Canada" – or wait patiently in the hallway while their friends do so?

Millett was certainly not the first Canadian teacher to be denounced for failing to hold an anthem in high enough regard. In 1918, Toronto schoolteacher Freda Held was strong-armed into resigning after some members of the school board, apparently acting on lunchroom gossip concerning a discussion of war profiteering, accused her of disloyalty to the Crown. Procedural improprieties and lack of evidence resulted in almost six months of ongoing investigations and public furor over the issue. In the process, Held's critics highlighted her lack of patriotism by noting her concerns with the second verse of "God Save the King." Held made it a practice to have her students recite "the Golden Rule" – do unto others as you would have them do unto you – prior to singing the second verse of the anthem, which read,

> Oh, Lord, our God, arise
> Scatter his enemies
> And make them fall
> Confound their politics
> Frustrate their knavish tricks
> On Thee our hopes we fix
> God Save us all.

Moreover, on religious grounds she was known not to sing the verse at gatherings off school grounds.[48]

Some school trustees took this as disloyalty. But some members of the public defended Held's actions. A.B. Sissons, Professor at Victoria College, was keen to note that Held was not alone in her discomfort with the verse's militaristic tone. He explained in the *Toronto Telegram* that "an influential section of the Anglican Synod was opposed to its use even in war time."[49] Still, the Board refused to rescind Held's resignation. Moreover, in 1921 it changed its by-laws regarding teachers' duties. Whereas a 1904 by-law read "All teachers shall . . . refrain from the discussion in the schools of questions purely political or ecclesiastical" the Board now added the clause "and from expression anywhere opinions adverse to British Institutions or sentiments disloyal to the Crown."[50]

Since the 1950s English-speaking Canada has reconceptualized its notions of citizenship. It has moved away from a British world view and embraced a more inclusive, "civic" national identity – one that played down earlier militaristic visions of the country's past, present, and future.[51] However, events since September 11, 2001 have resulted in a North American political climate more favourable to linking national loyalty with military service. This is particularly true in the United States where in the months following the 9/11 attacks various state legislatures created new, or re-affirmed old, bills that encouraged or enforced patriotic exercises in schools.[52] While this form of patriotism was less pronounced in Canada, cries to "support our troops" proliferated dramatically. As Ian McKay and Jamie Swift note, this campaign boasted a concerted effort to have Canadians "wear special red shirts with yellow-ribbon logos as a gesture of support for the troops."[53] A more successful initiative featured yellow-ribbon decals and signs in store windows and on vehicle bumpers, including those operated by civic authorities such as fire fighters, police officers, and paramedics. "To oppose the support-our-troops loyalty display was politically risky," they note, "making the yellow-ribbon campaign useful in attempts to silence opposition to the war."[54]

As Canada took on a prominent military role in Afghanistan, businesses in communities around Base Gagetown, located a short drive from Belleisle Elementary, began to prominently display those yellow ribbons. Moreover, it was not unheard of for daycares in the provincial capital, Fredericton, to promote "wear red" days to support the troops or to invite military personnel to talk to children about Remembrance Day. In one such case a serviceman handed out souvenir bracelets to four-year-olds on which, unbeknownst to the preschool, the phone number for the local recruitment office was prominently displayed.

It was in this climate that Susan Boyd's supporters not only called for the daily singing of the anthem but also directly linked it to support and respect for the troops. They did so amid a political culture that ostensibly championed the idea that educational institutions ought to stand apart from politics. As the Held case suggests, there are longstanding expectations that educators be politically neutral. Underlying that expectation, critics argue, is an inference that neutrality means educators should adopt attitudes favourable toward the political status quo.[55] Hence, the Toronto Board of Education's 1921 proscription on denouncing British institutions. In many respects, Millett found himself caught between community standards that equated anthem singing with national loyalty and provincial educational policy that recognized diversity and individual rights.[56]

Since the 1970s, Canadian school curricula and regulations have increasingly been shaped by a multicultural framework.[57] Moreover, the Charter of Rights has, in many ways, prioritized individual over community rights. While the vision represented by Boyd and her supporters was loudest in public discourse, it frequently met what might be termed "passive resistance" within the school system itself. While avoiding the vitriol of the debate, many school administrators gave voice to their positions by immediately requesting exemptions from the daily singing for their schools. This debate thus reminds us that while Canadian society has become more multicultural and generally accepting of minority rights, visions of a "traditional" Canada continue to flare up when core values are perceived to be in danger.

○ ○ ○

The Belleisle controversy demonstrates that in Canada today the national anthem exists within a symbolic web of vague concepts and strong sentiments about Canadian values: freedom, democracy, loyalty, patriotism. In a conservative, rural, anglophone, and relatively ethnically homogeneous community located close to a major Canadian military base, rituals such as the anthem continue to evoke historic ties to Canada's military tradition and support for the idea of military duty as the ultimate expression of national loyalty. It is a vision of Canadian society held strongly by many others across Canada, as illustrated by the outpouring of support for the demands to reinstitute the daily singing of the anthem. Principal Millett himself attempted to disentangle the popular symbolic meaning of the anthem from the more tangible and structural elements of Canada's institutions and identity. "As Canadians we must realize that it is not our anthem or our flag that makes this country what it is. Every country in the world has a flag and an anthem," he explained. "It's the underlying laws and values and rules and practices and democratic institutions that guide a country that are important."[58] That he found it so difficult to articulate this vision successfully in 2009 highlights ongoing tensions between progressive rights-based discourses and more conservative pro-military ones.

The controversy also highlights the precarious nature of an educator's position in contemporary Canada. Principal Millett's vision of the treatment of children clearly differed from what he encountered in the school system. Rather than see children excluded from daily classroom activities, visibly cast as outsiders, he chose to eliminate the daily singing of the anthem. His decision did not contravene provincial education policy. He was well within his mandate and indeed in line with practices in other school districts. Those who perceived Millett's action as unpatriotic could be quick to denounce his (sometimes idiosyncratic) political activities and peace activism, indirectly reinforcing the notion that educators ought to be symbols of community propriety – and thus defer to the will of the majority. As a result, even though the decision was within his jurisdiction as principal, the broader cultural context of the community and the response of education authorities rendered his position untenable.

We should also note that national anthems, like official celebrations and remembrances, are one of the earliest and most frequent ways children are taught about national loyalty. And yet in the Canadian context there are many unanswered questions about how they are implemented within the education system. When did anthems become part of the school day and in the Canadian context switch from "God Save the Queen" to "O Canada?" How did the historical practice of anthem singing differ from the way it was described in school regulations? How do, and have, children understood the practice? What do they learn? How often is the anthem part of music education rather than simply a patriotic ritual? These questions and more highlight the need for further research. But what we can conclude is that far from being innocuous, or "inclusive," the anthem sparks a range of feeling and contested values and ideals about Canadian citizenship.

Writing about the importance of teaching a reflective national history, Ken Osborne argues that "dialogue and discussion are the essence of democracy and, if we are serious about educating citizens, this is what we must prepare students to engage in."[59] Yet the debate around the anthem reflected an authoritarian form of patriotism that refused to accept any questioning of the place or practice of singing the anthem. The nastiness of the debate led one parent to ask, "Is this our Canada, one where we become hateful and threatening toward other people who have a difference of opinion?"[60] The many case studies explored in this volume indicate that Canadians have been grappling with this question for some time. The Belleisle school anthem controversy suggests that on the issue of patriotism and military duty the answer, unfortunately, continues to be "Yes."

Notes

Introduction

1 J.L. Granatstein, "No Flanders Fields? Canadians, War, and Remembrance," *Who Killed Canadian History* (Toronto: HarperCollins, 1988), 111–35; J.L. Granatstein et al., "To Vimy Ridge and Back," *Nation: Canada Since Confederation* (Toronto: McGraw-Hill Ryerson, 1990), 167–33; Béatrice Richard, "La Mémoire des guerres au Québec: Un espace de résistance?" *Canadian Issues/Thèmes canadiens* (Winter 2004): 17–20. On the contested representations of the Second World War see David Bercuson and S.F. Wise, *The Valour and the Horror Revisited* (Montreal/Kingston: McGill-Queen's University Press, 1994). On the centrality of war and the military to Canadian history, see Desmond Morton, *A Military History of Canada* (Toronto: McClelland & Stewart, 2007).

2 Ian McKay and Jamie Swift, *Warrior Nation: Rebranding Canada in an Age of Anxiety* (Toronto: Between the Lines, 2012); Esyllt Jones and Adele Perry, eds., *People's Citizenship Guide: A Response to Conservative Canada* (Winnipeg: ARP, 2011); Yves Frenette, "Conscripting Canada's Past: The Harper Government and the Politics of Memory," *Canadian Journal of History* 49, no. 1 (2014): 50–65. See also Steven Chase, "Ottawa Spends More on Military History Amid Criticism Over Support for Veterans," *Globe and Mail*, June 16, 2014, accessed July 15, 2014. www.theglobeandmail.com/news/politics/ottawa-commemorates-military-history-while-under-fire-for-veteran-support/article19176795/. Chase writes that the federal government has "earmarked more than $83-million" over the rest of the decade to "commemorate" various aspects of Canadian military history.

3 Frenette, "Conscripting Canada's Past"; "Forum: History Under Harper," *Labour/Le travail* 73 (Spring 2014): 195–237. For just a few examples of this discussion, see Jocelyn Létourneau, "Multiculturalism Died, and Harper Replaced it with 'Royalization,'" *Globe and Mail*, July 1, 2013; David Akin, "Harper Hit for History Rewrite," *Toronto Sun*, May 20, 2014; Christopher Moore, "Hot History: Conscripting Canada's Past Now Online," blogpost, *Christopher Moore's History News*, May 27, 2014; John Geddes, "How Stephen Harper is Rewriting History," *Maclean's*, July 29, 2013; Emmett Macfarlane, "Why Harper's Meddling with Canadian History Might Not be All Bad," *Globe and Mail*, May 6, 2013. See also Christopher Moore, "Maclean's: What if They Did the First World War Over, and Nobody Came?" blogpost, *Christopher Moore's History News*, July 30, 2014; Andrew Cohen, "Hard Truths about Canada in the First World War," *Ottawa Citizen*, July 29, 2014.

4 As Conrad Stoesz notes in his contribution to this volume, claiming conscientious objector status was reserved for members of the historic peace churches until the Second World War and the introduction of noncombatant service. On pacifism in Canada, see Thomas Socknat, *Witness Against War: Pacifism in Canada, 1900–1945* (Toronto: University of Toronto Press, 1987); Socknat, "Conscientious Objectors in the Context of Canadian Peace Movements," *Journal of Mennonite Studies* 25 (January 2007): 62–74; Marlene Epp, *Mennonite Women in Canada: A History* (Winnipeg: University of Manitoba Press, 2008); James Penton, "Jehovah's Witnesses and the Second World War: Resistance to Militarism and to Alternative Service," *Journal of Mennonite Studies* 25 (January 2007): 75–88. See numerous articles on religious conscience, war, and peace in the *Journal of Mennonite Studies*. Many North American feminists championed the First World War effort because politicians promised female suffrage in return for war support, while many socialists in the interwar peace movement supported military intervention against fascism.

5 Amy J. Shaw, *Crisis of Conscience: Conscientious Objection in Canada During the First World War* (Vancouver: UBC Press, 2009); Marlene Epp, "Heroes or Yellow-bellies? Masculinity and the Conscientious Objector," *Journal of Mennonite Studies* 17 (1999): 107–17; Socknat, *Witness Against War*; Mark Moss, *Manliness and Militarism: Educating Young Boys in Ontario for War* (Don Mills: Oxford, 2001). On entitlement and war service, see Lara Campbell, "'We Who Have Wallowed in the Mud of Flanders': First World War Veterans, Unemployment and the Development of Social Welfare in Canada, 1929–1939," *Journal of the Canadian Historical Association* 11, no. 1 (2000): 125–49; Desmond Morton and Glenn Wright, *Winning the Second Battle: Canadian Veterans and the Return to Civilian Life, 1915–1930* (Toronto: University of Toronto Press, 1987); James W. St.G. Walker, "Race and Recruitment in WWI: Enlistment of Visible Minorities in the Canadian Expeditionary Force," *Canadian Historical Review* 70, no. 1 (1989): 1–26; Desmond Morton, "The Canadian Veterans' Heritage from the Great War," in *The Veterans Charter and Post-World War II Canada*, ed. Peter Neary and J.L Granatstein (Montreal/Kingston: McGill-Queen's University Press, 1998), 15–31.

6 Robert Talbot, "'It Would Be Best to Leave Us 'Alone': First Nations Responses to the Canadian War Effort, 1914–1918," *Journal of Canadian Studies* 45, no. 1 (Winter 2011): 90–121. Socialist parties and organized labour in Canada were often split on support for the war effort during the First World War. Many organizations argued that war benefited the capitalist classes, divided the working class, harmed women and children, and forced workers and farmers to bear the greatest costs of wartime sacrifice. But such organizations struggled to retain this antiwar critique when the nation-state was actually at war. The Trades and Labour Congress, for example, despite resistance from mainly western locals, shifted from an antiwar and anti-conscription stance to ultimately supporting conscription. And many socialists who had been active in the interwar peace movement publicly pressed for military action against fascism, most famously in the Spanish Civil War. Linda Kealey, *Enlisting Women for the Cause: Women, Labour, and the Left in Canada* (Toronto: University of Toronto Press, 1998); Socknat, *Witness Against War*; A. Ross McCormack, *Reformers, Rebels, and Revolutionaries: The Western Canadian Radical Movement, 1899–1919* (Toronto: University of Toronto Press, 1977).

7 J.L. Granatstein and J.M. Hitsman, *Broken Promises: A History of Conscription in Canada* (Toronto: Copp Clark Pitman, 1985); Béatrice Richard, "Henri Bourassa and Conscription: Traitor or Saviour?" *Canadian Military Journal* 7, no. 4 (2006): 75–83; Susan Mann Trofimenkoff, "Thérèse Casgrain and the CCF in Quebec," in *Beyond the Vote: Canadian Women and Politics*, ed. Linda Kealey and Joan Sangster (Toronto: University of Toronto Press, 1989), 139–68; Martin Auger, "On the Brink of Civil War: The Canadian Government and the Suppression of the 1918 Quebec Easter Riots," *Canadian Historical Review* 89, no. 4 (2008): 503–40; Patrick Bouvier, *Déserters et insoumis: Les Canadiens-français et la justice militaire (1914–1918)* (Outremon: Athéna Éditions, 2003).

8 Socknat, *Witness Against War*; Barbara Roberts, "Women's Peace Activism in Canada," in Kealey and Sangster, eds., *Beyond the Vote*.

9 Barbara Roberts, "Why Do Women Do Nothing to End the War? Canadian Feminist-Pacifists and the Great War" (Ottawa: Canadian Research Institute for the Advancement of Women, 1985); Roberts, "Women's Peace Activism"; Kealey, *Enlisting Women for the Cause*; Irene Howard, *The Struggle for Social Justice in British Columbia: Helena Gutteridge, the Unknown Reformer* (Vancouver: UBC Press, 1992). See also Frances Early, *A World Without War: How U.S. Feminists and Pacifists Resisted World War I* (Syracuse: Syracuse University Press, 1997). Note that the Canadian WILPF branch was originally the Women's International Congress for a Permanent Peace. Roberts, "Why Do Women," 3.

10 Kenneth McNaught, "J.S. Woodsworth and War," in *Challenge to Mars: Essays on Pacifism from 1918–1945*, ed. Peter Brock and Thomas Socknat (Toronto: University of Toronto Press, 1999), 186–98; McNaught, *J.S. Woodsworth* (Don Mills: Fitzhenry and Whiteside,

1980); Allen Mills, *Fool for Christ: The Political Thought of J.S. Woodsworth* (Toronto: University of Toronto Press, 1991).

11 The Combined Universities Campaign for Nuclear Disarmament (CUCND) was formed in 1959 in Montreal to lobby against Canadian participation in the nuclear arms race. Dimitri Roussopoulos, "Canada: 1968 and the New Left," www.ghi-dc.org/files/publications/ bu_supp/supp006/bus6_039.pdf; Bryan Palmer, *Canada's 1960s: The Ironies of Identity in a Rebellious Era* (Toronto: University of Toronto Press, 2009). The Canadian Peace Congress, founded in 1948 by United Church minister James Endicott, for example, enjoyed support for its Ban-the Bomb campaign but was hampered by Endicott's pro-Mao stance, allowing the state to condemn it as pro-Soviet and leading to increased surveillance of its leaders throughout the 1960s. Victor Huard, "The Canadian Peace Congress and the Challenge to Postwar Consensus, 1948–1953," *Peace and Change* 19, no. 1 (January 1994): 25–49. Examples of other organizations in this era include the Canadian Committee for the Control of Radiation Hazards, the Canadian Campaign for Nuclear Disarmament, and the Canadian Peace Research Institute. On state surveillance, see Steve Hewitt, "'Information Believed True': RCMP Security Intelligence Activities on Canadian University Campuses and the Controversy Surrounding Them, 1961–1971," *Canadian Historical Review* 81, no. 2 (June 2000), 191–228; Reginald Whitaker and Gary Marcuse, *Cold War Canada: The Making of a National Insecurity State, 1945–1957* (Toronto: University of Toronto Press, 1996).

12 Members of VOW were mainly middle-class and mostly white, many with connections to government officials, with strong English- and French-Canadian participation. The historical accounts, biographies, and autobiographies of key players, such as Kay Macpherson, Thérèse Casgrain, Ursula Franklin, and Muriel Duckworth, have added a great deal to our historical knowledge of women's political activism in this period. See Frances Early, "Re-imaging War: The Voice of Women, the Canadian Aid for Vietnam Civilians, and the Knitting Project for Vietnamese Children, 1966–1976," *Peace and Change* 34, no. 2 (April 2009): 148–63; Early, "'A Grandly Subversive Time': The Halifax Branch of the Voice of Women," in *Mothers of the Municipality: Women, Work, and Social Policy in Post-1945 Halifax*, ed. Judith Fingard and Janet Guildford (Toronto: University of Toronto Press, 2005), 253–80; *Voice of Women: The First 30 Years*, directed by Margo Pineau and Cathy Reeves (Toronto: Full Frame Film and Video, 1992); Amy Swerdlow, *Women Strike for Peace: Traditional Motherhood and Radical Politics in the 1960s* (Chicago: University of Chicago Press, 1983); Susan Mann Trofimenkoff, "Thérèse Casgrain and the CCF in Quebec," in Kealey and Sangster, eds., *Beyond the Vote*; Kay Macpherson, *When in Doubt, Do Both: The Times of My Life* (Toronto: University of Toronto Press, 1994); Marion Douglas Kerans, *Muriel Duckworth: A Very Active Pacifist* (Halifax: Fernwood, 1996).

13 See Bruce Douville's chapter in this collection; Bryan Palmer, *Canada's 1960s*, 256–57; Simonne Monet-Chartrand, *Les Québécoises et le movement pacifiste (1939–1967)* (Montreal: Les Éditions Écosociété, 1993). Marie Hammond-Callaghan, "Bombings, Burning and Borders: Remembering Women's Peace Groups under Internment," *Canadian Journal of Irish Studies* 32, no. 1 (Spring 2006): 32–45. On the intersection of social movements in 1960s Montreal, see Sean Mills, *The Empire Within: Postcolonial Thought and Political Activism in Sixties Montreal* (Montreal/Kingston: McGill-Queen's University Press, 2010).

14 See Ian McKay's chapter in this volume; Brian Thorne, "Peace is the Concern of Every Mother: Communist and Social Democratic Women's Antiwar Activism in British Columbia, 1948–1950," *Peace and Change* 35, no. 4 (October 2010): 626–57; Tarah Brookfield, *Cold War Comforts: Canadian Women, Child Safety, and Global Insecurity* (Waterloo: Wilfrid Laurier University Press, 2012).

15 There is no easy correlation of either womanhood or feminism with an explicitly antiwar perspective. Women in the white feather campaigns during the First World War shamed men who were not fulfilling their masculine "duty" to the nation-state. And many first-

wave feminists championed that war effort because male politicians increasingly linked it to suffrage rights. Feminist theorists still debate the extent to which women have a differing perspective on issues of war and peace. Does their position as potential victims (often of wartime sexual violence) or as mothers facing the loss of husbands and sons mean that women have the ability to more cogently critique the state's position on war? Or are women, on the basis of their race, ethnicity, or nationality, just as likely to support the war effort using the rhetoric of protection of home and family? Many have critiqued maternal feminist peace politics as veering far too closely toward a biological essentialism reifying women's "inherent" peacefulness vs. men's militaristic aggression. On these issues, see Frances Early, "Feminism's Influence on Peace History," *Atlantis* 25, no. 1 (Fall-Winter 2000): 3–10; Jean Bethke Elshtain, *Women and War* (New York: Basic Books, 1987); Cynthia Enloe, *Does Khaki Become You? The Militarization of Women's Lives* (Boston: South End Press, 1983); Sara Ruddick, *Maternal Thinking: Toward a Politics of Peace* (Boston: Beacon Press, 1989); Carolyn Strange, "Mothers on the March: Maternalism in Women's Protest for Peace in North America and Western Europe, 1900–1985," in *Women and Social Protest*, ed. Guida West and Rhoda Lois Blumberg (New York: Oxford University Press, 1990), 209–24; Lois Ann Lorentzen and Jennifer Turpin, *The Women and War Reader* (New York: NYU Press, 1988).

16 Victor Levant, *Quiet Complicity: Canadian Involvement in the Vietnam War*; Brookfield in this collection; Jessica Squires, *Building Sanctuary: The Movement to Support Vietnam War Resisters in Canada, 1965–73* (Vancouver: UBC Press, 2013); David S. Churchill, "An Ambiguous Welcome: Vietnam Draft Resistance, the Canadian State, and Cold War Containment," *Social History/Histoire sociale* 27, no. 73 (2004): 1–26; Jay Young, "Defining a Community in Exile: Vietnam War Resister Communication and Identity in *AMEX*, 1968–1973," *Social History/Histoire sociale* 44, no. 87 (May 2011): 115–46.

17 Mark Leeming, "The Creation of Radicalism: Anti-Nuclear Activism in Nova Scotia, c.1972–1979," *Canadian Historical Review* 95, no. 2 (2014): 217–41; Steve Breyman, "Were the 1980s' Anti-Nuclear Weapons Movements New Social Movements?" *Peace and Change* 22, no. 3 (July 1997): 303–29; Mark Andrew Eaton, "Canadians, Nuclear Weapons, and the Cold War Security Dilemma" (PhD diss., University of Waterloo, 2007). Project Ploughshares was initially formed in 1976 as a coalition of churches (mainly Quaker and Mennonite) and development groups to study, lobby, and advocate for disarmament. Jacquetta Newman, "Surviving the Cold War: Project Ploughshares in the 1990s," *Peace Research* 31, no. 4 (November 1999): 3–4.

18 In February 2003 there were approximately 150,000–200,000 protesters in Montreal, 20,000–30,000 each in Vancouver and Toronto, 500,000 in New York City, and close to 2 million in London, U.K. Brendon O'Connor and Srdjan Vucetic, "Another Mars-Venus Divide: Why Australia said 'Yes' and Canada said 'Non' to Involvement in the 2003 Iraq War," *Australian Journal of International Affairs* 64, no. 5 (November 2010): 526–48. Scholars have argued about whether the reluctance of French-Canadians to participate in the world wars has shaped attitudes toward war in present-day Quebec. On the differing role of war in the French- and English-Canadian imaginaries, especially the battles of Vimy and Dieppe, see Richard, "La Mémoire des guerres." On the relationship between war, national identity, and the anti-Iraq movement in Quebec, see Jocelyn Létourneau, "Topique du conflit guerrier dans l'imaginaire et l'identitaire franco-québécois: argumentation exploratoire," *Canadian Issues/Thèmes canadiens* (Winter 2004): 29–32. On deconstructing the differences between Quebec and English Canada regarding foreign policy and international military interventions, see Stéphane Roussel and Jean-Christophe Boucher, "The Myth of the Pacific Society: Quebec's Contemporary Strategic Culture," *American Review of Canadian Studies* 38, no. 2 (2008): 165–87; Justin Massie, Jean-Christophe Boucher, and Stéphane Roussel, "Hijacking a Policy? Assessing Quebec's 'Undue' Influence on Canada's Afghan Policy," *American Review of Canadian Studies* 40, no. 2 (June 2010): 259–75.

19 Jerome Klassen and Greg Albo, *Empire's Ally: Canada and the War in Afghanistan* (Toronto: University of Toronto Press, 2013); Sherene Razack, *Dark Threats and White Knights: The Somalia Affair, Peacekeeping, and the New Imperialism* (Toronto: University of Toronto Press, 2004); Yasmin Jiwani, "Gendering Terror Post-9/11," in *Discourses of Denial: Mediations of Race, Gender, and Violence* (Vancouver: UBC Press, 2006), 177–201; Sunera Thobani, "White Innocence, Western Supremacy: The Role of Western Feminism in the 'War on Terror,'" in *States of Race: Critical Race Feminism for the 21st Century*, ed. Sunera Thobani, Sherene H. Razack, and Malinda S. Smith (Toronto: Between the Lines, 2010), 127–46.

20 Amy Shaw, *Crisis of Conscience*; Peter Brock, "Accounting for Difference: The Problem of Pacifism in Early Upper Canada," *Ontario History* 90, no. 1 (May 1998): 19–30; Marlene Epp, "Alternative Service and Alternative Gender Roles: Conscientious Objectors in BC during WWII," *BC Studies* 105–6 (Spring-Summer 1995): 139–58; Charles W. Humphries, "Two BC Pacifists and the Boer War," *BC Studies* 45 (Spring 1980): 116–27.

21 James Naylor, "Pacifism or Anti Imperialism: The CCF Response to the Outbreak of WWII," *Journal of the Canadian Historical Association* 8 (January 1997): 213–37; Stan Kerr and Don Hanson, "Pacifism and the Saskatchewan CCF and the Outbreak of World War II," *Prairie Forum* 23, no. 2 (October 1993): 211–23; Gregory Kealey, "State Repression of Labour and the Left in Canada, 1914–1920: The Impact of the First World War," *Canadian Historical Review* 73, no. 3 (1994): 281–314.

22 Desmond Morton and Glenn Wright, *Winning the Second Battle: Canadian Veterans and the Return to Civilian Life* (Toronto: University of Toronto Press, 1987); Morton, *Fight or Pay: Soldiers' Families in the Great War* (Vancouver: UBC Press, 2004); Ian Mosby, *Food Will Win the War: The Politics, Culture, and Science of Food on Canada's Home Front* (Vancouver: UBC Press, 2014).

23 On Canadian responses to war and displacement in Central America, see Maria Cristina Garcia, *Seeking Refuge: Central American Migration to Mexico, the United States, and Canada* (Berkeley: University of California Press, 2006); Kathryn Anderson, *Weaving Relationships: Canada-Guatemala Solidarity* (Waterloo: Wilfrid Laurier University Press, 2003). On nationalism and anti-Americanism, see Stephen Azzi, "The Nationalist Moment in English Canada," in *Debating Dissent: Canada and the Sixties*, ed. Lara Campbell, Dominique Clément, and Gregory S. Kealey (Toronto: University of Toronto Press, 2012), 213–28; David Meren, "'Plus que jamais nécessaires': Cultural Relations, Nationalism and the State in the Canada-Québec-France Triangle, 1945–1960," *Journal of the Canadian Historical Association* 19, no. 1 (2008): 279–305.

24 Peter Brock and Thomas P. Socknat, eds., *Challenge to Mars: Essays on Pacifism from 1918–1945* (Toronto: University of Toronto Press, 1999), ix. On nonviolent resistance, see Theodore Olson and Gordon Christiansen, *Thirty-One Hours: The Grindstone Experiment* (New London: Grindstone Press, 1966). For an alternate way to define terms relating to war resistance, see Roussel and Boucher, "The Myth of the Pacific Society."

25 Ruth Roach Pierson, *"They're Still Women After All": The Second World War and Canadian Womanhood* (Toronto: McClelland & Stewart, 1986); Jeff Keshen, *Saints, Sinners and Soldiers: Canada's Second World War* (Vancouver: UBC Press, 2004); Kealey, *Enlisting Women for the Cause*; *And We Knew How to Dance: Women in World War I*, directed by Maureen Judge (Montreal: National Film Board, 1993).

26 Note that Canadian historiography, particularly when discussing international peace and antiwar movements, is intimately connected to the Canadian experience. Collections on pacifism and war resistance include: Socknat and Brock, *Challenge to Mars*; Harvey L. Dyck, ed., *The Pacifist Impulse in Historical Perspective* (Toronto: University of Toronto Press, 1996); Janice Williamson and Deborah Gorham, eds. *Up and Doing: Canadian Women and Peace* (Toronto: Women's Press, 1989).

1 "Scruples of Conscience" and the Historic Peace Churches

1 See Alan Taylor, *The Civil War of 1812: American Citizens, British Subjects, Irish Rebels and Indian Allies* (New York: Knopf, 2010).

2 On the general impact of the militia see J.C.A. Stagg, *The War of 1812: Conflict for a Continent* (New York: Cambridge University Press, 2012), 161; cf. Alan Taylor, *The Civil War of 1812*. On the militia myth see L.F.S. Upton, *The United Empire Loyalists: Men and Myths* (Toronto: Copp Clark, 1967); Jo-Anne Fellows, *The Loyalist Myth in Canada* (Ottawa: Canadian Historical Association, 1971); Murray Barkley, "The Loyalist Tradition in New Brunswick," *Acadiensis* 4, no. 2 (Spring 1975): 3–45; Norman Knowles, *Inventing the Loyalists: The Ontario Loyalists Tradition and the Creation of Usable Pasts* (Toronto: University of Toronto Press, 1997).

3 This is summarized in John Allemang, "The Myth of 1812: How Canadians See the War We Want to See," *Globe and Mail*, March 10, 2012.

4 See Jonathan Seiling, "Lamenting the War of 1812," *Intotemak* 42, no. 1 (Spring 2013): 8–9. Echoing the militia myth, Stephen Harper has called the war "the beginning of a long and proud military history in Canada." See Ian McKay and Jamie Swift, "The Trouble with Celebrating the War of 1812," www.rabble.ca, June 18, 2012; cf. McKay and Swift, *Warrior Nation: Rebranding Canada in an Age of Anxiety* (Toronto: Between the Lines, 2012), 6, 10, 31.

5 Ironically the study manual designed for citizenship applicants, called *Discover Canada*, lauds the role of "Canadian Volunteers" (meaning militia) in the War of 1812. www.cic.gc.ca/english/pdf/pub/discover.pdf. See p. 17. More accurately, Canadian *conscripts* tried repeatedly to evade duty in order to tend to agricultural needs or, among other reasons, because they were pro-American.

6 For example, see the published muster roll for 1818, Lincoln County in J.A.C. Kenney, "Lincoln Militia Return, 1818," *Families* 10 (1971): 14–15. In the case of militia records, some register a separate list of the "Menonists and Tunkers" who appeared dutifully for muster to pay their exemption tax. Quakers are generally absent from the muster rolls because they forbade compliance with the exemption tax laws. Family records of Mennonites, Brethren in Christ, and Quakers can be found in numerous collections, such as the Archives of the Mennonite Historical Society of Ontario, Conrad Grebel University College, Waterloo; the Brethren in Christ archives at Messiah College in Mechanicsburg, PA; the Canadian archives of the Society of Friends (Quakers) at Pickering College in Newmarket, Ontario. In the Niagara region, two particularly helpful archives are the L.R. Wilson Heritage Research Archives in Port Colborne and the Mayholme Foundation Family Research Centre in St Catharines.

7 See chapter 4, "'A Parcel of Quakers?' Militia Service, 1813–15," in George Sheppard, *Plunder, Profit, and Paroles: A Social History of the War of 1812 in Upper Canada* (Kingston: McGill-Queen's Press, 1994), 68–99, and Peter Brock, "Accounting for Difference: The Problem of Pacifism in Early Upper Canada," *Ontario History* 90, no. 1 (Spring 1998): 19–30.

8 Located at the Niagara Historical Society Museum. images.ourontario.ca/1812/70988/data?n=23. Willcocks, who had been a member of the Legislative Assembly of Upper Canada, became a Major in the American army and raised a band of treasonous soldiers in Niagara starting in the summer of 1813. Donald Edward Graves, "Joseph Willcocks and the Canadian Volunteers: An Account of Political Disaffection in Upper Canada During the War of 1812" (master's thesis, Carleton University, 1982).

9 Karl Koop, ed., *Confessions of Faith in the Anabaptist Tradition: 1527–1660* (Kitchener: Pandora Press, 2006), 285–310.

10 In 1755 Pennsylvania, for example, Mennonites had stated in a petition to the House of Representatives that "We do with the utmost fidelity acknowledge George upon the

British throne to be our lawful king and sovereign, we ... account ourselves faithful and loyal subjects to his Majesty, being willing and ready to submit and to be faithful and obedient to him.... This we are willing to evidence by a cheerfulness to pay the duty, tax etc., that the law of Great Britain, and this province requires, and to comply with every other particular relating thereunto wherein our consciences are free and clear." Richard MacMaster, Samuel Horst, and Robert Ulle, eds., *Conscience in Crisis: Mennonites and Other Peace Churches in America, 1739–1789* (Scottsdale: Herald Press, 1979), 91–93.

11 In their "Founding Statement of Faith," they stated, "it is also completely forbidden to bear the sword for revenge or defence.... We are not to withstand authority, but be obedient in all that is right and good, paying them tax and toll and protection-money." "Concerning Oaths, the Sword and the State" in Carlton O. Wittlinger, *Quest for Piety and Obedience: The Story of the Brethren in Christ* (Nappanee, Indiana: Evangel Publishing, 1978), 551–54.

12 *Rules of Discipline of the Yearly Meeting of Friends Held in Philadelphia* (1806), 127.

13 Arthur G. Dorland, *The Quakers in Canada: A History*, 2nd ed. (Toronto: Macmillan, 1968), 94.

14 See image, courtesy of the Jordan Historical Museum, images.ourontario.ca/1812/70627 /data?n=15.

15 See published sources in Peter Brock, ed., *Liberty and Conscience: A Documentary History of the Experiences of Conscientious Objectors in American Through the Civil War* (Toronto: Oxford University Press, 2002), 71–74.

16 James Moore, "A Lamentation for Pennsylvania," *Friends' Miscellany* 6 (1835): 150–54.

17 Richard Feltoe, *Redcoated Ploughboys: The Volunteer Battalion of Incorporated Militia of Upper Canada, 1813–1815* (Toronto: Dundurn Press, 2012).

18 *An Act for the Relief of Minors of the Societies of Menonists and Tunkers*, 1810, 50 Geo. 3, c. 11; Frank Epp, *Mennonites in Canada, 1786–1920: The History of a Separate People* (Toronto: MacMillan, 1974), 103.

19 E. Morris Sider, "History of the Brethren in Christ (Tunker) Church in Canada" (master's thesis, University of Western Ontario, 1955).

20 *Act for Quartering and Billeting, on Certain Occasions, his Majesty's Troops, and the Militia of this Province, 1809*, 49 Geo. 3, First Session, c. 2.

21 Home District/York Court of General Sessions of the Peace, Minute Books (series RG22–94), MS 251, Reel 1, 1800–1899, Archives of Ontario.

22 Sandra Fuller, "'A Parcel of Quakers' and the War of 1812–14 in Upper Canada," *Canadian Quaker History Journal* 72 (2007): 11–43, 29.

23 Fuller, "'A Parcel of Quakers,'" 32.

24 Fuller, "'A Parcel of Quakers,'" 25.

25 Peter Brock, *Against the Draft: Essays on Conscientious Objection from the Radical Reformation to the Second World War* (Toronto: University of Toronto, 2006), 90.

26 Sandra Fuller, "'A Parcel of Quakers.'"

27 Elma Starr, "Quakers Opposed War Preparations in Upper Canada," *Canadian Friend* 69, no. 1 (1973): 10.

28 Albert Schrauwers, *Awaiting the Millennium: The Children of Peace and the Village of Hope, 1812–1889* (Toronto: University of Toronto Press, 1993), 44–45.

29 The Waterloo settlement was established by Mennonites and Brethren in Christ around 1801. See Epp, *Mennonites in Canada, 1786–1920*, 57–58.

30 On this context and the battle see Robert S. Allen, *The Battle of Moraviantown October 5, 1813*, Canadian War Museum Canadian Battle series no. 11 (Toronto: Balmuir Book Publishing, 1994); Sandy Antal, *A Wampum Denied: Procter's War of 1812*, 2nd ed. (Montreal/ Kingston: McGill-Queen's University Press, 2011).

31 H.S. Bender, "New Source Material for History of Mennonites in Ontario," *Mennonite Quarterly Review* 3 (1929): 43.

32 Letter from William Ellis on Waterloo Wagons and Price (June 28, 1823), Jacob Erb file,

Department of Finance – Upper Canada: War of 1812 Losses Claims, RG19 E 5(a), vol. 3741, file 2, Archives of Ontario.

33 Miriam Helen Snyder and Joseph Meyer Snyder, *Hannes Schneider and His Wife Catharine Haus Schneider: Their Descendants and Times, 1534–1939* (University of Waterloo, Conrad Grebel Milton Good Library), 298–99.

34 Genealogical notes on Christian Jacob Burkholder, www.laurencebarber.ca/Families/People/Barber/Roberts/Nicholson/Burkholder/christian_burkholder.htm.

35 Miller Family File, no. 5, ML-66, Haldimand County Museum and Archives. Sarah Miller (1794–1881) later married Benjamin Shoup.

36 On women's experience during the war in general, see Dianne Graves, *In the Midst of Alarms: The Untold Story of Women and the War of 1812* (Montreal: Robin Brass Studio, 2012).

37 Department of Finance – Upper Canada: War of 1812 Losses Claims, RG19 E 5 (a) vol. 3752, file 3, Archives of Ontario.

38 Department of Finance – Upper Canada: War of 1812 Losses Claims.

39 T.W. Acheson, "M'Coll, Duncan," in *Dictionary of Canadian Biography*, vol. 6, University of Toronto/Université Laval, 2003, www.biographi.ca/en/bio/m_coll_duncan_6E.html.

40 Robert Lochiel Fraser III, "Overholser, Jacob," in *Dictionary of Canadian Biography*, vol. 5, University of Toronto/Université Laval, 2003, www.biographi.ca/en/bio/overholser_jacob_5E.html.

41 Journal of George Ferguson, 1986.131C; f. 3122; 1986.111C/TR; f. 3102, United Church of Canada Archives.

42 E. Morris Sider, "Nonresistance in the Early Brethren in Christ Church in Ontario," *Mennonite Quarterly Review* 31, no. 4 (October 1957): 282–83.

2 A Mixed Blessing

1 See Ezra E. Eby, *A Biographical History of Waterloo Township and Other Townships of the County: Being a History of the Early Settlers and their Descendants, Mostly All of Pennsylvania Dutch Origin, as also Much Other Unpublished Historical Information Chiefly of a Local Character* (Berlin, Ontario: n.p., 1895); Arthur Garrett Dorland, *A History of the Society of Friends (Quakers) in Canada* (Toronto: MacMillan, 1927); E. Morris Sider, "Nonresistance in the Early Brethren in Christ Church in Ontario," *Mennonite Quarterly Review* 31 (October 1957): 278–86; G. Elmore Reaman, *The Trail of the Black Walnut* (Toronto: McClelland & Stewart, 1957); Frank H. Epp, *Mennonites in Canada, 1786–1920: The History of a Separate People* (Toronto: MacMillan, 1974). I explore the theme of loyalty in "'Theirs was a Deeper Purpose': The Pennsylvania Germans of Ontario and the Craft of the Homemaking Myth," *Canadian Historical Review* 87, no. 4 (December 2006): 653–84.

2 Ross Fair, "Model Farmers, Dubious Citizens: Reconsidering the Pennsylvania Germans of Upper Canada, 1786–1834," in Alexander Freund, ed., *Beyond the Nation? Immigrants' Local Lives in Transnational Cultures* (Toronto: University of Toronto Press, 2012), 79–106; Robynne Rogers Healey, *From Quaker to Upper Canadian: Faith and Community among Yonge Street Friends, 1801–1850* (Montreal/Kingston: McGill-Queen's University Press, 2006).

3 C.P. Stacey, *Canada and the British Army, 1846–1871*, rev. ed. (Toronto: University of Toronto Press, 1963); J. Mackay Hitsman, *Safeguarding Canada, 1763–1871* (Toronto: University of Toronto Press, 1968); Desmond Morton, *Canada and War: A Military and Political History* (Toronto: Butterworths, 1981); Morton, *A Military History of Canada*, 5th ed. (Toronto: McClelland & Stewart, 2007).

4 For studies of pacifism in the colonial era see Peter Brock, *Freedom from Violence: Sectarian Nonresistance from the Middle Ages to the Great War* (Toronto: University of Toronto Press, 1991) and "Accounting for Difference: The Problem of Pacifism in Early Upper Canada," *Ontario History* 90 (1998): 19–30.

5 Upper Canada, *Statutes*, 1793, 33 Geo. 3, c. 1.

6 "Notice is Hereby Given," *Niagara Herald*, May 23, 1801. This 1801 notice of the militia muster for Lincoln County suggests that many pacifists avoided paying fines.

7 John McGill to William Jarvis, York, November 29, 1807, Samuel Jarvis Papers, Toronto Reference Library (TRL); List of Names of Markham Militia and of Those Exempt, 1800–07, Miscellaneous Collection 1807 #1, Archives of Ontario (AO).

8 Between February 1808 and January 1810, more than £243 worth of property was seized from Yonge Street Quakers in response to non-payment of exemption fines. Healey, 45. Peter Brock suggests that Mennonites and Tunkers adopted "a much less aggressive attitude, and consequently there existed in their case fewer possibilities of confrontation between military obligations and sectarian conscience." Brock, "Accounting for Difference," 22, 27–28.

9 Petition of Sundry Inhabitants, March 5, 1808: 2917–20, RG5 A1, Upper Canada Sundries (UCS), Library and Archives Canada (LAC).

10 Upper Canada, *Statutes*, 1808, 48 Geo. 3, c. 1. Eight men belonging to the Yonge Street Quaker settlements were imprisoned for one-month terms in 1808 and 1809. Healey, 45.

11 The main advocate for changes to the militia laws in 1808 and 1810 was likely Bishop John Winger, leader of the Tunker community in the Niagara peninsula. *Origin and History of the Tunker Church in Canada as Gathered from Authentic and Reliable Sources* (Ridgeway: M.V. Disher, 1918), Special Collections, Brock University Library; Sider, "Nonresistance in the Early Brethren in Christ Church in Ontario," 281. J. Boyd Cressman claimed that the preachers and elders who submitted the first petition were from the Waterloo settlement. Cressman, "History of the First Mennonite Church of Kitchener, Ontario," *Mennonite Quarterly Review* 8 (July 1939): 159–86.

12 Upper Canada, House of Assembly, *Journals*, February 8, 10, 1810.

13 Upper Canada, House of Assembly, *Journals*, February 10, 12, 15, 16, 20, 24, 26, 28, and March 12, 1810; Legislative Council, *Journals*, February 16, 17, 19, 20, 27, and March 12, 1810; *Statutes*, 1810, 50 Geo. 3, c. 11.

14 Upper Canada, *Statutes*, 1811, 51 Geo. 3, c. 7.

15 Circular, Inspector General's Office, York, December 18, 1813, Rogers Papers, AO.

16 John McGill to Robert Loring, York, June 22, 1814: 8523–26, RG5 A1, UCS, LAC; William Allan to Edward McMahon, York, January 3, 1815: 9197–99, RG5 A1, UCS, LAC; John McGill to Lieutenant Governor Gore, November 16, 1815: 11001–05, RG5 A1 UCS, LAC. Also see inconsistencies in the Adjutant General's report of 1829. Statement of the amount of Money . . ., March 19, 1829: 51601–04, RG5 A1, UCS, LAC; Statement of the amount of Money . . ., enclosed in N. Coffin to Z. Mudge, York, March 19, 1829: 51601–04, RG5 A1, UCS, LAC.

17 Upper Canada, *Statutes*, 1814, 54 Geo. 3, c. 1; Healey, 144.

18 Brock concludes that the conflict's end meant the "military question lost much of its urgency for the Canadian peace sects." Brock, "Accounting for Difference," 27–28.

19 Upper Canada, *Statutes*, 1816, 56 Geo. 3, c. 31.

20 Fair, "Model Farmers, Dubious Citizens," 95.

21 Fair, "Model Farmers, Dubious Citizens," 93–98.

22 Evidence of numerous amendments and divisive votes provides proof of considerable debate. Upper Canada, House of Assembly, *Journals*, January 23, February 14, 17, 23, 27, and March 1, 1830; Legislative Council, *Journals*, March 1, 2, 3, 1830.

23 Gerald M. Craig, *Upper Canada: The Formative Years* (Toronto: McClelland & Stewart, 1963), 191.

24 See notice of the petition in *Kingston Chronicle and Gazette*, July 6, 1833. House of Assembly, *Journals*, November 28, 30, 1833, January 2, 4, 8, February 17, 18, 22, March 6, 1834; Legislative Council, *Journals*, February 19, 20, 21, 22, 1834.

25 Upper Canada, *Statutes*, 1834, 4 Wm. 4, c. 13.

26 House of Assembly, *Journals*, February 3, 28, March 17, 18, 1835; Legislative Council, *Journals*, March 18, 19, 20, 1835.

27 House of Assembly, *Journals*, January 19, 25, 29, 30, 1836; Legislative Council, *Journals*, February 10, 11, 12, 1836.

28 House of Assembly, *Journals*, March 24, 25, 1836; Legislative Council, *Journals*, Appendix K, Report on an Address from the Assembly to the King, Complaining of the Rejection by the Council of Various Bills, April 18, 1836.

29 House of Assembly, *Journals*, November 10, 14, 1836, February 17, 1837; Legislative Council, *Journals*, February 20, 1837.

30 Upper Canada, *Statutes*, 1838, 1 Vic., c. 8, s. 49. A subsequent *Militia Act* maintained the strict terms for pacifist exemption. *Statutes*, 1839, 2 Vic., c. 9, s. 52.

31 Petition, People of Norwich to Charles Poulett Thompson, January 8, 1840: 129701–2, RG5 A1, UCS, LAC. Another instance of non-payment of fines is recorded in Summonses to Henry Moyer and David Reist, July 12, 1840, MU 2108, 1840 Miscellaneous Collection #5, AO.

32 Upper Canada, Legislative Council, *Journals*, December 10, 12, 14, 1839, January 3, 6, 9, 13, 14, 17, 21, 22, 23, 1840; House of Assembly, *Journals*, January 6, 14, 16, 21, 22, February 6, 1840.

33 Province of Canada, Legislative Assembly, *Journals*, June 15, 24, 28, July 30, August 2, 3, 11, 17, 1841; Legislative Council, *Journals*, August 4, 5, 6, 10, 1841. To the Right Honorable Charles, Baron Sydenham . . ., June 1841: 24073–5, Provincial Secretary, Canada West: Correspondence, file 551, RG5, c. 1, vol. 62.

34 Province of Canada, *Statutes*, 1841, 4 & 5 Vic., c. 2.

35 Before Draper presented the bill, a petition was read from Rev. Jacob Gooft and other Mennonites and Tunkers residing in the Home District requesting that the exemption fine be reduced. Province of Canada, Legislative Assembly, *Journals*, April 3, 9, 24, May 15, 26, 27, 28, 29, June 4, 5, 9, 1846; Legislative Assembly, *Journals*, May 29, 30, June 2, 3, 4, 6, 1846.

36 Province of Canada, *Statutes*, 1846, 9 Vic., c. 28, s. 30 and s. 31. A draft bill recommended a fine of twenty shillings in peace and £10 in time of war. Draft of Militia Bill, June 9, 1846: 138389–90, RG5 A1, UCS, LAC.

37 John Simpson, Acting Clerk, to William H. Merritt, M. P. P., Niagara, May 4, 1847, Merritt Papers, MS 74 vol. 3, Package #22, AO; Province of Canada, Legislative Assembly, *Journals*, June 9, 14, 17, 18, 25, 30, July 1, 1847; Legislative Council, *Journals*, July 1, 2, 5, 6, 1847. For the debate on Merritt's motions, see Elizabeth Cobbs, ed., *Debates of the Legislative Assembly of United Canadas 1841–1867* (Montreal: Presses de L'Ecole des Hautes Etudes Commerciales, 1975), June 17, 1847; *Montreal Gazette*, June 19, 1847; *British Whig*, June 25, 1847; *The Pilot and Journal of Commerce*, June 19, 1847.

38 Province of Canada, Legislative Assembly, *Journals*, March 6, 1848.

39 Province of Canada, Legislative Assembly, *Journals*, February 26, 28, March 21, April 2, 23, May 18, 19, 22, 25, 30, 1849; Legislative Council, *Journals*, May 22, 23, 25, 1849.

40 While several historians have hailed this 1849 legislation as freeing the pacifist sects from payment of annual militia exemption fines, this is incorrect. See Sider, "Nonresistance in Ontario," 283–84; Frank Epp, *Mennonites in Canada*, 107; Peter Brock, *Freedom from Violence*, 229.

41 Province of Canada, *Statutes*, 1849, 12 Vic., c. 88; 1846, 9 Vic., c. 28; 1841, 4 & 5 Vic., c. 2.

42 Morton, *A Military History of Canada*, 86.

43 Province of Canada, *Statutes*, 1855, 18 Vic., c. 77, s. 7.

44 The 1859 act declared the terms of the 1855 law to be permanent. *Statutes of the Province of Canada*, 1859, 22 Vic., c. 18, s. 1.

45 Province of Canada, *Statutes*, 1863, 27 Vic., c. 2, s. 4.

46 Canada, *Statutes*, 1868, 31 Vic., c. 40, s. 17.

47 Canada, *Statutes*, 1883, 46 Vic., c. 11, s. 15.

3 Dissent in Canada against the Anglo-Boer War, 1899–1902

1 Carman Miller makes a strong argument for more attention to the war in South Africa as a means of understanding aspects of Canada's First World War. See "Framing Canada's Great War: A Case for Including the Boer War," *Journal of Transatlantic Studies* 6, no. 1 (April 2008): 3–21. A similar argument could be made for examining dissent against the Boer War to help understand antiwar protest during that war.

2 For the international peace conventions see William I. Hull, *The Two Hague Conferences and Their Contributions to International Law* (New York: Garland, 1972); Arthur C. F. Beales, *The History of Peace: A Short Account of the Organised Movements for International Peace* (New York: Garland, 1971). On the social gospel movement in Canada see Ramsay Cook, *The Regenerators: Social Criticism in Late Victorian English Canada* (Toronto: University of Toronto Press, 1985).

3 speeches.empireclub.org/62387/data?n=2.

4 Thomas Socknat, *Witness against War: Pacifism in Canada, 1900–1945* (Toronto: University of Toronto Press, 1987), 23.

5 Report of the Peace and Arbitration Department, Report of the Convention of the Dominion Woman's Christian Temperance Union (n.p., 1901), 67.

6 "Let Loose for a Day: The People of Toronto Celebrate Buller's Great Achievement," *Toronto Globe*, March 8, 1900, 8.

7 The First Anglo-Boer War, or Transvaal War, was fought from December 16, 1880, to March 23, 1881. The British were defeated at several battles and in the aftermath the Transvaal regained its independence. The Pretoria Convention (1881) and the London Convention (1884) laid down the terms of the peace agreement. The memory of those losses helped shape British and colonial attitudes during the Second Boer War.

8 The first concentration camps were used by the Spanish in Cuba during the Spanish-American War in 1898. These "reconcentrados" were intended to move Cuban civilians to central locations where they would be under the control of the Spanish army until the Spanish were victorious. The camps were poorly administered and thousands died as a result of poor conditions. The camps were a central aspect of American antipathy toward the Spanish in the war.

9 "Boer" was the Dutch term for "farmer." By the late nineteenth century the term referred to Afrikaans-speaking descendants of the original Dutch settlers in South Africa.

10 For an overview of Canadian reactions to and participation in the war see Carman Miller, *Painting the Map Red: Canada and the South African War, 1899–1902* (Montreal: McGill-Queen's University Press, 1993); Robert Page, *The Boer War and Canadian Imperialism* (Ottawa: Canadian Historical Association, 1987). For a contemporary British discussion see Theodore Caldwell, *The Boer War: Why was it Fought, Who was Responsible?* (Boston: D.C. Heath, 1965).

11 "Canadian Outlanders," *Toronto Globe*, September 16, 1899, 1.

12 See a summary of the prewar negotiations at newsimages.worldvitalrecords.com/books %5C2009JUN14%5CCDAustraliaAU6007_TasmanianInTransvaalWar%5C50.pdf, accessed January 22, 2014.

13 For examples of contemporary attitudes see P. Edward Fields, *Poetry, on the Departure of the first Canadian Contingent for South Africa* [S. l.: s.n., 1899?], CIHM/ICMH collection de microfiches, no. 46154; Thomas Guthrie Marquis, *Canada's Sons on Kopje and Veldt: A Historical Account of the Canadian Contingents* (Toronto: Canada's Sons, 1900).

14 *Canadians in Khaki* (Montreal: Herald Publishing, 1900; Ottawa: Eugene Ursual, 1994), 8.

15 See, for example, Jean-Guy Pelletier, "La presse canadienne-française et la guerre des Boers" *Recherches sociographiques* 4, no. 3 (1963): 337–49.

16 Carman Miller, "English-Canadian Opposition to the South African War as Seen Through the Press," *Canadian Historical Review* 55, no. 4 (December 1974): 422–38.

17 Thomas Socknat, *Witness Against War*, 25.

18 *The Casket*, July 20, 1899, 7.

19 Charles W. Humphries, "Two B.C. Pacifists and the Boer War," *B.C. Studies* 45 (Spring 1980): 116–27, 117.

20 By "Hindostan" he was referring to India, and "Turkish despotism" is a reference to British participation in the Crimean War. See Goldwin Smith, *In the Court of History: An Apology for Canadians who were Opposed to the South African War* (Toronto: William Tyrrell, 1902).

21 Letter from M.F. Fallon, Dunnville, Ontario, *The Casket*, August 17, 1899, 4. Manitoba abolished funding for Catholic schools in 1890. This engendered great controversy and debate about provincial vs. federal powers and the rights of religious minorities. See Paul Crunican, *Priests and Politicians: Manitoba Schools and the Election of 1896* (Toronto: University of Toronto Press, 1974). Anti-Catholic practices in the United Kingdom included test acts according to which members of parliament had to swear oaths that violated Roman Catholic beliefs. This practice was ended in 1867, after which only the monarch had to make such a declaration at the beginning of their reign. At the turn of the century there was a movement in Canada and the Commonwealth to end the practice, and it was abolished in 1910.

22 *The Casket*, July 20, 1899, 7. The term "jingo" for aggressive and threatening patriotism came into use during the 1870s to describe Britain's bellicose attitude toward Russia.

23 "Civilization Advances," *Methodist Reporter*, October 18, 1899, cited in Carman Miller, *Painting the Map Red*, 18. For a discussion of the connection between imperialism, civilization, and Christianity see Gordon Heath, *A War with a Silver Lining: Canadian Protestant Churches and the War in South Africa* (Montreal: McGill-Queens University Press, 2009).

24 *The Casket*, Aug 31, 1899, 1. *Meum* is Latin for "what is mine," and *tuum* is Latin for "what is thine." If a man is said not to know the difference between *meum* and *tuum*, it is a polite way of saying he is a thief.

25 *Victoria Times*, October 28, 1899. Cited in Humphries, "Two B.C. Pacifists and the Boer War," 117.

26 *Victoria Times*, October 28, 1899. Cited in Humphries, "Two B.C. Pacifists and the Boer War," 118.

27 *Victoria Times*, October 30, 31, 1899. Humphries, "Two B.C. Pacifists and the Boer War," 118–20. For a present-day parallel concerning educational authorities and war resistance see Michael Dawson and Catherine Gidney's chapter in this volume.

28 Humphries, "Two B.C. Pacifists and the Boer War," 120. Few clergy spoke out against the war. For examples of those who did, see Socknat, *Witness Against War*, 24.

29 Goldwin Smith (*Toronto Sun* n.d.), quoted in *The Casket*, November 16, 1899, 1.

30 See a review of Hobson's book *The War in South Africa* in the *Toronto Globe*, May 26, 1900, 16.

31 Smith, *In the Court of History*, 20. Another aspect of the economic argument against the war concerned the degree to which its prosecution took away money for social improvements at home.

32 S.B. Spies, *Methods of Barbarism? Roberts and Kitchener and Civilians in the Boer Republics, January 1900 – May 1902* (Cape Town: Human & Rousseau, 1977); John Fisher, *That Miss Hobhouse* (London: Secker & Warburg, 1971).

33 Smith, *In the Court of History*, 52. Wrigley also kept up a criticism of the scorched earth policy in his *Citizen and Country*.

34 Smith, *In the Court of History*, 52.

35 Brereton Greenhous, "The South African War," in *We Stand on Guard: An Illustrated History of the Canadian Army*, ed. John Marteinson (Montreal: Ovale, 1992), 75.

36 For the interpretation that this was not Canada's responsibility see O.D. Skelton, ed., *Life and Letters of Sir Wilfrid Laurier* (Toronto: McClelland & Stewart, 1965). For Canada's distinctive reluctance to appraise this conflict critically see Robert Teigrob, "Glad Adven-

tures, Tragedies, Silences: Remembering and Forgetting Wars for Empire in Canada and the United States," *International Journal of Canadian Studies* 45–46 (2012): 441–65.

37 Roland H. Bainton, *Roly, Chronicle of a Stubborn Non-conformist* (New Haven: Yale University Divinity School, 1988).

38 Miller, "English-Canadian Opposition to the South African War as Seen Through the Press," 436–37. There were fairly frequent editorials on socialism in *The Casket*, evidence of the obstacles facing dissenting groups who wished to come together (e.g., "Religion and Civilization," October 26, 1899, 7).

39 Peter Brock argues, "It was not until 1916 that Christian pacifists, socialist antimilitarists, and rationalist and humanitarian objectors to war were brought together in united opposition to wartime conscription." Brock, *Twentieth Century Pacifism* (New York: Van Nostrand Reinhold, 1970), 290.

40 Humphries, "Two B.C. Pacifists and the Boer War," 126.

4 With Thought and Faith

1 The author would like to thank the Social Sciences and Humanities Research Council for the funding that made this research possible, as well as the editors of this collection for their patience, attention to detail, and hard work.

2 See Tim Cook, *At the Sharp End: Canadians Fighting the Great War, 1914–1916* (Toronto: Viking Canada, 2007); Tim Cook, *Shock Troops: Canadians Fighting the Great War, 1917–1918* (Toronto: Viking Canada, 2008). A worthwhile examination of gas warfare is Tim Cook, *No Place to Run: The Canadian Corps and Gas Warfare in The First World War* (Vancouver: UBC Press, 1999).

3 Jonathan Vance examines the dominant memory of the postwar era in English Canada in *Death So Noble: Memory, Meaning, and the First World War* (Vancouver, UBC Press, 1997). He describes the problem of French and English Canada as not agreeing with the "proper combination of remembering and forgetting" (8) on the events of the war, which could be applied to any who did not agree with the English-Canadian narrative. Alan Gordon outlines the "contested terrain" of French-Canadian memory of the war through commemorations of the Rebellions of 1836–37; see Alan Gordon, "Lest We Forget: Two Solitudes in War and Memory," in *Canadas of the Mind: The Making and Unmaking of Canadian Nationalisms in the Twentieth Century*, ed. Norman Hillmer and Adam Chapnick (Quebec: McGill-Queen's University Press, 2007), 159–73. For an examination of French-Canadian veterans, see Geoff Keelan, "'Il a bien merité de la Patrie': The 22nd Battalion and the Memory of Courcelette," *Canadian Military History* 19, no. 3 (Summer 2010): 28–40.

4 See Kenneth McNaught, *A Prophet in Politics: A Biography of J.S. Woodsworth* (Toronto: University of Toronto Press, 1959).

5 Ewart admits as much in a letter to Bourassa. See Ewart to Bourassa, December 1, 1916, and Ewart to Bourassa, January 21, 1918, Henri Bourassa fonds, MG27-IIE1, Library and Archives Canada (hereafter Henri Bourassa fonds).

6 See Michael Oliver, *The Passionate Debate: The Social and Political Ideas of Quebec Nationalism, 1920–1945* (Montreal: Véhicule Press, 1991), 56–61.

7 Réal Bélanger, "Bourassa, Henri," in *Dictionary of Canadian Biography*, vol. 18, University of Toronto/Université Laval, 2003 – , accessed September 20, 2013, www.biographi.ca/en/bio/bourassa_henri_18E.html.

8 For the best and most recent work on Bourassa's unique fusion of conservative Catholicism and Liberal nationalism, see Réal Bélanger, *Henri Bourassa: Le fascinant destin d'un homme libre (1868-1914)* (Québec: Les Presses de l'Université Laval, 2013). Bélanger describes the liberal tenets that informed Bourassa's intellectual development, which included respect for individual freedom, constitutional law, tolerance, justice, equality, and

social conservatism. He inherited his idea of liberalism from Wilfrid Laurier, who was influenced by the British Whigs of the eighteenth and nineteenth centuries. See Bélanger, 44. Still, Bourassa's Ultramontanism remained paramount. From early in his career he placed his Catholic faith above his political ideology after Liberals condemned one of his first cautious forays into combining liberal ideology and Catholicism. See Bélanger, 56–57 for a description of that decisive moment in 1897. A shorter but equally useful overview is cited above from the *Dictionary of Canadian Biography Online*.

9 James I.W. Corcoran, "Henri Bourassa et la guerre sud-africain (suite)," *Revue d'histoire de l'Amérique Française* 19, no. 1 (1965): 84. See also Jacques Monet, "Canadians, Canadiens and Colonial Nationalism: 1896–1914: The Thorn in the Lion's Paw," in *The Rise of Colonial Nationalism*, ed. John Eddy and Deryck Schreuder (Sydney: Allen & Unwin Australia, 1988), 166–72.

10 "Les Canadiens-français du peuple n'ont d'autre patrie que le Canada," Bourassa argued. "Ils sont prêts à lui rendre tout ce qu'ils lui doivent; mais n'estimant rien devoir à l'Angleterre ni à aucun autre pays, ils n'en attendent rien." See Henri Bourassa, *Les Canadiens-français et l'Empire britannique* (Québec: Imprimerie S.A. Demers, 1903), 40. All translations are the author's and any mistakes are his own.

11 Monet, "Canadians, Canadiens and colonial nationalism," 188.

12 Ramsay Cook and Robert Craig Brown, *Canada 1896–1921: A Nation Transformed* (Toronto: McClelland & Stewart, 1974), 76–79.

13 Yvan Lamonde, *Histoire sociale des idées au Québec 1896–1929 vol. II* (Quebec: Éditions Fides, 2004), 25.

14 Joseph Levitt, *Henri Bourassa and the Golden Calf: The Social Program of the Nationalists of Quebec 1900–1914* (Ottawa: Les Éditions de l'Université d'Ottawa, 1972), 140–44.

15 Henri Bourassa, "Le Discours de Notre-Dame au Congrès Eucharistique de 1910," *Hommage à Bourassa* (Montréal: Le Devoir, 1952), 108–14. See also Joseph Levitt, *Henri Bourassa on Imperialism and Bi-culturalism, 1900–1918* (Toronto: Copp Clark, 1970), 125–29; Levitt, *Henri Bourassa – Catholic Critic* (Ottawa: Canadian Historical Association, 1976), 9.

16 The original statement reads: "Royalistes, impérialistes, républicains, socialistes, tous ne paraissent avoir qu'un Coeur." Henri Bourassa, "En France et en Alsace au Début de la Guerre," *Le Devoir*, August 22, 1914.

17 Carl Berger, *The Sense of Power: Studies in the Ideas of Canadian Imperialism 1867–1914* (Toronto: University of Toronto Press, 1970), 277. For an opposing view of imperialism, see Douglas L. Cole, "Canada's Nationalistic Imperialists," *Journal of Canadian Studies* 5, no. 3 (1970): 44–49.

18 Sylvie Lacombe, *La rencontre de deux peuples élus: Comparaison des ambitions nationale et impériale au Canada entre 1896 et 1920* (Sainte-Foy, Québec: Presses de l'Université Laval, 2002), 18.

19 Bourassa, "En France et en Alsace."

20 See their editorials in *Le Devoir* on August 5 and 18, 1914.

21 The original statement reads as follows: "cet acte d'élémentaire justice et de politique intelligente fera plus pour assurer l'unité de l'Empire et de la nation canadienne que tous les dons de farine ou d'argent." See Henri Bourassa, "Le Partage Des Responsabilités," *Le Devoir*, August 29, 1914.

22 Ewart to Bourassa, January 10, 1918, Bourassa fonds.

23 René Durocher, "Henri Bourassa, les évêques et la guerre de 1914–1918," *Canadian Historical Association Historical Papers* 6 (1971): 252–53.

24 The *White Papers* were first published publicly on August 5, 1914, when they were presented to the British House of Commons "to inform Parliament as to the events which had brought about the war and the part taken in them by the British Government." See G.P. Gooch, D. Litt, and Harold Temperley, *British Official Documents on the Origins of the War, 1898–1914* (London: His Majesty's Office, 1926). Other governments had already pub-

lished similar collections of the official documents concerning their entry into the war, such as the *French Yellow Book* or the *German White Book.*

25 See Bourassa's editorials from *Le Devoir,* September 8–12 and September 14, 1914.

26 Lamonde, *Histoire sociale des idées au Québec,*" 40–41.

27 Henri Bourassa, "Le Devoir National," *Le Devoir,* September 8, 1914.

28 Henri Bourassa, "Apres la Guerre, la Famine," *Le Devoir,* September 2, 1914.

29 Lettre Pastorale de NN. SS les Archevêques et Evêques des Provinces Ecclésiastiques de Québec, de Montréal, et d'Ottawa sur les Devoirs des Catholiques dans la Guerre Actuelle, September 23, 1914. See *L'Action Social,* September 11, 14, 16, 1914.

30 Twice Bourassa was unable to give a scheduled talk. See the introduction to Henri Bourassa, *The Duty of Canada at the Present Hour* (Le Devoir, 1915), for copies of pamphlets handed out in advance. For a description of the event, see Robert Rumilly, *Henri Bourassa: La vie publique d'un grand Canadien* (Montréal: Éditions Chantecler, 1953), 521–22.

31 In Bourassa's words, "les conséquences effroyables qui découleraient d'une décision hâtive." See Henri Bourassa, "Le Désastre du 'Lusitania' et l'Attitude de Président Wilson," *Le Devoir,* May 12, 1915.

32 Henri Bourassa, "La Démission de M. Bryan: La Crise politique en Angleterre," *Le Devoir,* June 10, 1915.

33 Henri Bourassa, "L'Appel du Pape," *Le Devoir,* August 3, 1915.

34 Henri Bourassa, "Le Pape et la Guerre," *Le Devoir,* December 31, 1915. Bourassa first examines the British organization's peace goals in June 1915. See Henri Bourassa, "La Saine Opinion Anglaise," *Le Devoir,* June 12, 1915.

35 Bourassa suggested that "l'effondrement du système politique élevé par la fausse sagesse des hommes, par la diplomatie orgueilleuse, par la soif des conquetes et le culte paien de l'or et de la force brutale." Bourassa, "Le Pape et la Guerre."

36 Bourassa describes the possible triumph of the "militarisme scientifique des Allemands, de l'impérialisme mercantile des Anglais, de la démocratie débilitante de la Révolution française, ou du mysticisme sauvage et perfide du panslavisme." Bourassa, "Le Pape et la Guerre."

37 Sandra Gwyn, "Papineau, Talbot Mercer," in *Dictionary of Canadian Biography,* vol. 14, University of Toronto/Université Laval, 2003–, accessed September 20, 2013, www.biographi.ca/en/bio/papineau_talbot_mercer_14E.html.

38 Geoff Keelan, "Talbot Mercer Papineau: Memory, Myth and the Search for Meaning" (master's thesis, University of Waterloo, 2010), 34–39.

39 An English version of Bourassa's letter is cited here. See Captain Papineau's Letter to M. Henri Bourassa (editor of *Le Devoir*), Talbot Mercer Papineau fonds, vol. 4, LAC; Captain Papineau's Letter to M. Henri Bourassa (editor of *Le Devoir*), Talbot Mercer Papineau fonds, vol. 4, LAC. He published it in French as "Reponse de M. Bourassa à la letter du Capitaine Talbot Papineau," *Le Devoir,* August 5, 1916, 1.

40 Captain Papineau's Letter to M. Henri Bourassa, Talbot Mercer Papineau fonds, vol. 4, LAC.

41 For an expansion on this argument, see Geoff Keelan, "Catholic Neutrality: The Peace of Henri Bourassa," *Journal of the Canadian Historical Association* 22, no. 1 (2012): 99–132.

42 In Bourassa's words, these smaller nations were falling victim to "l'ambition et [les] infâmes calculs de leurs grands voisins, manipulateurs sans scrupules de l'équilibre européen." See Henri Bourassa, "La Démarche de L'Allemagne: Espoirs de paix – Obstacles probables," *Le Devoir,* December 14, 1916.

43 James Brown Scott, *Official Statements of War Aims and Peace Proposals, December 1916 to November 1918* (Washington: Carnegie Endowment for International Peace, Division of International Law, 1921), 13–15.

44 Henri Bourassa, "Espoirs de Paix," *Le Devoir,* December 27, 1916.

45 This reached its height in 1918 when Bourassa warned that ignoring the Pope's call for

peace would lead to the downfall of society, famine, and revolution. As it was for so many fighting the war, it became an issue of life or death. See Henri Bourassa, "Vers la Paix, Partie. 2," *Le Devoir*, January 30, 1918.

46 John English, *The Decline of Politics: The Conservatives and the Party System, 1901–20* (Toronto: University of Toronto Press, 1977), 129–35.

47 English, *The Decline of Politics*, 194–203.

48 Norman Ward, ed., *A Party Politician: The Memoirs of Chubby Power* (Toronto, 1966), 61, quoted in John English, *The Decline of Politics*, 190.

49 Henri Bourassa, "La Conscription," *Le Devoir*, July 26, 1915.

50 Henri Bourassa, "Why Canada Should Not Adopt Conscription," *New York Evening Post*, July 10, 1917.

51 Rumilly, *Henri Bourassa*, 590.

52 Henri Bourassa, "'L'isolement' des Canadiens-Français: II Pas de Basses Compromissions," *Le Devoir*, December 27, 1917.

53 André Bergevin, Cameron Nish, and Anne Bourassa, *Henri Bourassa. Biographie. Index des écrits. Index de la correspondance publique, 1895–1924* (Montréal: Éditions de l'Action nationale, 1966), L-LI.

5 A Better Truth

1 The author would like to thank Kimberley Wilson for her help with research.

2 This interpretation of the war and its significance is the official one and is widely promoted in official commemoration, particularly by the current federal government and particularly on Remembrance Day (November 11). The web site of Veterans Affairs Canada (www.veterans.gc.ca) is, not surprisingly, a good example. It presents the war as a heroic sacrifice and instructs readers to remember it that way. Most popular histories of various kinds offer versions of that message. The elevation of soldiers into mythological heroes is termed "high diction" by scholars of the First World War. Jonathan Vance's book *Death so Noble: Memory, Meaning, and the First World War* (Toronto: University of Toronto Press, 1997) is an excellent source on the origins of the sacrificial myth of the war in the period immediately after the armistice.

3 Ian McKay and Jamie Swift, *Warrior Nation: Rebranding Canada in an Age of Anxiety* (Toronto: Between the Lines, 2012), 2. McKay and Swift also wrote an article in the popular history magazine *Canada's History* that bemoaned the federal government's limiting national commemoration to "Sanitized wars, fought for freedom" ("Fighting Words," *Canada's History*, February – March 2013, 50.) The article prompted two enraged letters to the editor in the following issue, including one from the chair of the organization that publishes *Canada's History*, vividly illustrating the ruthlessness with which the sacrificial myth of the war is maintained.

4 The definition of democracy used here is roughly that of Charles Tilly: "the extent to which the people subject to a given state's authority exercise broad, equal, binding, and protected voice when it comes to state performance. If popular voice becomes broader, more equal, more binding on state performance, and better protected against arbitrary action by state agents, democratization is occurring. De-democratization, in these terms, includes narrowing, rising inequality, decreased binding of state action by popular voice, and/or declining protection of that popular voice against state agents' arbitrary action." See "Extraction and Democracy," in *The New Fiscal Sociology: Taxation in Comparative Historical Perspective*, ed. Isaac William Martin, Ajay K. Mehrotra, and Monica Prassad (New York: Cambridge University Press, 2009), 174. Much could be added to this definition, including the slogan from the 2011 Occupy Wall Street protests: "There can be no political freedom without economic justice." See Eli Schmitt, Astra Taylor, and Mark Greif, *Occupy! Scenes From an Occupation* (New York: Verso, 2011), viii. Tilly would point out that the

goal of economic justice requires the state capacity to influence the economy, as well as democratic power over that state capacity.

5 Electoral law in Canada has been enormously complex, owing to a combination of federalism (which creates, at any given time, up to eleven electoral jurisdictions with different rules) and decidedly mixed feelings about universal citizenship. A good accessible introduction to the history of the federal electoral franchise is a government publication, *A History of the Vote in Canada* (Ottawa: Elections Canada, 2007). Although poverty and gender were the most common barriers to participation, race-based restrictions were regularly imposed in various places, particularly in British Columbia. The *Franchise Act* of 1885, the first federal legislation on voting rights, explicitly denied the right to vote to Asians and status Indians west of Ontario. When that act was overturned in 1898, federal voting rights reverted to the provinces, and race restrictions became more uneven across the country. This was the policy in place when the war began.

6 Constance Backhouse's *Colour-Coded: A Legal History of Racism in Canada, 1900–1950* (Toronto: University of Toronto Press, 1999) is an excellent source on race-based limitations on civil rights in Canada. Backhouse argues that racism was not simply an unconscious characteristic of Canadians in the past, but was a central way of thinking about legal questions. Patricia E. Roy's *A White Man's Province: British Columbia Politicians and Chinese and Japanese Immigrants, 1858–1914* shows that attacks on the civil rights of Chinese and Japanese Canadians in BC actually increased in the lead-up to the war. Racism and a willingness to use the legal system to enforce racial hierarchies were the norm well into the twentieth century. Denying the rights of non-whites to work in Canada was a key focus of elements of the labour movement, as David Goutor has shown in *Guarding the Gates: The Canadian Labour Movement and Immigration, 1872–1934* (Vancouver: UBC Press, 2007).

7 "Whichever side succeeds, the country it is well known will be governed in just the same way: the only difference will be in the *personnel* of the government." Andre Siegfried, *The Race Question in Canada* (London: Eveleigh Nash, 1907), 142, emphasis original. The broad similarity of the parties was a common theme in political writings of the period leading up to the war.

8 Donald Avery, *Dangerous Foreigners: European Immigrant Workers and Labour Radicalism in Canada, 1896–1932* (Toronto: McClelland & Stewart, 1979), 16–17, 19, 28–29, 37.

9 R.T. Naylor, "The Canadian State, the Accumulation of Capital, and the Great War," *Journal of Canadian Studies* 16, nos. 3–4 (Fall-Winter 1981): 26–27.

10 A general perception held that the roles of men and women were changing, and enfranchisement was simply a question of time. Ramsay Cook's introduction to Catherine L. Cleverdon's *The Woman Suffrage Movement in Canada* (Toronto: University of Toronto Press, 1974) provides a good overview of attitudes toward feminism in the prewar years. He concludes that by 1910 "the tide seemed to be turning" (vi). This sense intensified after the war began. Stephen Leacock, who opposed woman suffrage, asserted in 1916 that "women are going to get the vote. Within a very short time … woman suffrage will soon be an accomplished fact." Stephen Leacock, *Essays and Literary Studies* (Toronto: S.B. Gundy, 1916), 148–49).

11 In 1913, at the height of prewar non-British immigration, British immigrants were still 52 per cent of the total. See Avery, *Dangerous Foreigners*, 37.

12 J.L. Granatstein and J.M. Hitsman, *Broken Promises: A History of Conscription in Canada* (Toronto: Oxford University Press, 1977), 23.

13 See in particular Mark Moss, *Manliness and Militarism: Educating Young Boys in Ontario for War* (Toronto: Oxford University Press, 2001).

14 Craig Heron and Myer Siemiatycki, "The Great War, the State, and Working-Class Canada," in *The Workers' Revolt in Canada, 1917–1925*, ed. Craig Heron (Toronto: University of Toronto Press, 1998), 18.

15 Ian McKay, *Reasoning Otherwise: Leftists and the People's Enlightenment in Canada, 1890–1920* (Toronto: Between the Lines, 2008), 420.

16 Naylor, "The Canadian State," 39.

17 Naylor, "The Canadian State," 29.

18 McKay, *Reasoning Otherwise*, 420.

19 W.A. Mackintosh noted shortly after the war that "issue after issue of tax exempt bonds put a premium on large incomes to be paid out of the taxes of the ordinary consumer." Cited in Hugh Grant, "Revolution in Winnipeg, 1919," *Labour/Le travail* 60 (Fall 2007): 174. Richard Krever notes that "raising revenue through bonds would mean that the poorer pay to the richer citizens of the country." Richard Krever, "The Origin of Federal Income Taxation in Canada," *Canadian Taxation* 3, no. 2 (Winter 1981): 184.

20 Martin Robin notes that, "by 1917, [Ontario] was the best organized in the dominion." Martin Robin, "Registration, Conscription, and Independent Labour Politics," in *Conscription 1917* (Toronto: University of Toronto Press, 1979), 72.

21 The link between "conscription of wealth" and the threat of either industrial or political unrest is documented in my "'The rich . . . should give to such an extent that it will hurt': 'Conscription of Wealth' and Political Modernism in the Parliamentary Debate on the 1917 Income War Tax," *Canadian Historical Review* 93, no. 3 (September 2012): 382–407.

22 Myer Siemiatycki comments, "the war-induced epidemic of general strikes, which one prominent unionist dubbed 'Winnipegitis,' found its earliest germination in Toronto." Myer Siemiatycki, "Munitions and Labour Militancy: The 1916 Hamilton Machinists' Strike," *Labour/Le travail* 3 (1978): 141.

23 Cited in Robin, "Registration," 62.

24 Cited in Robin, "Registration," 69.

25 Tarah Brookfield, "Divided by the Ballot Box: The Montreal Council of Women and the 1917 Election," *Canadian Historical Review* 89, no. 4 (December 2008): 488.

26 Adam Crerar, "Ontario and the Great War," in *Canada and the First World War: Essays in Honour of Robert Craig Brown*, ed. David MacKenzie (Toronto: University of Toronto Press, 2005), 244.

27 McKay, *Reasoning Otherwise*, 432.

28 Kealey, "1919," 297.

29 Heron and Siemiatycki, "The Great War," 25.

30 Avery's *Dangerous Foreigners*, the classic account of the cost ethnic minorities paid in the wake of the labour uprisings, notes that "it was the 'foreigner' who bore the brunt of the attack" on labour that followed. Avery later wrote in *Reluctant Host: Canada's Response to Immigrant Workers, 1896–1994* (Toronto: McClelland & Stewart, 1995, 79) that after the Russian Revolution "many Anglo-Canadians equated Bolshevism with the recent immigration from eastern Europe," which fed into anti-immigrant sentiment. Among more recent sources, Ian McKay devotes the final chapter of *Reasoning Otherwise* (497–501) to the aftermath of the Winnipeg General Strike, though his emphasis is on the "show trials," the very public legal process that Anglo-Canadian leaders were subjected to, rather than the more secretive and ruthless state activity meted out to ethnics and immigrants.

31 Kealey, "1919," 294.

32 This is the central theme of Carol Lee Bacchi's classic critique *Liberation Deferred? The Ideas of the English-Canadian Suffragists, 1877–1918* (Toronto: University of Toronto Press, 1983). See also my "'Civilization Had Given Him a Vote': Citizenship and the Ballot in Sara Jeannette Duncan's *The Imperialist*," *Journal of Canadian Studies* 40, no. 3 (Fall 2006): 120–34.

33 Asian Canadians were denied the vote in various places at various times, and federal legislation generally replicated these provincial restrictions. Status Indians could only vote under some conditions, the most common of which was that they revoke their status and leave their communities or serve in the military. The federal government explicitly elimi-

nated racial barriers to voting in 1960. Racial barriers to political participation were declared unconstitutional by the Charter of Rights and Freedoms in 1982.

34 Crerar, "Ontario," 245.

35 This position was articulated by Liberal members in the House of Commons when the Income War Tax was being debated, but it reflected a much wider feeling of what the tax ought to do. See my "'The rich ... should give to such an extent that it will hurt.'"

6 Challenging Strathcona

1 I am dedicating this to the memory of my cousin and dear friend, Daniela Fogal Nesbitt, May 22, 1964 – May 20, 2014.

2 "Physical and Military Training in the Schools: Lord Strathcona's Patriotic Offer to Dominion Government; Offer Stirs the House to an Outburst of Patriotism," *Globe*, March 25, 1909.

3 On early twentieth-century militarism and imperial nationalism, see Carl Berger, *The Sense of Power: Studies in the Ideas of Canadian Imperialism, 1867–1914* (Toronto: University of Toronto Press, 1971); Don Morrow, "The Strathcona Trust in Ontario, 1911–1939," *Canadian Journal of Sport and Physical Education* 8 (1977): 72–89; Desmond Morton, "The Cadet Movement in the Moment of Canadian Militarism," *Journal of Canadian Studies* 13, no. 2 (1978): 56–68; Mike O'Brien, "Manhood and the Militia Myth: Masculinity, Class and Militarism in Ontario, 1902–1914," *Labour/Le travail* 42 (1998): 115–41; Mark Moss, *Manliness and Militarism: Educating Young Boys in Ontario for War* (Don Mills: Oxford University Press, 2001); James Wood, *Militia Myths: Ideas of the Canadian Citizen Soldier, 1896–1921* (Vancouver: UBC Press, 2010); R. Blake Brown, "'Every Boy Ought to Learn to Shoot and to Obey Orders': Guns, Boys, and the Law in English Canada from the Late Nineteenth Century to the Great War," *Canadian Historical Review* 93, no. 2 (2012): 196–226.

4 James L. Gear, "Factors Influencing the Development of Government-Sponsored Physical Fitness Programmes in Canada from 1850 to 1972," *Canadian Journal of History of Sport and Physical Education* 4, no. 2 (1973): 1–25; Morton, "The Cadet Movement," 58–63.

5 On Empire Day, see Moss, *Manliness and Militarism*; Susan Fisher, *Boys and Girls in No Man's Land: English Canadian Children and the First World War* (Toronto: University of Toronto Press, 2011), 82, 88–89. On "the boy problem," see Bryan Hogeveen, "'The Evils with Which We are Called to Grapple': Elite Reformers, Eugenicists, Environmental Psychologists, and the Construction of Toronto's Working-Class Boy Problem, 1860–1930," *Labour/Le travail*, 55 (2005): 37–68; Cynthia Comacchio, "Lost in Modernity: 'Maladjustment' and the 'Modern Youth Problem,' English Canada, 1920–50," in *Lost Kids: Vulnerable Children and Youth in Twentieth-Century Canada and the United States*, ed. Mona Gleason, Tamara Myers, Leslie Paris, and Veronica Strong-Boag (Vancouver: UBC Press, 2010), 53–71. On Boy Scouts see Patricia Dirks, "Canada's Boys: An Imperial or National Asset? Responses to Baden-Powell's Boy Scout Movement in Pre-War Canada," in *Canada and the British World: Culture, Migration, and Identity*, ed. Phillip Buckner and R. Douglas Francis (Vancouver: UBC Press, 2006), 111–28.

6 *Constitution of the Strathcona Trust: For the Encouragement of Physical Training and Military Drill in Public Schools* (Ottawa: Government Printing Bureau, 1910); Morton, "The Cadet Movement," 62–64; Morrow, "The Strathcona Trust in Ontario, 1911–1939," 82–84; Frank Cosentino and Maxwell L. Howell, *A History of Physical Education in Canada* (Toronto: General Publishing Company, 1971), 28–29.

7 Ontario Department of Education, *Annual Report* (Toronto: King's Printer, 1915), 34.

8 In 1916, the McGill University physical education expert Ethel Mary Cartwright openly questioned the military premises of physical education; see Gear, "Factors," 14–15.

9 Ontario Department of Education, *Annals of Valour, Empire Day, Friday May 23rd, 1919* (Toronto: A.T. Wilgress, 1919), 5.

10 Thomas P. Socknat, *Witness Against War: Pacifism in Canada, 1900–1945* (Toronto: University of Toronto Press, 1987), 102.

11 Ontario Department of Education, *Annual Report* (Toronto: King's Printer, 1920), 56. In Ontario the high school population quadrupled during the 1920s; see Cynthia Comacchio, *The Dominion of Youth: Adolescence and the Making of Modern Canada* (Waterloo: Wilfrid Laurier University Press, 2006), 99–103.

12 "Cadet Training," letter to the editor, *Toronto Daily Star*, November 25, 1924, signed "A MOTHER." See also Barbara Roberts, "Women's Peace Activism in Canada," in *Beyond the Vote: Canadian Women and Politics*, ed. Linda Kealey and Joan Sangster (Toronto: University of Toronto Press, 1989), 276–308.

13 Comacchio, *The Dominion of Youth*, 114–16.

14 "Cadet Training, Sugar Tax, Proxies, Opposed by U.F.'s," *Toronto Daily Star*, September 16, 1922; "UFO Annual Convention in Toronto," *Toronto Daily Star*, December 18, 1924.

15 "Conference Deplores Gambling Under All Forms, Condemns Militarism," *Toronto Daily Star*, June 10, 1924; "Church Will Work for World Peace," *Toronto Daily Star*, September 12, 1928.

16 On Toronto's "Britishness" and militarism, see Ian Miller, *Our Glory and Our Grief: Torontonians and the Great War* (Toronto: University of Toronto Press, 2002); Morton, "The Cadet Movement," 62–64.

17 "Trustees Deadlock on Permit Question," *Toronto Daily Star*, November 22, 1924; "Anti-Cadet Speech from Miss Macphail Perturbs Trustees," *Toronto Globe*, November 22, 1924; "Agnes Macphail Ill and Cannot Speak," *Toronto Globe*, November 24, 1924.

18 "Let's Face the Facts," letter to the editor, *Toronto Daily Star*, December 23, 1924, signed "Pro Patria." See also "The Spotlight: L.H. Martell," *Toronto Daily Star*, July 25, 1924. Macphail became the first president of the Canadian WILPF in 1930; Terry Crowley, *Agnes Macphail and the Politics of Equality* (Toronto: James Lorimer, 1990), 65–68.

19 "Citizens Join in Discussing Cadet Problem," *Edmonton Journal*, March 18, 1927.

20 These modifications are reflected in the *Militia Act*, R.S.C 1927, c. 132, s. 50 and, correspondingly, in the *Ontario High Schools Act*, R.S.O. 1927, c. 326, s. 9.

21 "Coercion Used," letter to the editor, *Toronto Daily Star*, September 20, 1932, signed "IMB"; "The Cadet System," letter to the editor, *Toronto Daily Star*, September 24, 1932, signed "Pro Pace."

22 "Cadet Training," letter to the editor, *Toronto Daily Star*, June 13, 1930, signed "A Cadet"; "Against Cadet Training," letter to the editor, *Toronto Daily Star*, June 5, 1931, signed "One Who Knows."

23 See, for example, "No Cadet Training," *Toronto Daily Star*, January 22, 1931; "Minimum Wage Defied Labor Man's Charge," *Toronto Daily Star*, September 4, 1931; "Buy Milk and Boots Instead of Uniforms," *Toronto Daily Star*, December 17, 1932; "Trustees Heckled on Cadet Training," *Toronto Globe*, December 23, 1932. The *Globe* favoured compulsory training; the *Star* preferred a voluntarist approach.

24 "Cadet Grant Cut Off, Toronto Out $12,000," *Toronto Daily Star*, May 16, 1931; Editorial, "Value of Cadet Training," *Toronto Globe*, October 8, 1932.

25 "Ask Principals' Views on Value of Cadet Plan," *Toronto Daily Star*, September 29, 1932; "Trustees to Study Voluminous Report on Cadet Training," *Toronto Globe*, October 13, 1932; "Principals Favor Abolition of School Cadet System," *Toronto Daily Star*, October 15, 1932. The *Star* endorsed the cancellation on October 19, 1932.

26 "Thinks Cadet Training Teaches Duty to God," *Toronto Daily Star*, November 10, 1932; "Shelve Abolition of Cadet Training," *Toronto Daily Star*, November 24, 1932.

27 "Trustees Censured for Dropping Cadets," *Toronto Daily Star*, January 21, 1933.

28 Antimilitarist demonstrations were held by the Toronto Communist Party; see "Plan Anti-War Meeting," *Toronto Daily Star*, January 18, 1930.

29 "School Cadet Training," letter to the editor, *Toronto Daily Star*, June 1, 1931. Similar views were expressed from a mother's viewpoint: Gayle Powell, "Away with War," *Toronto Daily Star*, September 27, 1932.

30 "Most Collegiates Drop Cadet Corps," *Toronto Daily Star*, January 24, 1933.

31 Patrick A. Dunae, "The Strathcona Trust and Physical Training in B.C. Public Schools," *The Homeroom*, www.viu.ca/homeroom/.

32 "Provisional School Lecture for Qualifying Cadet Instructors, Ottawa, 1933," *Cadet History – The Cadet Program Story*, Government of Canada, www.cadets.ca/history; Socknat, *Witness Against War*, 190.

33 "No Need to Copy Mussolini," *Toronto Daily Star*, October 21, 1938; "Cadet System is Approved by Vote of Three-to-One," *Toronto Daily Star*, April 29, 1939.

34 "Cadet Training," *Winnipeg Tribune*, July 12, 1939; Editorial, "School Cadet Corps," *Winnipeg Tribune*, September 25, 1939.

35 "Labour Men Opposed to Reviving Cadets," *Toronto Daily Star*, January 12, 1939.

36 "Cadet Training Viewed as One of Most Essential Preparations for Ultimate Victory," *Hamilton Spectator*, January 30, 1942; "No Delinquency Among Cadets," *Globe and Mail*, October 12, 1942; "School Board Approves Cadet Training Corps," *Winnipeg Tribune*, July 10, 1940; "Air Cadet Work Emphasized in National Appeal," *Hamilton Spectator*, March 20, 1944. On juvenile delinquency see Jeff Keshen, *Saints, Soldiers and Sinners: Canada's Second World War* (Vancouver: UBC Press, 2004), especially chapter 8.

37 Editorial, "Drill vs. Culture," *Guelph Mercury*, April 12, 1939.

38 Cited in Christine Hamelin, "A Sense of Purpose: Ottawa Students and the Second World War," *Canadian Military History* 6, no. 1 (1997): 40.

39 "Organize Girls As Naval Cadets," *Hamilton Spectator*, February 7, 1942; Stephanie Walker, "K-W Airettes," *Annual Volume of the Waterloo Historical Society* 92 (2004): 103; Magee High School, Vancouver, B.C., *Adventure*, 1944 (school yearbook), 46, 54; Bobbie Rosenfeld, "Armyette Cadets Thrill as Ottawa Recognition Due," *Globe and Mail*, January 6, 1945. Not until the mid-1970s were young women officially accepted into the cadet corps.

40 "Girls Cadet Corps Proposed for Postwar Program, *Winnipeg Tribune*, February 7, 1945; Socknat, *Witness Against War*, 286.

41 Canada, *House of Commons Debates*, July 9, 1947, 5338–41.

42 Socknat, *Witness Against War*, 286–88; "Guelph Labour Men Oppose Compulsory Cadet Training," *Toronto Daily Star*, April 21, 1947. Drew, who served as Minister of Education, explains his commitment to continue in "Cadet Training Plans Must Go On: Drew," *Globe and Mail*, July 11, 1947.

43 "Cadet Training," letter to the editor, *Toronto Daily Star*, April 1, 1947, signed "Mrs. Edna Barnett." Barnett, a former school board trustee, had taken an active part in earlier board discussions against cadet training.

44 "Cadet Training," letter to the editor, *Toronto Daily Star*, April 24, 1947, signed "Christine Chadwick."

45 Gallup Poll of Canada, "56 PC Favour Cadet Training as Part of School Course," *Toronto Daily Star*, June 7, 1947.

46 "Citizenship Corps Plans Announced by Premier Drew," *Globe and Mail*, August 27, 1947. The new course was "Physical Education and Citizenship Corps Training." See also "School Head Raps Drew's 'Last Minute Curtailment,'" *Toronto Daily Star*, August 27, 1947. Calls for reinstatement included "Cut Out Patronage, Veterans Tell Drew," *Toronto Daily Star*, May 9, 1947, and "Veterans Favor Youth Training," *Regina Leader-Post*, December 12, 1950.

7 "This Thing Is in Our Blood for 400 Years"

1 John F. Kennedy Presidential Library and Museum, www.jfklibrary.org/Research/Research-Aids/Ready-Reference/JFK-Quotations.aspx#C. Thank you to the reviewers and editors for helping to build this chapter. Most importantly, thank you to the conscientious objectors and their families for their service and witness.

2 Conrad Stoesz, "Scattered Documents: Locating the CO Record in Canada," *Journal of Mennonite Studies* 25 (2007): 147. The most detailed estimate of Canadian COs during the Second World War suggests that they comprised 10,851 men. See John A. Toews, *Alternative Service in Canada During World War II* (Winnipeg: Publication Committee of the Canadian Conference of the Mennonite Brethren Churches, 1959), 95.

3 Within the historic peace church communities, families were usually aware of their relatives' work in some obscure forest, mine, or farm, but the CO experience and what it meant for the men, their communities, and the country was (and is) poorly understood. Indeed, some families were uninterested in or embarrassed by their relatives' decision to pursue alternative service.

4 Jesus' life embodied love for self, neighbour, and enemy, and a call to follow His example through discipleship – which includes a lifelong, everyday attempt to follow the principles of nonresistance.

5 It is important to note the diversity of thought among pacifist groups. Hutterites and many Mennonites understood faithfulness to include separation from society. Following Peter Brock, Thomas Socknat calls these groups "separational pacifists." Thomas P. Socknat, *Witness Against War: Pacifism in Canada 1900–1945* (Toronto: University of Toronto Press, 1987), 12. While not usually considered part of the Historic Peace Church group, Doukhobors had a similar separation ethic. Peter Brock, *Twentieth-Century Pacifism* (New York: Van Nostrand Reinhold, 1970), 5. In contrast, Quakers viewed faithful living as engagement with the world in order to bring about change and have been labelled "integrational pacifists." Other groups of pacifists have been labelled "eschatological pacifists" and include Jehovah's Witnesses, Christadelphians, and Seventh-Day Adventists. They embraced nonviolence but accepted the possibility of fighting for Christ when the final battle with Satan and evil is waged. Socknat, *Witness Against War*, 18. For further discussion on the types of pacifism see John Richard Burkholder and Barbara Nelson Gingrich, eds., *Mennonite Peace Theology: A Panorama of Types* (Akron: Mennonite Central Committee, 1991).

6 Ted Regehr, *Mennonites in Canada 1939–1970: A People Transformed* (Toronto: University of Toronto Press, 1996), 38–39.

7 Laureen Harder-Gissing, "Companions on the 'lonely path': the Conference of Historic Peace Churches, 1940–1964," *Canadian Quaker History Journal* 76 (2011): 2.

8 Regehr, *Mennonites in Canada*, 46–47.

9 The Quakers were pleased to be invited to join the committee and sent Fred Haslam as their representative. Their inclusion added more voices for active alternative service. Socknat, *Witness Against War*, 231.

10 Prime Minister Mackenzie King grew up knowing the Mennonite community, which was strong in his hometown of Kitchener, Ontario, and had a positive view of them. King's journal suggests that he respected people who believed in pacifism but saw it as impractical. He was, however, against censure of people with this belief. When conscientious objectors were disenfranchised in 1917, King forcefully recorded his opposition: "To take away the vote from 'conscientious objectors' Quakers etc. is very outrageous. They are among the best class of citizens. Because a man won't agree to kill another, that he should be deprived of citizenship is hideous." The Diaries of William Lyon Mackenzie King, September 6, 1917, Library and Archives Canada, www.collectionscanada.gc.ca/databases/king/001059-119.02-e.php?&page_id_nbr=6443&interval=20&&PHPSESSID=3dcpltng0ej8ol9f5p97gmq511.

11 Regehr, *Mennonites in Canada*, 48. The historic peace churches were not the only group to appeal to the government for special consideration regarding military exemption. The Doukhobors had also come to Canada with strong Christian beliefs against taking up arms and an important factor in their immigration was the Order-in-Council of December 6, 1898, that promised them military exemption. Two delegations of Doukhobors travelled to Ottawa but were informed that the government reserved the right to change its commitment to the Order-in-Council. Koozma J. Tarasoff, *Plakun Trava: The Doukhobors* (Grand Forks: Mir Publication Society, 1982), 155. Similarly, Jehovah's Witnesses were opposed to military involvement. However, they dared not seek an audience with the government because they were outlawed by Order-in-Council on July 4, 1940, and remained an illegal organization until 1943. James Penton, "Jehovah's Witnesses and the Second World War: Resistance to Militarism and to Alternative Service," *Journal of Mennonite Studies*, 25 (2007): 75. See also "Jehovah's Witnesses," *Historica Canada*, thecanadianencyclopedia.com/en/article/jehovahs-witnesses/.

12 Regehr, *Mennonites in Canada*, 48–49. David W. Fransen, "Canadian Mennonites and Conscientious Objection in World War II" (PhD diss., University of Waterloo, 1977), 103.

13 Fransen, "Canadian Mennonites," 108.

14 Bill Waiser, *Park Prisoners: The Untold Story of Western Canada's National Parks 1915–1946* (Saskatoon: Fifth House, 1995), 129.

15 Regehr, *Mennonites in Canada*, 53.

16 This was not welcomed by the separational pacifists, such as the *Aeltestenkomitee*. However, Fred Haslam advocated for exemption based on individual conviction on behalf of all people with moral aversion to war. This view was echoed by organizations such as the Christian Social Council and the United Church. Socknat, *Witness Against War*, 231, 233.

17 Toews, *Alternative Service in Canada During World War II*, 48.

18 Regehr, *Mennonites in Canada*, 46.

19 Kenneth Wayne Reddig, "Manitoba Mennonites and the Winnipeg Mobilization Board in World War II" (master's thesis, University of Manitoba, 1989), 52, 99–100.

20 Reddig, "Manitoba Mennonites," 162.

21 David Schroeder, "Theological Reflections of a CO: Changing Peace Theology since World War II," *Journal of Mennonite Studies* 25 (2007): 192, note 11. Adamson writes in the introduction "I am delighted to see Major Wadge's treatise on this subject and hope that it will go a long way in not only giving an answer to Conscientious Objectors, but in keeping the minds of the people at large on the right path." Herbert W. Wadge, *Should a Christian Fight? The Position of Conscientious Objectors* (Ottawa: Hignell Printing, 1944), viii. Reddig, 163.

22 "We are convinced that the younger people would gladly co-operate with the government and are only prevented by superior influence," they noted. Letter from Mr. Justice J.F.L. Embury to Bishop David Toews, May 22, 1942, Mennonite Heritage Centre, vol. 1321, file 922.

23 Benjamin B. Janz to Prime Minister Mackenzie King, October 24, 1942, Centre for Mennonite Brethren Studies, vol. 982, file 67.

24 Stoesz, "Scattered Documents," 146.

25 Henry Funk, "C.O. Experiences During World War II: The Manitoba School for Mentally Defective Persons, Portage la Prairie," *Alternative Service Memoirs*, ed. John C. Klassen and Jake Krueger (Morden: John C. Klassen & Jake Krueger, 1995), 138.

26 John C. Klassen, "Experiences as a C.O. During World War II" *Alternative Service Memoirs*, ed. Klassen and Krueger, 23.

27 Mennonite Heritage Centre, vol. 1015, file 67. See also www.alternativeservice.ca/sacrifice/prison/index.htm.

28 Waiser, *Park Prisoners*, 135.

29 Regehr, *Mennonites in Canada*, 35.

30 Tarasoff, *Plakun Trava*, 158.

31 Marlene Epp, *Mennonite Women in Canada: A History* (Winnipeg: University of Manitoba Press, 2008), 204–8.

32 Henry H. Funk, "Mennonites in Canada, A Pacifism – CMBC student project on C.O.'s in WWII," Mennonite Heritage Centre, vol. 1015, file 23.

33 Regehr, *Mennonites in Canada*, 41.

34 Penton, "Jehovah's Witnesses and the Second World War," 76.

35 William Janzen and Frances Greaser, *Sam Martin went to Prison: The Story of Conscientious Objection and Canadian Military Service* (Winnipeg: Kindred Productions, 1990). See also www.alternativeservice.ca/sacrifice/prison/CO-Sacrifice-Prision-Martin.htm.

36 Letter from Jacob Gerbrandt to David Toews, February 7, 1941, Mennonite Heritage Centre, vol. 1322, file 933. Translated from the German by Jake K. Wiens.

37 Henry H. Funk, "C.O. Experiences During World War II," 139.

38 "In Memory of Private Leslie Abram Neufeld," Veterans Affairs Canada, www.veterans.gc.ca/eng/remembrance/memorials/canadian-virtual-war-memorial/detail/2628195.

39 *Prince Albert Daily Herald*, October 25, 1941, 5. Quoted in Tarasoff, *Plakun Trava*, 155–56.

40 When Peter Unger of Coaldale, Alberta, was on his way to a CO camp in Jasper National Park, some of his former classmates taunted him and called his manhood into question. Waiser, *Park Prisoners*, 146. See also Amy Shaw, *Crisis of Conscience: Conscientious Objection in Canada during the First World War* (Vancouver: UBC Press, 2009).

41 Interview with Gordon Toombs by Conrad Stoesz, Mennonite Heritage Centre audiocassette 2386; Socknat, *Witness Against War*, 252.

42 Waiser, *Park Prisoners*, 131–34.

43 Henry Sawatzky, "C.O. Memoirs," *Alternative Service Memoirs*, ed. Klassen and Krueger, 8. Waiser, *Park Prisoners*, 139–41.

44 Sawatzky, "C.O. Memoirs," 7.

45 Noah W. Bearinger, "No Spears of Iron," *Alternative Service Memoirs*, ed. Klassen and Krueger, 105.

46 Peter Dueck and Conrad Stoesz, *Alternative Service in the Second World War: Conscientious Objectors in Canada 1939–1945* (Winnipeg: Mennonite Heritage Centre; 2004), www.alternativeservice.ca/service/camps/support/mail.htm.

47 In 1942 and 1943 COs fought 234 forest fires. Regehr, *Mennonites in Canada*, 52.

48 A.J. Klassen, ed., *Alternative Service for Peace* (Abbotsford: Mennonite Central Committee B.C., Seniors for Peace, 1998), inside front and back covers. See also www.alternativeservice.ca/service/maps/.

49 In total 44,115 acres of snags were cleared. Dueck and Stoesz, *Alternative Service in the Second World War*; alternativeservice.ca/sowhat/.

50 A.J. Klassen, ed., "Gordon Dyck," *Alternative Service for Peace*, 59–60.

51 Waiser, *Park Prisoners*, 173–74.

52 Waiser, *Park Prisoners*, 138. The COs appreciated the sporting activities but found the boxing amusing and it was not taken seriously.

53 "Camp GT-1 News," *Beacon* 3, no. 2 (February/March 1944): 5.

54 Marlene Epp, "Heroes or Yellow-bellies? Masculinity and the Conscientious Objector," *Journal of Mennonite Studies* 17 (1999): 111, 113. It is unclear if the men who left the CO camps for military service entered restricted enlistment, serving in the medical corps, or if they joined regular active service.

55 Mennonite Heritage Centre, alternativeservice.ca/service/camps/work/habukkuk.htm. See also www.cbc.ca/ideas/episodes/2012/09/17/iceberg-ship-habbakuk/#igImgId_50898.

56 Conrad Stoesz, "Gerhard Ens (1922–2011): Historian, Minister and Educator," *Preservings* 31 (2011): 85.

57 One wonders to what extent some may have seen such service as legitimizing the Japanese internment camps.

58 Dueck and Stoesz, *Alternative Service in the Second World War*; alternativeservice.ca/service/teachers.

59 Conrad Stoesz, "Are you Prepared to Work in a Mental Hospital?: Canadian Conscientious Objectors' Service during the Second World War," *Journal of Mennonite Studies* 29 (2011): 62.

60 The role of the medic was to care for the wounded in body and soul regardless if they were friend or foe. A.J. Klassen, ed., *Alternative Service for Peace*, 113. Some medics were killed in action including Rudolf Goetz who pounced on a live grenade, absorbing its impact to save others. Regehr, *Mennonites in Canada*, 37. Andrew Vogt of Steinbach was in the dental corps and received two military medals for his service. Email from Andrew Vogt's sister, Margaret Kroeker, to Conrad Stoesz, June 28, 2013. The two medals were the Canadian "Volunteer Service Medal" and the "War Medal 1939–1945." 227 Mennonites served in this capacity. Regehr, *Mennonites in Canada*, 54.

61 Stoesz, "Are you Prepared to Work in a Mental Hospital?" 63–68; Herbert J. Brandt, "Serving in Alternative Service as a C.O. in the Brandon Mental Hospital from 1943 to 1946," in *Alternative Service Memoirs*, ed. Klassen and Krueger, 123; Lawrence Klippenstein, *That There be Peace: Mennonites in Canada and World War II* (Winnipeg: Manitoba CO Reunion Committee, 1979), 49; Regehr, *Mennonites in Canada*, 53.

62 Toews, *Alternative Service in Canada During World War II*, 103.

63 David F. Friesen, "Mennonites in Canada, A Pacifism – CMBC student project on C.O.'s in WWII," Mennonite Heritage Centre, vol. 1015, file 56.

64 A.J. Klassen, ed., *Alternative Service for Peace*, 278–80.

65 Waiser, *Park Prisoners*, 155.

66 Lucille Marr, "Taves, Harvey W. (1926–1965)," *Global Anabaptist Mennonite Encyclopedia Online*, gameo.org/index.php?title=Taves,_Harvey_W._(1926-1965). Other examples include the Mennonite Central Committee and Mennonite Disaster Service Program.

67 Ed Brooks, camp boss at Clear Lake, noted at a thirty-year reunion that he became a better person because of his contact with the COs. Waiser, *Park Prisoners*, 156.

68 Speech by Brian Minnaker at the dedication of the City of Winkler Veterans Memorial Cenotaph, September 18, 2011.

69 This temporary display opened at the Canadian War Museum in Ottawa on May 31, 2013.

8 Principal Purdie Objects

1 The research for this chapter was funded in part by a grant from the Laurentian University Research Fund. The author wishes to thank her research assistant, David Scott, for his careful work on this project and her colleague in the LU History Department, Daniel Byers, for sharing his enthusiasm and expertise about Canadian military history. James Craig and the late Marilyn Stroud of the Pentecostal Assemblies of Canada Archives provided valuable support to this research. Portions of this chapter were published in Linda M. Ambrose, "On the Edge of War and Society: Canadian Pentecostal Bible School Students in the 1940s," *Journal of the Canadian Historical Association* 24, no. 1 (2013): 215–45.

2 J.E. Purdie to Rev. D.N. Buntain and C.M. Wortman, April 20, 1944, Pentecostal Assemblies of Canada Archives (PAOC Archives).

3 While it is impossible to know how many times Principal Purdie intervened on behalf of his students, correspondence surrounding at least five cases is preserved in his personal files at the PAOC Archives. It is likely, however, that this number is only a fraction of the cases, since Purdie described himself in a 1942 letter to officials at the Department of National War Services saying "you will recall having had correspondence with me regarding theological students and the war, and also several interviews." Purdie to Colonel C.D. McPherson, October 15, 1942, PAOC Archives. The 1944 student yearbook from the Bible College listed the names of twenty-nine students "On Active Service." These included sixteen who had enlisted in the army, five in the navy, seven in the air force, and one, Horace

Ross, who had died in action. It is not possible to determine whether these students had enlisted willingly, or if Purdie had tried unsuccessfully to intervene on their behalf. "On Active Service," *The Portal 1944*, PAOC Archives, 16.

4 Thomas P. Socknat, *Witness Against War: Pacifism in Canada, 1900–1945* (Toronto: University of Toronto Press, 1987); J.L. Granatstein and J.M. Hitsman, *Broken Promises: A History of Conscription in Canada* (Toronto: Oxford University Press, 1977); C.P. Stacey, *Arms, Men and Governments: The War Policies of Canada, 1939–1945* (Ottawa: Queen's Printer, 1970).

5 Michael Wilkinson, ed., *Canadian Pentecostalism: Transition and Transformation* (Montreal/Kingston: McGill-Queen's Press, 2009), 4–5.

6 Rev. J.E. Purdie played a significant leadership role among Canadian Pentecostals throughout the twentieth century through his work as an educator, particularly in developing the curriculum that was used to train ministers and laypeople in PAOC Bible Colleges across the country. Several scholars concur on this point including Peter Althouse, "The Influence of Dr. J.E. Purdie's Reformed Theology on the Formation and Development of the Pentecostal Assemblies of Canada," *Pneuma* 19, no. 1 (1996): 3–28; James Craig, "Out and Out for the Lord: James Eustace Purdie An Early Anglican Pentecostal" (master's thesis, University of St. Michael's College, 1995); Bruce L. Guenther, "Pentecostal Theological Education: A Case Study of Western Bible College, 1925–50," in *Canadian Pentecostalism*, ed. Wilkinson, 99–122; Brian Ross, "James Eustace Purdie: The Story of Pentecostal Theological Education," *Journal of the Canadian Church Historical Society* 17, no. 4 (1975): 94–103.

7 By the time the 2001 Canadian census was taken, there were almost 370,000 people who identified as Pentecostals. Wilkinson, *Canadian Pentecostalism*, 4.

8 Thomas William Miller, *Canadian Pentecostals: A History of the Pentecostal Assemblies of Canada* (Mississauga: Full Gospel Publishing House, 1994), 267.

9 *Yearbook of the Pentecostal Assemblies of Canada* (Toronto: PAOC, 1943), 59, PAOC Archives; *Pentecostal Testimony* (hereafter *PT*) October 15, 1941, 2; Wilkinson, *Canadian Pentecostalism*, 4.

10 Adam Stewart, ed., *A Handbook of Pentecostal Christianity* (DeKalb: Northern Illinois University Press, 2012).

11 Adam Stewart, "A Canadian Azuza? The Implications of the Hebden Mission for Pentecostal Historiography," in Michael Wilkinson and Peter Althouse, eds., *Winds from the North: Canadian Contributions to the Pentecostal Movement* (Leiden: Brill, 2010), 17–38; "Hebden, James (d. c. 1919) and Ellen K.," *The New International Dictionary of Pentecostal and Charismatic Movements*, ed. Stanley M. Burgess and Eduard M. van der Maas (Grand Rapids: Zondervan, 2010), 711–12; Thomas William Miller, "The Canadian 'Azuza': The Hebden Mission in Toronto," *Pneuma* 8, no. 1 (1986): 5–29.

12 Amy Shaw, *Crisis of Conscience: Conscientious Objection in Canada during the First World War* (Vancouver: UBC Press, 2009), 166–88; Socknat, *Witness Against War*, 81–84. One account of a Pentecostal conscientious objector in WWI is that of Elmer Morrison, whose story was recounted in "My Call to China," *PT* July 1923, 5. Morrison, of Kitchener, Ontario, had refused to be conscripted under the *Military Service Act* and in June 1918 was sentenced to imprisonment for a term of two years. He served nine months of that sentence.

13 "How he won the V.C.: A True Story," *PT* December 15, 1944, 14–15.

14 Zelma Argue, "The Outlook of the Unregenerate World: What is the World Getting Ready for? Is There Any Hope But in Christ?" *PT* January 1922, 2. For an explanation of "eschatological pacifism" see Peter Brock, *Pacifism in Europe to 1914* (Princeton: Princeton University Press, 1972), 472.

15 G.A. Chambers, "Should Christians Go to War?" *PT*, November 1935, 14; December 1935, 13; January 1936, 6; February 1936, 10.

16 Miller, *Canadian Pentecostals*, 42; "Chambers, George Augustus (1879–1957)" *The New International Dictionary of Pentecostal and Charismatic Movements*, 472.

17 Miller, *Canadian Pentecostals*, 247.

18 "Buntain, Daniel Newton (1888–1955)," *The New International Dictionary of Pentecostal and Charismatic Movements*, 449–50.

19 D.N. Buntain, "If I Were Caught in the Draft," *PT*, September 1, 1941, 4.

20 Buntain, "If I Were Caught in the Draft," 4.

21 Purdie to Rev. D.N. Buntain and C.M. Wortman, April 20, 1944, PAOC Archives.

22 Purdie to Col. C.D. McPherson, Department of National War Services, Winnipeg, March 27, 1941, PAOC Archives.

23 C.D. McPherson, Divisional Registrar, Department of National War Services, to Purdie, March 31, 1941, PAOC Archives.

24 H. Wuerch to Dr. Perdie [sic], July 29, 1942, PAOC Archives.

25 Purdie to McPherson, October 15, 1942. PAOC Archives.

26 Leslie Tausendfrende to Dr. J.E. Purdie, July 16, 1942, PAOC Archives.

27 Purdie to Tausendfrende, July 20, 1942, PAOC Archives.

28 M. James Penton, *Jehovah's Witnesses in Canada: Champions of Freedom of Speech and Worship* (Toronto: Macmillan Canada, 1976). See especially chapter 7, "Banned as Seditious," 129–55.

29 Purdie to McPherson, October 15, 1942, PAOC Archives.

30 Purdie to McPherson, October 15, 1942.

31 The best-known historical writing about military chaplaincy in Canada has concentrated on the First World War. See Duff Crerar, *Padres in No Man's Land: Canadian Chaplains and the Great War* (Montreal/Kingston: McGill-Queen's University Press, 1995); Crerar, "The Church in the Furnace: Canadian Anglican Chaplains Respond to the Great War," *Journal of the Canadian Church Historical Society*, 35 (1993): 75–103. On chaplains during the Second World War see Richard E. Ruggle, "Canadian Chaplains: A Special Issue," *Journal of the Canadian Church Historical Society*, 35 (1993): 65–74; Thomas Hamilton, "'The Delicate Equilibrium': Canada's Protestant Chaplains during the Second World War," *Journal of the Canadian Church Historical Society*, 35 (1993): 105–20; Peter Dueck, "'The Sword of the Lord': Honorary Captain Waldo E.L. Smith and the Second World War," *Journal of the Canadian Church Historical Society*, 48 (2006): 55–84; Albert G. Fowler, *Peacetime Padres: Protestant Military Chaplains, 1945–1995* (St. Catharines: Vanwell, 1996), 13–45; Yves Yvon J. Pelletier, "Faith on the Battlefield: Canada's Catholic Chaplaincy Service During the Second World War," *CCHA Historical Studies* 69 (2003): 64–84; Pelletier "Fighting for the Chaplains: Bishop Charles Leo Nelligan and the Creation of the Canadian Chaplaincy Service (Roman Catholic), 1939–1945," *CCHA Historical Studies* 72 (2006): 95–123.

32 Fowler, *Peacetime Padres*, 288, note 10.

33 Purdie to C.M. Wortman, January 17, 1945, PAOC Archives.

9 Margaret Ells Russell

1 Marie Smith, "500 Women Picket for Peace," *Washington Post/Times Herald*, November 2, 1961; Dennis Hevesi, "Dagmar Wilson, Anti-Nuclear Leader, Dies at 94," *New York Times*, January 23, 2011 (Kennedy quotation); Terry Golway and Les Krantz, *JFK Day By Day: A Chronicle of the 1,036 Days of John F. Kennedy's Presidency* (Philadelphia: Running Press, 2010), entry for February 16, p. 119.

2 Catia Cecilia Confortini, *Intelligent Compassion: Feminist Critical Methodology in the Women's International League for Peace and Freedom* (Oxford: Oxford University Press, 2012), 28.

3 Confortini, *Intelligent Compassion*, 4, 12.

4 I shall often simply call Margaret Ells Russell "Margaret" to avoid confusion, not to imply any personal connection with, or condescension toward, her. Canadians who remember her will know her as "Margaret Ells," the name under which she published her numerous articles and reports. Americans will know her as "Margaret Russell," from her peace activism. She is also often referred to in the contemporary press as "Mrs. Ralph Russell."

5 The consensus is that meeting was held on September 21 and included Margaret Ells Russell, Dagmar Wilson, Holly F. Fodor, Janie Holland, Jeanne Bigby, Eleanor Garst, Lawrence Scott, and Christopher Wilson. Dagmar Wilson, untitled document, November 1, 1960, Women Stike for Peace fonds, Peace Collection, Swarthmore College, Swarthmore, Pennsylvania (hereafter WSP fonds), series A2, box 1.

6 Inigo [Margaret Ells], "Canning in the 'Seventies,'" n.d. [c.1929], 16, Margaret Ells fonds, MG1, vol. 2676, Public Archives of Nova Scotia (PANS).

7 She was fearful in 1931 of the British Labour Party, for instance: see Margaret Ells to "Boys" [Donald and Theodore Ells], October 11, 1931, Margaret Ells fonds, MG1, Microfilm 10239, PANS.

8 Norah Story to "My friends" [James Martell and Margaret Ells], n.d. [1944], Phyllis Blakeley fonds, MG1, vol. 3070, file no. 1, PANS. Story writes: "First and foremost, I rejoiced in the C.C.F. victory, because I realized that it would please you. For myself, I have my doubts about the party. . . ." Story is likely referring to the CCF's victory in Saskatchewan. Many "middle-of-the-road" liberals were tempted by the CCF in the 1940s.

9 Although not formally affiliated with the Antigonish Movement, the Halifax Co-operators were inspired by its vision of a "Third Way" of grassroots democracy and equitable economic relations, an alternative to both classical liberalism and communism. For recent discussions of the movement, see Rusty Neal, *Brotherhood Economics: Women and Co-operatives in Nova Scotia* (Sydney: UCCB Press, 1998) and Santo Dodaro and Leonard Pluta, *The Big Picture: The Antigonish Movement of Eastern Nova Scotia* (Montreal/Kingston: McGill-Queen's University Press, 2012). The remains of the Halifax Co-operative Library can be found with the author.

10 In Asia, she visited the Philippines, Indonesia, China, Malaysia, Cambodia, Thailand, and Ceylon.

11 Margaret Ells to "Everybody," March 3, 1937, April 7, 19, 1937, MG1, vol. 2786, Ells Papers, file 4, PANS.

12 Margaret Ells to Donald Ells, December 9, 1930, Microfilm 10239, Margaret Ells fonds, PANS; unsigned and untitled biographical note by Ralph Russell, Margaret Ells fonds, MG1, vol. 2676, PANS.

13 Wilson was born in Manhattan in 1916 but lived abroad for much of her childhood; she graduated from London's Slade School of Fine Art in 1937.

14 As Agnes Macphail told one of its meetings in 1924, "Conditions are driving people to think. Increasing numbers are realizing that our problems are world problems, and we must solve them together or perish together." Annual Reports of the Women's International League for Peace and Freedom, *Report of the Fourth Congress of the Women's International League for Peace and Freedom, Washington, May 1 to 7, 1924.* English Edition. Women's International League, U.S. Section, 1924, 118. For an overview of global women's peace activism, see Carolyn Strange, "Mothers on the March: Maternalism in Women's Protest for Peace in North America and Western Europe, 1900–1985," in *Women and Social Protest*, ed. Guida West and Rhoda Lois Blumberg (New York: Oxford University Press, 1990), 209–24.

15 At Dalhousie, Margaret was a stalwart supporter of the Model League of Nations. See *Pharos: The Year Book of Dalhousie*, 1930, 102, Margaret Ells fonds, MG1, vol. 2788, no. 3, PANS.

16 Confortini, *Intelligent Compassion*, 4, 12.

17 In the early WSP of 1962, for example, there remained the persistent hope that, if only the

women could reach him through the White House, John F. Kennedy himself would become one of their followers. WSP, *Washington Newsletter* 1, no. 1 (January 1962), WSP fonds.

18 Abraham Bloom, Vice-President Washington Committee, Dagmar Wilson, Secretary, Holly F. Fodor, Janie Holland and Margaret Russell, to the National Committee for a Sane Nuclear Policy, August 23, 1960, National Committee for a Sane Nuclear Policy, WSP fonds, Washington Office fonds, DG58, series E, box 22, file Correspondence – District of Columbia, 1960–1966. There were other issues in the air as well, such as the recent imprisonment of philosopher Bertrand Russell – an act that generated minimal response from SANE.

19 See Frank Parkin, *Middle Class Radicalism: The Social Bases of the British Campaign for Nuclear Disarmament* (Manchester: Manchester University Press, 1968); Richard Taylor and Colin Pritchard, *The Protest Makers: The British Nuclear Disarmament of 1958–1965: Twenty Years On* (Oxford: Pergamon, 1980); and, for a transnational perspective, Holger Nehring, "National Internationalists: British and West German Protests against Nuclear Weapons, the Politics of Transnational Communications and the Social History of the Cold War, 1957–1964," *Contemporary European History* 14, no. 4 (2006): 223–41.

20 Tarah Brookfield, *Cold War Comforts: Canadian Women, Child Safety, and Global Insecurity* (Waterloo: Wilfrid Laurier University Press, 2012); Frances Early, "'A Grandly Subversive Time': The Halifax Branch of the Voice of Women in the 1960s," in *Mothers of the Municipality: Women, Work, and Social Policy in Post-1945 Halifax*, ed. Judith Fingard and Janet Guildford (Toronto: University of Toronto Press, 2005), 253–80; Kay Macpherson, *When in Doubt, Do Both: The Times of My Life* (Toronto: University of Toronto Press, 1994); Mick Lowe, *One Woman Army: The Life of Claire Culhane* (Toronto: Macmillan Canada, 1992). For contemporary accounts of VOW/WSP interactions, see "Local VOW Members Demonstrate at UN," *Globe and Mail*, November 2, 1963.

21 Other versions of the story have the Women's Strike emerging at a Washington garden party. In the more commonly accepted version, it is noteworthy that although writers have generally assumed the meeting took place in the Wilsons' home, Dagmar Wilson does not actually say that it did: it merely took place in a "comfortable" living room.

22 Dagmar Wilson, untitled document, November 1, 1960, WSP fonds, series A2, box 1. The document came to be attributed to Wilson alone, but it is better interpreted as a statement of the emergent collective.

23 Women Strike for Peace, Leaflet, *Information: Women's March for Peace, Nov 1, 1961. Keep This List – You'll Need It*, WSP fonds, series A2, box 1. Although we will never be certain of the authorship of this unsigned leaflet, it was characteristic of Margaret Ells to resort to the ironically grandiloquent reference to "The Day" at the end of this document. If not the document's author, she was, as manager of the Washington demo, responsible for it.

24 "Say, Fellows! Where's that Men's Auxiliary you keep muttering about? We sure would like a barbecue at the end of The Day!" Women Strike for Peace, Leaflet, *Information*.

25 One might even wonder if "strike" was being used as a verb or a noun. If the action was the "Women Strike for Peace," then strike could be taken to be a verb, and the action's name was a complete sentence. But if it was the "Women's Strike for Peace" – the more common usage – then the suggestion was that "strike" was a noun, applied to one particular event. Eventually, "Strike" acquired a third, highly unconventional connotation – it was applied to an entire group, rather than to an occurrence.

26 WSP, *Washington Newsletter* 1, no. 2 (1962), WSP fonds.

27 Dagmar Wilson, untitled document, November 1, 1960, WSP fonds, series A2, box 1.

28 She was strongly in favour of the Antigonish Movement, one of whose core texts was *Masters of Their Own Destiny*, a paean of praise to grassroots activism. As librarian of the Halifax Co-operative Society, she circulated down-to-earth accounts of how ordinary

people around the world could wrest back control of their lives from merchants and industrialists without resorting to revolutionary socialism.

29 In Winnipeg, member Ester Reiter recalls, "VOW members would dress in good clothes when they went to protests and marches, to show the police and potential critics they were respectable ladies and mothers." Brookfield, *Cold War Comforts*, 86–87.

30 In a private letter of December 5, 1962, James B. Day of SANE likened the WSPers to St. George taking on the Dragon. Maybe supporters of the peace movement were convinced that HUAC was a sham, but "I doubt very much that the general American public, the crowd both sides are trying to please, will see it so clearly. After all, HUAC is a legitimate Congressional committee with the power to subpoena for investigative purposes." National Committee for a Sane Nuclear Policy, Washington Office fonds, DG58, series E, box 1, file HUAC Investigation of Women Strike for Peace, WSP fonds.

31 Catharine Stimpson, introduction to Amy Swerdlow, *Women Strike For Peace: Traditional Motherhood and Radical Politics in the 1960s* (Chicago: University of Chicago Press, 1993), xi. Political philosopher Jean Bethke Elshtain underlines the extent to which WSP "showed the grand deconstructive power of a politics of humor, irony, evasion and ridicule. The Women's Strike for Peace didn't proclaim that the Emperor had no clothes; rather they put in him a position where, to his own astonishment, he found he had disrobed himself with his own tactics and strategies." Elshtain, *Women, Militarism, and War: Essays in History, Politics, and Social Theory*, ed. Jean Bethke Elshtain and Sheila Tobias (Totowa: Rowman & Littlefield, 1990), 40, as cited in Swerdlow, *Women Strike*, 119.

32 George Bain, "Women Strike for Peace," *Globe and Mail*, December 17, 1962.

33 *Washington WSPer, Women Strike for Peace Newsletter, Greater Washington Area* (December 1965), 2, WSP fonds.

34 This amorphousness means that one should take generalizations about WSP's base with a few grains of salt. The WSP women, Swerdlow argues, "not only sounded alike, they looked alike. They came, for the most part, from the same class, race, and age group. They wore their status of middle-class wifehood and motherhood proudly, while asserting their responsibility for nurturance, moral guardianship, and life preservation" (Swerdlow, *Women Strike*, 25). Yet Margaret Ells Russell reminds us, as a Canadian, that not all the "women" came from the same country nor likely sounded the same way; Wilson herself, though born in the U.S., had been raised in Britain and had a strong British accent. Other historians (Confortini, *Intelligent Compassion*, 47) suggest that it was *younger* members of WILPF who gravitated to the WSP – not everyone in this crowd, it seems, was over 50. Struggles in Detroit raised by women of colour over the centrality of civil rights also suggested that the ideal of WSP spoke to some African Americans. And many men admired the WSP and supported its ideals. Elise Boulding, "Who Are These Women? A Progress Report on a Study of the Women Strike for Peace," unpublished essay, WSP fonds, DG115, series A1, box 2, 1963. It seems valid to suggest, in general terms, a "middle-class sensibility" to WSP, but it seems inherently hazardous to generalize too dogmatically about the "members" of any movement without an official membership.

35 For wrenching memories of her own personal experience of learning that some of her close associates in the WSP were spies, see Ethel Barol Taylor, *We Made A Difference: My Personal Journey with Women Strike for Peace* (Philadelphia: Camino Books, 1998), 41–77.

36 Its full name was the Treaty Banning Nuclear Weapons Tests in the Atmosphere, in Outer Space, and Under Water. It expressly forbade nuclear test detonations above ground and committed the signatories to "the speediest possible achievement of an agreement on general and complete disarmament." It was officially ratified by the Senate on September 24 and signed by Kennedy on October 7, 1963. Though a partial victory for WSP, it still allowed underground testing and did not impede the global proliferation of

nuclear weapons, as the examples of China, India, and Pakistan would soon demonstrate.

37 Wilson specifically singled out "our churches, bridge clubs, group meetings" in her appeal to women in September 1961.

38 It should always be remembered that the WSPers were also often members of WILPF and SANE and functioned within highly differentiated peace movements that differed from place to place, but almost always included Quakers, college professors and students worried about the Bomb, and some adherents of older Popular Front and Old Left groups.

39 In their cases, it was obviously groundless to imagine that they hankered after the organizational principles of the Communist Party.

40 For critical evaluations of IR "realism," see Robert W. Cox's path-breaking *Production, Power, and World Order: Social Forces in the Making of History* (New York: Columbia University Press, 1987); John Agnew, *Hegemony: The New Shape of Global Power* (Philadelphia: Temple University Press, 2005); Mark McNally and John Schwarzmantel, eds., *Gramsci and Global Politics: Hegemony and Resistance* (London: Routledge, 2009); Michael C. Williams, *The Realist Tradition and the Limits of International Relations* (Cambridge: Cambridge University Press, 2005).

41 It might have reminded her of the eighteenth-century Loyalists, whom she described as confronting "two rather unpleasant alternatives" – survival as best as possible at home, or leaving the comforts of home for an uncertain future in distant parts. Margaret Ells, "Loyalist Attitudes," in G.A. Rawlyk, ed., *Historical Essays on the Atlantic Provinces* (Toronto: McClelland & Stewart, 1967), 47.

42 Some believed that the entire group had decided on this name-change on January 15, 1962, and for a time they applied it even to the movement's central national newsletter. Despite efforts to play with "WISP" as a name that evoked the wind, blowing down the male warrior power structure, it had unavoidable connotations, not of raging storms and unstoppable gales, but of something quiet, insubstantial, and fleeting.

43 Swerdlow, *Women Strike*, 187.

44 One is tempted to suggest a parallel with the "Occupy" movement in the twenty-first century: a dazzling success in that it aroused a worldwide public to the inequities of neoliberalism, but – at least at this time of writing – not discernibly a "moment" within a larger, sustained political process of contesting the planetary neoliberal agenda.

45 WSP, *Washington Newsletter* 1, no. 2, 1962, WSP fonds.

46 W.S.P. [Washington] Minutes February 12, 1962, WSP fonds, DG115, series A1, box 1. Many steering committee meetings were held in Margaret's home, which she frequently left through 1963 and 1964 to engage actively with WSPers throughout the Northeast. W.S.P. [Washington], Steering Committee Minutes May 16, 1963; January 16, 1964, WSP fonds, DG115, series A1, box 1.

47 She proposed they make unilateral demands upon the Soviets: the unilateral renunciation of all future nuclear tests, progressive reduction of Soviet forces and Warsaw Pact bases, the opening of Soviet newspapers to American writers, and an immediate 5 per cent cut in military expenditures. *National Information Memo* no. 3, WISP NICH, report on National Conference, WSP fonds, *National Information*, vols. 1–2, 1962.

48 "We gave them our propaganda, and they gave us theirs," she remarked after visiting the Russian embassy at the time of the November 1961 "Strike." Smith, "500 Women Picket for Peace."

49 Margaret defensively noted that it was headquartered in *West* Berlin, led by a non-communist Frenchwoman, had millions of women in ninety countries as members, and had met previously in Sweden, Denmark, Poland, and Austria. Margaret Ells Russell, Report, Women International Strike for Peace, National Information Clearing House (WISP NICH), May 15, 1963, WSP fonds, *National Information*.

50 Margaret Ells Russell, Proposal, WISP NICH, April 19, 1963, WSP fonds, *National Information*.

51 Margaret Ells Russell, Report, May 15, 1963.

52 *National Information Memo* 30, April 19, 1963, WSP fonds, *National Information*, vols. 1–2.

53 *National Information Memo* 2, no. 8, October 4, 1963, WSP fonds, *National Information*.

54 *Washington Newsletter* 1, no. 3 (July 10, 1962), WSP fonds.

55 Margaret Ells Russell, Proposals Re: Viet Nam, WISP NICH, Washington, D.C, *National Information* 2, no. 8 (October 4, 1963), 2–3.

56 Margaret Ells Russell, "WSP Committees in Action. Committee on Vietnam," *Washington WSPer, Women Strike for Peace Newsletter, Greater Washington Area* (February 1964), 2, WSP fonds.

57 The others include WILPF, the Washington Peace Center, Washington Professors for World Peace, the Peace Committee of the Friends Meetings of Washington and Sandy Springs, and the Washington and Baltimore chapters of the National Committee for a Sane Nuclear Policy.

58 "Appeal to Reason Ad – A Success," *Washington WSPer*, November 1964. *Women Strike for Peace Newsletter, Greater Washington Area*, 2, WSP fonds. In December 1964, as chair of this ad hoc committee, Margaret noted that the local Washington Committee had distributed 20,000 leaflets to Christmas shoppers and 10,000 to churchgoers, and had participated in an international conference for Solidarity with South Vietnam. And in March 1965, Margaret joined radical journalist I.F. Stone in a Washington Universalist Church and urged the audience to write to their congressmen – "TODAY!!" Margaret Ells Russell, "Viet Nam News," *Washington WSPer, Women Strike for Peace Newsletter, Greater Washington Area* (January 1965), 1; see also March 1965, 1.

59 WISP NICH, *National Information*, October 2, 8, 4, 1963, WSP fonds.

60 WISP NICH, *National Information*, February 2, 16, 28, 1964, Re: Campaign for peace in South Vietnam (co-written with Mary Clarke, Alice Richards, and Jacqueline Hoyt), October 1963, WSP fonds.

61 It was suggestive of the importance attached to this meeting by the Vietnamese that one of their delegation was Nguyen Thi Binh, a member of the Viet Cong's central committee and eventually the Vice President of the Socialist Republic of Vietnam from 1992 to 2002.

62 As Judy Tzu-Chun, "Journeys for Peace and Liberation: Third World Internationalism and Radical Orientalism during the U.S. War in Vietnam," *Pacific Historical Review* 76, no. 4 (November 2007): 575–84 remarks, "the experience of travel fostered and solidified a sense of internationalism, a conviction of political solidarity, with Third World peoples and nations among U.S. activists of varying racial backgrounds.... Through travel and correspondence, they learned to regard Third World female liberation fighters as exemplars of revolutionary womanhood" (582). Such a generalization would perhaps overstate Margaret's transformation – nowhere can I find her endorsing revolution – but it suggests that an initial romanticization of Third World "Others" could grow into more substantial acts of solidarity, as it did in her case.

63 Later, Claire Culhane became a radical activist against the War in Vietnam because of her experience in the country itself; see Mick Lowe, *One Woman Army: The Life of Claire Culhane* (Toronto: Macmillan Canada, 1992), 171–203. Kay Macpherson of VOW visited Hanoi in 1967: see Frances Early, "Canadian Women and the International Arena in the Sixties: The Voice of Women/La Voix des femmes and the Opposition to the Vietnam War," in *The Sixties: Passion, Politics and Style*, ed. Dimitry Anastakis (Montreal/Kingston: McGill-Queen's University Press, 2008), 29. Women from war-torn Vietnam visited an international women's conference in Toronto in 1969.

64 *Washington WSPer, Women Strike for Peace Newsletter, Greater Washington Area* (July-August 1965), 3, WSP fonds.

65 One year before the National Mobilization March on Washington in 1968, WSP militants "literally stormed the military citadel, having removed their shoes to bang against Pentagon doors locked in their faces. Front page photos of this action were featured in hundreds of U.S. newspapers and in the media around the world." Amy Swerdlow, "WSP's Long March," clipping, WSP fonds, series A1, box 2.

66 There are saddening indications from the mid-1960s that Russell, perhaps carrying the after-effects of a bout with encephalitis in the mid-1950s, was no longer functioning at full capacity. The Steering Committee in January 1964 expressed, on her urging, its sincere regrets for the long delay in announcing an important Nevada Vigil against underground atomic testing on the grounds of an "unlucky mis-filing" of the key documents; later in August, a woman was appointed to "help Margaret re-establish phone chain connections south of Washington." Steering Committee Meeting Minutes, January 16, 1964, handwritten notes by Margaret Russell; Steering Committee Meeting Minutes, November 19, 1964, WSP fonds, DG115, series A1, box 1.

67 Midge Dector, "The Peace Ladies," *Harpers*, March 1963, 48–53, citation at 52.

68 "Possessing little awareness of their contribution to sex-role stereotyping and female oppression, they [the WSPers] were not aware in their early years that they were fighting a battle of the sexes, a woman's battle against the male elites who decided issues of life and death for all of humanity. They had no notion that they were also challenging the gendered division of labor and power in the political culture of the Left as well as the Right." Swerdlow, *Women Strike*, 233–34.

69 And, of course, a good number of the WSPers, Margaret included, were not mothers.

70 There are certainly moments when WSPers appealed to "motherhood ideals," but there were many others, including in the movement's founding documents, when the campaign used a more general discourse of humanism. Both men and women were thought to hold the future of human civilization in their hands; women, purportedly less abstract and more inclined to spontaneity and compassion, were placed in a privileged position to articulate this sensibility. Swerdlow contends (*Women Strike*, 246n10) that "WSP was a movement that build on women's traditional role as mothers." Frances Early (following Swerdlow) characterizes both WSP and VOW as exponents of a "motherist ideology" (Early, "'A Grandly Subversive Time,'" 279n82). In fact, much early WSP discourse conforms to Simone de Beauvoir's position – i.e., that women should desire peace as human beings, not as women – more exactly than it does to the sanctification of mothering. And one strongly doubts Margaret would have found the notion of fighting a perpetual "battle of the sexes" an analytically or ethically interesting proposition.

71 Among whom, it should be noted, the Women's Question in general and the specific interests of many women in peace were both popularly developed themes. See especially Kate Weigand, *Red Feminism: American Communism and the Making of Women's Liberation* (Baltimore: Johns Hopkins University Press, 2001).

72 A reference to the multi-lateral [nuclear] fleet. In 1964 WSP mobilized opposition to a scheme for a NATO-controlled fleet of twenty-five ships, with American and West German personnel – a disturbing sign, according to WSPers, that Germany might re-arm.

73 *Washington WSPer, Women Strike for Peace Newsletter, Greater Washington Area* (November 1964), 1, WSP fonds.

10 Bridging and Breaching Cold War Divides

1 I am grateful for generous research funding from the President's Research and Creativity Activities and Crake Awards and the Provost's Development Fund at Mount Allison University, Sackville, New Brunswick. I would particularly like to acknowledge the invaluable assistance of staff at Library and Archives Canada (LAC) – including Christine

Barrass and Sophie Tellier – as well as other archivists I have consulted, Jennifer Anderson (Canadian Museum of History), Myron Momryk (formerly of LAC), Brent Lougheed, Tyyne Petrowski, and James Kominowski (University of Manitoba Archives & Special Collections). Also, I am very thankful for the help of my student research assistant, Lydia Blois, and library staff at Mount Allison University. In addition, I am indebted to colleagues and friends for offering important suggestions, critical insights, or much valued support at various stages of this project: Lara Campbell (Simon Fraser University), Catherine Gidney (Saint Thomas University), Michael Dawson (Saint Thomas University), Robert Cupido (Mount Allison University), Elaine Naylor (Mount Allison University), Christabelle Sethna (University of Ottawa), and Steve Hewitt (University of Birmingham). Finally, I greatly appreciated the discussions and general support of the Canadian Voice of Women for Peace (VOW), Brigid Grant (Fredericton NB VOW), Ursula Franklin (Professor Emeritus, University of Toronto), Betty Peterson (Halifax VOW), Janis Alton (VOW Chair, Toronto) and members of the VOW Book Project Committee. And as always, I am deeply thankful to my partner, Kevin Callaghan, for his attentiveness and encouragement.

2 Voice of Women and the Communist Smear: Some Thoughts from the National President as a Consequence of Many Recent Conversations, January 1965, 1–2, Memoranda from National Office, 1962–1974, Voice of Women fonds, MG28, I218, Library and Archives Canada (hereafter VOW fonds), vol. 23, file 7.

3 Helen Laville, *Cold War Women: The International Activities of American Women's Organizations* (U.K.: Manchester University Press, 2002); Helen Laville, "The Memorial Day Statement: Women's Organizations in the Peace Offensive," *Intelligence and National Security* 18, no. 2 (2003): 103–6; Francisca de Haan, "Continuing Cold War Paradigms in Western Historiography of Transnational Women's Organizations: The Case of the Women's International Democratic Federation (WIDF)," *Women's History Review* 19, no. 4 (September 2010): 547–73; Weston Ullrich, "Preventing Peace: The British Government and the Second World Peace Congress," *Cold War History* 11, no. 3 (August 2011): 341–62; Melissa Feinberg, "Battling for Peace: The Transformation of the Women's Movement in Cold War Czechoslovakia and Eastern Europe," in *Women and Gender in Post-War Europe: From the Cold War to the European Union*, ed. Joanna Regulska and Bonnie G. Smith (U.K.: Routledge, 2012), 22–27; Ruud Van Dijk, ed., "Peaceful Co-existence," in *Encyclopedia of the Cold War*, vol. 1 (London: Routledge, 2008); Steve Hewitt, *Spying 101: The RCMP's Secret Activities at Canadian Universities, 1917–1997* (Toronto: University of Toronto Press, 2002), 11; Franca Iacovetta, *Gatekeepers: Reshaping Immigrant Lives in Cold War Canada* (Toronto: Between the Lines, 2006), 104–5.

4 Francesca Miller, "Feminism and Transnationalism," *Gender and History* 10, no. 3 (1998): 569, 575; Leila J. Rupp, "Transnational Women's Movements," *European History Online*, www.ieg-ego.eu/en/threads/transnational-movements-and-organisations/international-social-movements/leila-j-rupp-transnational-womens-movements; Rupp, *Worlds of Women: The Making of an International Women's Movement* (Princeton: Princeton University Press, 1997); Marilyn Porter, "Transnational Feminisms in a Globalized World: Challenges, Analysis and Resistance," *Feminist Studies* 33, no. 1 (Spring 2007): 44; Patricia Clavin, "Defining Transnationalism," *Contemporary European History* 14, no. 4 (2005): 421.

5 Harriet Hyman Alonso, "Why Women's Peace History?" *Peace and Change* 20, no. 1 (1995): 48–52; Sandi Cooper, "Peace as a Human Right: The Invasion of Women into the World of High Politics," *Journal of Women's History* 14, no. 2 (2002): 202.

6 de Haan, "Continuing Cold War Paradigms"; Wendy Pojmann, "For Mothers, Peace and Family: International (Non-)Co-operation Among Italian Catholic and Communist Organizations During the Early Cold War," *Gender and History* 23, no. 2 (August 2011): 415–29; Frances Early, "'A Grandly Subversive Time': The Halifax Branch of the Voice of Women in the 1960s," in *Mothers of the Municipality: Women, Work and Social Policy in Post-1945 Hali-*

fax, ed. Judith Fingard and Janet Guildford (Toronto: University of Toronto Press, 2005), 154; Barbara Roberts, "Women's Peace Activism in Canada," in *Beyond the Vote: Canadian Women and Politics*, ed. Linda Kealey and Joan Sangster (Toronto: University of Toronto Press, 1989); Lawrence S. Wittner, "Gender Roles and Nuclear Disarmament Activism, 1954–1965," *Gender and History* 12, no. 1 (April 2000): 197–222.

7 Bryan D. Palmer, *Canada's 1960s: The Ironies of Identity in a Rebellious Era* (Toronto: University of Toronto Press, 2009), 256–57.

8 Lara Campbell, Dominique Clement, and Gregory S. Kealey, eds., *Debating Dissent: Canada and the Sixties* (Toronto: University of Toronto Press, 2012), 17, 20.

9 Education Report – VOW May, 1965, and VOW and WILC [Women's International Liaison Committee] for ICY [International Cooperation Year] (Background Paper), January, 1965, MG14 C19, box 3.f. VOW 1965, Provincial Archives of Manitoba (PAM); VOW Annual Meeting May 28–29, 1965, Ottawa, and photograph of Dagmar Wilson, in *VOW National Newsletter* 3, no. 3 (July 1965), 5–6, 10; "The Way of the WSP," *VOW National Newsletter* 2, no. 5 (Autumn-Winter 1964), 31–32, MG14 C19 box 3.f. VOW 1964, PAM.

10 The Soviet Women's Anti-fascist Committee and the Union des femmes françaises (UFF) were groups that had "organized women to fight Nazi Germany" during the war years. de Haan, "Continuing Cold War Paradigms"; Pojmann, "For Mothers, Peace and Family"; Celia Donert, "Women's Rights in Cold War Europe: Disentangling Feminist Histories," *Past and Present* (2013, Supplement 8): 178–202; Jadwiga E. Pieper Mooney, "Fighting Fascism and Forging New Political Activism: The Women's International Democratic Federation (WIDF) in the Cold War," in *Decentering Cold War History: Local and Global Change*, ed. Jadwiga E. Pieper Mooney and Fabio Lanza (London: Routledge, 2013), 52–72; Melanie Ilic, "Soviet Women, Cultural Exchange and the Women's International Democratic Federation," in *Reassessing Cold War Europe*, ed. Sari Autio-Sarasmo and Katalin Miklossy (London: Routledge, 2010), 157–74.

11 Memorandum Classification Secret, To Supt. Kelly, March 6, 1964, Subject: Voice of Women, Canada, VOW Canada correspondence December 20, 1963 to March 15, 1964, RG146–3, vol. 2844, LAC; ATTENTION: Col. H.T. Fosbery from (J.R.W. Bordeleau), Assistant Commissioner, Director Security and Intelligence, August 27, 1962, 2, VOW Canada Correspondence, from July 31, 1962 to September 12, 1962, RG146–3, vol. 2844, LAC. The communication is labelled "SECRET" and "BY HAND."

12 Hewitt, *Spying 101*, 120, 128–33; Steve Hewitt and Christabelle Sethna, "Sex-Spying: The RCMP Framing of English-Canadian Women's Liberation Groups During the Cold War," in *Debating Dissent*, ed. Campbell, Clement, and Kealey, 137, 148.

13 Early, "A Grandly Subversive Time," 253; Frances Early, "Re-Imaging War: The Voice of Women, the Canadian Aid for Vietnam Civilians, and the Knitting Project for Vietnamese Children, 1966–1976," *Peace and Change* 34, no. 2 (April 2009): 148–63; Frances Early, "Canadian Women and the International Arena in the Sixties: The Voice of Women/La Voix des femmes and the Opposition to the Vietnam War," in *The Sixties: Passion, Politics, and Style*, ed. D. Anastakis (Montreal: McGill-Queen's University Press, 2008), 25–41; Tara Brookfield, *Cold War Comforts: Canadian Women, Child Safety, and Global Insecurity* (Waterloo: Wilfrid Laurier University Press, 2012).

14 "Secret" Report: The VOW, May 1960-Jan. 1962, by the Research Section, Ottawa, March 8, 1962, VOW Canada correspondence February 27, 1962 to April 9, 1962, RG146–3, vol. 2844, LAC; "Secret" letter "BY HAND" Attention: Col. R.E. Holgarth, the Director of Military Intelligence, "A" Building, Department of National Defence, Army, Ottawa, Ontario, Signed: Superintendent (W.H. Kelly) Assistant Director of Security and Intelligence, July 18, 1962, VOW Canada correspondence from June 1, 1962 to July 30, 1962, RG146–3, vol. 2844, LAC; Christine Ball, "The History of the Voice of Women/La Voix des Femmes: The Early Years" (PhD diss., University of Toronto, 1994), 165–67.

15 Pamphlet, "Some Questions & Answers," 6, and "Declaration of VOW," *Voice of Women/*

Voco De Virinoj Newsletter 1, October 1, 1960, MG14, C19, box 3 f. VOW 1961, PAM; Ball, "The History of the Voice of Women," 243.

16 The term "Panopticon" refers to Michel Foucault's concept of a disciplinary society based on Jeremy Bentham's design of a model prison, in which inmates (or civilians) become their own jailers; and it is through this perpetual self-surveillance (censorship) that docile bodies are (re)produced. Michel Foucault, *Discipline and Punish: The Birth of the Prison*, trans. Alan Sheridan (New York: Vintage Books, 1979).

17 Landon R.Y. Storrs, "Attacking the Washington 'Femmocracy': Anti-feminism in the Cold War Campaign against 'Communists in Government,'" *Feminist Studies* 33, no. 1 (Spring 2007): 143; Joanne Meyerowitz, ed., *Not June Cleaver: Women and Gender in Post-war America, 1945–60* (Philadelphia: Temple University Press, 1994); Richard Cavell, "Introduction," in *Love, Hate and Fear in Canada's Cold War*, ed. R. Cavell (Toronto: University of Toronto Press, 2004); Patrizia Gentile, "'Government Girls' and 'Ottawa Men': Cold War Management of Gender Relations in the Civil Service," in *Whose National Security? Canadian State Surveillance and the Creation of Enemies*, ed. Gary Kinsman, Dieter K. Buse, and Mercedes Steedman (Toronto: Between the Lines, 2000), 131–42; Gary Kinsman, "The Canadian National Security War on Queers and the Left," in *New World Coming: The Sixties and the Shaping of Global Consciousness,* ed. Karen Dubinsky, Catherine Krull, Susan Lord, Sean Mills, and Scott Rutherford (Toronto: Between the Lines, 2009), 77–86.

18 Laville, *Cold War Women*, 128; Storrs, "Attacking the Washington 'Femmocracy,'" 143; Julie Guard, "Women Worth Watching: Radical Housewives in Cold War Canada," in *Whose National Security?*, ed. Kinsman, Buse, and Steedman, 79–87.

19 Report by the Security & Intelligence Branch, Winnipeg Manitoba, June 2, 1961, Re: The Voice of Women, Communist Activities Within, VOW Canada Correspondence, from April 29, 1961 to July 31, 1961, RG146–3, vol. 2843, LAC. On Cold War and RCMP masculine ideals see Gerda Ray, "Science and Surveillance: Masculinity and the New York State Police, 1945–80," in *A History of Police and Masculinities, 1700–2010*, ed. David G. Barrie and Susan Broomhall (U.K.: Routledge, 2012), 220–23; Steve Hewitt, "The Masculine Mountie: The Royal Canadian Mounted Police as a Male Institution, 1914–1939," *Journal of the Canadian Historical Association* 7, no. 1 (1996), 153–74; David G. Barrie and Susan Broomhall, "Introduction" in *A History of Police and Masculinities, 1700–2010*, ed. Barrie and Broomhall, 13–16.

20 The Canadian Intelligence Service, vol. 12, no. 4, Ottawa Reports Supplementary, Voice of Women Delegates Attend Red Meeting in Vienna (prepared by Mr. Pat Walsh, former RCMP undercover agent) Section No. 1, April 1962, VOW Canada correspondence April 17, 1962 to May 31, 1962, RG146–3, vol. 2844, pt. 9, LAC. Note: although Walsh was no longer an undercover RCMP agent, he maintained a high profile media campaign against communism. Walsh and other "highly active citizen Cold Warriors" – including members of the Imperial Order Daughters of the Empire (IODE) – saw communist "alert" services and "other anti-communist activities" as "tools of citizenship" and "supported multiple approaches to disarming Communists in Canada." Iacovetta, *Gatekeepers*, 104–5.

21 "V.O.W. and the Future," *Voice Of Women/Voco De Virinoj Newsletter* 14, October 15, 1961, 135, MG14, C19, box 3 f. VOW 1961, PAM; "Reports from Area Chairmen," *Voice Of Women /Voco De Virinoj Newsletter* 13, July 15, 1961, 98–99, MG14, C19, box 3 f. VOW 1961, PAM; VOW Canada Correspondence, from February 27, 1962 to April 9, 1962, "Secret," Voice of Women, May 1960 – January 1962, Research Section, Ottawa, March 8, 1962. VWG: MEL, 1–23, RG146–3, vol. 2844, LAC.

22 *Voice Of Women/Voco De Virinoj Newsletter* 1, October 1, 1960, the bi-weekly newsletter published by Voice of Women, MG14, C19, box 3 f. VOW 1961, PAM; Ball, "The History of the Voice of Women."

23 RG146–3, July 18, 1962, LAC; "SECRET" and "BY HAND": Director Security and Intelli-

gence, August 27, 1962, 2, RG146–3, vol. 2844, VOW Canada Correspondence, LAC; "Secret" letter "BY HAND" Attention: Col. R.E. Holgarth.

24 Alison Prentice et al., *Canadian Women: A History*, 2nd ed. (Toronto: Harcourt Brace, 1996), 413; Daniel Heidt, "'I Think That Would Be the End of Canada': Howard Green, the Nuclear Test Ban, and Interest-Based Foreign Policy, 1946–1963." *American Review of Canadian Studies* 42, no. 3 (2012): 343–69; Eric Bergbusch and Michael D. Stevenson, "Howard Green, Public Opinion and the Politics of Disarmament," in *Architects and Innovators: Building the Department of Foreign Affairs and International Trade, 1909–2009*, ed. Greg Donaghy and Kim Richard Nossal (Montreal: McGill-Queen's University Press, 2009), 191–206.

25 The erection of the Berlin Wall – dividing Eastern and Western Germany – in 1961; the Cuban Missile Crisis of October 1962 when the Soviet Union and the U.S. faced off over plans to deliver Soviet nuclear missiles to Cuba; and the Partial Test Ban Treaty – prohibiting all atmospheric testing of nuclear weapons (exempting only underground and underwater testing) – signed by the Soviet Union, the U.K., and the U.S. in the autumn of 1963, which was viewed as a victory for the disarmament movement.

26 "The Way of the WSP," in *VOW National Newsletter* 2, no. 5. (Autumn-Winter, 1964): 31–32, MG14 C19 box 3.f. VOW 1964, PAM; Amy Swerdlow, *Women Strike for Peace: Traditional Motherhood and Radical Politics in the 1960s* (Chicago: University of Chicago Press, 1993).

27 Susan Mann Trofimenkoff, "Thérèse Casgrain and the CCF in Quebec," in *Beyond the Vote: Canadian Women and Politics*, ed. Linda Kealey and Joan Sangster (Toronto: University of Toronto Press, 1989), 139–68; The Clio Collective, *Quebec Women: A History* (Toronto: Women's Press, 1987); Micheline Dumont, "The Origins of the Women's Movement in Quebec," in *Challenging Times: The Women's Movement in Canada and the United States*, ed. Constance Backhouse and David Flaherty (Montreal/Kingston: McGill-Queens University Press, 1992), 72–94; Thérèse F. Casgrain, *A Woman in a Man's World*, trans. Joyce Marshall (Toronto: McClelland & Stewart, 1972) (Also published in French under the title *Une Femme chez les hommes*); Ball, "The History of the Voice of Women," 372–416.

28 Letter to VOW members from Jo Davis, dated November 16, 1962, 2, RG146–3, vol. 2844, VOW Canada correspondence November 14, 1962 to December 21, 1962, LAC; Ball, "The History of the Voice of Women," 407, 451.

29 Ball, "The History of the Voice of Women," 153–56, 383–84; Brookfield, *Cold War Comforts*, 87–97; Andrew Burtch, *Give Me Shelter: The Failure of Canada's Cold War Civil Defence* (Vancouver, UBC Press, 2011), 197, 211.

30 Ball, "The History of the Voice of Women," 243; "Declaration of VOW," *Voice Of Women/ Voco De Virinoj Newsletter* 1, October 1, 1960, and pamphlet entitled "Some Questions & Answers," 6, MG14, C19, box 3 f. VOW 1961, PAM.

31 National Annual Meeting, 1962, VOW fonds, vol. 22, file 2; "Report of the National President," *VOW National Newsletter* 23, November 15, 1962, 14, vol. 7, file 19, VOW National Newsletters 1962–67, MG28, I218, LAC; Kay Macpherson, *When in Doubt, Do Both: The Times of My Life* (Toronto: University of Toronto Press, 1994), 97.

32 "Women's Voice is Stronger," *Globe and Mail*, November 6, 1962, VOW Canada correspondence November 13, 1962 to December 1, 1962, Access #AH 2001–00102, pt. 13, RG146, vol. 2844, LAC.

33 Letter to VOW members from Jo Davis, November 16, 1962, 2.

34 Candace Loewen, "Mike Hears Voices: Voice of Women and Lester Pearson, 1960–1963," *Atlantis* 10, no. 2 (Spring 1987): 24–30; "Secret" Letter "By Hand" to Mr. D.F. Wall, Secretary of the Security Panel, Privy Council Office, Ottawa, Signed: W.H. Kelly, Chief Superintendent, Director, Security and Intelligence, March 18, 1965, VOW Canada correspondence February 25, 1965 to March 19, 1965, RG146–3, vol. 2845, LAC.

35 Letter to VOW members from Jo Davis, November 16, 1962, 2; Memorandum Classification Secret. To Supt. Kelly, March 6, 1964.

36 A Message to All Voice of Women Members from the Acting President, signed Kathleen Macpherson, March 8, 1963, VOW fonds, vol. 23, file 14, President's Reports 1962–70; Macpherson, *When in Doubt, Do Both*.

37 Macpherson, *When in Doubt, Do Both*, 79, 101.

38 Davis Papers cited in Ball, "The History of the Voice of Women," 192; VOW, Alberta Branch Primer II, n.d., 9, Voice of Women, Reports Statements Announcements etc, 1961–64, 1972, 1988, MG14 C19, box 3, f. VOW, 1963, PAM; RCMP Report TO. October 11, 1961, plus attachments, VOW Canada correspondence August 1, 1961 to November 8, 1961, including part 5, pp. 31–41, RG146 3 Voice of Women Files (VOW Files), vol. 2843, LAC.

39 VOW, Alberta Branch Primer II, n.d., 10; Draft Report from the Closed Session of "Conference of Women for International Cooperation Year" LaReserve, St. Donat, Quebec, September 9–14, 1962, 2–3, Voice of Women, Reports Statements Announcements etc, 1961–64, 1972, 1988, MG14 C19, box 3, f. VOW, 1963, PAM; VOW and WILC for ICY (Background Paper), Jan 1965, 1–3, Voice of Women, VOW Official Reports, Announcements, Business, 1961–1969, MG14 C19, box 3, f. VOW, 1965, PAM.

40 "Message from the First Past-President, Voice of Women Canada – Helen Tucker," 2–3, *VOW National Newsletter* 23, November 15, 1962, VOW fonds, vol. 7, file 19, VOW National Newsletters 1962–67; Alberta Branch Primer II, n.d., 12; Draft Report from the Closed Session of "Conference of Women for International Cooperation Year," 2.

41 "VOW Speaker Hit At Moscow Congress," *Toronto Daily Star*, July 15, 1963, VOW Delegations to USSR & Soviet Bloc Countries June 13, 1963 to September 13, 1963, RG146 3 VOW Files – vol. 2, LAC; *VOW National Newsletter* 2, no, 3 (Spring 1964), 19, Voice of Women: Newsletters file, MG14 C19, box 3, f. VOW, 1964, PAM.

42 "World Congress on Women" by Ekaterina Shevelyova in *Soviet Union Today*, c. September 30, 1963, VOW Delegations to USSR & Soviet Bloc Countries, correspondence September 14, 1963 to June 27, 1966, RG146 3 VOW Files, vol. 3, LAC.

43 *National Newsletter* November 1963, VOW Delegations to USSR & Soviet Bloc Countries, correspondence June 13, 1963 to September 13, 1963, VOW Files, vol. 3, RG146 3 LAC; "Six VOW Members Visit the Soviet Union," *Winnipeg Free Press*, October 1, 1963, VOW Delegations to USSR & Soviet Bloc Countries, correspondence September 14, 1963 to June 27, 1966, VOW Files, vol. 3, RG146 3, LAC.

44 *The Voice of Women: The First Thirty Years*, Pineau Productions, 1992.

45 Soviet Women's Visit, October 1964, Voice of Women's First ICY Project, Voice of Women, Reports Statements Announcements etc, 1961–64, 1972, 1988, MG14 C19, box 3, f. VOW, 1964, PAM; *VOW National Newsletter* 11, no. 5 (Autumn-Winter 1964), File folder: Voice of Women National Newsletter, 1960–1964, VOW 1964, MG14 C19 box 3 f., PAM; *VOW National Newsletter*, January 1967, VOW fonds, vol. 7, file 19.

46 "Secret" Letter "By Hand" to Mr. D.F. Wall, March 18, 1965; Memorandum Classification Secret, to Supt. Kelly, March 6, 1964.

47 From H.Q. "I" Directorate, RE: Voice of Women (Communist Activities Within) Toronto, Ontario, January 26, 1965, VOW Canada Correspondence December 20, 1964 to February 24, 1965, Access # AH 2001–00109, pt 27, RG146, vol. 2845, LAC.

48 VOW Protesting MLF, From: Hague To: External, May 14, 1964 (stamped DSI, June 2, 1964, RCMP), VOW Canada Correspondence May 16, 1964 to May 30, 1964, RG146-3, vol. 2844, LAC; VOW Protesting NATO MLF, From: Hague To: External, 205 Priority, From Arnold Smith, Assistant Under-Secretary of State for External Affairs, May 12, 1964, VOW Canada Correspondence May 16, 1964 to May 30, 1964, RG146-3, vol. 2844, LAC; Department of External Affairs Ref. Slip To: The Commissioner, RCMP Ottawa. Attention: Directorate of Security and Intelligence, The Hague, May 12, 1964. RE: VOW Protesting NATO Multi-Lateral Nuclear Force, JJ McCardie for Under-Secretary of State for External Affairs, VOW Canada Correspondence May 16, 1964 to May 30, 1964, RG146-3, vol. 2844, LAC; Swerdlow, *Women Strike for Peace*, 206.

49 VOW Protesting NATO MLF From: Hague To: External, 205 Priority, From Arnold Smith, Asst Under-Secretary of State for External Affairs. May 12, 1964; Department of External Affairs Ref. Slip To: The Commissioner, RCMP Ottawa. Attention: Directorate of Security and Intelligence, The Hague, May 12, 1964. RE: VOW Protesting NATO Multi-Lateral Nuclear Force, JJ McCardie for Under-Secretary of State for External Affairs.

50 "Dutch Lift Entry Ban on VOW Delegates," *Winnipeg Free Press*, May 12, 1964, in VOW Media Clippings, MG14 C19, PAM; Swerdlow, *Women Strike for Peace*, 210.

51 Swerdlow, *Women Strike for Peace*, 206–7, 212; Kay Macpherson, President, Voice of Women, Report on Women's NATO Peace Conference, The Hague, Netherlands, May 12–14, 1964, MG14 C19 box 3 f. VOW 1964, PAM.

52 Kay Macpherson (Mrs. C.B.), President, Voice of Women, Members of the Canadian Delegation attending the NATO meetings, May 13, 1964, MG14 C19 box 3 f. VOW 1964, PAM; Macpherson, "Report on Women's NATO Peace Conference."

53 The handwritten note was stamped "DSI" June 2, 1964 and was likely authored by someone in the Directorate of Security and Intelligence in Ottawa; VOW Protesting MLF, From: Hague To: External, May 14, 1964.

54 La Voix des femmes/Voice of Women, Quebec Bulletin, December 1964, Ottawa Report, 2–3, MG14 C19 box 3 f. VOW 1964, PAM. See also Memorandum of PM Lester Pearson meeting with VOW delegation, November 16, 1964, VOW Canada correspondence October 31, 1964 to December 19, 1964, RG146–3, vol. 2845, LAC.

55 "Voices" was a term of endearment VOW members often used to refer to themselves and other VOW members.

56 Macpherson, *When in Doubt, Do Both*, 107–8.

57 José E. Iguarta, "The Sixties in Quebec," in *Debating Dissent*, ed. Campbell, Clement, and Kealey, 249–68; Ball, "The History of the Voice of Women."

58 Macpherson, *When in Doubt, Do Both*, 107.

59 Swerdlow, *Women Strike for Peace*, 214.

60 George Ignatieff, *The Memoirs of George Ignatieff: The Making of a Peacemonger* (Toronto: University of Toronto Press, 1985), 190. Macpherson notes that Ignatieff later became the President of Science for Peace; Macpherson, *When in Doubt, Do Both*, 106.

11 Fighting the War at Home

1 I would like to acknowledge the collection editors and anonymous reviewers of this article for their helpful input. I would also like to thank Karen Dubinsky for providing indispensable feedback on earlier versions of this argument.

2 Voice of Women was a Canadian women's peace organization founded in 1960 with a focus on nuclear disarmament and peace building. The organization was responsible for numerous awareness programs and lobbying efforts on issues including nuclear weapons, east-west détente, and the Vietnam War.

3 Kay Macpherson, *When in Doubt Do Both: The Times of My Life* (Toronto: University of Toronto Press, 1994), 140.

4 The Cuban Missile Crisis and U2 Spy Plane Incident are two events that significantly raised Cold War tensions between the USSR and the U.S. The downing of an American U2 spy plane on May 1, 1960 in the Soviet Union and the open revelation of U.S. espionage targeted at the USSR and its allies led directly to the failure of the Four Powers Summit. The Cuban Missile Crisis was a conflict between the U.S. and USSR over the Soviet deployment of nuclear capable missiles in Cuba during October of 1962. In response to the USSR's bold move, the U.S. opted to blockade Cuba. The resulting standoff brought the world to the brink of nuclear war.

5 See Sean Mills, *The Empire Within: Postcolonial Thought and Political Activism in Sixties*

Montreal (Montreal: McGill Queen's University Press, 2012); Stewart Henderson, *Making the Scene: Yorkville and Hip Toronto in the 1960s* (Toronto: University of Toronto Press, 2011); Karen Dubinsky, Catherine Krull, Susan Lord, Sean Mills, and Scott Rutherford, eds., *New World Coming: The Sixties and the Shaping of Global Consciousness* (Toronto: Between the Lines, 2009); Brian Palmer, *Canada's 1960s: The Ironies of Identity in a Rebellious Era* (Toronto: University of Toronto Press, 2009).

6 Braden Hutchinson, "Objects of Affection: Producing and Consuming Toys and Childhood in Canada, 1840–1989," (PhD diss., Queen's University, 2013), 92–94.

7 Thomas P. Socknat, "Canadian Feminists and the Interwar Peace Campaign," in *Up and Doing: Canadian Women and Peace*, ed. Janice Williamson (Toronto: Women's Press, 1989), 68.

8 Socknat, "Canadian Feminists and the Interwar Peace Campaign," 75–76.

9 R. Blake Brown, *Arming and Disarming: A History of Gun Control in Canada* (Toronto: University of Toronto Press, 2012), 159.

10 "Permit No Toys That Suggest War," *Montreal Gazette*, August 30, 1928, 9; Augustus Bridle, "Too Much Gun Play in Themes of Films," *Toronto Star*, June 27, 1936, 9; "Spirit of Service, Not Destruction," *Ottawa Citizen*, September 4, 1924, 7.

11 "[Letter] Dear Homemaker," *Globe*, December 5, 1936, 12.

12 S. Young to George Archer, January 6, 1955, Women's International League for Peace and Freedom fonds, vol. 4, file 23, University of British Columbia Special Collections.

13 "Air Gun Ban Requested by Women's Council," *Montreal Gazette*, February 6, 1957, 20.

14 W.E. Blatz, *Hostages to Peace: Parents and the Children of Democracy* (New York: W. Morrow & Co., 1940), 156–73; "War Toys Good for Children, Noted Psychiatrist Holds," *Globe and Mail*, November 28, 1946, 17; "Let Children Have War Toys," *Saskatoon Star-Phoenix*, October 19, 1950, 11.

15 Hutchinson, "Objects of Affection," 262–63.

16 Christopher S. O'Brien, "'And Everything Would Be Done to Protect Us': The Cold War, the Bomb and America's Children, 1945–1963" (PhD diss., University of Kansas, 2002); Marc Joseph Richards, "Recruitment in the Nursery: The Cold War Mobilization of Children" (PhD diss., University of California Davis, 1998); Karen Dubinsky, "Children, Ideology and Iconography: How Babies Rule the World," *Journal for the History of Childhood and Youth* 5, no. 1 (2012): 5–13; Tarah Brookfield, *Cold War Comforts: Canadian Women, Child Safety, and Global Insecurity* (Waterloo: Wilfrid Laurier University Press, 2012), 71–97.

17 Brown, *Arming and Disarming*, 159.

18 Mona Gleason, *Normalizing the Ideal: Psychology, Schooling and the Family in Postwar Canada* (Toronto: University of Toronto Press, 1999), 37–51.

19 Hutchinson, "Objects of Affection," 197–251.

20 See Albert Bandura, *Social Learning and Personality Development* (New York: Holt, Rinehart & Winston, 1963); Bandura, *Adolescent Aggression: A Study of the Influence of Child Training Practices and Family Interrelationships* (New York: Ronald Press, 1959); Bandura, Joan E. Grusec, and Francis L. Menlove, "Observational Learning as a Function of Symbolization and Incentive Set," *Child Development* 37, no. 3 (1966): 499–506.

21 See Mona Gleason, "From 'Disgraceful Carelessness' to 'Intelligent Precaution': Accidents and the Public Child in English Canada, 1900–1950," *Journal of Family History* 30, no. 2 (2005): 230; Cynthia Comacchio, *Nations are Built of Babies: Saving Ontario's Mothers and Children, 1900–1940* (Montreal: McGill-Queen's University Press, 1993); Gleason, *Normalizing the Ideal*; Julia Grant, *Raising Baby by the Book: The Education of American Mothers* (New Haven: Yale University Press, 1998); Norah Lillian Lewis, "Advising the Parents: Child Rearing in British Columbia During the Interwar Years" (PhD diss., University of British Columbia, 1980); Hutchinson, "Objects of Affection," 228–29.

22 Kay Macpherson, *When in Doubt, Do Both*, 89–90.

23 Voice of Women fonds, MG 28 I218, Library and Archives Canada (hereafter VOW fonds), vol. 4, file 17.

24 Kay Macpherson and Sara Good, "Canadian Voice of Women for Peace," *Peace Magazine*, October-November 1987, 26.

25 Lisa Yaszek, "Stories 'That Only a Mother' Could Write: Midcentury Peace Activism, Maternalist Politics and Judith Merril's Early Fiction," *NWSA Journal* 16, no. 2 (2004): 72–75, and Susan Lynn, *Progressive Women in Conservative Times: Racial Justice, Peace and Feminism, 1945 to the 1960s* (Chapel Hill: Rutgers University Press, 1992).

26 VOW fonds, vol. 5, file 2.

27 VOW fonds, vol. 6, file 7.

28 Tarah Brookfield, *Cold War Comforts*, 71–97.

29 Press Release from War Toy Committee, VOW fonds, vol. 7, file 7–2.

30 Press Release from War Toy Committee.

31 Let's Repudiate War Toys This Christmas, VOW fonds, vol. 7, file 7–2.

32 War Toy Committee Update (memo), VOW fonds, vol. 7, file 7–2.

33 Dr. Benjamin Spock, VOW fonds, vol. 7, file 7–2; Kay Macpherson to Dr. Benjamin Spock, February 7, 1968, Kay Macpherson fonds, MG31-K36, vol. 4, file 4–13, LAC.

34 A Psychiatrist on War Toys, VOW fonds, vol. 7, file 7–2.

35 A Psychiatrist on War Toys.

36 Kay Macpherson to Dr. Benjamin Spock, February 7, 1968.

37 Report of War Toy Committee, September 14, 1964, VOW fonds, vol. 7, file 7–2.

38 Report of War Toy Committee.

39 War Toy Committee Report, 1965, VOW fonds, vol. 7, file 7–2.

40 Mark Moss, *Manliness and Militarism: Educating Young Boys in Ontario for War* (New York: Oxford University Press, 2001), 110–21.

41 Arnold Arnold, "Are Dolls Good Boys' Toys?" *Edmonton Journal*, August 23, 1968, 21.

42 Lotta Dempsey, "Christmas is Coming – So is Barbie's Luxury Yacht," *Toronto Star*, October 17, 1975, E1.

43 Christopher Dummitt, *The Manly Modern: Masculinity in Postwar Canada* (Vancouver: UBC Press, 2007), 2–7.

44 "Rootie Kazootie Routs War Toys – Maker," *Toronto Star*, November 13, 1961, 35; "Spectre of Atomic War Hangs Over Toyland," *Calgary Herald*, December 15, 1961, 18.

45 Muriel Nickel [letter to the editor], *Ottawa Citizen*, January 30, 1962, 6.

46 "War Toys Put Out to Pasture," *Vancouver Sun*, August 25, 1965, 28.

47 VOW fonds, vol. 16, file 16–13.

48 Gordon Baker, "Symbols of Hell," VOW fonds, vol. 7, file 7–2.

49 *Toys*, directed by Grant Munro (National Film Board of Canada, 1966), www.nfb.ca/film/toys.

50 Nadine Brozan, "Women's Liberation Turns Efforts to Nursery Set," *Calgary Herald*, May 17, 1971, 39.

51 San Francisco Women for Peace, VOW fonds, vol. 7, file 7–2.

52 Gary Cross, *Kid's Stuff: Toys and the Changing World of American Childhood* (Cambridge, MA: Harvard University Press, 1997), 185–86; Karen J. Hall, "A Soldier's Body: G.I. Joe, Hasbro's Great American Hero and the Symptoms of Empire," *Journal of Popular Culture* 38, no. 1 (2004): 34–54; Robert M. Bliss, "When Barbie Dated G.I. Joe: Analyzing Toys of the Early Cold War Era," *Material History Review* 45 (1997): 38–50; Roger Chapman, "From Vietnam to the New World Order: The G.I. Joe Action Figure as Cold War Artifact," *Studies in the Social Sciences* 36 (1999): 47–55.

53 Lionel Microscope (Advertisement), VOW fonds, vol. 7, file 7–2.

54 "Do War Toys Teach Young Children that War is Inevitable?" *Toronto Star*, October 27, 1966, 3.

55 "Do War Toys Teach Young Children that War is Inevitable?"

56 "Warlike Toys," *Toronto Star*, December 21, 1966, 2.

57 Philip Winslow, "A Protest Becomes a Ten-Day Fast," *Montreal Gazette*, October 5, 1968, 7.

58 Andrew Geller, "Shoop-Shoop; Hula-Hoop Back," *Montreal Gazette*, July 29, 1967, 34.

59 "Catalogue from Store Cuts Guns," *Ottawa Citizen*, September 23, 1968, 8.

60 "Toy Testing Council, Government Issue List," *Montreal Gazette*, November 24, 1970, 28.

61 "Disturbed by War Toys," *Vancouver Sun*, February 5, 1975, 6.

62 "Play Area Machine Guns Called Hazard," *Toronto Star*, October 25, 1977, B2.

63 "Torture is Out in U.S. Toy Business," *Montreal Gazette*, June 19, 1972, 29.

64 Roger Chapman, "From Vietnam to the New World Order," 47–55.

65 Braden Hutchinson, "'The Littlest Arms Race'? War Toys and the Boy Consumer in Eighties' Canada," in *Situating Child Consumption: Rethinking Values and Notions of Children, Childhood and Consumption*, ed. Anna Sparrman, Bengt Sandin, and Johanna Sjoberg (Stockholm: Nordic Academic Press, 2012), 234–35.

66 Toys have also been central to debates about class, race, gender, technology, and modernity. See Hutchinson, "'The Littlest Arms Race'?" and "Making (Anti)Modern Childhood: Producing and Consuming Toys in Late Victorian Canada," *Scientia Canadensis* [Forthcoming].

12 Project La Macaza

1 The author wishes to thank the interviewees for their participation in this research project, especially Dimitri Roussopoulos. The author also wishes to thank the archivists at the William Ready Division of Archives and Research Collections at McMaster University, and, last but not least, the editors of this volume.

2 See John Clearwater, *Canadian Nuclear Weapons: The Untold Story of Canada's Cold War Arsenal* (Toronto: Dundurn Press, 1998), 82–85; Michael Dufresne, "'Let's Not Be Cremated Equal': The Combined Universities Campaign for Nuclear Disarmament, 1959–1967," in *The Sixties in Canada: A Turbulent and Creative Decade* ed. M. Athena Palaeologu (Montreal: Black Rose Books, 2009), 38–41; Myrna Kostash, *Long Way From Home: The Story of the Sixties Generation in Canada* (Toronto: J. Lorimer, 1980), 4; Gary Moffatt, *History of the Canadian Peace Movement Until 1969* (St. Catharines: Grape Vine Press, 1969), 138–41; Simonne Monet-Chartrand, *Les Québécoises et le movement pacifiste, 1939–1967* (Montreal: Les editions écosociété, 1993), 132–35. There are passing references to Project La Macaza in Sean Mills, *The Empire Within: Postcolonial Thought and Political Activism in Sixties Montreal* (Montreal/Kingston: McGill-Queen's University Press, 2010), 49–50; Bryan Palmer, *Canada's 1960s: The Ironies of Identity in a Rebellious Era* (Toronto: University of Toronto Press, 2009), 261, 267; and Lawrence Wittner, *Resisting the Bomb: A History of the World Nuclear Disarmament Movement, 1954–1970* (Stanford: Stanford University Press, 1997), 202.

3 "For Freedom and Peace: Operation St. Jean Baptiste – The First Stage of the La Macaza Project," *Sanity*, June 1964.

4 Dufresne, "'Let's Not Be Cremated Equal,'" 19–20; Monet-Chartrand, *Les Québécoises et le movement pacifiste*, 40–43; Wittner, *Resisting the Bomb*, 197–98.

5 Wittner, *Resisting the Bomb*, 348–49, 389. See also Patricia McMahon, *Essence of Indecision: Diefenbaker's Nuclear Policy, 1957–1963* (Montreal/Kingston: McGill-Queen's University Press, 2009).

6 Dufresne, "'Let's Not Be Cremated Equal,'" 29. See also Jocelyn Maynard Ghent, "Did He Fall or Was He Pushed? The Kennedy Administration and the Collapse of the Diefenbaker Government," *International History Review* 1, no. 2 (April 1979): 255–57.

7 Clearwater, *Canadian Nuclear Weapons*, 67–68, 76–77.

8 Dufresne, "'Let's Not Be Cremated Equal,'" 29–34. See also Tom Hayden, *The Port Huron Statement: The Visionary Call of the 1960s Revolution* (New York: Thunder's Mouth Press, 2005), 53.

9 For a more detailed attempt at defining civil disobedience, see Adam Roberts' introduction to Adam Roberts and Timothy Garton Ash, eds., *Civil Resistance and Power Politics: The Experience of Non-violent Action from Gandhi to the Present* (Oxford: Oxford University Press, 2012), 2–4.

10 Henry David Thoreau, "On Civil Disobedience," in William Rossi, ed., *Walden, Civil Disobedience, and Other Writings*, 3rd ed (New York: Norton, 2007), 227–46; Judith M. Brown, "Gandhi and Civil Resistance in India, 1917–47: Key Issues," in Roberts and Ash, eds., *Civil Resistance and Power Politics*, 43–57; Doug McAdam, "The US Civil Rights Movement: Power from Below and Above, 1945–70," in Roberts and Ash, *Civil Resistance and Power Politics*, 58–74; Martin Luther King, Jr. "Letter from Birmingham Jail," *Liberation: An Independent Monthly* (June 1963), 10–16, 23.

11 John D'Emilio, *Lost Prophet: The Life and Times of Bayard Rustin* (New York: Free Press, 2003), 223–48; Maurice Isserman, *If I Had A Hammer ... The Death of the Old Left and the Birth of the New Left* (New York: Basic Books, 1987), 130, 175.

12 A.J. Muste and Bayard Rustin were Quakers. On Quakers and their role in the Canadian peace movement in these years, see Robynne Rogers Healey, "Thirty-One Hours on Grindstone Island: The Canadian and American Friends Service Committees' Experiment in Civil Defence," *Canadian Quaker History Journal* 71 (2006): 22–32.

13 Dimitri Roussopoulos, Skype interview with author, February 19, 2011.

14 Roussopoulos, Skype interview with author.

15 Dan Daniels, André Cardinal, and Dimitrios Roussopoulos to multiple recipients, March 28, 1964, Combined Universities Campaign for Nuclear Disarmament fonds, William Ready Division of Archives and Research Collections, McMaster University, Hamilton, Ontario (hereafter CUCND fonds), file 6, Operation St. Jean Baptiste – Correspondence, Background Information, etc.," box 10; "For Freedom and Peace: Operation St. Jean Baptiste," *Sanity*, June 1964.

16 Daniels, Cardinal, and Roussopoulos to multiple recipients, March 28, 1964.

17 Mills, *The Empire Within*; Palmer, *Canada's 1960s*, 311–65.

18 "For Freedom and Peace: Operation St. Jean Baptiste."

19 Dimitri Roussopoulos, interview with author, February 11, 2009.

20 "For Freedom and Peace: Operation St. Jean Baptiste."

21 "For Freedom and Peace: Operation St. Jean Baptiste."

22 Daniels, Cardinal, and Roussopoulos to multiple recipients, March 28, 1964.

23 Daniels, Cardinal, and Roussopoulos to multiple recipients, March 28, 1964.

24 Dimitrios Roussopoulos to Arthur Pape, May 19, 1964; Dimitrios Roussopoulos, André Cardinal, and Dan Daniels to multiple recipients, May 28, 1964; Peter Boothroyd to André Cardinal, Dan Daniels, and Dimitri Roussopoulos, June 9, 1964; Danny Drache to Art Pape, n.d., CUCND fonds, file 6, box 10.

25 Roussopoulos, Cardinal, and Daniels to multiple recipients, May 28, 1964.

26 Roussopoulos to Pape, May 19, 1964; Roussopoulos, Cardinal, and Daniels to multiple recipients, May 28, 1964; Boothroyd to Cardinal, Daniels, and Roussopoulos, June 9, 1964; Drache to Pape, n.d. The quote was from Drache's letter to Pape.

27 Roussopoulos, Skype interview with author.

28 See the "personal statements" in *Project La Macaza Bulletin* 1, no. 2 (July 6, 1964), 5–7, and similar statements in *Project La Macaza Bulletin* 1, no. 3 (September 1964), 3–10, CUCND fonds, file 6, box 10.

29 *Project La Macaza Bulletin* 1, no. 1 (June 18, 1964), 1, CUCND fonds, file 6, box 10.

30 *Project La Macaza Bulletin* 1, no. 1 (June 18, 1964), 1.

31 *Project La Macaza Bulletin* 1, no. 2 (June 1964), 5.

32 *Project La Macaza Bulletin* 1, no. 2 (June 1964), 4.

33 *Project La Macaza Bulletin* 1, no. 1 (June 18, 1964), 2; *Project La Macaza Bulletin* 1, no. 2 (June 1964), 4–5. See also "A Break-through at La Macaza," *Sanity*, July 1964.

34 Lucia Kowaluk, phone interview with author, February 21, 2011; Peter Light, phone interview with author, February 20, 2011.

35 *Project La Macaza Bulletin* 1, no. 2 (June 1964), 4.

36 *Project La Macaza Bulletin* 1, no. 2 (June 1964), 5.

37 *Project La Macaza Bulletin* 1, no. 2 (June 1964), 5.

38 *Project La Macaza Bulletin* 1, no. 2 (June 1964), 5.

39 *Project La Macaza Bulletin* 1, no. 2 (June 1964), 5; "A Break-through at La Macaza."

40 "A Break-through at La Macaza."

41 Ian Gentles, interview with author, Toronto, February 2, 2009.

42 The account in *Project La Macaza Bulletin*, published shortly after the event, indicated that the process was repeated thirty times. However, according to André Cardinal, the protesters were dragged to the ditch thirty-six times. *Project La Macaza Bulletin* 1, no. 2 (June 1964), 3; Dimitri Roussopoulos, e-mail correspondence with author, July 4, 1914.

43 Kowaluk, phone interview with author.

44 Eilert Frerichs, interview with author, June 18, 2009.

45 David Lewis Stein, "The Peaceniks go to La Macaza," *Maclean's*, August 8, 1964, 37. Stein has also written a fictionalized account of the protest at La Macaza in his novel *Scratch One Dreamer* (Toronto: McClelland & Stewart, 1967).

46 Margaret Beattie, *A Brief History of the Student Christian Movement in Canada* (Toronto: SCM Canada, 1975); Catherine Gidney, "Poisoning the Student Mind?: The Student Christian Movement at the University of Toronto, 1920–1965," *Journal of the Canadian Historical Association* 7, no. 1 (1997): 147–63. On the role of the SCM in nuclear disarmament activism, see Bruce Douville, "The Uncomfortable Pew: Christianity, the New Left and the Hip Counterculture in Toronto, 1965–1975" (PhD diss., York University, 2011), 112–26.

47 See Rev. Donald Heap's comments in *Project La Macaza Bulletin* 1, no. 3 (September 1964), 9. It is worth noting that several participants in both protests were Jewish (including leaders such as Art Pape).

48 For example, see Charles Marsh, *God's Long Summer: Stories of Faith and Civil Rights* (Princeton: Princeton University Press, 1997).

49 Roussopoulos, Skype interview with author; "La Macaza," *Sanity*, October 1964.

50 *Project La Macaza Bulletin* 1, no. 2 (June 1964), 1.

51 *Project La Macaza Bulletin* 1, no. 3 (September 1964), 2–3; "La Macaza," *Sanity*, October 1964.

52 The reported numbers of CD'ers vary: the *Globe and Mail* reported fifty-one, *Sanity* reported fifty-eight, and a list of prospective participants in the *Project La Macaza Bulletin* (which went to print shortly before the sit-in began) contains fifty-nine names. The *Sanity* article may be the most accurate, since it is the only account that went to print after the protests had finished. See "Sitdown Protests Bomarcs, Blocks Entrance to Base," *Globe and Mail*, September 8, 1964, 1; "La Macaza," *Sanity*, October 1964; and *Project La Macaza Bulletin* 1, no. 3 (September 1964), 3–4.

53 *Project La Macaza Bulletin* 1, no. 3 (September 1964), 3; "La Macaza," *Sanity*, October 1964.

54 *Project La Macaza Bulletin* 1, no. 3 (September 1964), 4.

55 Stein, "The Peaceniks go to La Macaza," 37.

56 "La Macaza," *Sanity*, October 1964.

57 "La Macaza," *Sanity*, October 1964; Light, phone interview with author.

58 "La Macaza" and "House of Commons," *Sanity*, October 1964.

59 "La Macaza Campaign Begins," *Sanity*, July-August 1963.

60 Wittner, *Resisting the Bomb*, 185–90, 249–50.

61 Moffatt, *History of the Canadian Peace Movement Until 1969*, 136.

62 Kowaluk, phone interview with author.

63 Clearwater, *Canadian Nuclear Weapons*, 82, 87–89.

64 "Sitdown Protests Bomarcs, Blocks Entrance to Base"; Jean Desraspes, "Des croisés de la

paix vont envahir la base de la mort," *La Patrie*, mai 28, 1964, 3; Stein, "The Peaceniks go to La Macaza," 10–13, 36–37.

65 Todd Gitlin, *The Sixties: Years of Hope, Days of Rage* (New York: Bantam, 1993), 151–66.

66 Arthur Marwick, *The Sixties: Cultural Revolution in Britain, France, Italy, and the United States, c.1958–1974* (Oxford: Oxford University Press, 1998), 536–41, 565–85.

67 Clearwater, *Canadian Nuclear Weapons*, 82–85.

68 Palmer, *Canada's 1960s*, 258. The protests at La Macaza, and other peace protests organized in co-operation with Montreal-based activists such as Roussopoulos, may have nurtured relationships between young English-Canadian radicals and their francophone counterparts in Quebec. In *Une Douce Anarchie: Les Anées 68 au Quebec* (Montreal: Boréal, 2008), 86, Jean-Philippe Warren argues that the pacifist movement served as an important link between English- and French-Canadian radical youth in the 1960s.

69 Light, phone interview with author.

70 For a detailed history of the Selma protests at the American consulate and their significance, see David Churchill, "SUPA, Selma, and Stevenson: The Politics of Solidarity in mid-1960s Toronto," *Journal of Canadian Studies* 44, no. 2 (Spring 2010): 32–69.

71 Kostash, *Long Way From Home*, 47–49.

72 Light, phone interview with author.

13 "A Very Major Wheel That Helped Grind the War Down"

1 For the purposes of this work, the term "war resisters" includes draft dodgers, deserters, and others who moved to Canada to express their opposition to the war. "Draft dodgers" are those who eluded being inducted into the military; "deserters" are those who enlisted or were inducted and later came to Canada to escape military service. These terms were used by resisters themselves and by the anti-draft movement. This article is drawn from the research conducted in support of my book, *Building Sanctuary: The Movement to Support Vietnam War Resisters in Canada, 1965–73* (Vancouver: UBC Press, 2013). The original research was conducted with the support of SSHRC.

2 An overview of the new nationalism is provided in Stephen Azzi, *Walter Gordon and the Rise of Canadian Nationalism* (Montreal/Kingston: McGill-Queen's University Press, 1999).

3 Squires, *Building Sanctuary*, esp. 178–83.

4 Other works regarding this movement include David S. Churchill, "An Ambiguous Welcome: Vietnam Draft Resistance, the Canadian State, and Cold War Containment," *Social History/Histoire sociale* 27, no. 73 (2004): 1–26; David S. Churchill, "Draft Resisters, Left Nationalism, and the Politics of Anti-Imperialism," *Canadian Historical Review* 93, no. 2 (June 2012): 227–60; and John Hagan, *Northern Passage: American Vietnam War Resisters in Canada* (Cambridge, MA: Harvard University Press, 2001).

5 *Sanity* was a publication of the Combined Universities Campaign for Nuclear Disarmament (CUCND) until 1965. Its publication ended in 1968. Jacquetta A. Newman, "Continuing Commitment: The Durability of Social Movements – Project Ploughshares in the 1990s" (PhD diss., Queen's University, 1998), 48–49.

6 Letter, Robert Feinstein to Hans Sinn, n.d., and reply from Sinn, February 7, 1966, Hans Sinn fonds, William Ready Division of Archives and Research Collections, McMaster University Libraries, Hamilton, Ontario (hereafter Hans Sinn fonds), box 1, file 2, Correspondence with Prospective Draftees Wishing to Come to Canada, 1966–67.

7 Letter, David John Goodwyn to Hans Sinn, n.d., Hans Sinn fonds, box 1, file 2.

8 Letter, Arlo Tatum, Central Committee for Conscientious Objectors, to Hans Sinn, March 4, 1966, Hans Sinn fonds, box 1, file 2.

9 Letter, Hans Sinn to Virginia and Lowell Naeve, February 28, 1966, and reply from Virginia Naeve to Sinn, March 4, 1966, Hans Sinn fonds, box 1, file 2. The War Resisters League is a U.S.-based pacifist organization.

10 Letter, Richard S. Gottlieb to Hans Sinn, March 25, 1966, Hans Sinn fonds, box 1, file 2.

11 Letter, Tom Hathaway to Hans Sinn, n.d. (c1966), Hans Sinn fonds, box 1, file 2; Exile Group Publications: Toronto, Montreal, Renée Kasinsky fonds, University of British Columbia Library Rare Books and Special Collections, University of British Columbia, Vancouver (hereafter Renée Kasinsky fonds), box 7, file 11.

12 It appears to have been in place by May 1966. Correspondence – VCAAWO, Renée Kasinsky fonds, box 1, file 2.

13 Various letters, April 1966, Hans Sinn fonds, box 1, file 2.

14 Various letters, January 1967 and n.d., Hans Sinn fonds, box 1, file 2.

15 Mark Satin, ed., *Manual for Draft-Age Immigrants to Canada*, 4th ed. (Toronto: Toronto Anti-Draft Programme, 1968), 69–71.

16 "American Deserters Committee of Toronto," *TADC Newsletter* 1, Canadian Student Social and Political Organizations, Hans Sinn fonds, box 1, file 7; Melody Killian, American Deserters Committee Program, "Canadian Press on Emigrants, Deserters, Exiles," *Yankee Refugee* 8 (1969), Renée Kasinsky fonds, box 6, file 2.

17 Ann Farrell, "Quakers in Action: Nancy Meek Pocock," *Quakers in the World*, www.quakersintheworld.org; Hans Sinn to Juanita and Wallace Nelson, July 4, 1967, Hans Sinn fonds, box 1, file 2.

18 Gene Hooyman and Paul Frazier, "Handbook for Training Draft Counsellors," May 1970, Pocock (Jack) Memorial Collection, Thomas Fisher Rare Book Library, University of Toronto (hereafter Pocock Memorial Collection), box 5, folders 1–5; Pocock Memorial Collection, box 3, Counselling Resource Binder 1; Pocock Memorial Collection, box 12, CCCO Publications; Sinn to Juanita and Wallace Nelson, July 4, 1967, Hans Sinn fonds, box 1, file 2.

19 Kenneth Fred Emerick, *War Resisters Canada: The World of the American Military-Political Refugees* (Knox: Knox, Pennsylvania Free Press, 1972), 231; "Canadian Publications: *AMEX*," "Ottawa: AMEXiles Who Settle in Ottawa Easily Forget from Whence They Came," *AMEX* 2, no. 6 (October–November 1970), Renée Kasinsky fonds, box 6, file 4.

20 Renée G. Kasinsky, *Refugees from Militarism: Draft-Age Americans in Canada* (New Brunswick, NJ: Transaction Books, 1976), 82–83.

21 For details see Squires, *Building Sanctuary*, esp. 178–83, and Donald Maxwell, "Religion and Politics at the Border: Canadian Church Support for American Vietnam War Resisters," *Journal of Church and State* 48, no. 4 (2006): 807–29.

22 Interview with Bill Spira of the Toronto Anti-Draft Program [sic], June 1970, Renée Kasinsky fonds, box 4, file 14.

23 Joan Wilcox, interview with the author, Ottawa, May 17, 2006.

24 Athena Palaeologu, ed., *The Sixties in Canada: A Turbulent and Creative Decade* (Montreal: Black Rose Books, 2009), xii.

25 Mark Satin, "About the Editor (Mark Satin bio)," *The Radical Middle Newsletter*, accessed April 26, 2005, www.radicalmiddle.com/editor.htm.

26 "War Resisters League," *War Resisters League News* (July – August 1963), Combined Universities Campaign for Nuclear Disarmament fonds, William Ready Division of Archives and Research Collections, McMaster University, Hamilton, Ontario (hereafter CUCND fonds), box 15, file 11.

27 "Stationery," Pocock Memorial Collection, box 2, TADP Records, folder 11.

28 Kasinsky, *Refugees from Militarism*, 77, 85, 140.

29 Pocock Memorial Collection, box 7, International and U.S. Legal Publications.

30 One Toronto Anti-Draft Programme (TADP) account record showed that the Midwest Committee for Draft Counseling, Chicago, had ordered three hundred copies; the American Friends Service Committee in Pasadena, one hundred; the Central Committee for Conscientious Objectors (CCCO), Western Region, headquartered in San Francisco, two hundred; and the Fellowship of Reconciliation, in Nyack, NY, one hundred. *Manual for Draft-Age Immigrants to Canada* – Sales records, Pocock Memorial Collection, box 2, TADP Records, folder 5.

31 Mark Satin, ed., *Manual for Draft-Age Immigrants to Canada* (Toronto: House of Anansi, 1968); Satin, ed., *Manual for Draft-Age Immigrants to Canada*, 2nd ed. (Toronto: House of Anansi, c1968); Satin, ed., *Manual for Draft-Age Immigrants to Canada*, 3rd ed. (Toronto: Toronto Anti-Draft Programme, 1969); Satin, ed., *Manual for Draft-Age Immigrants to Canada*, 4th ed. (Toronto: Toronto Anti-Draft Programme and House of Anansi, 1969); Satin, ed., *Manual for Draft-Age Immigrants to Canada*, 4th ed., rev. (Toronto: House of Anansi, 1970); Byron Wall, *Manual for Draft-Age Immigrants to Canada*, 5th ed. (Toronto: House of Anansi, 1970); Toronto Anti-Draft Programme, ed., *Manual for Draft-Age Immigrants to Canada*, 6th ed. (Toronto: Toronto Anti-Draft Programme, 1971). Some of these professors, including Elliott Rose, were also connected with the University of Toronto Faculty Committee to End the War in Vietnam. Lawyers included Vincent Kelly and Robert D. Katz; church officials included Rev. Roy G. de Marsh, Secretary, Board of Colleges, United Church of Canada.

32 Jason Young, "'To Define a Community in Exile': Producers, Readers, and War Resister Communication in *AMEX* Magazine, 1968–1977" (master's major research paper, York University, 2006); "Canadian publications: *AMEX*," Renée Kasinsky fonds, box 6, files 4–7.

33 Hardy Scott, interview with author by mail, October 31, 2006.

34 "Interview with Bill Spira of the Toronto Anti-Draft Program [sic], June 1970."

35 Commission on Canadian Affairs Minutes – Ministry to Draft-Age US Immigrants – Accountability Committee and Others, 1969–73, Canadian Council of Churches fonds, MG28, I 327, box 39, file 6, Library and Archives Canada (LAC); Emerick, *War Resisters Canada*, 234.

36 Correspondence with Potential Draftees, Hans Sinn fonds, box 1, file 2; Immigration Procedures and the Fact Sheet on Immigration to Canada, 1967, Hans Sinn fonds, box 1, file 3; Paul Copeland, interview with the author, Ottawa, June 5, 2006.

37 A Note on the Handling of Draft-Age Americans Who Apply for Entry Into Canada, Renée Kasinsky fonds, box 8, file 8; A Further Note on the Handling of Draft -Age Americans Who Apply for Entry Into Canada, Renée Kasinsky fonds, vol. 7, file 13.

38 Military Personnel – Draft Dodgers – General, Memorandum to the Minister, from Deputy Minister's office file, January 30, 1969, Department of Employment and Immigration fonds, RG76, vol. 983, file 5660–1, LAC; Military Personnel – Draft Dodgers – General, letter, J.C. Morrison to L.R. Vachon, January 9, 1968, Department of Employment and Immigration fonds, RG76, vol. 1209, file 5665–1, LAC. Military Personnel – Draft Dodgers – General, Memorandum, Assistant Deputy Minister (Immigration), signed by James S. Cross for [R.B. Curry], to Deputy Minister [Couillard], May 23, 1969, RG76, vol. 983, file 5660–1, LAC.

39 Interview with Bill Spira of the Toronto Anti-Draft Program [sic], June 1970.

40 Military Personnel – Draft Dodgers – Complaints and Criticisms, 1968–69, Department of Employment and Immigration fonds, RG76, vol. 725, file 5660–2, parts 1–13, LAC.

41 Frank H. Epp, ed., *I Would Like to Dodge the Draft-Dodgers, But ...* (Waterloo/Winnipeg: Conrad Press, 1970), 50–54; Draft Dodgers and Deserters – Complaints and Criticisms, press release, Toronto Committee for a Fair Immigration Policy, signed by D. Camp, J. Ludwig, F. Mowat, R. Fulford, B. Frum, J. Callwood, D. Anderson, H. Adelman, W. Kilbourn, V. Kelly, S. Clarkson, Mel Watkins, C. Templeton, Watson, Russell, M. Moore. Rev. Gordon Stewart, Jane Jacobs, W. Spira, Allen Linden, attached to memo, District Admin., Toronto, to Director, Home Services Branch, Ottawa, Military Deserters – Petition by Committee for Fair Immigration Policy, May 9, 1969, Department of Employment and Immigration fonds, RG76, vol. 725, file 5660–2, LAC; "Discrimination Alleged at Border," *Vancouver Sun*, March 5, 1969, Renée Kasinsky fonds, box 8, file 5, Newspaper Articles – Dodgers and Deserters.

42 Military Personnel – Draft Dodgers – General, Media release, Office of the Minister of Manpower and Immigration, March 5, 1969, Department of Employment and Immigration fonds, RG76 vol. 983 file 5660–1, part 5, LAC.

43 For a general overview of amnesty campaigns see Lacie Ballinger, "Amnesty," in *The Encyclopedia of the Vietnam War: A Political, Social, and Military History*, ed. Spencer C. Tucker (London: Oxford University Press, 2001), 45–46. See also Hagan, *Northern Passage*, 142–44, 152–79, and Frank Kusch, *All American Boys: Draft Dodgers in Canada from the Vietnam War* (Westport: Prager, 2001), 212–15, among others.

44 "Canadian Publications: *AMEX*," "The Parley in Montreal," *AMEX* 2, no. 4 (June 1970), Renée Kasinsky fonds, box 6, file 4; Materials for Chapters VII to IX, Report on the Pan-Canada Deserter/Resistor [sic] Conference, Renée Kasinsky fonds, box 7, file 25.

45 Deportation – Appeals Backlog, various documents and articles, Department of Employment and Immigration fonds, RG76, vol. 1135, file 5235-6, pt. 1, LAC; "Immigration Department Reviews 'Draft Dodger Rule,'" *Vancouver Sun*, September 25, 1970, Renée Kasinsky fonds, box 8, file 5, Newspaper Articles – Dodgers and Deserters; Selection and Processing – Applications – Revocation of Sec. 34 of the Regulations – Statistics, various documents, Department of Employment and Immigration fonds, RG76, vol. 994, file 5855-12-7-2, LAC; Manpower and Immigration Statements, Pocock Memorial Collection, box 14, Canadian Adjustment of Status Program, folder 18; TADP Statements and Lobbying, various documents, Pocock Memorial Collection, box 13, folder 1, Lobbying and Public Relations; Adjustment of Status Program – Correspondence, Press Releases, Notes, various documents, Pocock Memorial Collection, box 14, Canadian Adjustment of Status Program, folder 10; Adjustment of Status Program Clippings, Pocock Memorial Collection, box 27 [oversize], folder 2, continued from box 14, Canadian Adjustment of Status Program, folder 27.

46 The renewed Canadian Coalition of War Resisters included the Vancouver Committee to Aid American War Objectors, Calgary Committee on War Immigrants, Alexander Ross Society in Edmonton, Regina Committee to Assist War Objectors, Winnipeg Committee to Assist War Objectors, Toronto Anti-Draft Programme, Ottawa Aid Committee, American Refugee Service in Montreal, and the Halifax Committee to Aid War Objectors. Stationery, Pocock Memorial Collection, box 2, folder 11, TADP Records.

47 Nova Scotia Committee to Aid American War Objectors fonds, MS-10-7, file 1.2 [various publications], Dalhousie University Archives and Special Collections; "60 Days of Grace," TADP Information Sheet, Pocock Memorial Collection, box 14, Canadian Adjustment of Status Program, folder 5; Adjustment of Status Program clippings, 7 News, August 25, 1973, 4–5, Pocock Memorial Collection, box 27 [oversize], folder 2, continued from box 14, Canadian Adjustment of Status Program, folder 27; "Notice to All Counsellors"; Dick Brown, TADP, to Don Lumley, Public Service Announcements, CHLO radio, St. Thomas, Ontario, September 12, 1973.

48 Bus Promotion, Canadian Coalition of War Resisters – Personal Service Contract, n.d., Pocock Memorial Collection, box 14, Canadian Adjustment of Status Program, folder 26; Front Desk Inquiry Records, 1972–73, Pocock Memorial Collection, box 2, TADP Intake Records, Sales Records, Stationery, and Other Materials, folders 1–4; "Canadian Publications: *AMEX*," "Fewer Americans Than Expected," *AMEX* 4, no. 4 (September-October 1973), 32, Renée Kasinsky fonds, box 6, file 5.

14 The Fasting Granny vs. the Trudeau Government

1 The author wishes to thank Dara Culhane, the anonymous reviewers, and the editors of this collection for their support and feedback.

2 Canada, *House of Commons Debates*, March 4, 1971, 3940.

3 Canada, *House of Commons Debates*, March 4, 1971, 3940.

4 Transcript of trial and notes re: chaining to chair April 19, 1971, 22, Claire Culhane fonds, McMaster University William Ready Division of Archives and Research Collections (hereafter Claire Culhane fonds), box 48, file Regina vs. Claire Culhane. Since there was no evi-

dence that house debate was disturbed, the judge dismissed the charges against Culhane.

5 Peter C. Dobell, *Canada's Search for New Roles: Foreign Policy in the Trudeau Era* (London: Oxford University Press, 1972), 25; Douglas Ross, *In the Interests of Peace: Canada and Vietnam, 1954–1973* (Toronto: University of Toronto Press, 1984), 5.

6 Claire Culhane, *Why is Canada in Vietnam?: The Truth About Our Foreign Aid* (Toronto: NC Press, 1972), 8.

7 The exception to this is Mick Lowe's thoughtful and thorough biography of Culhane, *One Woman Army: The Life of Claire Culhane* (Toronto: Macmillan Canada, 1992).

8 Robert Bothwell, *Alliance and Illusion: Canada and the World, 1945–1984* (Vancouver: UBC Press, 2007), 197–200.

9 Ross, *In the Interests of Peace*, 378–81.

10 Andrew Preston, "Balancing War and Peace: Canadian Foreign Policy and the Vietnam War, 1961–1965," *Diplomatic History*, 27, no. 1 (2003): 74.

11 Preston, "Balancing War and Peace," 78.

12 Bothwell, *Alliance and Illusion*, 317.

13 Peter Sypnowich, "Canada Awakens to the Agony of Viet Nam's Maimed Children," *Star Weekly*, April 29, 1967, 4.

14 Jonathan Neale, *A People's History of the Vietnam War* (New York: The New Press, 2003), 129, 155.

15 Sean Mills, *The Empire Within: Postcolonial Thought and Political Activism in Sixties Montreal* (Montreal/Kingston: McGill-Queen's Press, 2010), 28.

16 On war resister activism see Jay Young, "Defining a Community in Exile: Vietnam War Resister Communication and Identity in AMEX, 1968–1973," *Social History/Histoire sociale* 44, no. 87 (2011): 115–46.

17 Tarah Brookfield, *Cold War Comforts: Canadian Women, Child Safety, and Global Insecurity* (Waterloo: Wilfrid Laurier University Press, 2012), 172–75.

18 Brookfield, *Cold War Comforts*, 181.

19 Lowe, *One Woman Army*, 20–22.

20 She also took courses toward being a medical records librarian. Biographical details are drawn from Lowe, *One Woman Army*, and the author's interview with Dara Culhane, June 25, 2010.

21 Lowe, *One Woman Army*, 150.

22 Culhane speculates the RCMP did not initially connect her married name with the original RCMP file under her maiden name. The majority of the file comprises press clippings tracking Culhane's activism. Copies of the file are in the Mick Lowe fonds (UBCSP-680) at Rare Books and Special Collections, University of British Columbia, Vancouver.

23 Greg Lockhart, *Nation in Arms: The Origins of the People's Army of Vietnam* (Sydney: Allen & Unwin, 1989), 119, 139–40.

24 The My Lai Massacre was the murder of 300–500 South Vietnamese civilians, the majority of whom were women, children, and the elderly, who American infantry patrolling Quang Ngai province in March 1968 suspected were NLF supporters. When the event was made public a year later, twenty-six American soldiers were charged with criminal offences, and platoon commander Second-Lieutenant Commander William Calley Jr. was found guilty of killing twenty-two Vietnamese residents of My Lai. Neale, *A People's History of the Vietnam War*, 121.

25 Neale, *A People's History of the Vietnam War*, 26.

26 Culhane, *Why is Canada in Vietnam?*, 36.

27 Culhane, *Why is Canada in Vietnam?*, 16

28 Culhane, *Why is Canada in Vietnam?*, 20.

29 Culhane, *Why is Canada in Vietnam?*, 54–83.

30 "Supplying the War Machine," *As it Happens*, January 27, 1975.

31 Culhane, *Why is Canada in Vietnam?*, 92.

32 Culhane, *Why is Canada in Vietnam?*, 54.

33 Culhane, *Why is Canada in Vietnam?*, 83.

34 Culhane to Vennema, August 4, 1968, Claire Culhane fonds, box 1, August 1968.

35 Ivan L. Head, *The Canadian Way: Shaping Canada's Foreign Policy 1968–1984* (Toronto: McClelland & Stewart, 1995), 181.

36 David S. Churchill, "An Ambiguous Welcome: Vietnam Draft Resistance, the Canadian State, and Cold War Containment," *Social History/Histoire sociale* 37, no. 73 (2004): 1.

37 Canada, *House of Commons Debates*, June 29, 1972, 36560–3663.

38 Sharman Apt Russell theorizes that the more frequent use of hunger strikes in the last hundred years was "partly to the media, the way a newspaper and now the internet can publicize drama. We may as well have a more modern way of seeing hunger, as an anomaly rather than the normal human condition, an affront to our ideas of who we are." Russell, *Hunger: An Unnatural History* (New York: Basic Books, 2005), 74.

39 In 1965, British antiwar protesters held a ten-day fast in London's Hyde Park, and in 1967 American Christian groups opposed to the war organized a national Fast for Peace day. There was also a three-day fast among students in Oklahoma and the 1969 hunger strike of imprisoned activists Daniel and Philip Berrigan, American priests arrested for burning their draft cards. "10-Day Fast For Peace in Vietnam – Hyde Park 1965,"
www.friendsreunited.com/10-day-fast-for-peace-in-vietnam-hyde-park/Memory/233447d1
-4e0e-4206-a924-a00c00a5f8d1;
"The Vietnam War," www.historyplace.com/unitedstates/vietnam/index-1965.html;
"Vietnam War Protests," digital.library.okstate.edu/encyclopedia/entries/V/VI005.html;
"Hunger Strike," www.infoplease.com/encyclopedia/society/hunger-strike.html,
all accessed August 23, 2013.

40 Hunger strikes were also the strategy of choice for anti-Iraq War activists Barbara Tucker and Cindy Sheehan, and most recently for Idle No More activist Theresa Spence.

41 Cynthia Cockburn, *From Where We Stand: War, Women's Activism, & Feminist Analysis* (New York: Zed Books, 2007), 177.

42 See, for example, "Fasting Grandmother Camps at MPs' Doors," *Globe and Mail*, October 4, 1968, 13; John Danylchuk, "Granny Fasts on Hill: She's Hungry but Not Lonely," *Ottawa Journal*, October 2, 1968.

43 Worried about the militancy of a hunger strike, VOW's national committee did not come out in favour of Culhane's fast until it was over. Meanwhile VOW branches in Montreal, Toronto, Ottawa, Hamilton, Winnipeg, and Victoria, and the Ontario provincial committee offered logistical and emotional support during the fast.

44 Judy Barrie, "Faster is No Slower," *Ottawa Citizen*, October 8, 1968.

45 Frank Jones, "'Don't Talk Silly' woman protester ticks off Sharp," *Toronto Star*, October 1, 1968; Robert Stall, "Grandmother's Viet Protest: Model 10-day 'Fast' on the Hill," *Montreal Star*, October 3, 1968.

46 Culhane Report to VOW, 2, Claire Culhane fonds, box 1, October 1968; VOW, "Vietnam Fast," *News Flash* 7, October 11, 1968.

47 Culhane Report to VOW, 4, Claire Culhane fonds, box 1, October 1968.

48 Denis Hudon, VP of CIDA, to Culhane, November 7, 1968, Mitchell Sharp fonds, MG32 vol. 49, file 5, Subject 10–3 Culhane, Claire 1969–1974, Library and Archives Canada.

49 Confidential Memorandum for the Minister, May 27, 1969, Mitchell Sharp fonds, MG32 vol. 49, file 5, Subject 10–3.

50 Confidential Memorandum for the Minister, May 27, 1969.

51 "Fasting Grandmother Camps at MPs' Doors," 13.

52 Lowe, *One Woman Army*, 192.

53 The first two adjectives were used in a memo between A.S. McGill, Senior Departmental Assistant, and Olga Maxwell, PMO, May 13, 1970, Mitchell Sharp fonds, MG32 vol. 49, file 5, Subject 10–3. The latter adjectives are attributed to Peter Clark, ISCS representative, in

his article "The Great and Galloping Granny of the Canadian Far Left," *Canada Month*, September 1971, 6, 10.

54 Even NDP supporter Douglas referenced Culhane's gender in his joke about women interrupting him during her later parliamentary protest.

55 Canada, *House of Commons Debates*, June 29, 1972, 3660. Note that Culhane was awarded the Order of Canada in 1995 for her lifelong career in social activism.

56 Confidential Memorandum, Jon Church to J.A. Beesley, October 5, 1970, Mitchell Sharp fonds, MG32 vol. 49, file 5, Subject 10–3.

57 McGill and Maxwell, PMO, May 13, 1970.

58 Culhane to Trudeau, January 10, 1969, Mitchell Sharp fonds, MG32 vol. 49, file 5, Subject 10–3.

59 "Claire Culhane & Mike Rubbo Buttonhole P.M. on Parl. Hill," January 12, 1970, Claire Culhane fonds, box 3, December 1969.

60 John English, *Just Watch Me: The Life of Pierre Elliot Trudeau 1968–2000* (Toronto: Vintage Canada, 2009), 213.

15 "A Good Teacher Is a Revolutionary"

1 This chapter grew out of my doctoral dissertation, "Including Women: The Establishment and Integration of Canadian Women's History into Toronto Ontario Classrooms 1968–1993" (PhD diss., University of Toronto, 2012). I thank all the Toronto teachers and educators who graciously shared their time and experiences.

2 Teacher L, interview by author, Toronto, February 12, 2010 (some teachers in this study remained anonymous).

3 Teacher O, email interviews with author, March 2009.

4 Over twenty Toronto teachers' oral testimonies were used for this chapter. The interviews were conducted between 2009 and 2013.

5 This study examines the former Toronto Board of Education. The school board had approximately 166 schools during the period examined here. In 1998, the Toronto Board amalgamated with the six school boards that were part of Metropolitan Toronto to form the Toronto District School Board (TDSB).

6 The majority of teachers discussed in this chapter began their teaching career in the 1960s and early 1970s and were working at the time of social movement activism. The interviews demonstrate that teachers were aware and/or part of public demands for social justice, the political mobilization of women, affirmative action initiatives, and the broader activism taking place outside of schools.

7 E.M. Hall and L.A. Dennis, *Living and Learning: The Report of the Provincial Committee on Aims and Objectives of Education in the Schools of Ontario* (Toronto: Ontario Department of Education, 1968/69).

8 Ontario Association for Curriculum Development (OACD), *Reconciliation of Means and Ends in Education*, Report, November 1968, 45. OACD themes for the years 1964–69 focused on changes taking place as a result of social movement activism and the subsequent shifts in curriculum.

9 Federation of Women Teachers' Associations of Ontario, *Dear Teacher* (Toronto, 1978), 34.

10 A number of book series were popular in the 1970s and 1980s, including "Canada: Issues and Options." That series included R.P. Bowles, *Protest, Violence and Social Change* (Scarborough, Ontario: Prentice-Hall, 1972).

11 *Community Schools 1971–1974*. Myra Novogrodsky, private collection. See also Kari Dehli et al., "The Rise and Demise of the Parent Movement in Toronto," in *Social Movements/Social Change: The Politics and Practice of Organizing*, ed. Frank Cunningham et al. (Toronto: Between the Lines/Society for Socialist Studies, 1988), 209–27.

12 Peter Hennessy, *Teacher Militancy* (Ottawa: Ontario Teachers Federation, 1975).

13 See Peace Education files and Parents for Peace files, TDSB Sesquicentennial Museum and Archives. See also Hennessy, *Teacher Militancy,* preface.

14 John Wadland, "Voices in Search of a Conversation: An Unfinished Project," *Journal of Canadian Studies* 35, no. 1 (Spring 2000): 52–75.

15 Russell Hann, interview by author, Toronto, November 25, 2010.

16 A look through the 1970s New Hogtown Press book titles reveals the diversity of published materials. Examples include: Greg Kealey, *Working Class Toronto at the Turn of the Century* (1974); Wayne Roberts, *Honest Womanhood: Feminism, Femininity, and Class Consciousness among Toronto Working Women, 1893 to 1914* (1976); and Daphne Read, ed., *The Great War and Canadian Society: An Oral History* (1978).

17 Frieda Forman, interview by author, Toronto, June 2013. Forman emigrated from New York to Toronto in 1970. She had been active in the 1960s American antiwar and women's movements and continued her activism in Toronto.

18 Barbara Todd, interview by author, Toronto, April 2010; Vancouver Women's Caucus, "Indochinese Conference," *The Pedestal: A Women's Liberation Newspaper* 3, no. 5 (May 1, 1971).

19 Andrea Lebowitz et al., "Women's Studies at the University of Alberta," in *Minds of Our Own*, Wendy Robbins et al., eds. (Waterloo: Wilfrid Laurier University Press, 2008), 178–88.

20 Interview with Barbara Todd, April 13, 2010. See *She Named It Canada: Because That's What It Was Called* (Vancouver: Vancouver Corrective Collective, 1971); *Never Done: Three Centuries of Women's Work in Canada* (Toronto/Vancouver: CWEP/Vancouver Corrective Collective, 1974). Both books were distributed by the Corrective Collective. The Ontario school system bought ten thousand copies of *Never Done* in 1974 to distribute to schools, which was quite a significant number at that time.

21 Interview with Barbara Todd, April 13, 2010.

22 John Hagan, *Northern Passage: American Vietnam War Resisters in Canada* (Cambridge, MA: Harvard University Press, 2001), 66.

23 Hagan, *Northern Passage*, 82.

24 Myra Novogrodsky, interview by author, Toronto, October 28, 2009, and June 2013.

25 Myra Novogrodsky, interview by author.

26 Margaret Wells, interview by author, Toronto, November 2009 and June 2013.

27 Teacher B, interview by author, Toronto, June 2010 and June 2013.

28 Margaret Wells, interview by author.

29 John Pendergrast, email interview by author, July 10, 2013.

30 See Susan Goldberg, ed., *Times of War and Peace: Dealing with Kids' Concerns* (Willowdale, Ontario: Annick Press, 1991).

31 Teacher K, interview by author, Toronto, November 30, 2009. This teacher developed a labour studies curriculum unit.

32 John Waksmundski, "Discussing Vietnam on 'Off days': Preplanning and Question Formulation," *Social Studies Journal* (November 1974): 245–46. A number of journals provided curriculum support, such as *Forum* (the Ontario Secondary School Teachers Federation journal), *The Social Science Teacher*, *This Magazine Is about Schools*, and *History Teachers' Magazine*, to name a few.

33 Teacher F, interview by author, Toronto, June 2010.

34 Margaret Wells, interview by author.

35 Teacher Y, interview by author, Toronto, March 17, 2012.

36 Sources such as Charles Tilly, *From Mobilization to Revolution* (Reading, MA: Addison-Wesley, 1978) and Lawrence Grinter and Peter Dunn, eds., *The American War in Vietnam: Lessons, Legacies and Implications for Future Conflicts* (Westport, CT: Greenwood Press, 1987) helped teachers with lesson ideas.

37 Teacher Q, interview by author, Toronto, November 12, 2009.

38 Teacher B, interview by author.

39 Teacher K, interview with author, Toronto, November 30, 2009.

40 Tim McCaskell, *Race To Equity: Disrupting Educational Inequality* (Toronto: Between the Lines, 2005), 3–5. McCaskell reflects on the 1970s "reform trustees" who "set into motion a series of initiatives" that would have a lasting impact on schools in the city.

41 It was later renamed the "Critical Issues in the Curriculum Committee." Directive, February 28, 1983, notes of a World Affairs Pilot Project for Secondary Schools, Parents for Peace files, Envelope 1, TDSB Archives. See John Pendergrast, "Critical Issues in Toronto," *Peace Magazine* 3, no. 3 (June 1987): 46–47.

42 Parents for Peace files, TDSB Archives.

43 Teacher N, interview by author, Toronto, October 13, 2009.

44 Parents for Peace files, Envelope 1, TDSB Archives. For example, speakers and film events were held each Wednesday evening at Northern Secondary School in the early 1980s and the school board offered a ten-week evening course on "Nuclear War and Peace."

45 Margaret Wells, interview by author.

46 The *Parents for Peace Newsletter*, June 1984, Parents for Peace files, Envelope 1, TDSB Archives notes that the Curriculum Committee of Parents for Peace had a number of events, speakers, and films for use in classrooms K-13 and a peace calendar. The peace curriculum was discussed by many of the interviewees, including Fiona Nelson (interview June 2010, Toronto) former Chair of the Toronto Board of Education, who noted that George Ignatieff, who had written human rights documents for the UN, also helped with the development of the peace curriculum for Toronto schools.

47 Christine Peringer, ed., *How We Work For Peace: Canadian Community Activities* (Dundas, Ontario: Peace Research Institute, 1987). The introduction notes that by 1985 the peace movement had more than two thousand active groups across Canada.

48 Wally Heinrichs and Rob Macintosh, eds., *The Canadian Peace Educators' Directory*, 2nd ed. (Drayton Valley, Alberta: Pembina Institute for Appropriate Development, 1990).

49 See Pendergrast, "Critical Issues in Toronto."

50 Sharon Anne Cook, "Give Peace a Chance: The Diminution of Peace in Global Education in the United States, United Kingdom, and Canada," *Canadian Journal of Education* 31, no. 4 (2008): 889–914.

51 Ian McKay and Jamie Swift, *Warrior Nation: Rebranding Canada in an Age of Anxiety* (Toronto: Between the Lines, 2012).

52 McKay and Swift, *Warrior Nation,* 196.

53 See the government announcements at www.pch.gc.ca/eng/1370873738331 and www.thememoryproject.com.

54 For an example of the former, see the Cleghorn Battlefield tours. For the latter, see the Laurier Centre for Military, Strategic and Disarmament Studies.
See also www.thememoryproject.com.

55 See, for example, Keith Barton and Linda Levstik, *Teaching History for the Common Good* (Mahwah, NJ: Lawrence Erlbaum Associates, 2004); Goh Bee Chen, B. Offord, and R. Garbutt, eds., *Activating Human Rights and Peace: Theories, Practices and Contexts* (Burlington, VT: Ashgate, 2012); Karina V. Korostelina, *History Education in the Formation of Social Identity: Toward a Culture of Peace* (New York: Palgrave Macmillan, 2013); www.facinghistory.org.

16 Rewriting History

1 Precise numbers are impossible to determine because many soldiers went underground or returned to the United States. See Dahr Jamail, *The Will to Resist: Soldiers who Refuse to Fight in Iraq and Afghanistan* (Chicago: Haymarket Books, 2009), 107.

2 This chapter is a modified version of an article originally published as "The Re-writing of History: The Misuse of the Draft 'Dodger' Myth Against Iraq War Resisters in Canada," Activehistory.ca, October 22, 2012.

3 The Uniform Code of Military Justice (UCMJ), which is the military equivalent of the U.S. Code, defines a deserter under Article 85 as a soldier who: "(1) without authority goes or remains absent from his unit, organization, or place of duty with intent to remain away therefrom permanently; [or] (2) quits his unit, organization, or place of duty with intent to avoid hazardous duty or to shirk important service." See James Branum, "AWOL in the Army: A Guide for Attorneys and GI Rights Counselors," Version 3, October 5, 2011, created for the Military Law Task Force of the National Lawyers Guild.

4 See War Resister Support Campaign Press Release, "Iraq War Resister Kimberly Rivera Sentenced to 14 Months in Military Prison After Deportation by Harper Government," April 30, 2013.

5 See "Army: Health Promotion, Risk Reduction, Suicide Prevention, Report 2010," July 29, 2010, 72, www.army.mil/article/42934/.

6 "Principles of International Law Recognized in the Charter of the Nüremberg Tribunal and in the Judgment of the Tribunal, 1950," www.icrc.org.

7 The relevant provisions of the U.N. Charter state:

> Chapter I, Article 2(4): "All Members shall refrain in their international relations from the threat or use of force against the territorial integrity or political independence of any state, or in any other manner inconsistent with the Purposes of the United Nations."
>
> Chapter VII, Article 39: "The Security Council shall determine the existence of any threat to the peace, breach of the peace, or act of aggression and shall make recommendations, or decide what measures shall be taken in accordance with Articles 41 and 42, to maintain or restore international peace and security."
>
> Chapter VII, Article 51: "Nothing in the present Charter shall impair the inherent right of individual or collective self-defence if an armed attack occurs against a Member of the United Nations, until the Security Council has taken measures necessary to maintain international peace and security. Measures taken by Members in the exercise of this right of self-defence shall be immediately reported to the Security Council and shall not in any way affect the authority and responsibility of the Security Council under the present Charter to take at any time such action as it deems necessary in order to maintain or restore international peace and security."

See also Michael Byers, *War Law: Understanding International Law and Armed Conflict* (New York: Grove Press, 2005), 6–8.

8 Quoted in Ewen MacAskill and Julian Borger, "Iraq War was Illegal and Breached UN Charter, says Annan," *Guardian*, September 16, 2004.

9 See Michael Mandel, *How America Gets Away with Murder: Illegal Wars, Collateral Damage and Crimes Against Humanity* (London: Pluto Press, 2004), 5–6, and Howard Friel and Richard Falk, *The Record of the Paper: How the "New York Times" Misrepresents US Foreign Policy* (London: Verso, 2004), 144–48.

10 The whole statement reads: "War is essentially an evil thing. Its consequences are not confined to the belligerent states alone, but affect the whole world. To initiate a war of aggression, therefore, is not only an international crime; it is the supreme international crime differing only from other war crimes in that it contains within itself the accumulated evil of the whole." Quoted in Mandel, *How America Gets Away with Murder*, 5–6. Mandel's first chapter methodically refutes the claims by the George W. Bush administration in 2002 and 2003 about Iraq and demonstrates that Security Council Resolutions (678, 687, and 1441) did not authorize unilateral American intervention in March 2003. The Nuremberg Principles placed individual criminal liability on perpetrators and codified, under customary international law, crimes against peace (or waging a war of aggression), crimes against humanity, and war crimes. Luke Stewart, "'A New Kind of War': The Nuremberg Principles and the Vietnam War, 1964–1968" (PhD Diss., University of Waterloo, 2014).

11 Chapter I, Article 1(A)(2) Convention Relating to the Status of Refugees, July 28, 1951; Article I (2) Protocol Relating to the Status of Refugees, January 31, 1967.

12 UN High Commissioner for Refugees (UNHCR), *Handbook on Procedures and Criteria for Determining Refugee Status under the 1951 Convention and the 1967 Protocol relating to the Status of Refugees*, Section B, Article 171. January 1992, HCR/IP/4/Eng/REV.1, www.refworld.org/docid/3ae6b3314.html (emphasis added). See also Rachel Brett, *International Standards on Conscientious Objection to Military Service*, November 2008, www.refworld.org/docid/494f8e422.html.

13 War Resisters Support Campaign, *AWOL in Canada: A Counseling Memo*, April 2006, 2.

14 See Thomas Walkom, "Deserter poses a problem for Ottawa," *Toronto Star*, November 30, 2004, A25. A background paper, "Americans Seeking Asylum," from October 18, 2004, released to the author under the *Access to Information Act*, stated: "The Department [of Citizenship and Immigration Canada] will actively argue against a refugee claim at the formal hearing where it considers the claim manifestly unfounded or the claimant is a candidate for the exclusion for refugee determination under the Geneva Convention to war crimes or involvement in terrorism. In particular, refugee hearing officers have been advised to be particularly vigilant about claims from Western democracies particularly the United States. The integrity of the determination process demands that such claims be actively opposed."

15 "Canada Won't Join Military Action Against Iraq without Another UNSC Resolution," March 17, 2003, wikileaks.org/cable/2003/03/03OTTAWA747.html#.

16 Hinzman v. Canada (Minister of Citizenship and Immigration) [2006] FC 420, March 31, 2006. See especially paragraphs 158, 159, and 164.

17 Robert E. Murdough, "'I Won't Participate in an Illegal War': Military Objectors, the Nuremberg Defense, and the Obligation to Refuse Illegal Orders," *The Army Lawyer*, July 2010, 4–14; Patrick J. Glen, "Judicial Judgment of the Iraq War: United States Armed Forces Deserters and the Issue of Refugee Status," *Wisconsin International Law Journal* 26, no. 4 (2009): 965–1032.

18 Stewart, "'A New Kind of War.'"; Francis Boyle, *Protesting Power: War, Resistance and Law* (Lanham: Rowman & Littlefield, 2009); Staughton Lynd, "Someday They'll Have a War and Nobody Will Come," in *From Here to There: The Staughton Lynd Reader*, ed. Andrej Grubacic (Oakland: PM Press, 2010), 265–78; "Report of the Citizens' Hearing on the Legality of US Actions in Iraq: The Case of Lt. Ehren Watada," January 20–21, 2007, Tacoma, Washington, www.ehrenwatada.com/REPORT.pdf.

19 For polls, see Gloria Galloway, "Canadians Oppose Iraq War, Poll," *Globe and Mail*, June 29, 2008, and "Most Canadians Would Grant Permanent Residence to U.S. Military Deserters," *Angus Reid Strategies,* June 27, 2008, www.angusreidforum.com/Admin/mediaserver/3/documents/2008.06.27_Soldiers.pdf. See also Patricia Molloy, *Canada/US and Other Unfriendly Relations: Before and After 9/11* (New York: Palgrave Macmillan, 2012), 109–10.

20 In response, war resister lawyer Alyssa Manning adopted a new legal strategy in 2008 that focuses instead on whether the U.S. military justice system was a fair and impartial body and whether soldiers who publicly opposed the wars were punished more harshly. See Manning's contribution in Sarah Hipworth and Luke Stewart, eds., *Let Them Stay: U.S. War Resisters in Canada, 2004–2014* (Toronto: Iguana Books, forthcoming).

21 For an academic study, see, for instance, Robert Bothwell, "Thanks for the Fish: Nixon, Kissinger, and Canada," in *Nixon in the World: American Foreign Relations, 1969–1977*, ed. Fredrik Logevall and Andrew Preston (Oxford: Oxford University Press, 2008), 309–28. Bothwell concludes that for Nixon and Kissinger "draft dodgers were, like Canada, a problem of lesser magnitude." Bothwell reproduces the myth that only draft dodgers were an issue in Canada and does not mention deserters in his chapter.

22 Deputy Minister [Janice Charette] to Minister [Joe Volpe], July 11, 2005. Released to the author under the *Access to Information Act*, the memorandum stated that Citizenship and

Immigration Canada were waiting for Jeremy Hinzman's appeal to Federal Court before they moved on the war resister file. Moreover, the memorandum pointed out that the U.S. government had not yet contacted the department with regard to the Iraq war resisters.

23 "A Deserter, Not a Refugee," *Globe and Mail*, December 9, 2004, A24 (emphasis added). These sentiments were expressed again by a *Globe and Mail* editorial after Hinzman was denied refugee status on March 24, 2004, which declared that Hinzman's "testimony showed that his opinions and actions over the past several years have been confused at best." Why? "Unlike the roughly 50,000 Vietnam-era draft dodgers who fled to Canada in the 1960s and 70s, Mr. Hinzman was a volunteer." "The Ruling Against Jeremy Hinzman," *Globe and Mail*, March 25, 2005, A14. See also "Kenney's Comments Prejudice Hearings for War Resisters, Critics Say," *CBC News*, January 9, 2009; Peter Worthington, "No Room for U.S. Deserters," *Whig Standard*, January 9, 2009, and Worthington, "U.S. War Deserters Insult our Troops," *Toronto Sun*, September 30, 2010.

24 There are no precise numbers on the number of draft dodgers and military deserters who came to Canada during the Vietnam War. The U.S. Department of Defense tracked soldiers who deserted to foreign countries between 1966 and 1973, estimating that 4,404 soldiers fled to other countries and that 71 per cent of these went to Canada. However, these numbers were imprecise because soldiers did not inform the Pentagon when and where they were going AWOL. D. Bruce Bell's 1979 report noted that "the best non-DOD estimate would be between 8,000 and 24,000" deserters fleeing abroad. The DOD's low estimate of 4,404 meant 3,127 Vietnam-era soldiers deserted to Canada and the higher estimate of 24,000 meant 17,040 deserted to Canada. See D. Bruce Bell, *Characteristics of Army Deserters in the DOD Special Discharge Review Program* (Alexandria: U.S. Army Research Institute for the Behavioral and Social Sciences, October 1979), 2–3. Renée Kasinsky estimated in *Refugees from Militarism: Draft-Age Americans in Canada* (New Brunswick, NJ: Transaction Books, 1976) that there were 20,000 to 26,000 draft dodgers and 10,000 to 14,000 military deserters. Lawrence M. Baskir and William A. Strauss estimated in *Chance and Circumstance: The Draft, the War, and the Vietnam Generation* (New York: Knopf, 1978) that there were 12,482 to 23,556 draft dodgers and 10,000 to 30,000 military deserters. John Hagan estimated in *Northern Passage: American Vietnam War Resisters in Canada* (Cambridge, MA: Harvard University Press, 2001) that 25,865 men and 26,804 women migrated to Canada during the Vietnam era. Joseph Jones therefore concludes, after including statistics for women, family members, and men beyond the ages 19–25, that "estimates for the Vietnam-era influx of Americans to Canada credibly extend to 100,000 and beyond." See Joseph Jones, *Contending Statistics: The Numbers for U.S. Vietnam War Resisters in Canada* (Vancouver: Quarter Sheaf, 2005), 34.

25 Tom Kent to Mr. Cadieux, November 17, 1967, RG76, vol. 983, file 5660–1 (Part 1), Library and Archives Canada (LAC). See also Allan J. MacEachen to R.B. Curry, February 20, 1969, RG76, vol. 725, file 5660–1 (Part 1), LAC; Memorandum to Cabinet, "Admission to Canada of Draft Dodgers and Military Deserters," March 12, 1968, RG76, vol. 983, file 5660–1 (Part 5), LAC.

26 The memorandum instructed border officers not to "refuse an immigrant" on the basis of suspected draft evasion, but that U.S. military personnel should submit "proof" of discharge. Appendix B: Development of Immigration Policy on Draft Dodgers and Military Deserters, Deputy Minister of Immigration to Assistant Deputy Minister of Immigration, November 26, 1969, RG76, vol. 983, file 5660–1(Part 6), LAC. For an excellent overview on shifting regulations, see Appendix 2, "Shifts in Immigration Regulations and Tactics of Counseling at Border Crossing," in Jessica Squires, *Building Sanctuary: The Movement to Support Vietnam War Resisters in Canada, 1965–73* (Vancouver: UBC Press, 2013), 235–38.

27 Quoted in Hagan, *Northern Passage*, 42–43.

28 During the Vietnam War there were 27 million men available for conscription. Of these, over 2 million were drafted, 8,720,000 enlisted or volunteered, and an estimated 16 million

did not serve in the armed forces (with over 15 million receiving deferments, exemptions or disqualifications). Of those who were on active duty, roughly 2 million actually served in Vietnam. This was roughly 10 per cent of the total male population who came of age during the Vietnam era. For in-depth analysis of the available statistics, see Figure One in Baskir and Strauss, *Chance and Circumstance.*

29 David Cortright, *Soldiers in Revolt: G.I. Resistance During the Vietnam War* (Chicago: Haymarket Books, 2005), 10–15. Cortright's research, utilizing U.S. government and newspaper sources, revealed that of the more than five hundred thousand incidents of desertion during the Vietnam War, the majority of deserters were those who had voluntarily enlisted. The Army and Marine corps had the highest rate of desertion within the armed services. Cortright's book was originally published in 1975 and was reprinted by Haymarket Books with a new chapter on the GI movement from Vietnam to Iraq.

30 Bell, *Characteristics of Army Deserters in the DOD Special Discharge Review Program*, vii – viii, 1–5, 7, 10, 34. While the study does not specify what countries the exiles fled to and only includes those in the Army, it does note the majority went to Canada.

31 Kasinsky, *Refugees from Militarism*, 37–42. Both Kasinsky's and Cortright's numbers correlated with G. David Curry's in *Sunshine Patriots: Punishment and the Vietnam Offender* (Notre Dame: University of Notre Dame Press, 1985). See Table 2–1, p. 16; Table 2–3, p. 23; Table 3–2, p. 29; Table 4–1, p. 40; Table 4–2, p. 41; and Table 4–10, p. 44.

32 For immigration regulations during the Vietnam War, see Kasinsky, *Refugees from Militarism*, 60, 67–69. For immigration regulations during the twenty-first century, see "AWOL in Canada: A Counseling Memo," War Resisters Support Campaign, April 2006, www.resisters.ca/AWOL_in_Canada.pdf.

33 Bill Nichols, "8,000 Desert During Iraq War," *USA Today*, July 7, 2006, www.usatoday.com/news/washington/2006-03-07-deserters_x.htm; Sig Christenson, "US Army Desertion Rate at Lowest Since Vietnam," *Agence France Presse*, November 7, 2011.

34 Carl Mirra, *Soldiers and Citizens: An Oral History of Operation Iraqi Freedom from the Battlefield to the Pentagon* (New York: Palgrave, 2008).

35 For instance, the *New York Times* reported that, according to U.S. Army statistics, the number of incidents of soldiers going AWOL during their two weeks of R&R was increasing. Paul von Zielbauer, "Army, Intent on Sending a Message, Cracks Down on Deserters," *New York Times*, April 9, 2007.

36 Quoted in "Kenney's Comments Prejudice Hearings for War Resisters, Critics Say," *CBC News*, January 9, 2009. See also Peter Worthington, "U.S. War Deserters Insult our Troops," *Toronto Sun*, September 30, 2010.

37 OB 202 advised all Canadian border guards that "some individuals who may have deserted the military or who may have committed an offence equivalent to desertion of the military in their country of origin have sought refuge in Canada. Desertion is an offence in Canada under the *National Defence Act.* . . . Consequently, persons who have deserted the military in their country of origin may be inadmissible to Canada." See Operational Bulletin 202, July 22, 2010, www.cic.gc.ca/english/resources/manuals/bulletins/2010/ob202.asp.

38 Alex Neve to Jason Kenney, September 27, 2010, www.resisters.ca/Amnesty_International_OB_202_sept_2010.pdf. See also Peter Showler to Jason Kenney, September 29, 2010, reprinted in *Embassy*, September 29, 2010, 7.

39 For an excellent critique of the contemporary U.S. military definition of conscientious objector status, see Lynd, "Someday They'll Have a War and Nobody Will Come," 265–78.

40 These pertain to the 1951 United Nations Convention Relating to the Status of Refugees and the 1967 Protocol Relating to the Status of Refugees.

41 Emphasis added. UN High Commissioner for Refugees (UNHCR), *Guidelines on International Protection No. 10: Claims to Refugee Status related to Military Service within the context of Article 1A (2) of the 1951 Convention and/or the 1967 Protocol relating to the Status of Refugees*, December 3, 2013, HCR/GIP/13/10, www.refworld.org/docid/529ee33b4.html.

17 "There Is Nothing More Inclusive Than O Canada"

1 Many thanks to our research assistant, Katrin MacPhee, whose work was funded by the St. Thomas University J.O.B.S. program. Thanks also to Alan Sears, Lara Campbell, and the anonymous peer reviewers for their constructive suggestions on an earlier draft of the chapter.

2 Bruce Cheadle, "Sing O Canada, or Learn Canadian History? Students do Neither in 2009," June 28, 2009, www.600ckat.com/news/national/more.jsp?content=n263817226.

3 Patrick White, "Decision to Omit O Canada Hits Patriotic Nerve," *Globe & Mail* online, January 31, 2012, www.globecampus.ca/in-the-news/article/decision-to-omit-o-canada-hits-patriotic-nerve/.

4 On contemporary militarism in Canada, see Ian McKay and Jamie Swift, *Warrior Nation: Rebranding Canada in an Age of Anxiety* (Toronto: Between The Lines, 2012).

5 Neither Millett nor educational administrators ever identified the families or their religious affiliation. Nor did the media do so. We found only one reference to religious identity – where the students were identified as members of a "minority Christian sect." Initial public response jumped to the conclusion that the families in question were recent immigrants. See Alison Ménard, "O Canada Issue Shows an Ugly Side," *Moncton Times & Transcript*, February 13, 2009, D7. Members of a number of Christian groups, including Jehovah's Witnesses and Mennonites, oppose active participation in anthem singing on the grounds that anthems encourage allegiance to the state rather than to God.

6 "Irate Parents Force School to Reinstate O Canada," *Daily Gleaner*, February 3, 2009, A4.

7 Tammy Scott-Wallace, "Belleisle Mom Stands on Guard for 'O Canada,'" *Telegraph-Journal*, January 23, 2009, A1.

8 Pte. Greenslade was killed by a roadside bomb.

9 Scott-Wallace, "Belleisle Mom Stands on Guard for 'O Canada,'" A1.

10 CTV News Staff, "N.B. School Stops Playing 'O Canada' Over Complaints," *CTV News*, January 29, 2009, www.ctv.ca/CTVNews/TopStories/20090129/o_canada_090129/.

11 Canada, *House of Commons Debates* (Hansard), January 30, 2009.

12 Tammy Scott-Wallace, "Anthem Controversy Divides Small N.B. Community," *Moncton Times & Transcript*, February 4, 2009, C1.

13 "New Brunswick. Once Again, School Begins Day with O Canada," *Ottawa Citizen*, February 3, 2009, A6.

14 "Principal Who Cut Anthem Getting Angry Responses," *Daily Gleaner*, February 10, 2009, A4.

15 He received a conditional discharge and eight months probation. "Man Guilty of Threats," *Moncton Times & Transcript*, July 24, 2009, A1, and Tammy Scott-Wallace, "Conditional Discharge for Threatening Principal," *Telegraph-Journal*, August 29, 2009, B1.

16 Chuck Brown, "Greenie's Shtick Falls Flat," *Telegraph-Journal*, January 13, 2006, B3.

17 Megan O'Toole, "Outrage Grows Over Cancelled Anthem," *National Post*, January 30, 2009, A1.

18 Kevin Newman, "Anthem Dispute," *Global National*, February 6, 2009, www.fpinfomart.ca.proxy.hil.unb.ca/doc/doc_print.php?key=ar|5558368|bcwg|20090206|2209100, accessed August 22, 2013.

19 Tammy Scott-Wallace, "Parents Step Up Fight for 'O Canada' in School," *Telegraph-Journal*, January 31, 2009, A1.

20 Tammy Scott-Wallace, "Students get OK to Sing Anthem," *Telegraph-Journal*, February 2, 2009, A1.

21 Tammy Scott-Wallace, "Resignation Saddens Parents," *Telegraph-Journal*, April 2, 2009, C8.

22 Tammy Scott-Wallace, "Resignation Saddens Parents."

23 Tammy Scott-Wallace, "Anthem Controversy Divides Small N.B. Community."

24 *New Brunswick Education Act,* Regulation 97–150 (1997) 25(2), 13. Emphasis added.

25 *New Brunswick Education Act,* Regulation 97–150, 29.1 and 29.2, laws.gnb.ca/en/showfulldoc/cr/97-150/20120914.

26 According to reporter Adam Huras, administrators defended the requests, "saying that patriotism can be taught in other ways, while the national anthem cuts into class time and is difficult to co-ordinate." See "Roughly 40 Francophone Schools Don't Want to Sing Anthem Daily," *Telegraph-Journal,* November 2, 2009, A3.

27 Michael Tutton, "Irate Parents Force School to Reinstate O Canada," *Daily Gleaner,* February 3, 2009, A4.

28 Ashfield was also the Secretary of State for the Atlantic Canada Opportunities Agency. Bruce Cheadle, "School Slammed for Dropping 'O Canada,'" *St. John's Telegram,* January 31, 2009, B11.

29 "Dominion Institute Reacts to Belleisle Elementary School's Decision on National Anthem," January 30, 2009, www.dominion.ca/release30012009.pdf.

30 See, for example, Walter O'Toole, Miramichi, letter to editor, *Moncton Times & Transcript,* February 3, 2009, D6; Cheryl Barber, letter to editor, *Moncton Times & Transcript,* February 3, 2009, D6; Angela Nielsen, Qualicum Beach, letter to editor, "Anthem Removal Shocking," *Oceanside Star,* February 5, 2009, 6; Roland Smith, "Why Ban Singing Anthem?" *Alberni Valley Times,* February 9, 2009, A5.

31 Canada, *House of Commons Debates* (Hansard), January 30, 2009, www.parl.gc.ca/HousePublications/Publication.aspx?Language=E&Mode=1&Parl=40&Ses =2&DocId=3635351#SOB-2574683.

32 Canada, *House of Commons Debates* (Hansard), January 30, 2009.

33 Sheilagh Bailey, Airdrie, Alberta, "If You Don't Like the Anthem, You're Free to Leave," *Daily Gleaner,* February 3, 2009, C7.

34 Keith J. Tindale, Shediac, letter to editor, *Moncton Times & Transcript,* February 3, 2009, D6.

35 Editorial, "Oh, Canada! True North Strong and Politically Correct," *Calgary Herald,* February 2, 2009, A8. See also Charles W. Moore, "No 'Right' to Not Be Offended," *Moncton Times & Transcript,* February 4, 2009, D6.

36 See "N.B. School Stops Playing 'O Canada' Over Complaints," January 29, 2009, in the comments section at www.ctv.ca/CTVNews/TopStories/20090129/o_canada_090129/, accessed April 26, 2012.

37 Jennifer Dunville, "O Canada Controversy Sparks Discussion," *Daily Gleaner,* February 2, 2009, A3.

38 Eric Lewis and Mary Moszynski, "Schools Told to Play Anthem," *Moncton Times and Transcript,* February 3, 2009, A1. See also Reagan Johnston, letter to editor, "Build Patriotism Through Teaching," *Moncton Times & Transcript,* February 4, 2009, D8.

39 Jennifer Dunville, "O Canada Controversy Sparks Discussion."

40 Patrick White, "Decision to Omit O Canada Hits Patriotic Nerve," *Globe & Mail* online, January 31, 2012, www.globecampus.ca/in-the-news/article/decision-to-omit-o-canada-hits-patriotic-nerve/, accessed 25 September 2012.

41 Bruce Cheadle, "Sing O Canada, or Learn Canadian History? Students do Neither in 2009."

42 See, for example, Frances Helyar, "'Gladly Given for the Cause': New Brunswick Teacher and Student Support for the War Effort, 1914–1918," *Journal of New Brunswick Studies* 3 (2012): 75–92; Susan R. Fisher, *Boys and Girls in No Man's Land: English Canadian Children and the First World War* (Toronto: University of Toronto Press, 2011), 79–92; José Igartua, *The Other Quiet Revolution: National Identities in English Canada, 1945–71* (Vancouver: UBC Press, 2006), chapter 3; Amy von Heyking, *Creating Citizens: History and Identity in Alberta's Schools, 1905 to 1980* (Calgary: University of Calgary Press, 2006), chapter 1; Mark Moss, *Manliness and Militarism: Educating Young Boys in Ontario for War* (Toronto: University of Toronto Press, 2001); Harro Van Brummelen, "Shifting Perspectives: Early British Columbia Textbooks from 1872 to 1925," *BC Studies* 60 (Winter 1983–84): 3–27; David W.

Brown, "Militarism and Canadian Private Education: Ideal and Practice, 1861–1918," *Canadian Journal of History of Sport* 17, no. 1 (1986): 46–59; Robert M. Stamp, "Empire Day in the Schools of Ontario: The Training of Young Imperialists," *Journal of Canadian Studies* 8, no. 3 (1973): 32–42; Katherine F.C. MacNaughton, *The Development of the Theory and Practice of Education in New Brunswick, 1784–1900* (Fredericton: University of New Brunswick, 1946), 245–46.

43 The practice of anthem singing differs widely across Canada. At the time of the Belleisle controversy, the B.C. Ministry of Education required the singing of the anthem at a minimum of three school assemblies during the year. Ontario required the daily playing or singing of the anthem, with children opposed to the practice being able to leave the room. In Quebec, no legal requirement existed. Michael Tutton, "Irate Parents Force School to Reinstate O Canada"; Jennifer Dunville, "O Canada or No Canada in Schools?" *Daily Gleaner*, January 31, 2009, A1.

44 Carlos Abril, "Functions of a National Anthem in Society and Education: A Sociocultural Perspective," *Bulletin of the Council for Research in Music Education* 172 (Spring 2007), 72.

45 Abril, "Functions of a National Anthem," 73–74.

46 Abril, "Functions of a National Anthem," 71.

47 Joel Westheimer, "Politics and Patriotism in Education," *The Phi Delta Kappan* 87, no. 8 (April 2006): 608–20.

48 Bruce Vance, ed., *The Status of Women in the Toronto School System: A Series of Case Studies Based on Documents In the Archives of the Toronto Board of Education. No. 2 Miss Held and 'Pro-German Sentiments' From the Toronto Evening Telegram* (Toronto: Affirmative Action Office and Records, Archives and Museum of the Toronto Board of Education, 1990), 10.

49 Vance, *The Status of Women in the Toronto School System*, 39.

50 Vance, *The Status of Women in the Toronto School System*, front matter.

51 Igartua, *The Other Quiet Revolution.*

52 Westheimer, "Politics and Patriotism in Education," 608–9. See also Abril, "Functions of a National Anthem," 81.

53 McKay and Swift, *Warrior Nation*, 253.

54 McKay and Swift, *Warrior Nation*, 253.

55 See for example, Deirdre M. Kelly and Gabriella Minnes Brandes, "Shifting Out of 'Neutral': Beginning Teachers' Struggles with Teaching for Social Justice," *Canadian Journal of Education* 26, no. 4 (2001): 437–54. That perspective has implications for teaching more generally. The Atlantic Canada social studies curriculum encourages a "critical and engaged citizenship." Yet, as Alan Sears argues, "the mandated, unexamined, daily singing of the national anthem for patriotic purposes is wholly inconsistent with that vision. There is considerable evidence that the structures of schooling are much more powerful in terms of citizenship education than the curriculum and the message here is that good citizens do as they're told." Correspondence with Alan Sears, November 11, 2013.

56 That the province's revised policy on school anthems retained these emphases is telling. Despite forceful rhetoric from the Education Minister about the necessity of daily anthem playing, when it came time to codify his wishes, it appears that cooler, and legally astute, heads prevailed.

57 Ken Osborne, "Public Schooling and Citizenship Education in Canada," *Canadian Ethnic Studies* 32, no. 1 (2000), 24.

58 Bruce Cheadle, "National Identity Crisis 101," *Daily Gleaner*, June 29, 2009, A1.

59 Osborne, "Public Schooling and Citizenship Education in Canada," 16.

60 Tammy Scott-Wallace, "Anthem Controversy Divides Small N.B. Community."

Author Biographies

Linda M. Ambrose is Professor of History at Laurentian University. She is currently researching the gender history of Canadian Pentecostalism through the biographies of women in ministry. Her publications on this subject have appeared in *Winds from the North: Canadian Contributions to the Pentecostal Movement*, edited by Michael Wilkinson and Peter Althouse (Brill, 2010), the *Journal of the Canadian Historical Association* and *Pneuma: The Journal of the Society for Pentecostal Studies*.

Tarah Brookfield is Associate Professor in History and Youth and Children's Studies at Wilfrid Laurier University's Brantford campus. She is the author of *Cold War Comforts: Canadian Women, Child Safety, and Global Insecurity* (Wilfrid Laurier University Press, 2012). Her new book project is "Educating for Peace: Adults, Youth, and Families on Grindstone Island, 1939–1989."

Lara Campbell is Associate Professor of Gender, Sexuality, and Women's Studies at Simon Fraser University, where she teaches women's history and the history of social activism. She is the author of *Respectable Citizens: Gender, Family, and Unemployment in Ontario's Great Depression* (University of Toronto Press, 2009) and co-author, with Willeen Keough, of *Gender History: Canadian Perspectives* (Oxford University Press, 2014). Her current project focuses on the gender politics of war resistance in the Vietnam era.

Cynthia Comacchio, Professor of History at Wilfrid Laurier University, is interested in Canadian social and cultural history, particularly the history of children, youth, and families. She has published three books on those subjects, most recently *The Dominion of Youth: Adolescence and the Making of Modern Canada, 1920–1950* (Wilfrid Laurier University Press, 2006). She is currently collaborating, with Neil Sutherland, on *Ring Around the Maple: A Sociocultural History of Children and Childhood in Canada, 19th and 20th Centuries*, for Wilfrid Laurier University Press.

Michael Dawson is Professor of History at St. Thomas University. His research has focused primarily on consumerism, tourism, and popular culture and their relationship to regional, national, and imperial identities. With Catherine Gidney and Susanne Klausen, he recently edited E. Maud Graham's *A Canadian Girl in South Africa: A Teacher's Experiences in the South African War, 1899–1902* (University of Alberta Press, 2015). His current projects include (separate) studies of Jell-O and the Muppets.

Bruce Douville is an adjunct professor of Canadian history at Algoma University. His research centres on the relationship between Christianity and the radical and countercultural youth movements in 1960s English Canada. He is currently working on a monograph titled "The Uncomfortable Pew: Christianity and the New Left in Toronto, 1959–1975."

Ross Fair is an adjunct professor in the Department of History at Ryerson University, where he serves as Academic Coordinator, Continuing Education. His academic interests focus on pre-Confederation Canada, particularly Upper Canada and early Toronto. His work has appeared in the *Canadian Historical Review, Journal of the Canadian Historical Association, Ontario History,* and elsewhere.

Rose Fine-Meyer teaches in the Masters of Teaching and Bachelor of Education programs at the Ontario Institute for Studies in Education, University of Toronto. Her publications examine the history of teacher pedagogy in Ontario, how social movement activism has influenced the work of teachers in altering curricula, and the importance of place-based educational programming in schools. She is guest editor of a special edition of *Ontario History* on the history of women and education (2015) and has developed a women's history talk series, herstoriescafe.com, that was recognized with a Heritage Toronto Community Award in 2012. She is the recipient of the Queen Elizabeth II Diamond Jubilee Medal (2012) and the Governor General's Award for Excellence in Teaching Canadian History (2007).

Catherine Gidney is an adjunct professor in the History Department at St. Thomas University. She is the author of *A Long Eclipse: The Liberal Protestant Establishment and the Canadian University, 1920–1970* (McGill-Queen's University Press, 2004) and *Tending the Student Body: Youth, Health, and the Modern University* (University of Toronto Press, 2015). Her current research focuses on the commercialization of schools in Canada.

Marie Hammond-Callaghan is Associate Professor in History and Women's and Gender Studies at Mount Allison University, Sackville, New Brunswick. Her current research focuses on transnational women's peace movements in Cold War Canada and Europe. She has contributed to scholarly journals and edited collections on peace movements and Irish history. She is co-editor of *Mobilizations, Protests and Engagements: Canadian Perspectives on Social Movements* (Fernwood, 2008).

Braden Hutchinson is a high school teacher with the Ottawa-Carleton District School Board. He completed his Ph.D. in 2013 at Queen's University on the social, cultural, and economic history of toys in Canada from the mid-nineteenth to the late twentieth century. His articles have appeared in the *Alberta Journal of Educational Research, Scientia Canadensis*, and the *Journal of the History of Childhood and Youth*. His current research focuses on historical thinking and history education and the history of video games.

Geoff Keelan is a Ph.D. Candidate in the Department of History at the University of Waterloo working on a study of Henri Bourassa and the First World War. He has published on topics relating to French Canada and the First World War.

Ian McKay is Professor of History at Queen's University. In 2012 he co-authored, with Jamie Swift, *Warrior Nation: Rebranding Canada in)n Age of Anxiety* (Between the Lines, 2012).

Jonathan Seiling is a Research Associate at the Institute for Peace Church History in Hamburg, Germany, and specializes in the history of radicalism and dissent in Christianity, with a focus on the Anabaptist-Mennonite tradition. He was the Chair of the 1812 Bicentennial Peace Committee, comprised of Quakers, Mennonites, and Brethren in Christ. He also publishes translations of early modern sources, primarily from German.

Amy Shaw is Associate Professor of History at the University of Lethbridge. She is the author of *Crisis of Conscience: Conscientious Objection in Canada during the First World War* (UBC Press, 2009) and the co-editor, with Sarah Glassford, of *A Sisterhood of Suffering and Service: Women and Girls in Newfoundland and Canada during the First World War* (UBC Press, 2012).

Jessica Squires is an independent scholar of Canadian political, social, and cultural history who lives and works in Gatineau, Quebec. She is the author of *Building Sanctuary: The Movement to Support Vietnam War Resisters in Canada, 1965–1973* (UBC Press, 2013).

Luke Stewart is a historian and grassroots activist from Brantford, Ontario. His doctoral dissertation, from the University of Waterloo, focuses on the Nuremberg Principles and the anti-Vietnam War movement in the United States. He is an independent researcher with the War Resisters Support Campaign (WRSC) and is co-editor, with Sarah Hipworth, of *Let Them Stay: U.S. War Resisters in Canada, 2004–2014* (Iguana Books, forthcoming).

Conrad Stoesz is the archivist at the Mennonite Heritage Centre and the Centre for Mennonite Brethren Studies in Winnipeg, Manitoba. His research on the topics of conscientious objectors and Mennonite midwives has been published in *Journal of Mennonite Studies* and *Manitoba History*. He is the co-editor of the *Mennonite Historian* and manages the award-winning web site www.alternativeservice.ca.

David Tough is a postdoctoral fellow in Canadian Studies at Trent University, studying the politics of anti-poverty in the 1960s. His doctoral dissertation is being revised for publication as *The Terrific Engine: Income Taxation and Canada's Modern Political Imaginary, 1910–1945.*

Index

Note: "n" after a page number indicates an endnote; "nn" after a page number indicates two or more consecutive endnotes. The page number for a figure is indicated in **boldface**.